Touring Exhibitions

Touring Exhibitions

The Touring Exhibitions Group's Manual of Good Practice

Edited by

Mike Sixsmith

Butterworth-Heinemann Ltd
Linacre House, Jordan Hill, Oxford OX2 8DP

OXFORD LONDON BOSTON
MUNICH NEW DELHI SINGAPORE SYDNEY
TOKYO TORONTO WELLINGTON

First published 1995

British Library Cataloguing in Publication Data
Touring Exhibitions
I. Sixsmith, Mike
707.4

ISBN 0 7506 2518 X

Library of Congress Cataloguing in Publication Data
Touring exhibitions/edited by Mike Sixsmith,
p. cm.
Includes bibliographical references (p.) and index.
ISBN 0 7506 2518 X (pbk.)
1. Travelling exhibitions – Handbooks, manuals, etc
2. Exhibitions – Handbooks, manuals, etc. 3. Museum techniques – Handbooks, manuals, etc. I. Sixsmith, Mike.
AM151.M33 95–24198
069′.5–dc20 CIP

Typeset by Avocet Typeset, Brill, Aylesbury, Bucks
Printed in Great Britain

Contents

Preface

This manual complements the *Standards for Touring Exhibitions*, in the series of Standards documents published by the Museums and Galleries Commission. As such, it provides guidance on how to achieve the requirements and carry out the obligations set out in the Standards.

But the manual also looks back to twenty years ago, when the Arts Council of Great Britain (ACGB), as it then was, published *Organising Exhibitions*, 'a manual outlining the methods used to organise temporary exhibitions of works of art', by Teresa Gleadowe. This handy booklet has been out of print for some years, and a replacement is overdue. The ambition of the present manual is to be as useful as its predecessor and – with any luck – to last as long. However, the manual is substantially different from – as well as considerably larger than – *Organising Exhibitions* for several reasons.

First, it is not solely concerned with the visual arts. The Touring Exhibitions Group (TEG) was founded in 1985 as a response to the withdrawal of museum-based exhibitions when the Victoria & Albert Museum closed its Circulation Department. Although many of its members are involved in touring exhibitions of contemporary art and craft, TEG has always taken an interdisciplinary approach, embracing historical material and areas other than the visual arts.

A second reason is that the science of conservation now gives as much attention to preventive measures as to remedial work. Lenders are increasingly requiring evidence of borrowers' ability to look after their objects, and this publication deliberately builds bridges between the world of the exhibition-user and that of the conservator. Our concern is to reinforce the responsibilities and the professionalism of everyone involved in exhibitions.

A third reason is that there is now a greater interest in how an exhibition is used once it goes on tour, so more attention is given in this manual to the business of touring and to guidance for venues. In many cases, the manual covers areas that are relevant to all exhibitions (and not just those that tour), where a venue might be expected to make a greater effort or to enter unfamiliar territory because of the arrival of an incoming exhibition. For example, a venue would ideally undertake market research in relation to its whole programme, no matter whether its exhibitions are bought-in or generated in-house, but an incoming exhibition might provide it with its first opportunity to do so.

The method we adopted for compiling the manual was quite different from that used for *Organising Exhibitions*. The latter was a conscious attempt to disseminate the experience and procedures of the ACGB's Art Department (or at least that part of it which now runs the Hayward Gallery and National Touring Exhibitions) which then had a dominant position in touring in the United Kingdom. Twenty years later, National Touring Exhibitions is still a force to be reckoned with, but expertise and good practice are now widespread throughout Great Britain, and TEG felt that this manual should be an opportunity to share this knowledge.

As a result, my task has been to locate experts from the whole of the UK to discuss and describe all aspects of touring. I am very grateful to all those who provided contributions to this publication. Without their expertise – and, let it be said, without their willingness to be bullied by myself – this publication would not have been possible. With only one or two exceptions, most of the contributors drafted their texts without knowing what others were writing, so the blame for any gaps or overlaps lies at my door, not at theirs. Because the manual is designed to be consulted, rather than read from cover to cover, I hope that the cross-references will be more useful than any attempt at continuity from section to section.

In addition to the contributors, many other individuals have helped to make this manual possible, and I should like to thank in particular Lindsay Brooks of Arts About Manchester, Cynthia Gilliland of the Hood Museum of Art, New Hampshire, Susan Pratt of Pratt Contemporary Art, Denise Reid of Momart Ltd and Sue Rose of the Arts Council of England. Steve Brake, Jane Bywaters and Caroline Krzesinska provided invaluable assistance and moral support during the editing process, while Neil Warnock-Smith and Michael Wright were extremely helpful on the publishing side.

I am grateful to National Touring Exhibitions from the Hayward Gallery for permission to quote the hire agreement discussed in section 16. In the same Chapter, the consortium agreement is reproduced by kind permission of the institutions that collaborated on *'The Woodcarver's Craft'* exhibition: Bradford Art Galleries and Museums; the Crafts Council, London; Glasgow Museums; Hove Museum and Art Gallery; and Lincolnshire County Council: Usher Gallery, Lincoln. Glasgow Museums also permitted the use of the draft budget forms in Chapter 9. I am indebted to Michael Dibdin and Faber and Faber Ltd for permission to quote the text that opens Chapter 32. Finally, I would like to acknowledge the help of the Department of National Heritage and Her Majesty's Stationery Office, which gave their permissions to reproduce the application forms that appear in Chapter 56.

This publication would not have been possible either without financial assistance from the Museums and Galleries Commission. We gratefully acknowledge the Crafts Council's grant aid, which was an early expression of the importance of the bridge between historical collections and contemporary practice. This was reinforced by the financial support of the Arts Council of England, for which we are particularly grateful because, amongst other things, it enabled us to offer payment to all our contributors!

Mike Sixsmith
Secretary, Touring Exhibitions Group

Introduction

The intention of this manual is to prescribe methods and procedures for the production of touring exhibitions, but not to proscribe their nature and scope. This important distinction is one which the contributors to this publication have been ever vigilant to observe. Furthermore, they have been mindful of the particular features which characterize a touring exhibition, as distinct from any other museum or gallery installation.

In many ways, a temporary exhibition is akin to a newspaper: it is ephemeral, up-to-the-minute and likely to be 'read' only once. In contrast, the relatively permanent installation may be revisited like a favourite book or used as a basic text or a standard work of reference.

The single showing of a temporary exhibition raises a whole series of questions which are further multiplied with a touring exhibition. Whatever its content, the touring show must be constructed, both metaphorically and literally, for tour. It may be ephemeral, but it must also be strong and hard-wearing. Short of starting from scratch again, there is no such thing as converting a one-off temporary exhibition into a touring show.

There is one central point which we in the museum and gallery professions should never lose sight of, no matter how burdensome the technicalities of our work may become. We enjoy the privilege of presenting the riches of the world, the treasures of the past and the vitality of the present, to the wider public. In an age of second-hand images, we offer the first-hand experience of real 'things'. It is a resource we must husband with great sensitivity.

In producing in the same year the *Standards for Touring Exhibitions* and this *Manual of Touring Exhibitions*, the Museums and Galleries Commission and the Touring Exhibitions Group hope to engender greater care in the preparation, presentation and circulation of exhibitions. Both publications were conceived at the same time to provide information which is intended to be so fundamental as to be, by definition, neutral. History demonstrates that this has often been an aspiration of didactic publishing. A suitably interdisciplinary example is Charles Haytor's *Introduction to Perspective and Practical Geometry* (London, 1832 – first published 1815) which touches on the sciences and social history as well as on the visual arts. Despite its 'practical' intentions, the title page declares it to be 'properly adapted for the Instruction of Females'. Such a precedent demonstrates the dangers inherent in a catechism, a dialogue in which the questions confine the answers to the prejudices of their time.

What then, are these open-ended questions concerning touring exhibitions? It seems to me that there is, within the museum professions, a constant need for balance between the 'front of house' and the 'backstage'. This equilibrium has been endangered by the technology of our time, by conservation departments which have, in effect, been presented with the power of veto. The legitimate demands of the care and conservation of collections are considered in this volume, but it also seeks to establish the reasonable limits of such power. In practice, public access to public collections should be a constant preoccupation for us all.

Paradoxically, a concern for the wider public is often less evident in publicly-funded institutions, and more commonly encountered in independent establishments which are necessarily responsive to the demands of the paying public. Commercial pressures, though, may be associated with even greater pitfalls. The market-place may result in exhibitions which are popular rather than innovative, amusing rather than instructive, provocative rather than original. In view of the costs involved in these ventures, it is perhaps inevitable that the administrators of many independent museums and galleries put the likely commercial success of a planned exhibition ahead of virtually any other consideration.

With all these hazards and costs, it is remarkable that exhibitions, temporary or touring, ever get organized.

Presumably, many organizations believe that the benefits outweigh the difficulties. So what are the benefits?

Because of its temporary nature, an exhibition is able to reflect the latest thinking in a chosen field. It will provide an opportunity to show new discoveries in science, or developments in technology, the work of a living artist or of a person engaged in one of the crafts. Alternatively, an exhibition might comprise recently-excavated items from an archaeological dig or demonstrate some new theory concerning the natural sciences. It might provide the opportunity to exhibit objects from a private collection or, dare one say, from the museum store.

'Temporary' can mean 'available' if the exhibition comes from a little-known private source or a distant foreign collection or is composed of materials – for example, textiles or drawings – which are too fragile or fugitive to be permanently exhibited. Furthermore, new research may bring to the surface items that were previously considered to be trifles. Above all, a temporary exhibition may provide an opportunity for a museum or gallery to present a full dress-rehearsal for a projected permanent display. This may be particularly useful with a contentious subject and 'deniable' if brought in from elsewhere.

As 'birds of passage', exhibitions are often newsworthy and offer the public a deadline: 'see me now or never'. Because an exhibition is usually greater than the sum of its parts (if it isn't, there must be something seriously wrong), it may influence a new tide of opinion or a new current of understanding. This may result from the coming together of previously unrelated objects, or the ebb and flow of material culture, or fluctuating theories in the natural sciences.

Organizing an exhibition, on the sciences as much as on the arts, is a creative activity. In common with all the arts, the temporary exhibition observes certain very basic conventions, a grammar rather than a language, which is peculiar to itself. This is why an exhibition should never resemble anything else, not even a book or a film (especially when it is about books or films). Exhibitions exist because there is no other way to communicate what they have to express.

Exhibitions of the temporary kind are best suited to respond to this fascinating and ever-shifting frame of our perceptions. It is only possible for museums to respond to these ever-changing interpretations if the institution involved has imaginative personnel and has not succumbed to that dangerous and negative activity known as 'de-accessioning', for yesterday's trash may become tomorrow's treasure.

Exhibitions of the permanent kind provide a useful fixed point for comparison with the more fugitive issues which concern us here. In part, permanent installations in the primary galleries are about past achievements in curatorial expertise. Also, the weighty responsibilities and importance of these galleries is such that those involved in their preparation may suffer the inhibition of third-person thinking rather than first-person singularity. In contrast, the temporary exhibition offers great freedom, for nothing in their presentation is permanently engraved in tablets of stone: stick-on letters may be prosaic, but at least they are flexible. It is in ways such as this that the temporary exhibition resembles a living organism, existing on the premiss that its days are numbered.

These, then, are just a few of the many reasons why temporary exhibitions are important, and why they should be considered almost compulsory in all museums and galleries. In some institutions, they already are, for example in museums of science and industry and in contemporary art galleries where rapidly evolving ideas are reflected in ever-changing installations. As we have seen, the fragile nature of items in a particular department, like Prints and Drawings, may necessitate constant revolution, which is to say a rotating programme of exhibitions.

Up and down the country, there are institutions (not all of them either museums or galleries as such) which have exhibition spaces but which lack any permanent collection. Venues of this kind may be used by a local art society, but for the other eleven months of the year they are generally dependent upon brought-in shows. For them, the absence of a permanent collection makes cooperative ventures difficult, so touring exhibitions are their life-blood.

Most museums, of course, have more in store than on show, so why should they venture into a touring exhibition, still less host a show from another institution? It is perhaps the presence of all those riches in the basement which will inspire the creation of an exhibition. However, in reviewing the material in the reserve collection, it may be found that only part of a particular story may be told on the basis of what is available there. Collaboration with other museums or galleries may establish other parts of the story by the provision of additional items. In these circumstances, several showings may be suggested, and an exhibition will almost of its own volition establish a travel itinerary, one which is virtually pre-ordained. Provided the decision to tour is made at an early enough stage in the preparations, there are almost as many reasons why an exhibition should tour as there are reasons for creating a temporary, but static, show in the first place.

Touring is important because it is the best way in which real objects may reach the widest possible audience regionally, nationally and internationally. It may be objected that some exhibitions, like some wines, will not travel. Some will cite, as reasons for not getting an exhibition 'off the ground' as a touring show, the fragile nature or parochial importance of exhibits. It has to be accepted that some questions relating to conservation and environmental controls are insurmountable. However, it is open to question whether any topics exist that are so localized as to be meaningless beyond their region or nation. Even a subject like 'vernacular architecture' is best understood if seen within a national or international context and against the yardstick of 'polite architecture'.

Another example might be a raw material which may have an importance well beyond its source. As far as I am aware, the calamine mines of Somerset have never been the subject of an exhibition. Nevertheless, calamine – or the zinc that was extracted from the ore – is one of the components of bronze. These mines played a part in the bronze industry of eighteenth-century Bristol and therefore in the triangular trade in slavery and molasses, not to mention the zinc-based pigments used by painters and the medical use of calamine lotion and zinc ointments. These calamine mines of Somerset were a research interest of James Smithson (1765–1829), whose bequest made possible the foundation of that great conglomerate of museums known as the Smithsonian Institution in the United States of America.

Most subjects – and calamine or Smithsonite is but one example – though rooted to a particular district, nevertheless have regional, national and international significance, provided they are presented in a stimulating way. It is our duty as a profession not only to facilitate physical access to objects in our care but also to create an enticing ambience which will incite our potentially very wide audience to demand that access as of right.

For many years, exhibitions have been created at a financial loss, and subsidy has been the order of the day. Touring can provide a useful way of sharing costs with other institutions and of achieving an economy of scale which will make more ambitious schemes possible. Whilst exhibitions will seldom make money, there are signs that more realistic – or at least less unrealistic – hiring fees are being introduced. To offset some of these costs, the public visibility of an exhibition may attract funding or sponsorship, although it has to be said that this is more likely to be forthcoming with a large international art exhibition. Ethnographic exhibitions may for good reason be seen as 'art', but there is certainly a pecuniary advantage to be derived from describing them as such. More often than not, lesser funding for smaller non-art based shows is directly related to the theme of the exhibition and the commodity a sponsor wishes to sell or promote.

With all this often loss-making investment, there is a great obligation to maximize use. This is another important reason for touring. Sponsorship may compel a museum to think through the project to the 'end-user', to promotion, marketing and education. Furthermore, each venue should make the most of the exhibitions it receives. The great problem with so many exhibitions that are 'parachuted in' is not the exhibition itself but the inertia that spoon-feeding may cause. The best venues use exhibitions to promote their presence within a particular community, and in doing so, maximise the use of their own resources, their collections, their education department and, lest it be forgotten, their sales outlet.

In popular imagination, the museum curator, if not the gallery director, is seen as a retiring character immersed in a past which is beyond all understanding. Sadly, this popular view of us all may too often contain a germ of truth. The touring exhibition does more than give dynamism to an otherwise static collection. It is the curator who is seen to be metamorphosed from a desiccated academic into a vital entrepreneur with press-releases and photo-opportunities. Touring exhibitions can work miracles.

James Ayres
Director, John Judkyn Memorial: American Exhibitions, Bath (and Chairman, Touring Exhibitions Group 1992–5)

The touring exhibitions manifesto

The Museums Association's definition of a museum as an organization that 'collects, documents, preserves, exhibits and interprets' is all too often used as an order of priority which puts collections first and interpretation last. Museums need collections but that does not mean that museums can only exist if they are next to a store door!

Museums can exist anywhere – wherever people come into contact with collections – in arts centres, libraries, exhibition galleries, schools, community centres. These organizations can often be better 'museums' (by interesting people more deeply in what they exhibit) than those institutions that call themselves museums and just sit on their collections and do little for the public.

This manifesto is written for all those who take, show and initiate touring exhibitions. I have called them all 'museums' because that is what they become when they show objects to people.

Just as exhibitions are essential to individual museums, so touring exhibitions are essential to the museum community as a whole. Disagreement with the latter is usually based on failure to understand the reality of the former.

Rather than write a reasoned argument justifying these assertions, which would not be read by those who do not approve of exhibitions in any form (because they would not be reading this manual in the first place), I have decided to write it in the form of a Manifesto, to give heart to those whose ambitions for touring exhibitions might temporarily falter and provide them with some rallying cries against those who oppose, by downright obstruction or by stealthily doing nothing, their worthy ambitions.

I have based my Manifesto on deeply-buried memories of the one written for Communism by Marx and Engels, with the odd dash from Wyndham Lewis's *Blast*. If they are around anywhere, I hope they will forgive me. Every manual needs a Manifesto. Here it is.

Manifesto

People, the world over, have a right of access to world culture.

Many of the objects of world culture are in museums, and it is the museum's job to make these objects accessible to everyone, the world over.

Museums are not equally distributed throughout the world, nor are the collections of world culture equally distributed throughout museums. As museums spread through the world, they will provide opportunities for a more equitable distribution of world culture. Much of this will be achieved through loan exhibitions, to ensure that people can have equal access to world cultures, particularly to those that are far removed from their own.

Museums cannot expect the whole world to come to them; they also have a duty to go out to the world.

Museums should not be bound by their buildings or circumscribed by their collections. Museums should be defined by their areas of interest. These can exist wherever there are people. A museum, therefore, can exist wherever these interests are or can be generated.

A museum exists when and wherever someone becomes interested in something it has. A museum can be in many places at once, at home or on tour.

TOURING EXHIBITIONS ARE MUSEUMS.

Museums are where people and objects meet.

A museum with objects but no people is not a museum; it is a store. A museum with people but no objects is not a museum; it is a theme park.

The museum's job is to look after objects for people, both now and for the future. If it loses its objects by not looking after them, it will cease to be a museum. If it loses its public by not looking after them, it will cease to be a museum.

The museum's job is to make its objects safely accessible. If the objects are just made safe, it has only done half its job (the easier half, too). A job half done is a job not done. Beware half-done jobs masquerading as jobs done. They are a cover for hegemony!

Classes and races appropriate cultures to differentiate themselves from others. (There is no intrinsic harm in the adoption and creation of a distinct culture; the harm comes when it is used as a means to exclude or denigrate others).

Museums, public museums that is, must be generous

institutions, welcoming all, excluding none. They must ACTIVELY RESIST all attempts to turn them into bastions of privilege.

To do this, since wealth and opportunity are not yet equally distributed throughout the world, public museums should, of course, provide free access. ALL MUSEUMS THAT NOW CHARGE SHOULD ASPIRE TO BE FREE.

Due to the current unequal distribution of ownership of museums (though the contents of public museums belong to everyone, their costs, as of yet, do not), whereas free access to static museums is sociologically and economically desirable, the considerable additional cost of touring exhibitions cannot be fairly borne solely by the current 'owner' of the collections, except in those circumstances where a museum in a wealthy region has been capitalizing on the possession of objects derived from a poorer region, and then proposes to charge that region for the loan of the objects that originated from it. In other cases, it is fair that the recipient of a touring exhibition contributes to the cost, and that can legitimately be through charging an entrance fee, unless a sponsoring organization has the foresight to subsidize it so that the exhibition can be free and truly accessible to everyone, no matter what their fortune.

As museums should treat their objects with equal care, so they should treat their public with equal care.

Care of a museum's public has to be founded on equality of access. Anything else is favoured cosseting and builds divisions in society. Achieving equality of access is an ambition beset with difficulties – both physical and mental – in the location of museum services and in the attitudes of people who run them.

The physical obstacles to equality of access are addressed – most simply – by sending objects out of the museum and – most easily – in touring exhibitions to those people who can't, for whatever reason, get themselves to where the objects, at that historical moment, happen to be. TAKE THE OBJECTS TO THE PEOPLE!

National museums have a responsibility to serve their nation – and nations to serve other nations – so that understanding and enjoyment can be spread equally throughout the world.

Why should someone living a hundred pounds' journey away from London pay for a local amenity for those living in South Kensington? Why should someone living a thousand pounds' journey away never have a chance to see the culture that an imperialist power looted from it?

The answer is not only to re-allocate the local product. That path, if narrowly pursued, leads to Nationalism. Touring exhibitions are the answer – that way leads to true Internationalism.

Why are so many obstacles put in the way of this comparatively simple process? Why do people have to beg to borrow the objects that belong to them? Why does anyone wanting to organize a touring exhibition have to genuflect and be ever so grateful to the temporary custodians of the objects they have a right to borrow? The pads should be on the other knees! The temporary custodians should bow and be thankful to the organizers of touring exhibitions, who are helping them to do their work!

TOURING EXHIBITION ORGANIZERS, DO NOT STOOP! THE CULTURE OF THE WORLD BELONGS TO YOU!

Do not believe the cries of the custodians when they say they are only being responsible for their objects. Only for whom? Of course they should care for their objects, but never forget they care for them for you!

Do not believe them when they say that their objects are safer at home. Most damage occurs in museums and stores – and how better it is to diversify risk by distributing loans!

Most of all, do not believe these custodians when they hide behind the science of conservation. The job of a conservator is to make a museum's objects safely accessible. If it is only safe, the conservators are doing only half their job. Huge investment has been made in the science of conservation in recent years, and we must expect as a result great improvements in both safety and accessibility. Demand your rights! Conservators are there to find a way of doing what the organizers of touring exhibitions want! Man has gone to the moon. Man can make culture equally accessible to all.

Do not be deceived by those who argue that permanent collections must be given priority over temporary exhibitions. Nothing is permanent. Everything changes, even permanent collections! Both 'permanent' and 'temporary' should be barred from the vocabulary of museums. There should only be 'collection' and 'exhibition' – object and display. One cannot exist without the other in a museum. Exhibition is as essential as collection to museums.

Do not be deterred by those curators who turn down requests for loans because the exhibition is not sufficiently 'serious' or 'scholarly' or 'important'. What right have they to restrict other people's access to objects and to restrict people's enjoyment of them? Suspect all who obstruct access to culture in order to preserve it! Preserve for people!

Once museums accept the ultimate reality of change (whatever its pace, from the imperceptibly slow to the visibly evident) and stop pretending they represent 'permanent' values, they will cease to be the pawns of a dominating society or a mad individual seeking immortality, and will become instead a living, breathing, responding, creative force in society.

Museums must be able to respond to human need. This responsiveness cannot be just mouthed or marginal; it has to be central to the museum's whole being.

Only then will the need to respond be given its proper priority, not as a token activity to be undertaken grudgingly so that the museum can get on with its 'real' work. A museum's 'real' work is to put people in touch with objects. To do that, the museum has to respond to what people are really interested in.

The onus is on the museum to respond to people because it has (or can get) what they want.

Museums must learn to listen to people. They cannot just dole out what they think people should have – the imperial ambitions of the Europeans are over – they are merely numerically outnumbered, even in many of the territories they claim as their own.

Museums have to ask people what people want from them. Museums have to invite people into the stores and select what interests them and then take what they have out to where most people can see it.

Whole sections of society, whole generations, have been or are in danger of being excluded from our museums because the latter only reflect the interests of one section or one generation. Museums should look at the whole of society and see what interests they can serve – not by attracting new audiences in, but by going out to serve these communities of interest. In that way, new museums and new museums services will be formed.

TOURING EXHIBITIONS ARE THE HARBINGERS OF MUSEUMS.

Touring exhibitions are also the laboratories of museums. They provide museums with occasions to experiment with new approaches, new interpretive methods, new ways of interesting new people. From their experiments will be built the museums of the future.

TOURING EXHIBITIONS ARE MUSEUMS.

THEY ARE THE MEANS BY WHICH MUSEUMS WILL LOSE THEIR CHAINS.

Julian Spalding
Director, Glasgow Museums

List of contributors

ABSA (Association for Business Sponsorship of the Arts), London.

Josie Adams, Keeper of Art, Scarborough Art Gallery.

John Asquith, press and publicity consultant, London W2 3SG.

John Benington, Senior Exhibitions Officer, Cheltenham Art Gallery and Museums.

John Bevin, Head of Estates, The Science Museum, London.

Celine Blair, Touring Exhibitions Officer, Glasgow Museums.

Scot Blyth, Managing Director, Momart Ltd, London.

Hilary Bracegirdle, Registrar, Victoria & Albert Museum, London.

Steve Brake, County Arts and Exhibitions Officer, Clwyd County Council, Wrexham.

David Breuer, Managing Director, A Zwemmer Ltd, London.

Christina Bridgwater, formerly Assistant Exhibitions Officer, City Museum and Art Gallery, Stoke-on-Trent.

Anne Buddle, Registrar, National Galleries of Scotland, Edinburgh.

Rosalie, Cass, Registrar, National Gallery, London.

May Cassar, Environmental Adviser, The Conservation Unit, Museums & Galleries Commission, London.

Bob Child, Head of Conservation, National Museum of Wales, Cardiff.

Birthe Kruse Christensen, Principal Keeper (Conservation and Design), Royal Pavilion, Art Gallery and Museums, Brighton.

Sue Clive, freelance gallery education consultant, London, SW1V 2LD.

Margot Coatts, exhibition curator and writer, Richmond, TW10 7HU.

Mike Collier, Lecturer in Art History, Newcastle College, Newcastle-upon-Tyne.

Bryan Dovey, formerly Museums Security Adviser, Museums and Galleries Commission, London.

Julia Ellis, Director, Craftspace Touring, Birmingham.

Brendan Flynn, Keeper of Fine Art, Wolverhampton Art Gallery.

Elizabeth Goodall, Head of Heritage, Arts and Entertainments Southampton City Council.

Michael Harrison, Director, Kettle's Yard, Cambridge.

Mary Heathcote, Administrator, Oriel Mostyn, Llandudno.

Philip Hughes, Craft Development Officer, Ruthin Craft Centre, Ruthin.

John Johnson, Lightwaves Ltd, London, N5 2TE.

Louise Karlsen, Principal Galleries and Museums Officer, Oldham.

Judith Kelly, freelance writer and *Museums Journal* correspondent, Cardiff, CF4 1UL.

Hilary Lane, exhibition organizer, Lewes, BN7 2DS.

Jem Legh, Film, Video and Broadcasting Department, Arts Council of England, London.

Kate Lowry, Chief Conservation Officer, Art Department, Amgueddfa Genedlaethol Cymru/National Museum of Wales, Cardiff.

Helen Luckett, Education Officer, National Touring Exhibitions, London.

Roger Malbert, Head of National Touring Exhibitions, Hayward Gallery, London.

David McNeff, Registrar Fine Art, National Museums & Galleries on Merseyside, Liverpool.

Janet Moore, Touring Exhibitions Organizer, Museum of Modern Art, Oxford.

Gerri Morris, Arts Marketing Consultant and Trainer, Manchester, M4 4DE.

John Wm Morris, Assistant Director (Technical), Yorkshire and Humberside Museums Council, London.

Roy Pateman, Director, Wingate & Johnston, London.

David Phillips, Lecturer in Art Gallery and Museum Studies, History of Art Department, University of Manchester.

Kevin Richardson, Shipping Director, Momart plc, London.

Jacqueline Ridge, Head of Painting Conservation, National Museums and Galleries on Merseyside, Liverpool.

Sally Rousham, interpretation consultant, Loughborough, LE11 2EA.

Sarah Shalgosky, Curator Mead Gallery, Univesity of Warwick.

Nicholas Sharp, solicitor, London, NW1 8XN.

James Shea, Arts Development Officer, Brighton Health Care NHS Trust, Brighton.

Tracy Teasdale, Education Officer, Ferens Art Gallery, Hull.

Jeremy Theophilus, Senior Visual Arts Officer, Arts Council of England, London.

Linda Theophilus, freelance exhibitions consultant, Colchester, CO2 7BL.

Giles Velarde FCSD FMA FRSA, museum designer, Pett Level, TN35 4EF.

Ian Vines, Assistant Exhibitions Officer, City Museum and Art Gallery, Stoke-on-Trent.

Valmai Ward, Visual Arts Department, Arts Council of Wales, Cardiff.

Heather Wilson, Capital Taxes Officer, Museums & Galleries Commission, London.

Nick Winterbotham, Director, Tullie House, Carlisle.

1

Policy

Christina Bridgwater and Ian Vines

1.1 The reasons for a written policy

Any institution involved in either organizing or hosting touring exhibitions will need a policy. A formal, written policy should not be seen either as a block to further thinking about which exhibitions should be considered or as a device for restricting the ambitions of the institution. Instead, it should be seen as a means of agreeing aims and objectives and providing a practical framework in which these can be achieved.

In particular the institution will need a written policy to:

- agree within the organization the character of the exhibitions it will tour or host, so that all members of staff know why a programme takes a certain shape;
- assess the implications and establish the priorities for staff and resources;
- relate touring exhibitions to its other policies, e.g. overall exhibitions policy, service delivery, collections, education, publications, promotions, design and equal opportunities;
- relate the exhibitions it wants to tour or those it wishes to attract from other sources, to the policies of other institutions;
- attract funding and other support from outside bodies.

1.2 Drafting a policy

The process of devising a policy may need a lead-time of several weeks or months, depending on the size of the institution and the number of other interested parties. In a large institution with several members of staff (e.g. educational, technical) directly involved in or affected by the exhibition programme, an 'exhibitions working party' including the Director and key members of staff might be set up to address the role of touring exhibitions. The process would need to involve any outside bodies (e.g. Regional Arts Board or Area Museum Council) likely to be affected by the policy. Finally, the policy will need to be approved by local authority representatives, trustees or funding bodies.

Whether the policy is drafted by one person or in committee, the first consideration will be to establish the reasons for organizing and/or hosting touring exhibitions and to balance the advantages and disadvantages of either or both strategies.

Organizing such exhibitions might raise the profile of the institution, but could also result in little or no financial benefits when the full costs of touring (including staff time) are taken into account.

Hosting such exhibitions can add breadth and variety to an overall programme. The organizer may have access to a collection and/or resources which are beyond the scope of the venue. However, hosting touring exhibitions might be something of a gamble. Often exhibitions are still in the planning stage when first advertised, so it could be difficult to gauge the precise nature of the exhibition from the material supplied by the organizer.

The resources currently and potentially available will dictate whether touring exhibitions form a major or a minor part of the institution's activities.

1.3 Considerations for an organizer

As an organizer of touring exhibitions, the institution should establish general parameters for the types of exhibition that will be considered.

How far touring exhibitions will be drawn from any permanent collection held by the institution and/or from material borrowed from other sources. Either choice will have implications in terms of cost and conservation. If exhibitions are formed from borrowed material, should they reflect the specific disciplines of the institution or include other kinds of subjects.

Whether the institution will organize tours in the traditional manner (i.e. taking overall responsibility for content, administration and financing of the exhibition), or whether it will enter into some form of collaboration with other institutions (i.e. where some or all of the responsibilities are shared, see 13.1, 13.2).

The effect of touring on the overall policy and balance of the programme must be borne in mind. A tour can allow an institution to undertake different categories of exhibition such as historical/contemporary, popular/special interest, etc., or to respond to factors such as age range, anniversaries, etc.

The public(s) that the institution would like to reach, e.g. particular age-groups, special needs, community groups (see 3.6).

Consideration should be given to the policies of other institutions involved in touring on a regional, national or international level. The policy should aim for a programme that is distinctive, in order to attract other showings and/or funding from outside sources.

1.4 Considerations for a venue

As a venue, the institution should similarly establish general parameters for the types of exhibition that will be considered.

It must consider how far the subject area of hired-in exhibitions must relate to the disciplines represented by the venue. This includes not only any permanent collection held by the institution but also the interests and specialities of members of staff. Touring exhibitions can be used to bring in other subjects.

The effect of incoming exhibitions on the overall policy and balance of the programme must be borne in mind. A touring exhibition can allow a venue to experiment with different approaches (to special needs, cultural diversity, etc.) and allow it to show different types of exhibition or to respond to the needs of different sectors of its public (see 2.5, 28.4). At the same time, the venue must be prepared to tolerate the aims and objectives of organizers of touring exhibitions that are different from its own. Ideally, its policy on incoming exhibitions should be sufficiently flexible to take account of different policies of other institutions, rather than to seek to exclude certain types of exhibition.

1.5 Resource implications

The organization of touring exhibitions will involve considerable amounts of staff time and will require a major investment of money and other resources. At the stage when the policy is being drafted, it is important to ensure that all members of staff who are likely to be directly involved in or affected by the touring programme are consulted so that the overall allocation of time and resources can be resolved. It is vitally important to resolve the issue of resources at this early stage. Failure to do so will probably result in serious practical problems, certainly during the process of organizing exhibitions, but also at the venues.

A policy will normally require a budget adequate to cover all the normal costs associated with organizing exhibitions and any additional costs for touring them to other venues, e.g. onward transport (see 9.4).

It should be established in principle what will be provided by the organizer, and what will be outstanding for the venue to provide. Custom and practice may limit what the venues will pay as hire fees and/or provide as services. The policy should indicate if the aim is: to recoup the costs of the tour alone, to contribute to the costs of originating the exhibition; or even to generate a profit for the institution.

A policy may be influenced by the possibility of additional funding in the form of grants or sponsorship (see 10.1, 11.1).

Unless there is significant sponsorship, the cost of a touring programme or even a single touring exhibition may require a large proportion of the annual exhibitions budget, which will have implications for the rest of the programme, perhaps requiring reductions in expenditure on other exhibitions and/or a reliance on touring exhibitions from other sources.

Researching, financing and commissioning work for a major project can be time-consuming for the organizer and can divert this person from other work for the institution during a long lead-time. It may be necessary to formally second specialist exhibition staff or curators of collections if they can be spared. External specialists might be brought in on occasion, e.g. to select and organize exhibitions (see 5.1).

After the exhibition has opened, managing a tour can still be time-consuming for the organizer.

Designing and building an exhibition for tour can be time-consuming for design and technical staff, diverting them from other work for the institution for an extended period before the opening of the exhibition. There may need to be formal agreement relating to the amount of time that design and technical staff should be involved.

Display equipment may be away from the institution for the duration of the tour.

Collaborations can help to reduce the level of financial commitment by an organizer, but it does involve additional work in the liaison that is necessary. Collaborations also involve the venues – or partners – in a higher level of liaison that is usual in traditional touring, and a significant increase in the financial commitment (see 13.3).

For the venue, hosting the traditional form of touring exhibitions should be generally less demanding than organizing them. However, they still require considerable input in terms of coordination, promotional and educational work and a budget to cover hire fees, publicity, display, events and activities and transport. Staff must plan to devote sufficient time; additional help may be required (and will then need to be supervised) for technical or educational purposes. Advisory groups may need to be set up, including individuals from outside the institution (see 2.5).

For a small venue, a touring exhibition can be a significant financial commitment and a principal item in the programme. Both the organizer and the venue itself will expect a larger proportion of time and funding to be devoted to promotion and education than may be normal with the rest of programme.

Larger venues have sometimes regarded a touring exhibition as an easy option for filling a gap in a programme in a way which enables other work to be done. Not unnaturally, the organizer will regard this as a poor use of the resource that it has made available, and it will be unlikely to offer showings to the same venue in future. The organizer has saved the venue the time and expense of bringing the exhibition together, and as a result it will expect a commitment of time and funding for publicity and promotion that is at least equivalent to other exhibitions in the programme.

1.6 Evaluating the policy

Evaluation of a policy is quite distinct from the evaluation of individual exhibitions, and will take place separately, though taking account of what has been learnt from individual projects (see 6.11), as well as from market research (see 3.17). An annual review will ascertain:

- what objectives have been achieved;
- where resources have been inadequate; and
- what should be provided in future, or
- where ambitions need to be curtailed.

2

Cultural diversity

Roger Malbert

2.1 What is 'cultural diversity'?

The subject of cultural diversity is too often obscured by clichés and stereotypes. This is due partly to the generality of the term itself, with its implication of everything 'other' than mainstream, white, European culture, and partly to the standard conservative reaction to anything that smacks of 'political correctness'.

The issue is, unavoidably, contentious. Diversity implies relativism, the recognition of equality between different cultures. Yet, even today, many Europeans find it difficult to relinquish the old imperialist myth of racial and cultural superiority. In the world of galleries, it is only necessary to recall Hitler's persecution of progressive museum directors in Germany in the thirties and the purge of 'non-Aryan' art from their collections to be reminded of the extremes of ideological disagreement that are possible in the interpretation of a museum's function.

2.2 Representing diversity

During the past decade, some of the most stimulating discussion about the exhibition as a medium, and the status of the exhibited object, has occurred within the academic discipline of cultural anthropology. Although focused principally on ethnographic exhibitions, many of the issues addressed there have wider application. Anthropologists tend to be aware of the political and epistemological problems associated with the representation of other cultures, and of the necessity for self-analysis and careful reflection upon the relationship between the observer and the observed, particularly given the imbalance of power between rich and poor countries of the world.

Similarly, many museum curators are now sensitive to the effect of traditional ethnographic exhibitions on visitors who identify with or belong to the cultures represented. The issue has been sharply felt in North America and Australia, where indigenous peoples have sought to reclaim their cultures and to re-define them in displays of their own making, pushing to the foreground the questions of power and ownership.

2.3 The role of exhibitions

In Britain the situation is different, but no less complicated, and the working out of these questions follows a parallel course. Britain's museums and galleries are largely a product of the Victorian era, containing the wealth of an empire which a century ago encompassed a quarter of the world's population. Today they are in a delicate, somewhat contradictory position in relation to the changing realities of a post-colonial, multicultural society. They are required, on the one hand, to represent and interpret the 'national heritage' – which is no simple matter in a society divided by differences of class, gender, region, religion, generation and ethnicity. On the other hand, they have a constructive role to play in defining the cultural values of the present.

Museums remain impressive institutions with the authority to validate as well as educate. Yet, with a few exceptions, their financial resources for new acquisitions have dwindled almost to nothing; many barely have funds to re-design old displays. In these circumstances, the temporary exhibition can be the most economical way to explore new ideas and approaches to issues of difference and diversity. Temporary exhibitions drive museums' thinking about the ways that collections should be displayed, and touring exhibitions can be used to bring in the ideas and exhibits that the museum might not have the resources or the experience to acquire itself.

Many museums in areas of the country with a culturally-diverse population have made positive efforts to engage with minority groups, often employing curatorial staff from those communities. This is an ongoing – and in some places unduly slow – process. In many instances, these efforts involve exhibitions focusing on traditional artefacts and the history of a particular community. However, it would be patronizing in the extreme to suggest that all 'the ethnic minorities' require are 'ethnic minority arts', any more than a diet of Elizabethan miniatures could satisfy a quest for a native English tradition. There is no reason why a young black student should not be as interested as her white counterpart in Gainsborough or Goya or Hieronymous Bosch.

Equally, a venue does not need to have a multicultural community on its doorstep before it introduces exhibitions of material from beyond the European tradition. Such exhibitions should be of interest to everybody, for their intrinsic excellence and for the experience they bring in broadening horizons. Every lover of twentieth-century art will appreciate the truth of Derain's dictum that an African sculpture can be as beautiful as the Venus de Milo. In that sense, there is no dichotomy between the 'canon' and other voices; the Graeco-Roman tradition was subverted from within, almost a century ago.

Western artists have borrowed freely from sources throughout the world, but the international rates of exchange have not encouraged reciprocal relations. The suspicion that artists of colour have been arbitrarily excluded from the official history and institutions has inspired many of the polemics and activities of the Black Arts movement during the past decade. The curator wishing to engage with these issues should be familiar with the arguments and history of the movement, and should be aware that the situation changes from year to year.

What might have been appropriate a decade ago, e.g. the 'ghetto' exhibition of black and Asian artists revolving exclusively around the issue of race and 'identity', would seem anachronistic today. New institutions, the growth of experience and confidence among artists and curators of colour, international exhibitions and exchanges and an ongoing, vigorous debate have altered the terms of reference significantly. A number of galleries have opened up to the plurality of voices within contemporary art practice, a plurality which is increasingly recognized as crucial to art's revitalization.

2.4 The exhibition

An organizer or a venue might use the following checklist when devising a programme or considering an exhibition:

- Does this exhibition include exhibits that present one cultural perspective only?
- Is this deliberate or accidental?
- If it is accidental, is there any way of redressing the imbalance within the exhibition?
- Are there plans to present other cultural perspectives?
- Is this exhibition aimed at visitors from a particular cultural group, and if so how will they be attracted?
- Is this exhibition intended to inform and stimulate other cultural groups, and how will we appeal to or inform them?

A distinction should be made between exhibitions of historical material and those of work by living artists. In the latter, the organizer's role is usually subordinated to the wishes of the artist, and exactly the same rules apply in the presentation of contemporary 'culturally diverse' art as in any exhibition of contemporary art. Exhibitions of work from the past, or representing other cultures, are open to more curatorial intervention, but where any exhibits have a sacred significance, there must be a similar dialogue with the relevant cultural group, about appropriate methods of display and installation and – above all – about their interpretation.

In weighing the balance between contextual and aesthetic considerations, it is important for the organizer to be aware of the codes governing the display of art in museums and galleries. These are influenced by contemporary art practice, and today (Victorian revivalism aside) the tendency is towards a sparse display, allowing the exhibits space to be appreciated on their own terms. Rather than crowding them with didactic texts, less obtrusive ways should be found of presenting that information without demeaning the exhibits.

This is all the more relevant when the exhibits are from another culture, because museums often present this material artlessly, submerged in text and badly lit. The typical 'Masterpieces from . . .' exhibition confirms the view that the greater the imputed value of the exhibit, the less text is given on the label. If one aim of an exhibition of artefacts from another culture is to affirm that culture in a society where it is generally undervalued, then subtle display and good graphics are paramount. The need for contextualization is anyway relative: no Sikh will need to be informed about the significance of Ranjit Singh's throne.

What constitutes key information will be different for each cultural group, and can only be drafted with the advice of representatives of the relevant communities. Translations of key information into appropriate languages can be expensive and needs to be budgeted for and planned well in advance.

Back-up can and should be provided, in the form of publicity, interpretive and explanatory material, including an audio–visual programme, lists of possible speakers, etc (see 25.3).

2.5 The tour

No venue is the same as another, ideologically and demographically as well as physically. Every exhibition will look different and be experienced differently even by the same visitor going to each of the venues in a tour. The use made of an exhibition which was not originated locally ultimately depends upon circumstances beyond the control of the organizer. An exhibition's impact depends on the venue's rapport with its diverse constituencies. At worst, an exhibition may receive practically no visits from the community it was intended to interest, and will serve no other purpose than as a sop to political pressure from the powers that be.

The touring exhibition organizer will need to know the situation at each venue, and seek to work in co-operation with the relevant staff to ensure that the exhibition relates to the local context, and can be used effectively. Ideally, group meetings should be arranged, allowing curators from all the venues to meet each other and share their experiences (see 49.3).

A venue with a well-established multicultural programme and good working relationship with local communities (perhaps through the efforts of a highly-committed curator who represents an alternative 'voice' within the institution) can provide an invaluable example and source of information for other venues. Equally, a venue with a dynamic education department might draw out unexpected potential in a show (e.g. by using local artists as a source of inspiration).

The long-standing role of touring exhibitions, of enabling venues to experiment with new ideas and approaches, applies to issues of difference and diversity. A venue with no real link with a particular community might have a motivated, albeit inexperienced, curator who may be keen to use the exhibition as a starting point to a connection that can be built on in the future.

Special efforts may be necessary to publicize a show if the aim is to interest people who are not regular visitors, and this requires research into local media and other community networks (see 31.6).

Education departments, where they exist, are likely to be alert to the possibilities of a show with wider cultural reference, but without adequate support from their director and curators, their efforts may remain peripheral, concentrated on school and other formally-organized groups (see 25.2).

The community 'targeted' may be suspicious of, even antagonistic to, the venue as an institution, and the venue should be prepared to open itself up for public discussion – possibly of a more heated kind than normal. First-time contacts should be made at the planning stage (in the case of the organizer) and well in advance of the exhibition's arrival (in the case of a venue). It might be appropriate to organize some educational projects away from the building, before as well as during the showing. Community centres and other less formal venues may provide a more congenial setting. Close liaison at grass-roots level is essential.

Opening receptions are significant social events (see 30.19). They provide an opportunity to welcome people to the venue for the first time. It is worth putting real energy into re-defining the ambience, thinking about a special invitation list and suitable supporting activities. A radical departure from the conventional private view may be called for, even at the risk of upsetting some of the regulars!

2.6 Further reading

Araeen, R. *The Other Story, Afro-Asian artists in post-war Britain,* 1989, South Bank Centre, London.

Fisher J. *Global Visions,* 1994, Institute for Internationalism in the Visual Arts, London.

Karp, I. and Lavine, S.D. *Exhibiting Cultures: the poetics and politics of museum display,* 1991, The Smithsonian Institution, Washington.

3

Market research

Gerri Morris

3.1 Why do market research?

Market research and marketing go hand in hand. As exhibition galleries develop closer relationships with their visitors – perhaps through recognizing the need to be more accountable, or through a desire to attract a wider range of people – then the role of marketing develops in significance, and market research becomes an important tool to understand the market and to discover how better to communicate with it.

The more marketing-focused a venue is, the more important market research becomes. Market research is indispensable if a venue's priorities include any of the following: improving access; keeping existing visitors; attracting new visitors; maintaining visitor satisfaction; enhancing quality of experience; working with minority groups; developing education; building up shop sales; increasing income; and battling for survival.

For the organizer, defining the market for an exhibition can inform its selection of venues and the information it gives them. For the venue, knowledge of the market for an exhibition can inform programming, planning, publicity, information, events and interpretation.

In addition, market research is the most direct means of evaluating visitor response to an exhibition (see 6.7).

3.2 Planning market research

When considering market research, remember that: it need not always involve additional time and money; it can generally tell you more than you think you know; it is the only way to explode myths and misconceptions about your visitors; it need not take the form of streams of superfluous statistics; it dispels uncertainty and offers the only valid alternative to guesswork; and a little amount of research is better than none at all.

The three key steps in any market research project are:

- to establish what the information is needed for (see 3.3);
- to identify the most appropriate method (see 3.9); and
- to decide how to use the information and act on the results (see 3.18).

3.3 What information is needed and why?

The first steps in any market research project are to establish clear objectives, in terms of what information do we need, why do we need it and how will we use it. Market research can be used to address any of the following issues: to justify the venue's existence and activity (see 3.4); to identify the profile or character of the existing market (see 3.5); to identify the size and character of the potential market (see 3.6); to identify the needs, wants, attitudes and motivations of actual and potential visitors (see 3.7) and to evaluate visitors' reactions to exhibitions (see 3.8).

3.4 Justifying the venue's existence and activity

Being able to quote statistics on

- the number of existing visits,
- the size of the actual market,
- the size of the potential market,
- the number of people who regularly visit exhibitions in general, and
- the relative success of the venue in reaching the potential market

helps to justify the venue's operation, promotes confidence, helps to set strategic targets, and strengthens its position with funding bodies, collaborators and decision-makers.

3.5 The profile or character of the existing market

Knowing

- the age of people who come,
- their profession,
- who they come with,
- what motivates them,
- what they like about the venue and its services,
- what they dislike,
- how often they come,
- what else they do in their leisure time,
- where they live and work, and
- where they go for information about the arts and the heritage

helps in developing a portrait of existing visitors, explodes myths and identifies gaps. Knowing who comes helps the venue to communicate better with organizers of touring exhibitions and artists. It informs decisions on approaches to interpretation. Knowing the types of existing visitors and where they live helps to identify potential visitors with similar characteristics. This information informs future planning decisions.

3.6 Identifying the needs, wants, attitudes and motivations of actual and potential visitors

Asking people to talk about

- what they like about the venue,
- what they dislike,
- what they might welcome by way of information and opportunities to find out more about the exhibits,
- new ideas that the venue would like to explore,
- the image that non-visitors might have

can all help in making the most of good points and planning to overcome weaknesses.

3.7 Size and character of the potential market

Identifying the size and character of the potential market can help in programming, setting attendance targets and designing information and interpretation.

Knowing what information to request will help an organizer of a touring exhibition to identify appropriate venues, to note weaknesses in other venues, to identify the market for that venue and how to go about reaching it.

3.8 Evaluating visitors' responses to an exhibition

Measuring

- the number of visitors
- how long they stay
- how they use the space
- how they use and respond to interpretation
- how they respond to the exhibition
- what they say about the exhibition

will help to evaluate the exhibition against its objectives, find out more about visitor reactions and inform future planning (see 6.6).

3.9 Identify the most appropriate method

The key to successful market research is identifying the most appropriate and cost-effective method for achieving the research objectives. Market research information is of two different types: quantitative and qualitative.

Quantitative information deals with statistics and data which can be analysed mathematically into percentages, columns, graphs, etc., to show trends and patterns.

Qualitative information deals with abstract findings concerning the reactions, thoughts, needs and wants, perceptions and beliefs that people hold.

It is important to decide whether the information needed is of a quantitative or qualitative nature, as this informs the method of obtaining that information.

There are also two levels of research: secondary and primary. Secondary data has already been collated for other purposes but is nevertheless useful. It is often known as desk research, as it can be carried out without moving very far, and it is generally less costly to gather than primary data. As a general rule, the researcher explores secondary sources before commissioning new research, in case the information required already exists.

Primary research is that which an organization commissions or carries out itself or in collaboration with a group of similar organizations.

3.10 Internal records as a source of secondary data

When analysed, a venue's internal records can provide valuable information, from:

- visitor books
- admissions records
- feedback from members of staff/volunteers
- comments cards
- suggestion boxes
- sales records.

3.11 ACE as a source of secondary data

The Marketing Department of the Arts Council of England (ACE) gathers and analyses an enormous amount of secondary data on behalf of organizations in receipt of ACE or Regional Arts Board (RAB) funding:

ACORN and TGI data provide numbers and profiles of arts attenders (including separate figures for art gallery visitors), the degree of cross-fertilization between art-forms, and numbers of potential gallery visitors in each postcode sector in England.

Site reports provide potential numbers of arts attenders within 30 minutes' driving time of all major towns in England.

The *Visual Arts Research Digest* is a compilation of statistics on visual arts attendances and visitor profiles.

A directory of existing visual arts surveys and research projects and their availability is included in the *Market Research Index for the Arts*.

Audiences for Contemporary Visual Arts, conducted by Denis Robb of The Research Practice.

3.12 Other sources of secondary data

The Policy Studies Institute's *Cultural Trends* is a series of publications which includes statistics on attendances at galleries and museums.

British Tourist Authority and regional tourist boards compile annual reviews and summaries of attendances at heritage and visitor attractions.

Local authority planning departments generally publish summaries of Census data, local population statistics which give overviews of relative wealth, cultural and demographic make-up, etc.

Other sources of secondary data include RABs, Area Museums Councils, government departments, local authority economic development and tourism departments.

3.13 Primary Research

New information can be gathered in a number of ways, not all of them expensive and time-consuming. Each of the following methods has its own strengths and weaknesses. Some can be carried out on a shoestring; others require professional involvement.

Observation of visitors can be done cheaply and unobtrusively, to provide valuable information on the type of visitor, on approximate age, cultural background, numbers of families, how long visitors stay, how long they look at exhibits, how they use the building, their reactions, and what they say to one another (see 6.8).

Conversations with visitors can discover what they think of the venue and the exhibits, how they found out about the exhibition, whether they will tell their friends, what they would like to see, and other qualitative feedback.

Interviewing visitors is a more formal approach, which takes them through a questionnaire to generate both quantitative and qualitative data: it gathers statistics on who the visitors are, as well as offering an opportunity to ask their opinions on various aspects of the venue or the exhibition. Catching people as they leave is therefore advisable (see 6.10).

Self-completion questionnaires are an efficient and cost-effective method of establishing a profile of the general characteristics and habits of visitors. Self-completion monitoring/comment cards are a shorter alternative to the long questionnaire, which can gain useful insights into visitors' response to an exhibition, as well as monitoring where they came from and how they found out about the exhibition (see Figure 3.1).

A postal survey can help to reach non-visitors by using other organizations' mailing lists. It is a reasonably cheap method, but the response rates are never very high. An incentive to respond, in the form of a prize draw and a freepost facility, can help.

A telephone survey is time-consuming, but speaking to people on the mailing list provides high-quality information. If they support the organization, people are generally flattered to be contacted and asked for their opinions.

A household survey can be expensive and time-consuming, but is useful for establishing levels of awareness about the venue, attitudes to it, frequency of attendance, how respondents find out what's on, and what would motivate them to go more often.

A street survey can again be expensive and time-consuming, but is an immediate method of reaching non-visitors and exploring their attitudes.

Focus groups entail inviting groups of actual or potential visitors to the venue to discuss their responses to it and its exhibitions, to explore what they like and dislike, and to discover their needs, wants and attitudes. Focus groups should be facilitated by an experienced group leader to draw out the issues. When conducted successfully, they provide a rich source of data. This makes them expensive to have conducted professionally.

Visitor panels involve asking groups of actual or potential visitors to attend more regular meetings, to explore the potential of a number of proposals and to test their response to possible projects. This can build

MUSEUM & ART GALLERY
QUESTIONNAIRE

We are constantly trying to improve our services. Please help us by spending a few moments completing this questionnaire.

1 Why did you visit the museum and art gallery today? (please ✔ tick)

❑ just a general visit

❑ interested in a particular exhibition or event. If so which? . . . .

. . . .

2 Have you also used the library, cafe or shop today? (please ✔ tick)

❑ library ❑ cafe ❑ shop

3 Before your visit, which of the following publicity had you seen or heard during the past month? (please ✔ tick only those you definitely remember)

❑ signs on the outside of the building

❑ posters or leaflets inside the building

❑ posters displayed elsewhere

❑ preview leaflet

❑ special exhibition or event leaflet

❑ piece in local newspaper or magazine

❑ piece in national newspaper or magazine

❑ mention on the radio

❑ mention on the television

❑ leaflet or brochure received in the post

❑ display elsewhere

4 Could you say if any of the following prompted your visit? (please ✔ tick)

❑ felt that it would appeal to the children

❑ brought friends or visitors on day out

❑ it was recommended by a friend

❑ found out about it at school/college

❑ other

Figure 3.1 Sample questionnaire

5 How often have you visited the museum and art gallery in the last 12 months? (please ✔ tick)

- ❑ this is my first visit
- ❑ I've been before but not in the last 12 months
- ❑ once in the last 12 months
- ❑ 2 or 3 times
- ❑ 4 or more times

6 Please ✔ tick one or more of the following expressions which best describe your overall impression of the museum (glass, ceramics, local history) and art gallery (paintings, sculptures)

	Museum	Art gallery
welcoming	❑	❑
too old fashioned	❑	❑
stimulating	❑	❑
uninformative	❑	❑
educational	❑	❑
unwelcoming	❑	❑
interesting	❑	❑

We welcome other comments . . . .

It would help us if you could give us the following information about yourself, although it will be treated in the strictest confidence:

7 Your full postcode

8 Sex (please ✔ tick)

❑ male ❑ female

9 Age (please ✔ tick)

❑ under 15	❑ 15–19	❑ 20–24	❑ 25–34
❑ 35–44	❑ 45–54	❑ 55–64	❑ over 65

10 How would you describe your ethnic background? (please ✔ tick)

❑ Asian	❑ white British	❑ black British
❑ African	❑ Caribbean	❑ other................................

Would you like to receive information about our Friends organization? All Friends receive advance information about exhibitions and events.
Simply fill in your name and address:

Name..

Address ....

Post code ....

Thank you for your time.
Please put this form in the box provided.

loyalty and good will as well as provide valuable feedback.

Community consultation: if it is important to explore the needs and wants of a group that does not presently use the venue, it may be necessary to go into the community, to ask it what it wants and to explore ideas with it (see 2.5). This might require the appointment of a specialized member of staff, to establish community contacts and to build trust.

3.14 Rules for simple do-it-yourself research

Many of the methods outlined above lend themselves to DIY research. Important points to remember are:

- be clear about your research objectives;
- decide in advance how the data will be analysed;
- be clear on which part of the market you are researching;
- don't try to collect too much information at once.

If it proves difficult to prioritize what information is needed, establish what information the organization is in a position to act upon. If there is no possibility of the information influencing any aspect of the organization, then save it for a subsequent research project. A little but often is better than too much, too soon. Differentiate information which you need to know from that which would be nice to know, and forsake the latter.

Decide on the method of analysis for the data before embarking on a DIY project. Computer analysis is preferable for quantitative data, as it offers more scope for cross-analysis of data. If the only option is manual analysis, then the questionnaire should be structured to take into account how the data is to be collated and by whom. Computer analysis can sometimes be obtained from local authority departments, colleges and university computing departments, and marketing resource agencies at reasonable cost.

3.15 Designing a questionnaire

For analysing quantitative data, questions should:

- be close-ended, i.e. requiring a specific answer;
- offer a multiple choice of answers, e.g. yes/no/don't know, poor/fair/good/excellent, agree/disagree/don't know;
- be easy to understand;
- not be open to misinterpretation;
- follow a logical sequence.

Open-ended questions, seeking data of a more qualitative nature should be kept to a minimum on self-completion questionnaires. Otherwise they become very difficult to analyse, and the results are laborious to represent.

Devising the questionnaire requires careful consideration, see *List of Visitor Survey Questions for the Visual Arts*, published by ACE's Marketing Department. When designing a questionnaire:

- give it a title, and use a logo or letter-heading;
- provide an introduction on the reasons for the research;
- leave enough room for answers;
- use a clear, uncluttered layout;
- keep to a maximum of two sides of A4;
- instruct where to return the completed questionnaire;
- conclude by thanking the respondent and promising confidentiality.

3.16 Sample sizes

Sampling is a complex area of market research. For DIY research, decide on the nature of the sample according to the information required, and whether the research is addressing existing, frequent, infrequent, potential or lapsed visitors or non-visitors. For simple research, the following rules can help in obtaining a representative sample:

- aim for a minimum sample of 150;
- do not analyse quantitatively any sample below 100;
- if interviewing, approach a new visitor only when the interview with the previous visitor is finished;
- when handing out questionnaires, give only one copy to a party or group of visitors;
- if handing out questionnaires, take up a central position or staff all entrances, and ask visitors to complete the questionnaire on their way out;
- allow for a varied mix of visitors by handing out questionnaires at different times of day, on weekdays as well as weekends, term-time as well as holidays, etc.

3.17 Commissioning market research

ACE maintains lists of individual consultants and commercial agencies. Professional services will regard as central to their role the selection of the most appropriate method for achieving the research objectives. When commissioning research, the following points should be borne in mind.

Write a brief, stating clearly the research objectives, the budget available, which segment of the market the research is addressing, and how the organization plans to use the research findings.

Send the brief to a number of agencies/consultancies, asking them to quote for the job by a specified date and to describe the method they would adopt.

Select the successful tender on the basis of that agency's sensitivity to the organization and its experience with similar organizations.

Be prepared to challenge, edit, re-write certain parts of the questionnaire to ensure that it makes sense to those filling it in and that it correctly represents how respondents experience the organization.

Ensure that the method will meet your objectives and that the questionnaire asks the questions you want answers to: if they do not, ask the agency how these questions will be answered.

Remember that if you don't get the answers you seek, you haven't asked the right questions!

3.18 Acting on the results

Market research is worthless if the results sit as an indecipherable pile of statistics on a shelf. Time must be allowed for a full scrutiny and analysis of the findings, to ensure that the full meaning and implications are drawn out. The results and implications should be written up into a report which should be then used to inform future decisions.

Highlighting the implications of the findings is the first step to taking action. Market research should provide one link in a continuous, circular process of analysis, planning and action, informing future activities and monitoring the effect of those activities.

The findings of market research are an empowering tool, enabling an organization not only to shape strategy, but to justify it and then evaluate its effectiveness. Market research is the organization's way of establishing and maintaining a dialogue with its visitors. Listening to these visitors will help the organization to become more effective.

3.19 Examples

Example 1: Justifying the venue's existence and activity (see 3.4). An art gallery attracts about 80 000 visits a year. Research shows that people visit the gallery an average of twice a year, which makes an actual market size of 40 000. The town has a population of 190 000. ACE research shows that 21 per cent of the population currently visit art galleries. Since the market size of 40 000 is very close to 21 per cent of the town's population, i.e. 39 900, the gallery feels that its programme is reaching a representative proportion of its local population. This helps to remind people of the gallery's effectiveness and justify the programming policy.

Example 2: Identifying the profile or character of the existing market (see 3.5). A venue's visitors are predominantly 25–44 years old, earn £15 000–£25 000 a year, and 56 per cent are in professional employment. Three-quarters of them also go to the theatre. This contradicts the impression that the venue had that most of its visitors were students, and suggests that the venue could do more to attract younger visitors. This might influence programming decisions and the design and distribution of publicity material.

Example 3: Identifying the size and character of the potential market (see 3.6). An exhibition gallery providing a programme for a town of 200 000 people will calculate that there are 42 000 potential visitors (21 per cent of the population, see Example 1). Ten per cent of the population of the town are people from the Asian sub-continent, of whom the largest majority are Pakistani Muslims. The gallery is addressing the cultural isolation of this percentage, partly through a policy of providing at least one exhibition a year which will appeal to Muslim people. Other under-represented groups are younger, lower-middle class and working class families, teenagers and older people, and the gallery is developing children's events and reminiscence sessions around its exhibitions. This will influence programming, outreach and publicity decisions.

Example 4: Identifying the needs, wants, attitudes and motivations of actual and potential visitors (see 3.7). Research shows that a venue's visitors appreciate the exhibitions but require more information of a factual nature, rather than subjective interpretation. They also appreciate family guides which will help their children to enjoy the exhibits. Publicity material that includes information on the nature of the exhibition written in simple, everyday language will help to attract new visitors. This will help in the planning of interpretation.

4

Concept

Michael Harrison

4.1 Defining the concept

Having an idea is one thing. Defining, developing and presenting it is another. The progress from initial idea to realization is a process of constant questioning. All of the following questions – including whether the exhibition can and should tour (see 4.6) – should be considered at the outset, and should be addressed at various stages as the project advances. Answers will help to form a written outline for the exhibition, identifying its intention and scope.

Education staff who will be working with the exhibition should contribute from the outset (see 22.2). At various stages in the development of an exhibition, other colleagues, boards of management, funders and sponsors, potential lenders of exhibits, potential hirers of the exhibition and, eventually, the press and the public will need to be convinced of the exhibition idea and the desirability and feasibility of its realization.

4.2 Policy and programme

The idea will need to be tested against the exhibition policy and programme of the originating gallery (see 1.2). Does it fit the policy, and contribute to it more than other exhibitions would? How does it relate to other recent and planned exhibitions? In relation to other exhibitions elsewhere, has the subject been covered before, and if so, how recently? Is the idea sufficiently distinct from other projects?

4.3 Is it an exhibition?

An exhibition is primarily a gathering of objects for public presentation, selected and arranged so that they speak fully for themselves and, in combination, contribute to our perception of each. A theme should not be imposed on objects but should appear or emerge from them. Will the theme of the exhibition emerge from the juxtaposition of exhibits, or will they illustrate an otherwise verbal argument?

Is it really necessary to the concept to bring exhibits together at great expense and at no little risk? The visitor's direct experience of the real thing should be crucial to what the organizer intends with the exhibition. Forget the exhibition if the idea could be explored better or as effectively as an article, a book, a video or a television programme.

What is the exhibition trying to achieve? Is it attempting to be comprehensive or authoritative on a particular subject, or is it being speculative or provocative?

4.4 Testing the idea in relation to available exhibits

Research may be necessary to develop the idea and locate the exhibits (see 36.4). Does the organizer have the time and the experience to research the idea, not least through visits to see potential exhibits for their contribution to the concept and their availability to the planned exhibition?

Are there experts in the field? It may be sensible to involve others who may know more about the subject. A specialist, with particular knowledge of the subject can be brought in on a freelance basis to shape the concept and contents (and often to compile the catalogue). Does the organizer have the budget to engage such a specialist and the time to allow for this person's research (see 5.11, 5.12)? The responsibility of the organizer as editor and overall presenter of the exhibition remains, and the organizer should play an active part in shaping the exhibition with any subject specialist who may not be so well versed in exhibition-making or whose intentions might be scholarly rather than communicative (see 5.8).

Whether carried out in-house or by an external curator, the first objective of any research is to draw up a 'wish list' of key exhibits with their whereabouts (see 36.4). On the basis of this list, the organizer will be able to investigate the likelihood of loans. A small amount of money spent on research at this early stage may avoid wasting more on an impractical proposal.

Does the idea hold up to the evidence of the objects? The idea may change in response to the work as selection progresses. How many exhibits – or, rather, how few – are needed to serve the purpose? Exhibits are the all-important 'material evidence'. They should be selected, first because of their intrinsic value – for the experience and/or information each individual item can convey – and second, because together they contribute to an overall experience and/or more general story which reinforces the significance of each item.

The 'wish list' of key exhibits with their whereabouts will in turn affect the feasibility of the exhibition and define the resources necessary to realize it. The costs of transport, packing, couriers and insurance may be very high if the exhibits are to be borrowed from a number of widely-scattered lenders, rather than from the organizer's collection (if applicable) or from a single lender. How dependent is the exhibition on the loan of objects from distant collections?

Some objects might not be available in view of their fragility, vulnerability to atmospheric changes, size or value. Exhibits require respect and care. Some material might also be expensive to borrow if the loan agreements specify special conservation or display measures e.g. display-cases, plinths, framing (see 39.2). Again, how dependent is the exhibition on these objects?

Are the policies of the lender(s) compatible with your aims? Are they likely to be sympathetic to the idea? Some material might be difficult to borrow if it has been lent and exhibited in the recent past, since lenders will set restrictions on the amount of time that their objects will be on loan or even on display (see 37.4). The selection of exhibits should not be dictated by what has been exhibited recently, when further research could reveal comparable – and, possibly, even better – material that has not been seen for some time.

4.5 What interpretation will be necessary

An exhibit's capacity to stimulate and satisfy the visitor will depend on its intrinsic interest, its presentation in the design and installation of the exhibition, and the style and language in which its significance might be communicated. Apart from the exhibits, what will be needed to allow visitors to grasp what the exhibition is intending to do? Research will provide raw material which should be selected and edited to suit the knowledge, reading age and stamina of visitors (see 22.3).

Understanding the exhibition should not depend on anything that every visitor will not experience, e.g. catalogues, lecture programmes etc. Is explanatory material best presented in wall texts, in take-away leaflets, in pick-up-and-replace laminated sheets or in some audio–visual form? Is the exhibition designed to cater for any special needs, e.g. using large print or Braille versions of texts or sound loops (see 28.3)? Is different material needed for different sectors of the target visitors, e.g. different age or language groups (see 25.5)? But having considered all the options, how little can be used to make it effective?

4.6 Testing the idea for a tour

An exhibition should be considered at the outset for its potential for touring to other venues. Often the decision to tour is taken too late in the organizing process, after lenders have been approached or after decisions have already been taken on design.

Often a decision to tour is also taken too late from the point of view of the venues, which have their own schedules to meet. Exhibition ideas should be questioned from conception to realization, and it can be useful to engage curators at potential venues in this process at the outset, so they are not mere recipients of the show (see 13.5). An idea for a touring exhibition needs to be tested against the following criteria.

Its wider appeal: Would the exhibition be relevant to other galleries or is its interest mainly local? Does it carry a message which other venues are interested in promoting, or does it use a method which they may wish to try?

Its timeliness: Is there a particular reason for organizing it at this moment, perhaps an anniversary, a climate of interest or debate, a context of other exhibitions? Would it be better at a certain time of the year, perhaps to reach a particular target group.

Availability of exhibits: Some material might not be available for a tour: how seriously would the removal of these exhibits affect the exhibition? If this material is available, is it still sensible to tour exhibits that are fragile, vulnerable to environmental changes, valuable, etc. If so, are the costs of the tour containable, in terms of extra costs to be incurred on transport, insurance, packing, couriers, display-cases, framing?

Optimum number of showings: How many venues should be planned? How long a tour will lenders tolerate? How does this balance with economy of effort and finance?

Possible causes of offence (see 34.3). Some venues may be sensitive to issues of gender or race, perhaps involving culturally-sensitive material (see 2.5).

Compatibility of venues: Are the venues comparable in terms of size, accessibility, environmental and security conditions? Will it be necessary to build some flexibility into the selection, to allow for exhibits to be left out at some venues. This may be easier if exhibits are borrowed direct from artists, and may be more difficult for loans from private collections or from museums.

The staff available: Does the organizer have the manpower resources to be responsible for a tour while running its own programme (see 1.5)? Does the organizer have the knowledge and experience to realize and tour the exhibition? Should other specialists be involved who may know more about making and touring that kind of exhibition (see 5.1)?

The budget available: Does the organizer have the financial resources to meet all the extra costs associated with preparing an exhibition for tour and then with managing this operation? Can sponsorship and/or grants be obtained in time to support the tour (see 10.3, 11.5).

5

External curators

Mike Collier

5.1 Why employ an external curator?

In this section, the term 'external curator' is used for any person brought in, usually on a short-term contract, to select or manage an exhibition on behalf of the organizer. For employing temporary staff for education programmes, see 25.8. An external curator can be an artist, critic, dealer, researcher, freelance consultant or other person with a specialist knowledge of the proposed subject and/or expertise in the mechanics of organizing and touring exhibitions. This person might be contracted to:

- organize a large or complicated exhibition which the employer might not have the capacity to do itself;
- manage a tour that needs expertise the organization does not possess;
- bring a specialist knowledge of a subject or period; or
- introduce the institution to different insights.

These roles are not mutually exclusive, but can be combined according the needs of the exhibition, the finance available and the skills of the external curator. There are many reasons why employing an external curator can be desirable or even necessary.

5.2 Extra capacity and expertise

Organizing an exhibition that is more ambitious or larger than normal, e.g. thematic exhibitions or survey exhibitions of national or international importance will stretch to the maximum the in-house expertise and capacity of all but a few institutions. Employing an external curator can help to compensate for limited administrative or service support or restrictions of procedure.

5.3 Tour managers

Touring an exhibition can be more complicated and time-consuming still. A tour can divert staff and services away from their normal responsibilities (see 1.5). This is increasingly difficult to justify, especially within local authority museums and galleries which are expected to service their own areas. Employing an external curator buys time for the whole duration of the tour, ensuring consistency.

Managing a tour involves skills additional to those normally required for administering a programme within one centre. Some institutions do not have in-house the expertise in the mechanics of touring to undertake such a task. For employing agents on such work, see 52.1.

An organizer planning a touring exhibition should make an objective assessment, based on a careful reading of this manual, as to whether the organization has the expertise and the capacity to manage the organization and tour. Freelance organizers and consultants with touring expertise can be contacted, either by personal recommendation by galleries that have successfully employed such freelance people, or via the indexes of consultants held by the national arts and crafts councils, regional arts boards and area museums councils.

5.4 Selectors

With changing patterns of work within museums and galleries, it is not always possible for full-time staff to set aside time for research and personal development (see 4.4). The demands of marketing and the increased levels of bureaucracy eat into their time. The need for greater accountability also reduces the freedom to engage in research and speculative travel, when such activities cannot be seen to bring immediate benefits to the institution. An external curator is a way of buying into the organization some of the knowledge and research which it has been unable to invest in its own staff.

An external curator is also a way of buying into the organization a diversity of knowledge and research which it could never hope to represent in its full-time staff, especially where the latter might be diversifying into managerial or administrative functions.

For example, most National Touring Exhibitions projects will involve a specialist who has a particular knowledge of the subject and who will be brought in on a freelance basis to shape the overall concept and contents of the exhibition and (usually) to compile the catalogue (see 12.3). The first task of this type of external curator is to draw up a list of key works with their whereabouts, from which the organizer will be able to investigate the likelihood of loans, the general feasibility of the exhibition, and the resources needed.

An external curator can make proposals and suggestions without having to worry about the long-term political consequences. Museum and gallery staff are increasingly involved in the cultural politics of their region. This can make objective decision-making awkward and problematic, and compromises have to be made for the sake of longer-term regional relationships. External curators can bring a fresh eye to bear on a complex political situation.

By their nature, many institutions are resistant to change and unwilling to take risks. An external curator can help to bring change, and is often in a better position to take risks.

Few museums or galleries allow their staff the time or the flexibility to travel widely abroad. It is therefore important that overseas curators are given the opportunity to present exhibitions from their own countries. Contact with potential curators can be established through the British Council or Visiting Arts, or by working closely with artists and museum professionals who are involved in exchange programmes abroad.

5.5 The disenfranchised

Museums and galleries in the United Kingdom are run very largely by white, able-bodied staff. It has been difficult for people from minority groups to gain employment in this field. As a result, many are working independently, outside the system. It is important to redress this imbalance by employing them to create exhibitions within museums and galleries. This will help to change attitudes towards employment practice within these institutions, as well as bringing a much-needed change of emphasis in overall programmes and in individual exhibitions (see 2.4).

5.6 Artists

Many artists are capable of selecting and organizing their own exhibitions, with a member of the institution's staff acting as enabler. Most of the decisions about catalogue images, touring venues and the presentation of the poster can be taken by the artist, advised by the member of staff and subject to the institution's financial controls. The process of making art is very often fundamentally different from the work of a museum professional, whose academic background can lead to exhibitions which are didactic rather than visual. Employing an artist or crafts-person can help to bring a visual dimension into the selection of an exhibition, especially a thematic or mixed exhibition.

In addition, the work of many conceptual artists is narrowing the gap between the artist and the museum curator. The processes revealed by such artists are often more intellectual than skills-based, and it is a logical step to move from making their own work to presenting the work of their contemporaries in mixed or thematic shows.

The involvement of artists in selecting and organizing exhibitions not only gives the museum an insight into the practice of making art, but also has a long-term benefit to the artistic community. Because they have often been excluded from the decision-making process, many artists do not understand the very business they have chosen to work in. Working as an external curator can help to inform them.

The payment of fees and expenses to artists when mounting an exhibition can prove difficult for museums. This is especially so when new work is being commissioned, since it is likely that expenditure will be required at short notice and often will be left to the last minute (this is the nature of the creative process, not bad organization, see 34.2). One way of coping with this problem is to ask the external curator to handle all exhibition costs.

5.7 Two-way traffic

External curators can not only bring a fresh perspective, but can also take away with them an important knowledge of the context in which they have been working. Artists working in a region far from London can often become very isolated from the mainstream of the London art world. Even if they have opportunities to show their work in the region, it is highly unlikely that their work will be seen by, for example, dealers or curators from the national institutions in London. This problem can be alleviated by hiring such people to select mixed exhibitions which will include the work of artists working in that region and which will therefore require a range of studio visits. Regional and local authorities should ensure that decision-makers do have the opportunity to experience the excellent work which at present never gets shown where it can attract critical attention or significant patronage.

One of the main problems faced by exhibition galleries outside London is the lack of critical coverage given to exhibitions. By employing critics as external curators, institutions are not only hiring their knowledge, but also their visibility as a critic and their access to the media, all of which can help to put the museum or gallery on the national or international map. The same point can be made about hiring freelance curators who operate across Europe and internationally. They move around the world and have contacts across the continents. A good external curator can serve the institution well as an international marketing agent.

5.8 Anchor-person

Remember that some of the reasons given above for employing an external curator relate to the problems and shortcomings faced by full-time staff. Such problems do not necessarily disappear when employing an external curator, who can exacerbate them when things go wrong. However, with careful handling, an external curator should be able to circumnavigate many of the obstacles.

Appoint a member of staff to be the anchor- or link-person, acting as the liaison between the external curator and the organization. Do not assume that an external curator will replace the work done in-house. This is not an opportunity for staff to take a well-earned break! In fact the staff will have to work very hard as well during the period that the external curator is employed.

The example quoted above of National Touring Exhibitions (see 5.4) inevitably involves a member of staff who is responsible for all aspects of administration, budgeting and co-ordination, and who works with the external specialist with the knowledge of the subject. The ideal relationship is a partnership or collaboration. For this partnership to work, the anchor-person will carry out the following tasks.

- Define to whom the external curator is responsible. As well as being necessary for the external curator, it is also important that other members of staff in the institution are aware of the line-management structure.
- Provide administrative support. On the basis of a list of possible exhibits provided by an external curator, the organizer can investigate the likelihood of loans and the general feasibility of the exhibition. Although the external curator may be able to help with approaches to owners and may sign the loan requests on the organizer's behalf, the organizer remains responsible for these loans, and for transport, insurance, installation, printing and publicity.
- Be accountable for the finances of the exhibition. The contract should define the extent to which an external curator is responsible for preparing estimates, securing resources and agreeing expenditure, but the organizer will remain accountable for controlling expenditure. The contract should authorize the external curator to incur any necessary expenditure within the overall aims of the project and the itemised headings of the budget. It is up to the organizer to monitor expenditure and to take appropriate action where there are variations.
- Provide support within the organization and ensure that colleagues accept and welcome a temporary addition to the professional staff.
- Smooth out any procedural or administrative difficulties. Because they are self-employed, external curators do not have the benefits of full-time employment, and it is unrealistic to expect them to adapt suddenly to the procedures and timescales of the institution. It will be necessary to safeguard the interests of the external curator, who is often being employed precisely for their independence. Do not underestimate the time-consuming nature of this part of the job. For public liability, see 29.5.

5.9 Briefing

Brief the external curator on the institutional background. Many people working outside the system (or outside the UK) will not be aware of the bureaucracy to be faced, for example, when working for a local authority museum. Nor will they be aware of the hierarchical structures that exist within the institution, or the latter's relationship to local authority departments, Area Museum Council, Regional Arts Board, etc. It is always worth taking the time to explain these factors and to arrange for the external curator to meet key figures within the organization. The external curator may have to be paid for their time, but it will be money well spent if it saves a lot of time, trouble and money later.

Employing an external curator may also have an impact on the community outside the institution. Some artists, researchers or administrators can be suspicious of outsiders who are brought in to do a job they feel can be done by people based in the region. The organizer should consider whether this is in fact the case. Too often, local expertise is by-passed because it is always assumed that a professional from London or abroad will do a better job. The organizer should take the trouble to introduce the external curator to the local community. This may not only allay the fears of colleagues, but also ensure that their ideas are shared and discussed within the community.

Special attention may be necessary where an external curator is employed from a minority group. For instance, if there are no significant black communities within the region served by a venue, a black curator may feel vulnerable and isolated. The venue needs to be sensitive to the situation and should be ready to provide advice if necessary. Or, if a person with a disability is employed, it may be necessary to make modifications to the office environment, to ensure equality of access to facilities and services. It is useful to approach an agency working in the disability field to undertake an audit of office provision for the disabled.

5.10 The contract

The organizer should define how the exhibition for which the external curator has been employed relates to the aims and objectives of the employing organization. Specify what the organization's expectations are.

The ground-rules should be established for the tasks that the external curator is being commissioned to carry out and where responsibilities begin and end. Is this person:

- keen to oversee all aspects of the project, from the design of the poster to its installation at every showing, and whose enthusiasm may need to tempered by considerations of cost and practicality?
- someone with particular knowledge of the subject, who has been brought in to shape the overall concept, to select the contents and to compile the catalogue?
- appointed to manage the mechanics of the project, making all the arrangements for the different stages of an exhibition and its tour?

Formalize thoughts and discussions into a letter of contract, which defines what decisions an external curator will be expected to make, as well as outlining responsibilities. If the exhibition is touring, the organizer should specify the external curator's duties in terms of liaising with venues, arranging transport, installing and dismantling the exhibition, etc., and should ensure that lenders and venues are informed of the extent of the external curator's role on its behalf.

After the job has been completed, it is useful to formally assess the success and failure of the exercise with colleagues. This will improve relationships internally, and will assist the organization when planning to employ an external curator in the future.

In some cases such as when new work is being commissioned from artists, it can be advantageous for the external curator to act as banker, since this person can pay bills without delay as and when work is completed. The organizer can advance funds before the event or reimburse spending afterwards, according to the particular circumstances and the external curator's own cashflow. In other cases, an external curator might handle all exhibition costs – designers, printers, etc – and present a final account for the whole operation at the end of the tour.

5.11 Scheduling

Agree a timetable for the tasks. The work an external curator is asked to do is all too often elastic in expectation. As far as possible, establish what are the expectations of both the organizer and the external curator and when and to what level the work should be completed. It should be clear that remuneration will not be automatic if the external curator chooses to do more work than has been requested. However, it is important to allow for changes to the exhibition, beyond the control of the organizer or the external curator, which require the latter to work many more days than quoted for. The timetable should include a number of formal sessions, when the external curator and organizer can review progress and decide on any corrective action.

5.12 Fees

Agree a fee for the job. It is essential that fees are discussed and agreed in writing at an early stage. Establish whether the external curator is registered for VAT, and whether the fee includes VAT. See also 19.3, for a discussion of fees for designers.

Fees are sometimes calculated as a percentage of the total cost. More frequently, they are based on an estimate of the amount of work and time which are needed. If the organizer has defined precisely what the external curator is expected to do, then the latter should be able to estimate how much time will be required. As a rule of thumb, consultants will currently (1995) base their calculations on a cost per diem in the range of £150–£250.

Working on this basis, the external curator estimates how much time the job will take, and then together with the organizer agrees an overall price for the work. It is best to agree a set fee and not pay for work by the day or the week. If, through no fault of the external curator, the project requires more time, it may be possible to renegotiate the fee halfway through a project.

Agree a method and schedule for payment, and confirm in writing. Most external curators, whether artist, critic, expert or consultant, will be self-employed, and will submit an invoice at the end of the job, or, for any work over an extended period, at stages agreed in the contract so that they receive their fees in instalments. The organizer may need to liaise closely with the finance department of the museum or local authority, to ensure that instalments will be paid swiftly. Fees should not be taxed at source if the external curator is registered as self-employed and quotes the Inland Revenue Registration Number on the invoice.

Agree whether expenses are to be paid, and what they will cover, and how they should be reimbursed. Expenses will depend on the amount of travelling or buying of services which the external curator will have to do. The extent of expenses will usually have an inverse relationship to the basic daily rate that is used for calculating the fee, i.e. a lower daily rate will normally mean that all expenses will be claimable. For fees to designers, see 19.3.

5.13 Credits

Last but not least, make sure that the role of the external curator is fully credited in press releases and other publicity and in formal acknowledgements (catalogue foreword, opening speeches, etc.).

6

Evaluation

David Phillips

6.1 What is evaluation?

Evaluation is the collection and analysis of the response of visitors to a particular event, such as an exhibition. It is different from market research, which is concerned with the perceptions of a venue and its overall programme by both those who do visit and those who do not (see 3.1).

Evaluation is often done systematically, by specialists in social psychology and statistics, to make it as objective as possible, but it is still valuable if done cheaply and intuitively, since that is how response is evaluated in everyday life. The important thing is that an evaluation appropriate to the scale of each project should be a routine part of practice.

Evaluation is increasingly required by grant-aid bodies and sponsors, and the information gathered can be invaluable not only for planning new exhibitions but also for making the case for grants and sponsorship (see 10.4, 11.3, 25.10, 30.23, 31.17).

6.2 Formative or summative

Evaluation may be done to test components of an exhibition during development, in which case it is called 'formative'. Formative evaluation is an indispensable part of the design of any installation which involves interaction, unusual display fittings, experimental modes of interpretation or untested features for disabled visitors (see 22.2, 24.4, 28.4).

Alternatively, evaluation may be done in order to assess completed installations, in which case it is called 'summative'. It is the second type of evaluation which is the main subject of the following section, although there are opportunities for cross-over. Formative evaluation may be usefully applied after the exhibition is open, when there is still scope for change in aspects of an installation e.g. the placing of labels, or when different arrangements are being considered for subsequent venues.

6.3 Planning evaluation

Generally, the planning of evaluation should be led by the organizer, but in discussion with venues. The collection of data should be the venues' responsibility, whilst analysis should be the organizer's. The plan should specify the methods to be followed by the venues or the contracted specialists.

6.4 Planning: the institutional context

The evaluation programme should be as consistent as possible across different venues, but those planning evaluation for a tour should bear in mind the constraints of varying contexts. Venues that have carried out little previous market research will have few visitor statistics to act as a base-line against which can be measured any difference in visiting patterns made by the exhibition. Where market research has already been done, there may be a reluctance to intrude upon visitors with yet more distractions.

6.5 Planning: costs and resources

Methods must be appropriate to the scale of the exhibition, but when planning evaluation for a tour, costs in time and resources should allow for both the collection and analysis of data. Typically collection of data might need:

- contracting-out of evaluation design;
- printing of questionnaires;
- supervised administration of questionnaires;
- expenses of observers and equipment;
- expenses of visitors invited for focus groups or controlled experiments.

Typically, the analysis of data might involve:

- contracting-out of analysis;
- access to special facilities;
- expenses of meetings between organizer and venues and any contracted-out staff.

6.6 Planning: specifying goals

Those planning evaluation should bear in mind who the exhibition is for. Any exhibition is likely to appeal to some more than others. For example, an exhibition scheduled for the Summer holidays might be intended mainly to attract groups including children between the ages of eight and twelve, whereas another exhibition might realistically only be expected to appeal to a specialist market, such as art students or Friends groups. Surveys by the English Tourist Board and the Scottish Development Department (see 6.12) give broad indications of the varying appeal of museum displays of different types across the socio-economic spectrum. Hooper-Greenhill provides an overview of results from numerous similar surveys (see 6.12).

Those planning evaluation should also bear in mind what kind of experience the exhibition is intended to offer. Exhibitions of science or natural history may be intended to teach information or to challenge assumptions. An installation by a contemporary artist may only be intended to provide a vivid experience. Most exhibitions offer a mixture of these kinds of experience, but the two kinds require different approaches if evaluation is to do more than simply assess patterns of visitors' attention.

6.7 Methods: the visitor profile

Statistics about visitors should strictly be considered a part of market research, rather than evaluation of the effect of individual installations, but it is useful to include some such figures in the evaluation of temporary exhibitions. An organizer will normally ask for a head-count from each of the venues as part of the feedback required in the hire agreement (see 16.4). Numbers in the exhibition may be recorded by ticket sales, by turnstiles, beam-operated counter or – most commonly – by invigilators provided with a mechanical counting device.

Socio-economic background can be assessed from questionnaires. Questions should seek to distinguish characteristics of visitors to whom the exhibition is principally expected to appeal. This might be apparent, for example, from where they come from, their age or what newspapers they read. Questions might therefore include age-group, gender, distance travelled, reasons for coming and previous attendance at the gallery. Questionnaires should end with space for comments about the exhibition.

Data will only be quantitatively reliable if the questionnaires and their administration are designed and carried out by trained evaluators, allowing for numerous technicalities. Miles (see 6.12) succinctly explains the principal difficulties. However, less formal evaluation by questionnaires may still be useful, if it is remembered that the results are only suggestive, and probably not representative of all visitors. Where questionnaires are left for visitors to pick up, the response assessed will clearly only be of visitors sufficiently engaged to return completed forms, and they are likely to represent a committed segment of the market. Where questionnaires are left out in this way, there should be a sign inviting visitors to help themselves, and pens should be provided.

It is impossible to give much guidance as to the minimum number of completed questionnaires which might be required without specification of the type of information sought, the variability of response amongst respondents, and the degree of confidence required in the results. Certainly, indications of any value would rarely emerge from less than 100 responses (see 3.16). Where visitor numbers are large, Miles (see 6.12) suggests that a sample of between 1 in 25 and 1 in 50 visitors may suffice, if the sample is truly random.

The simplest approach to tabulating data is simply to produce percentages of visitors, for example showing that 45 per cent came from out of town.

An exhibition which fails to attract the expected visitors may be at fault in some way. Alternatively, it may be in the wrong venue or it may not have been adequately publicized. The visitor profile achieved should be compared with any information held by the venue about previous response from the target visitors.

The visitor profile should also be compared with data, which the venue should research if it is not already held, on the extent of the presence of these target visitors as a potential local market. For an exhibition likely to appeal primarily to members of the local community, demographic data will be available as Census Reports for the area, held in main libraries or by local authority planning departments. For an exhibition with tourist potential, local tourist offices will have data on different visitors (local coach tour, day-visits, overnight stays, etc.).

6.8 Methods: attention

Whether the primary aim of an exhibition is formal learning or affective experience, nothing much is likely to have been achieved unless visitor attention has been manifestly engaged and held. This is the easiest response to assess. Most commonly, an observer with multiple copies of the exhibition plan can discreetly log routes and times at exhibits for a sample of visitors.

With museum studies students at Manchester, we have used time-lapse video filming. Earlier researchers found that observation affected visitor behaviour, but security cameras are now so ubiquitous that another camera (even if its presence is explained in a label) seems to pass unnoticed.

If an installation is particularly successful or unsuccessful in holding attention, it is often apparent on casual review of video records. The time taken to read key labels, for example, is known for most readers, so that their success in holding readers' attention is readily apparent, as is the extent to which visitors do or do not follow intended sequences through exhibitions, or the extent of interaction with interpretive devices.

Such methods record large amounts of data, which can reveal patterns of response which are not obvious, if analysed by statistically-competent researchers. However, the analysis of data is extremely time-consuming (and in the case of the video-tapes requires a video editing deck), and the resulting statistics are likely to be misleading if not expertly applied. Phillips describes some problems and possibilities of measures of attention, with particular attention to time-lapse video recording (see 6.12).

6.9 Methods: formal learning

Any gain in factual knowledge or change in attitudes or assumptions can be readily assessed, but only by systematic questioning of groups of visitors to the exhibition of a kind best designed by specialists. To provide a base-line for comparison, this method also requires assessment of control groups before they visit, the selection of whom is a similarly technical business. Where established specialists cannot be contracted, it may be possible to involve local students of educational psychology or recent graduates who retain access to academic expertise.

6.10 Methods: experience

This is the most difficult area for professional evaluation, but a great deal more than is yet normal practice can be done by informal discussion with visitors and study of comments books. It may also be thought acceptable to eavesdrop within a gallery, if it is apparent that an observer is within ear-shot, so that visitors can use normal social caution in what they choose to discuss.

As a next step, requiring time but not necessarily expertise, small groups of visitors of not more than eight at a time may be invited to return for focus group discussions. Evaluators who have not been involved in organizing the exhibition should lead the group sessions. Group members might be recruited by asking visitors who complete questionnaires to indicate willingness to be involved in further evaluation. Such groups need hospitality. To get a discussion going, they might be asked to note four things they liked and four they disliked about an exhibition.

More systematic research by specialists sometimes includes visits to visitors at home, or to teachers and parents to seek reflections of the reactions of children to an exhibition in subsequent discussions or activities at school or at home. On occasions, visitors are contacted again at a later date to correlate memories with earlier reactions. Such methods are tolerated for specialist research, particularly into educational projects, but would be intrusive and over-expensive except for the evaluation of ambitious exhibitions.

6.11 Evaluating evaluation

The benefits of formative evaluation should be inescapable if built into display improvements, but summative evaluation will be of little value unless time is set aside for considering the results. For a touring exhibition, this might take the form of a meeting, which might also be the best opportunity for peer-group criticism, i.e. comment invited from curators who were not involved in organizing the exhibition but who are respected by the organizer. Their comments, not only on their own responses to the exhibition but also on evaluation by non-curatorial specialists, may carry more weight than contributions from what may be perceived as an alien academic culture.

6.12 Further reading

Beer, V. 'Great expectations: do museums know what visitors are doing?' *Curator*, 1987, Vol 30, No 3, pp 206–215.

English Tourist Board, *Survey of Visitors to Museums*, 1982, ETB, London.

Grant, R. *Survey of Visitors to Scottish National Museums and Galleries*, 1981, Scottish Development Department, Edinburgh.

Hooper-Greenhill, E. 'Who goes to museums?', *Museums and Their Visitors*, 1994, Routledge, London, pp 54–68.

Loomis, R.J. *Museum visitor evaluation*, 1987, American Association for State and Local History, Nashville.

Miles, R. *et al. The Design of Educational Exhibits*, 1988, 2nd edition, Unwin Hyman Ltd, London.

Phillips, D. 'Evaluating Time-Lapse Video Evaluation', *International Journal of Museum Management and Curatorship* (in press).

Stevenson, S. 'The long-term impact of interactive exhibits', *International Journal of Science Education*, 1991, Vol 13, No 15, pp 521–531.

7

Documentation

Julia Ellis and Jacqueline Ridge

7.1 Definitions

For museums, 'documentation' has a particular significance in terms of recording the status and location of objects in a collection. This section is concerned with documentation in this sense, to mean the process of recording the movement and condition of each exhibit in a tour. Documentation has a special importance for touring, because a large number of objects may be transferred through several stages without the immediate supervision of their owners. Its purpose is to provide a continuous record of the status of each exhibit, keeping all the various parties – organizer, lenders, carriers and venues – informed as necessary. The following summarizes the features of each of the key parts in the documentation process, outlining how each is built up and how it is used.

7.2 Lenders' File

The selector of the exhibition, who might be the organizer or an external curator, will draw up a provisional list of exhibits, a 'wish list' of suitable loans. This list may be arranged in order of priority or in categories of preference, in terms of each exhibit's significance to the theme or story of the exhibition (see 4.4). This significance may eventually be registered in an entry in a published catalogue (see 7.6).

The list will also be the basis of a more factual form of research in terms of checking the whereabouts of each exhibit, and ensuring that contact names and addresses are correct and up-to-date (see 36.5). Potential lenders are identified, and a file arranged by the name of each person or institution. This file will include: name and address of lender, name/description of the exhibit(s), copies of any published material or bibliographic references, category of significance in relation to the theme of the exhibition.

It will record all informal contacts, preliminary requests and visits made to potential lenders (see 36.6). It will contain copies of the formal requests for loans, and log when action would be necessary if there is a delay in responding to a request (see 36.7). It will file unsuccessful requests, noting the reasons given for the refusal, in case action should be taken immediately or might be planned for the future.

The process of selecting and requesting loans must be logged, so that the organizer has a clear sense of how the exhibition is taking shape. Contacting potential lenders may lead to additional or alternative sources, perhaps not known or considered previously (see 37.2).

7.3 Inventory of Exhibits

Successful applications for loans will become a new sub-section, or even a separate file, which identifies each exhibit separately. Where exhibits are borrowed from other sources, this inventory will include the signed agreement with the lenders, any specific requirements for the object, and all variations, e.g. extensions to the loan. It may include notes by the selector, of the exhibit's historical or academic importance for the exhibition, which may be used later in a catalogue entry (see 7.6).

Each exhibit would be listed by its normal title or description, with dimensions and weight, and its condition. There should be a note of any special handling, lighting, etc. that is required, which a lender will normally include in the loan agreement. A lender may provide – or the initial visit (see 7.2) may have gleaned – information about narrow roads, awkward flights of stairs and other difficulties of access, which will be important in any instructions to carriers for the collection and return of exhibits (see 7.10).

Each exhibit should have a valuation agreed with its lender, which will form the basis of the Insurance list (see 7.4) and should be accompanied by a note of its insurance or indemnity cover, and a copy of the notification of this cover to the lender. The inventory will also include any additional information about the exhibits requested from their lenders, e.g. certificates of fumigation or licences for working objects or firearms.

Where exhibits are for sale, the inventory will include a discrete list of all such exhibits, with any numbering system for multiples, plus financial details, e.g. artist's price, commission, VAT and selling price (see 35.7). This information may change during the course of the tour, e.g. if exhibits are sold and therefore change their ownership for insurance purposes (see 35.1), or if exhibits are taken away when sold and replaced by similar material (see 35.2).

Together with the particulars of components and equipment (see 7.9), the inventory will make up a list of all the items in the exhibition.

7.4 Insurance list

This list provides a broker or underwriter with the necessary details to be able to arrange insurance cover. The details will be extracted from the loan agreements (see 7.3). Each exhibit will be described in terms of: name and address of owner; title; size and medium; agreed value; and any remarks about its status or fragility (see 40.3).

For the Government Indemnity Scheme, the list will be divided between loans from the National Museums and Galleries, to which separate applications are made, and loans from other sources, for which application is made to the Museums and Galleries Commission. The latter list should be sub-divided to exclude cover for loans by any of the venues on their premises, and should include a photograph for each item for which indemnity is required (see 41.3).

7.5 Label

A label should ensure that staff in each venue can identify the exhibit. It should have sufficient information to enable easy and unambiguous identification, using at least two points of reference (e.g. the number and the title used in the catalogue), and should relate to both the inventory of exhibits (see 7.3) and individual condition check dockets (see 46.2). Any label that a lender has attached to an exhibit and which bears its current accession or catalogue number, and any previous marking which is part of the exhibit's documentation, should not be removed from the exhibit or be covered in any way by the label relating to the exhibition. Exhibits should be identified using adhesive or tie-on labels with full regard to conservation requirements, in terms of the material(s) they are made from and their structural strengths and weaknesses (see 39.1).

7.6 Catalogue entry

The information provided in a catalogue will depend on the scale and intentions of the publication. It is normal practice to record all the exhibits in an exhibition, in sufficient detail to enable them to be recognized or located. Information authorized by the owner – title or description, dimensions, medium and support, acknowledgement to the lender, etc. – will be obtained from the loan agreement (see 7.3). Details of provenance and a discussion of a more critical or historical nature may be provided by the lender or by the selector (see 7.2). The lender may, in turn, update its own record about the exhibit, with details of the exhibition and the publication in which it was mentioned.

7.7 Condition Check Docket

A research visit or an initial inspection by a lender's conservator may be the first assessment of the condition of an exhibit and the conditions in which it is displayed or stored (see 7.2 and 39.1). By the time the exhibit is delivered to the organizer, this assessment may have prompted remedial treatment and preventive measures, and may have led to instructions for handling, movement, display and environmental control. It should also have led to the preparation for a condition check docket (CCD) for each exhibit. Usually a CCD will record the condition of one exhibit at entry and exit and at other specified times, and record its location and the environment in which it is stored or displayed (see 46.1).

7.8 Summary of materials used

The organizer should send a list of all materials used in the exhibition to each venue which can then obtain the relevant approvals from its Fire Officer (see 27.3).

7.9 Particulars of components and equipment

Parallel to the inventory of exhibits (see 7.3), there should be a separate list of all other items which travel as separate units. Each of the components of a display case dismantled for travelling should be marked with a unique code or number. The code or number and description of the component should be recorded in a checklist, so that any missing items can be identified. The code or number will also be important for any instructions for unpacking and assembly and for dismantling and repacking (see 21.3). Equipment should be marked for the same reasons, and so that it can be related to the manufacturer's information for each item (see 27.4).

7.10 Collection and return instructions

See 53.11 and 53.12 for instructions to carriers, which will be listed by the name, address and telephone number of each lender (with contact name, where appropriate), extracted from the lender's file (see 7.2). Signed receipts will record the entry and exit of exhibits, and the transfer from lender to carrier and from carrier to organizer. Other documentation may be necessary, e.g. export licences requested by or on behalf of the lender.

7.11 Contacts with venues

Potential venues will be identified at an early stage, and the organizer will normally open a file that is arranged by name of the institution, probably with some form of priority or preference against each name. This file will include the address, telephone and fax numbers and contact name. It will record the date and content of all informal contacts and preliminary agreements, especially in relation to dates, costs and any action necessary. As showings are confirmed, venues which have been contacted even at an informal level, but which are not included in the tour will be informed in writing before filing away the records.

The organizer will file any details of the facilities and resources of potential venues (see 38.2). It will transmit to the venues any special conditions made by the lenders, e.g. for environmental control or invigilation, which require action by the venues (see 37.4). The organizer will obtain the venue's confirmation that these conditions will be met. This will only be one part of a hire agreement which will define a wider range of responsibilities (e.g. on publicity, interpretation, evaluation, etc) for both parties (see 16.3).

7.12 Contents of crates

Each crate or package will have a list of contents, which in effect is a sub-division of the inventory of exhibits (see 7.3) and the particulars of components and equipment (see 7.9) into units that can be safely transported. The list should be attached to the inner face of the crate's lid, along with any diagram or instructions to help unpacking and repacking (see 46.9). A second copy of the list and any instructions should be sent to each venue (see 17.11). In conjunction with the transport manifest (see 7.13), a venue will be able to identify the contents of crates, in order to plan acclimatization, sequences of unpacking and repacking, placing of crates, etc.

7.13 Transport manifest

The transport manifest is a list of each crate, box or other separately-packed item that is actually loaded or unloaded on vehicles (see 53.10). Crates will be marked on the exterior with a unique number (see 45.9). The transport manifest should itemize each crate according to its number, giving dimensions, weights and any instructions on handling or the machinery to be used. It should be sent to the carrier with the transit instructions (see 7.14) and to the venue as part of its advance information (see 17.10), to provide a checklist against which carrier and venue can sign a receipt when they take delivery of the consignment.

7.14 Transit instructions

See 53.11 and 53.12 for instructions to carriers. The consignment will be itemized in the transport manifest (see 7.13). If the organizer is arranging transport, instructions to the carrier should be copied to the relevant venues; if the venue is arranging onward transport, copies of the instructions should be sent to the organizer and to the next venue (see 17.10).

7.15 Installation instructions

These instructions outline how the different parts of the exhibition work together, and give detailed information on the handling and display of individual exhibits (see 49.7). They should be provided whether or not the organizer supervises installation and dismantling at each venue. A copy should be sent to each venue a month prior to its showing, so that its staff can familiarize with the details and so that no time is lost once the exhibition has arrived (see 17.11). A second copy of the instructions should accompany the exhibition.

7.16 Disaster plan

Every venue should supplement its disaster plan with details of any exhibits or exhibition temporarily on its premises. The supplement should record the location of exhibits and any priorities for rescue (see 27.8, 44.5).

There should be a notification procedure in case of loss or damage. Even with the best will in the world, things do go wrong. It is essential that the process by which the relevant people are notified is clearly established at the outset. This will include a list of the names and addresses of organizer and lenders, indemnifiers and insurers, police, conservators, etc (see 40.8-40.10, 41.5, 43.5, 48.12).

8

Scheduling

Rosalie Cass

8.1 Introduction

Whether it is the organizer coordinating the different elements that make up the exhibition, or whether it is the venue preparing to receive an incoming show, it is necessary to prepare a programme, timetable or schedule of forthcoming duties, procedures and events and the desired sequence of tasks. Effective scheduling will help to achieve a successful exhibition, and can be a key element in budget control.

Of the various methods of scheduling, the bar chart is recommended as the most useful for exhibition use. A bar chart will:

- show when a task needs to be carried out, in relation to other tasks:
- set out the time needed to carry out each task;
- highlight the 'milestones';
- identify where bottlenecks may occur;
- indicate where additional resources or external contractors may be necessary; and
- provide an easy visual reference at all stages.

A 'milestone' is a key point at which certain tasks need to have been completed before moving on to other ones, e.g. hire agreements may need to be formalized or sponsorship and grants secured before further work can be undertaken.

8.2 Checklist

The starting point is to make a checklist of all the different factors relating to the exhibition. The checklist is necessary to avoid omissions which could be costly later on. All planning should begin with a checklist regardless of the size of the project. For the organizer, the checklist might include most of the following, while only the later items will be necessary for the venue:

- selector (or researcher, author, external curator, etc);
- research into locations of potential exhibits;
- requesting loans;
- conservation;
- research into suitable venues and agreeing showings;
- catalogue;
- installation;
- publicity;
- transport (collections/returns between venues);
- insurance;
- education;
- fund-raising.

8.3 Sub-projects

Large projects must be split into smaller sub-projects for effective management. Isolate each sub-project and plan the tasks associated with it in a practical working sequence. Always assume that there will be delays, and add extra time. Collaborations are time-consuming because of the amount of consultation involved, for which adequate time must be allowed (see 13.4).

Taking each item, construct a preliminary schedule by working backwards in time from the opening of the exhibition. In the early stages of the project, it may only be possible to estimate during which month an event should take place, but it is useful to break down the schedule into weeks so that it is easier to revise and introduce greater precision as time goes on.

8.4 Example 1: an installation and dismantling schedule

Venues programme exhibitions several years in advance, and the time allocated for exhibition turnarounds are frequently found to be unrealistically short. The schedule will reveal the amount of time required to bring in or despatch an exhibition, and alert those concerned to the bottlenecks during this critical period. The schedule will then be effective in redefining the time needed for the turnaround.

Although delivery and collection times will not be fixed until a time much nearer to the exhibition opening, adequate installation and dismantling periods must nevertheless be allowed for in the schedule. Installation and dismantling are the times when exhibits are exposed to the most risk, and it is essential to define as early as possible installation/dismantling schedules in as much detail as possible (see 49.2).

Serious problems will be met if the activities are not planned effectively. If exhibits arrive while the galleries are still being prepared or before the preceding exhibition has been collected, not only will the organizer and the venue experience problems with storing the exhibits until the galleries are ready, but there will be serious consequences relating to loans which are accompanied by couriers (see 51.4). Couriers will not allow their exhibits to be installed until the galleries are free from hazards and may insist on hotel accommodation with daily subsistence payments while they wait. In extreme circumstances, couriers can insist on taking their loans back again. Bad planning can have far-reaching results: it can put exhibits in danger and cause serious overspending, and lenders may be reluctant to lend to future exhibitions.

The installation and dismantling schedules must allow for sufficient time and manpower to ensure proper and careful handling of the exhibits (see 48.2). Other gallery activities must not coincide with periods when exhibits are being delivered or collected or when they are being handled within display-, unpacking- or storage-areas.

Every stage has to be carefully thought out and planned for. Depending on the nature of the exhibits and the installation time required, additional time must be included for 24-hour acclimatization of crated exhibits that have travelled from different climatic zones. Sufficient time must be allowed for unpacking and for condition-checking before the exhibits are installed (see 46.10).

The following example of an installation schedule illustrates some of the factors to be considered. Clearly a dismantling schedule would involve some of the same items, although the first half of the list would be taken in reverse order as shown in Table 8.1.

An installation schedule might also include such events as the:

- delivery of catalogue, posters, cards and other publicity materials;
- delivery of educational materials;
- deployment of invigilators during installation;
- erection of banners;
- sign-writing;
- arrival of caterers with wine, glasses, tables, flowers, etc.

Table 8.1 Dismantling schedule

Days prior to opening	*Action*
1	briefing invigilators
1	labelling (if outside frames or display cases)
2	lighting (if outside the display cases)
3	installation of exhibits completed
4	installation of exhibits in second shipment
4	condition checking
4	empty crates taken to store
4	unpacking of second shipment
5	installation of exhibits in first shipment
5	condition checking
5	empty crates taken to store
5	unpacking of first shipment
5	pay subsistence to couriers with second shipment
5	morning delivery of second shipment: acclimatization begins
6	place labels within display cases
6	adjust lighting within display cases
6	pay subsistence to couriers with first shipment
6	morning delivery of first shipment: acclimatization begins
7	display-surfaces and/or -cases ready
7	barrier rails to galleries
8	visit by Fire Officer to approve installation (see 27.16)
8	prepare receipts for incoming exhibits
8	repainting of galleries completed
8	painting and glazing of display cases completed
8	lighting check for replacement of bulbs
9	begin repainting of galleries
9	delivery of display cases
10	crates for previous exhibition collected
14	organize subsistence payments for couriers
20	make hotel reservations for couriers
30	go through updated installation schedule with gallery manager and technical staff
30	prepare Condition check docket for each exhibit (see 46.2)
30	preliminary visit by Fire Officer (see 27.13)
40	instruct carrier
60	propose transport and installation timetable to lenders (or organizer)
90	alert Fire Officer about proposed installation and arrange preliminary visit
90	alert gallery manager of dates of installation and details of any special requirements.

8.5 Example 2: a publishing schedule

The time allowed to produce a catalogue will depend on its size and the number of essays and illustrations

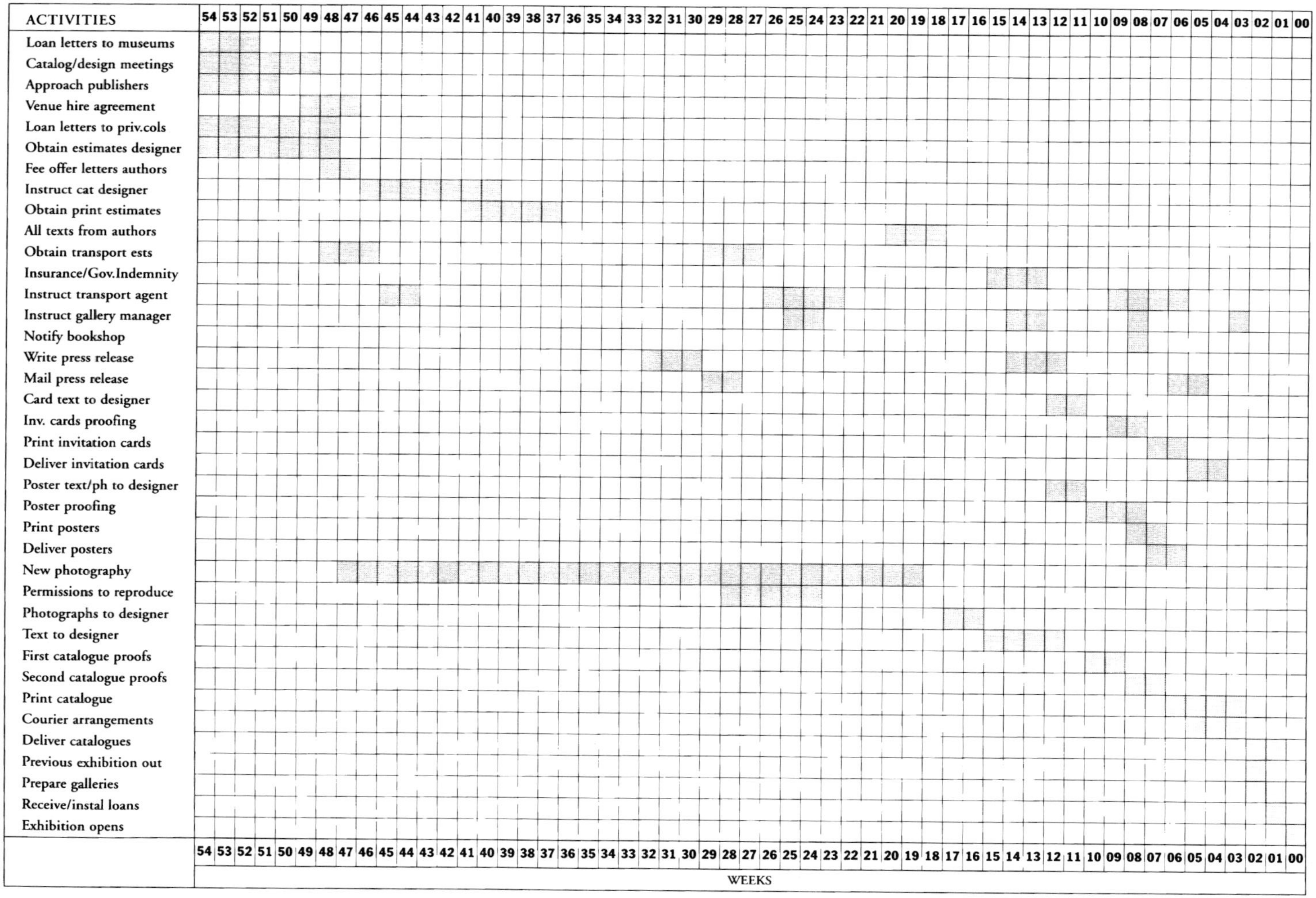

ACTIVITIES
Loan letters to museums
Catalog/design meetings
Approach publishers
Venue hire agreement
Loan letters to priv.cols
Obtain estimates designer
Fee offer letters authors
Instruct cat designer
Obtain print estimates
All texts from authors
Obtain transport ests
Insurance/Gov.Indemnity
Instruct transport agent
Instruct gallery manager
Notify bookshop
Write press release
Mail press release
Card text to designer
Inv. cards proofing
Print invitation cards
Deliver invitation cards
Poster text/ph to designer
Poster proofing
Print posters
Deliver posters
New photography
Permissions to reproduce
Photographs to designer
Text to designer
First catalogue proofs
Second catalogue proofs
Print catalogue
Courier arrangements
Deliver catalogues
Previous exhibition out
Prepare galleries
Receive/instal loans
Exhibition opens

Weeks: 54 53 52 51 50 49 48 47 46 45 44 43 42 41 40 39 38 37 36 35 34 33 32 31 30 29 28 27 26 25 24 23 22 21 20 19 18 17 16 15 14 13 12 11 10 09 08 07 06 05 04 03 02 01 00

WEEKS

EXAMPLE OF BAR CHART UP TO 54 WEEKS PRIOR TO THE EXHIBITION OPENING. PLEASE NOTE THAT LOAN NEGOTIATIONS WITH MUSEUMS SHOULD BEGIN AT 72 WEEKS.

Figure 8.1 Example of bar chart up to 54 weeks prior to exhibition opening (see 32.9). The schedule for publishing a catalogue will need to be considered in terms of weeks rather than days, and might be broken down as illustrated in Table 8.2.

Table 8.2 Catalogue publishing schedule

Weeks prior to opening	*Action*
1/2	first venue receives catalogues
2	notify second venue's retail manager
6	catalogue on the press
8	final proofs from printer
8	notify first venue's retail manager
10	first proofs from printer
12	camera-ready artwork to printer
14	photographs and transparencies to printer
16	all text, photographs and transparencies to designer
17	all photographs and transparencies labelled
18	assess sale price, notifying publicity staff and venues
18	receive all photographs and transparencies from lender(s)/author(s)
18	receive all text from author(s)
24	receive all permissions to reproduce
24	appoint printer and establish print schedule
36	request estimates from printers
40	appoint catalogue designer
40	exchange fee offer letters with author(s)
48	arrange any photography that is required
52	write to lender(s) and other sources to request photographs and transparencies and permissions to reproduce
56	finalize catalogue details with selector(s) and author(s)
100	meet selector to decide on type of catalogue

All individuals concerned with the production of the catalogue should be asked to provide an approximate timetable for how long their duties will take. However, if the designer or printer has not yet been appointed, seek advice from as many people working in these areas as possible.

If a large, academic volume is planned, the amount of work involved may suggest that a publishing house should be approached, and this should be allowed for in the schedule, e.g. Table 8.3.

Table 8.3 Inclusion of publishing house in publication schedule

Weeks prior to opening	*Action*
50	exchange contract with publishing house
54	approach publishing houses

This schedule is concerned principally with the production of a catalogue. It might be extended, or a different one compiled to cope with the particular timetable of distribution and accounting for each of a series of venues.

8.6 The bar chart

Once the initial checklist and preliminary schedules have been established for the different sub-projects, the information is ready to be included in the bar chart. The chart is really a calendar planner on which activities are identified by a bar to denote when a task should be started and completed. The calendar scale can be broken down into days, weeks or months, depending on the activities and the detail required. The bars can be colour-coded, e.g. to display the number of personnel required for each activity. During the early stages, this information can be interpreted or translated easily for programming, staffing and budgeting purposes. During the course of organizing the exhibition or while preparing for its arrival, the chart will be referred to constantly, in order to monitor progress and to check that all activities are in hand.

The example illustrated (see Figure 8.1) spans 54 weeks only, and begins towards the end of the period of researching and requesting exhibits. It does not include the early tasks such as preliminary negotiations with the exhibition selector or proposer, time required to research loans, sponsorship and venues, or setting out a budget. Contacts with potential venues might begin 100 weeks before the exhibition is due to open, while loan negotiations with institutions should commence 76 weeks in advance.

Because of the space available, it does not give detail of all the tasks associated with the exhibition installation. It culminates at the time the exhibition opens. It does not include activities which follow the opening of the exhibition, e.g. sending complimentary copies of the catalogue to the lenders, nor does it cover the period of the tour. The example is, in effect, the slice relating to the most intensive period in the organization of an exhibition, from a much larger bar chart which would cover initial research, discussions with the venues, the tour itself and the return of exhibits. Nevertheless it is hoped that this example will prove useful and easily adaptable, both to the wide variety of exhibitions and to use by venues as much as by organizers.

9

Budgets

Celine Blair

9.1 Institutional budgets

Any organization that organizes or hosts exhibitions on a regular basis will normally have a standard form for estimating expenditure and income, to ensure consistency in financial planning, control and evaluation.

Such forms will usually list key areas, such as research and development, conservation, etc. These key areas help those putting together the budgets to consider all the potential costs of their projects. They give an at-a-glance summary of what expenditure is planned in each key area.

Key areas are normally defined by the headings in the overall budgets for the organization, and usually given a budget code for computerized accounting. The figures in the 'Total Budget' column of the Exhibition Funding Summary (see Figure 9.1) helps Glasgow Museums to relate spending on every exhibition to the cost of the overall programme and overheads. Estimates are authorized, by signature and date, by the person with responsibility for the finances of the organization, as a sign that they are part of the overall financial picture.

9.2 Itemized budgets

To help to estimate spending, key areas can be subdivided on separate sheets, e.g. the detail on spending on graphic material on the Exhibition Estimate Drafting Sheet used by Glasgow Museums (see Figure 9.2). A standard format will normally give a separate line to each of the sub-divisions that is relevant to the project being costed.

The following checklist may be as useful for a large museum planning a new permanent display as for a small library preparing for the arrival of one of the National Touring Exhibitions' 'cased' exhibitions. Which areas are incorporated into its own format will depend on the scale and ambitions of each organization.

Research and development: allocation of cost of research by staff, or fees to consultants, researchers or selectors; travel for visits for study and to see potential loans; accommodation for such study visits; books; telephones; postage; photography (see 4.4, 5.12, 36.4).

Conservation: allocation of cost for work by the organization's own conservation department, or conservator's fees for advisory work and/or remedial treatment; preventive measures, including packing, crating, materials testing, mounting, framing and other preparation for display; monitoring costs, including photography, condition reports, monitoring equipment (see 21.9, 21.10, 39.2, 45.2, 46.1).

Transport: allocation of cost for administration, plus transport by the organization's own vehicles or cost of carriers; courier travel, accommodation and subsistence; insurance; crating and packaging not covered above, e.g. for panels, display cases, equipment and parts of the structure other than the exhibits themselves; administration of customs requirements or agent's fees; storage; lifting and handling gear (see 21.3, 21.4, 48.9, 51.6, 53.5, 56.6).

Installation and dismantling: allocation for in-house designer, or fee to freelance designer; writing and production of graphic panels, labels, title boards, internal signs; construction and painting of display cases and other structures; lighting, electrical equipment, e.g. audio–visual; other devices and equipment, e.g. mechanical interactive devices; allocation for costs of installation and dismantling by in-house staff and/or use of external contractors; allocation for costs of invigilation by in-house security; staff and/or use of external contractors; record photography (see 19.3, 22.4, 23.6, 24.2, 48.9, 52.8).

Marketing and evaluation: photography; copyright fees; printing of posters, publicity leaflets and invitations cards; postage; advertising; distribution fees; sign-writing; banners; road signs; press pack; press view; hospitality; allocation for in-house marketing officer, or fee

GLASGOW MUSEUMS
EXHIBITION FUNDING SUMMARY

Exhibition: ______________________ **Financial Year:** ______________________

Venue: ______________________ **Dates:** ______________________

Project Leader: ______________________ **Code:** 620-SUB-
619-SUB-

Element	Code	Budget Holder	Total Budget	Commitment Accounting Statement Split					
				620 Code 9 /9	619 Code 9 /9	**Total** 9 /9	620 Code 9 /9	619 Code 9 /9	**Total** 9 /9
Development	0553								
Publication	0401								
Marketing	0730								
PR/Posters	0712								
Events	0554								
Transport	0631								
Graphics/Photography	0711								
Construction	0343								
Audio Visual Element	0351								
Sundries	0731								
Maintenance	0373								
TOTALS									

Comments: ______________________

____

____

____

Prepared By: ______________________ **Date:** ______________________

Authorised By: ______________________ **Date:** ______________________
(Head of Corporate Services)

Figure 9.1 Glasgow museums: exhibition funding summary

to consultant; evaluation, whether in-house or contracted out (see 6.5, 30.5–30.14, 31.12).

Publication: photography; copyright and reproduction fees; allocation for in-house designer, or fee to freelance designer; allocation for writing in-house or fees to authors; printing of brochure and/or catalogue (see 19.1, 32.3–32.9, 33.4).

Events: materials, fees to speakers, workshop leaders, etc., costs of keeping building opening after hours, e.g. extra security (see 23.6, 25.2, 25.10).

9.3 Identifying touring costs

There are significant differences between a static one-venue exhibition and a touring exhibition, all of which will have budget implications. A tour will affect the exhibition production in a number of key areas – design, conservation, transport and often selection.

Touring is not something that happens once the exhibition has closed at the organizer's premises, nor something that is considered half-way through its production. Ideally, an exhibition will be perceived as touring right from its conception, and budgets will be constructed with touring in mind from the very start (see 4.1).

Costs associated with touring are peppered throughout the entire budget. Failure to recognize this often means that the resource implications are often realized too late. Regardless of the size of the exhibition and the duration of its tour, it is important that the costs incurred by the touring process are fully realized and integrated into both the exhibitions planning and its budget from the beginning.

On the one hand, it is most important that a touring exhibition budget should not be considered as an exhibition budget with a 'Touring Maintenance' heading tagged on to the end of it. On the other hand, the organizer may be required to account for the extra costs that touring may involve additional to those which would be incurred if the exhibition were shown only at the organizer's premises. In this case, it will be important to separate these two costs at the outset.

Both the Summary and the Drafting Sheet used by Glasgow Museums (see Figures 9.1 and 9.2) have columns with the budget code 620 to cover standard costs and with the code 619 to cover identifiable touring costs. Thus, the cost of producing graphic panels would be included in the first column, but the cost of laminating them so that they will better withstand the tour will be added to the second column. Clearly, this process can also work in the other direction, if touring means that panels of a higher quality of text and design can be produced in the first place.

GLASGOW MUSEUMS
EXHIBITION ESTIMATE DRAFTING SHEET

Exhibition: ______________ **Project Leader:** ______________

Venue: ______________ **Dates:** ______________

Element: GRAPHICS **Code:** 620 - 0711
619 - 0711

Budget Holder: ______________

Breakdown	Items	620 Estimate	619 Estimate	Total
Consumables				
Display Services				
Graphic Panels				
Labels				
Overtime				
Photography				
Printing				
Title Boards				
TOTALS				

Figure 9.2 Glasgow museums: exhibition estimate drafting

9.4 The costs of touring

Costs will reflect the overall standard and quality of the exhibition. Touring exhibitions have to be durable. The exhibits and their display aids – labels, text panels, mounts, etc. – have to look good in each venue regardless of the duration of the tour.

Costs are also dependent on the need to make touring exhibitions as accessible as possible to other venues. In this instance, 'accessible' means the exhibition must be easy to handle, install and transport, which means in turn that the organizer has to produce information, instructions and packaging of high quality (see 49.7). This does not mean complicated or lengthy written instructions: it means clear, simple information requiring the minimum effort to understand it.

The following paragraphs identify a few of the areas of extra cost incurred in the preparation stage because the exhibition is touring.

Graphic panels: More durable materials may be necessary, to ensure that corners do not get easily damaged, and that the surface is easy to clean, e.g. heat-sealed or laminated rather than just dry-mounted.

Labels; As above, but it may be worthwhile having several sets of labels made at the same time, to save time and money.

Posters: Ideally, the organizer will know how many posters are required for the duration of the tour. If not, e.g. for a long-running tour with an unspecified number of venues, it is much cheaper to get extra posters printed during the first run, than to get the press set up again for a re-run. All publicity should relate to the overall scale and aims of the exhibition and to the visitors for whom it is intended, in all the venues (see 30.1).

Display structure: If display cases, plinths, partitions and other parts of the original installation are to travel to other venues, they will have to be easy to assemble and dismantle, with sections which are easy to handle and transport when dismantled (see 21.3). This may mean more construction materials and hardware (e.g. nuts and bolts) to join these smaller sections together. Durability of the materials is also a consideration, but the use of alternative materials may not necessarily be more expensive. Complicated structures are particularly susceptible to inflation and last-minute emergencies which can prove expensive. The balance between display and the exhibits must be always borne in mind, since expensive installations may reduce the budget for securing a key loan.

Staff time: Unless the designer has favoured a minimalist approach, touring may tie up technicians for a long period of time, both for design and construction.

Installation photographs: For the cost of film, processing and printing, it is possible to show how the exhibition was displayed at the first place of showing, highlighting individual display areas/cases, and to give where necessary a step-by-step guide for constructing display elements or for installing exhibits (see 49.7). Photographs are generally easier to understand and quicker to produce than elaborate written installation instructions. If you intend to send out a construction team with the exhibition, then the amount of photographic material required in this instance would probably be reduced.

Conservation: A conservator, whether in-house or freelance, can advise on any remedial treatment or preventive measures that may be necessary for an exhibit, according to its nature and vulnerability, and whether or not the exhibition is going to be installed by a courier. Preventive measures are particularly relevant where the tour is a long one and has a large number of venues. Exhibits which may be fragile or awkward to display may have to be mounted in a way which will give them support or protection, make them easier to display and reduces the level of direct handling. Clearly it will not be practical to tour an exhibit that will cause problems, unless it is essential to the exhibition theme. Exhibits have to be identified earlier in the development of an exhibition that is to tour, and the work required to make them safe has to be assessed and costs estimated (see 39.2).

Packing: Factors governing the kind of packing include lenders' requirements, duration of the tour, number of venues, type of transportation, and the presence of couriers (see 45.2).

9.5 Ongoing costs

Once the exhibition goes on tour, there will be further costs that will have to be budgeted, if they are not 'hidden' in the organizer's overheads.

The ongoing management of the tour will involve transport (arrangements with carriers, whether in-house or contracted-out); installation and dismantling (including repairs and maintenance, couriers and other supervision, and might require the organizer to provide technical staff), publicity and publications (sending posters, press-releases, catalogues and educational materials on time).

The decorative condition of an exhibition space will affect the exhibition. Venues should consider painting and refurbishing as an essential part of the preparations for an exhibition and costed into their budgets. On occasions, the organizer may even have to assist these preparations.

Once the tour has finished, it may also involve costs especially if the exhibition includes a large number of loans which have to be returned to their owners.

9.6 Duration

Even a relatively-modest, medium-sized touring exhibition can cost as much as a major one-off exhibition, because of the extra precautions that are necessary. It will also take as long to administer, because of the longer timescale for negotiating loans, as well as the length of the tour itself. The budget should cover this length of time. The schedule will indicate when outside contractors – conservators, designers, agents, carriers, etc – should carry out their tasks (see 8.1). The budget will allow the organizer to estimate how much money needs to be spent in each financial year. There is no point in allocating money for one year, when there is no one available in that year to carry out the work.

Most exhibition-users budget on the basis of a financial year starting on 1 April. Other organizations might run over a different twelve-month cycle, but the principle is the same, i.e. budgets are set at the beginning of the cycle to cover all the costs expected to be incurred during the period. Keeping to financial years may also be important for funding bodies. As far as touring is concerned, the organizer must ensure that the exhibition appears in the organization's overall budgets for each financial year covered by its preparation or tour. An exhibition opening in January 1999 but needing three years' research may mean that its preparation costs will be spread over the period 1996–97, 1997–98 and 1998–99. Spending may be quite small in the first year (e.g. for the purchase of books and a few visits) and the bulk of expenditure (e.g. on construction materials, transport, insurance) might be scheduled to occur two years later. If the exhibition then tours for a year before the exhibits are returned to their lenders, the books may not be closed until the financial year 2000–01.

Its costs and its tour will generally mean that a touring exhibition will have an extended time-scale running parallel to the shorter-term exhibitions. Estimating how much is required to be spent on each project and when is vital for planning and budgeting for an organization's entire activity, including the programme in the organizer's premises as well as any long-running tour. From any sum allocated for the exhibition programme each year, it will be necessary to balance the costs of exhibitions that need to be kept 'on the road', with what can be afforded for showing on the organizer's premises, and with the amount of development money required to research future exhibitions.

9.7 Cost-centre budgeting

Which key areas an organization chooses to incorporate in its own standard format will depend on what costs it needs to pay from the funds allowed it to run a programme of exhibitions, e.g. an organizer who carries out research as part of her normal tasks may decide not to include a 'Research and Development' heading in her budgets.

At the simplest level, a budget for a tour can be an expansion of an exhibition budget (see 9.4). Different organizations will have different budgeting structures, but basically each budget will cover all the key areas of the normal process of exhibition production, encompassing all the potential costs associated with these areas. However, a more complicated tour can involve costs completely outside the normal budgeting process. Work that is normally handled in-house, e.g. on research, design, transport or conservation, may not be possible because of the scale of the project. What was previously 'lost' or 'hidden' in the organization's overheads suddenly appears in the open, and – what is worse – these costs can be much higher than the marginal extra cost of making frames more robust or printing more posters.

Clearly, such a budget shows what an exhibition actually costs in time and cash. It is a truer reflection than the tip of the iceberg which normally shows in exhibition budgets, and it is a clearer basis for approaches for grants and sponsorship. Difficulties arise where an organization has an exhibitions budget which is based on 'hidden' costs and then has to pay for a service. A gallery's technicians may have constructed crates in the past, but a lender may require an external contractor to do the work, in which case labour will become a real cost and have to be budgeted for (where applicable, the process of Compulsive Competitive Tendering will also take up time).

The answer is 'cost-centre budgeting', which allows all the costs for each project to be calculated. In this case, a figure would be included for each of the items into which the budget was sub-divided (see 9.2), whether work is carried out in-house or by external contractors. Realistic estimates can show where extra capacity has to be bought-in, e.g. if the time that an in-house designer needs to spend on one or more projects exceeds that person's salary for this period, then there is a clear signal that the work is too much to handle without either overtime or employing an external designer (for which, of course, the budget allows).

9.8 Comparison of estimates with actual spending.

Monitoring of actual spending (and income-generation) can be done on a day-to-day basis, at the end of a financial year and/or at the tour by providing appropriate columns alongside the 'budget' column, as in Glasgow Museums' Close of Project/Probable Spend in Financial Year form (see Figure 9.3). Where it is clear that additional spending is necessary (or savings can be made), revised figures should be entered. Once again, these revisions should be authorized by the person with financial responsibility, as a sign that this new spending (or saving) is taken into account in the organization's overall figures. In Glasgow's case, we need to prepare separate 'Close of Project' forms to summarize

GLASGOW MUSEUMS
CLOSE OF PROJECT/PROBABLE SPEND IN FINANCIAL YEAR REPORT

Exhibition: ____________ **Financial Year:** ____________

Venue: ____________ **Dates:** ____________

Project Leader: ____________ **Code:** 619 - SUB -

Element	Code	Budget Holder	Budget	Actual Spend	Probable Spend	Difference
Development	0553					
Publication	0401					
Marketing	0730					
PR/Posters	0712					
Events	0554					
Transport	0631					
Graphics/Photography	0711					
Construction	0343					
Audio Visual Element	0351					
Sundries	0731					
Maintenance	0373					
TOTALS						

Comments: ____________

____

Prepared By: ____________ **Date:** ____________

Seen By: ____________ **Date:** ____________
(Head of Corporate Services)

Figure 9.3 Glasgow museums: close of project

actual costs on basic production (i.e. budget code 620) and identifiable touring costs (i.e. budget code 619).

9.9 Income

When substantial income is anticipated from the sale of the exhibition catalogue, it should be considered in terms of recouping expenditure on this publication, not as general income for the exhibition or the institution. An expensive catalogue may only be justified if it makes a definitive contribution to the subject and will continue to sell after the exhibition closes, or if sales can be guaranteed and costs shared between the venues. It can be treated as a discrete project with its own budget separate from the exhibition with which it is associated (see 32.10). In some cases, exhibits may also be sold from the exhibition (see 35.6).

Touring exhibitions can be financed in different ways, but the two most common are: first, where an institution creates an exhibition and then offers it out to other venues for a hire fee; and second, where each member of a consortium contributes a share of the costs. In the first method, the organizer recoups, to a degree which is largely a policy decision, a proportion of the cost of organizing the exhibition (see 16.6). In the second method, the burden of the exhibition's cost is shared, so the initial financial outlay is considerably reduced (see 16.9). Pooling resources allows each contributor to share in an exhibition which each individually may not otherwise have been able to afford.

An organization which decides to tour must consider all the financial implications. It must be aware of its human and financial resources, and decide how much it can afford to subsidize the tour and how much it needs to retrieve through hire fees (see 1.3). There is no set formula for working out a hire fee, and each organization will take a different basis. The organizer may regard other elements, e.g. potential sponsorship benefits, publicity received through a tour and professional contacts and working relationships, as important as the income. This basis should be clearly stated, so that it can inform future financial decisions. Some of the following considerations may influence the fees venues are charged:

- Is the organizer subsidized or sponsored, to enable it to keep hire fees low ? In effect, this means that the subsidy or sponsorship is transmitted to other district and regional museum, library and gallery services.
- Is the organizer a service first and foremost, and allowed to write off all its losses?
- Does it have a guaranteed budget but need to cover all its costs?
- Does the organizer need to make a surplus to fund future projects?
- Is the income generated just seen as a bonus (e.g. no amounts are shown on individual exhibition budgets) and as a means of supporting the exhibition programme in general?
- Does the expected income allow the organizer to spend more money on the project in the first place, knowing that this additional expenditure will be recouped through the hire fee?

10

Sources of grant aid

Judith Kelly

10.1 The importance of grant-aid

Financing a touring exhibition usually involves seeking support from a variety of sources. With the current emphasis in the UK on partnership funding, museums and related organizations are under increasing pressure to match public subsidy with funds obtained from the private sector. However, in contrast to the tradition of corporate sponsorship and patronage in the US, the infrastructure of museums and galleries in the UK is the result of over 200 years of state subvention.

Touring exhibitions remain among the many cultural activities which rely on public investment to operate at a democratic level. Grants, and the aims and aspirations of the bodies which award them, are therefore an issue of major importance to all exhibition organizers and users. This section aims to summarize grant-aid schemes from public sources which might assist touring exhibitions at any stage from embryonic ideas to fully-fledged projects.

Without any initial injection of grant-aid, many touring exhibitions would never take place. Some projects, particularly smaller-scale exhibitions or those tackling unconventional or controversial subjects, are unable to attract private sector contributions. Geographic scope is also relevant: commercial sponsors may have little interest in sending exhibits, however significant, to a handful of remote locations with low populations, e.g. in the Scottish highlands and islands. Even large-scale, metropolitan initiatives often need pump-priming before they can develop sufficiently to interest sponsors. Putting an exhibition on the road involves major investments of staff-time and money and few organizations can meet these needs from existing staff and budgets.

10.2 Types of grant

Funding bodies can grant-aid touring in two ways:

- by aiding the making of exhibitions for tour through grants to organizers, e.g. research, travel and origination grants; and
- by subsidizing the circulation, display and use of existing exhibitions through grants to venues, e.g. hire-fee and transport subsidies.

The potential for subsidy should be viewed from both angles. Even where an exhibition is a joint venture between two or more organizations, it may still be possible for one of the partners to take the lead in applying for grant aid towards origination, while the other(s) applies for hire-fee subsidy (see 13.4).

10.3 Where to apply?

Both organizers and venues face a complex situation in the UK. Touring exhibitions suffer directly from the rigid compartmentalization of state support for museums and the arts. Figure 10.1 shows the division of responsibilities between various quangos ('quasi-autonomous non-governmental organizations'), which has created a fragmented, uncoordinated and restrictive system. Individual funding bodies expend time and resources in establishing parameters in relation to one another. Unfortunately, attempts to operate in a complementary manner to avoid duplication often create schisms.

Since the closure in 1993 of the Travelling Exhibitions Unit of the Museums and Galleries Commission (MGC), no single agency with an overview of the whole UK has grant aided museum-sector (i.e. non-arts) touring exhibitions. Moreover, until April 1994, the Department of National Heritage (DNH) had responsibility for the arts in Scotland and Wales via the Arts Council of Great Britain, but this was lost with the division of the UK into individual states with distinct cultural policies. These changes have exacerbated two major inconsistencies in the funding system:

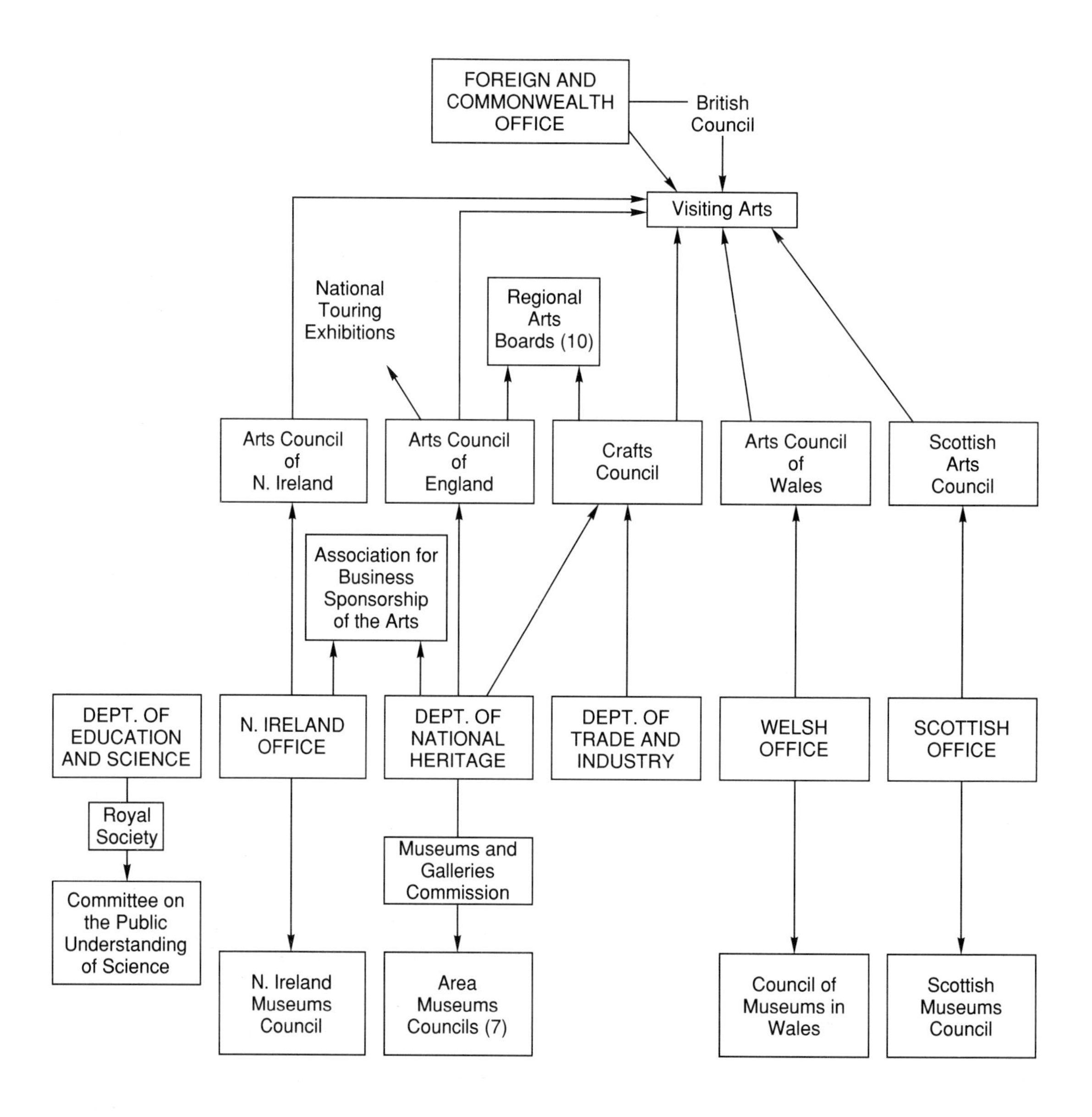

Figure 10.1 Government funding chart

- the wider the tour, the more difficult it is to find sources of grant-aid; and
- provision is not constant across all subjects.

For example, a gallery aiming to tour an exhibition of contemporary fine art to two other English venues will find it easier to locate grant aid, than a Scottish museum organizing a palaeontology exhibition in collaboration with venues in Wales and Northern Ireland.

Potential sources of grant-aid currently depend on:

- the subject matter of the exhibition e.g. contemporary fine art, craft, design, history, science, interdisciplinary; and
- the geographical scope of the tour, i.e.region, country, nationwide, international.

Figure 10.2 identifies funding bodies most appropriate to various types of exhibition. Crosses indicate gaps in provision, where no public agency has a clear funding responsibility and where the possibility of joint funding may need to be explored.

In addition, eligibility under schemes administered by the Association for Business Sponsorship of the Arts (ABSA, see 10.5) and the Committee on the Public Understanding of Science (COPUS) can be investigated (see 10.6). Note however, that funding bodies will frequently only support organizations and activities within their own geographical and subject remit.

Regional Arts Boards (RABs) and Area Museum Councils (AMCs) each operate their own schemes, and provision varies from region to region (see 10.7, 10.8).

Exhibitions of historical art, applied art and design fall between stools (the Design Council does not grant-aid exhibitions).

10.4 Eligibility and approach

Prospective applicants should ensure that they meet the following criteria.

The organizer or venue is eligible for support: The national museums and galleries (see 41.1), galleries receiving revenue grants from an arts council or RAB and commercial galleries are ineligible under some funding schemes. Freelance organizers can be eligible (e.g. for the Arts Council of England's schemes). Some AMCs restrict grant aid to their members and/or museums fully- or provisionally-registered by the MGC.

The exhibition is eligible for support: Generally, it should be fully accessible to the public, and must be relevant to subjects/activities the funder wishes to promote, preferably sharing current priorities. Grants to organizers often depend on the exhibition being shown in a minimum number of venues within the funder's geographical remit, unless the funder agrees to waive such a requirement because of the scale, complexity or environmental/security requirements of the exhibition.

The application takes account of the criteria used to assess it: Funders will consider some or all of the following: how well the exhibition fits the scope and purpose of the grant scheme; its likelihood of achieving its stated objectives; target audiences; innovation, originality, discernment; curatorial/organizational expertise; related educational activities; appropriateness to the overall programme of the organizer/venue; other aspects such as equal opportunities or payment of artists' fees.

The conditions of grant aid can be met: These may refer to other funding sources, acknowledgement of support, submission of audited accounts, evaluation procedures, etc.

The application is submitted on the correct form (if the funder issues one) by the specified deadline and accompanied by any required supporting information (budgets, schedules, etc) and visual material if appropriate.

Note that it is always advisable for the applicant to discuss the proposed exhibition with the funder before making a formal submission. This can prepare the funder to receive the application, identify potential difficulties and help the applicant to shape a more persuasive argument.

10.5 National bodies (visual arts and crafts)

The following is intended as a 'snapshot' of the variety of financial assistance currently (1995) available in the UK. It relates only to grants, and does not cover other forms of help in kind (e.g. transport, information) that funding bodies often provide. Grant-aid schemes are subject to constant revision, and prospective applicants should always contact the funding bodies for their current guidelines.

Arts Council of England (ACE). 14 Great Peter Street, London SW1P 3NQ. Tel 0171 333 0100. Fax 0171 973 6590. ACE's primary concern is promoting contemporary practice, but exhibitions of historical material may be supported if placed within a contemporary context. Exhibitions can include work from abroad (but see Visiting Arts, below). ACE provides a series of 'step' grants to organizers (e.g. development, then travel, then origination) which cover each stage of progress.

Arts Council of Northern Ireland (ACNI). 181A Stranmillis Road, Belfast BT9 5DU. Tel 01232 381591. ACNI has no formal scheme to grant aid touring but will support exhibitions of the visual arts and crafts coming to or touring within Northern Ireland under its projects scheme. This is fairly flexible, with each application being judged individually. ACNI does not rule out supporting collaborative tours to other parts of the UK, provided the exhibition has an impact on the cultural life of Northern Ireland.

Exhibition subject

Geographical scope

	Contemporary visual art*	Contemporary craft+	Interdisciplinary including visual art and/or craft	All others
One English region	RAB	RAB	Possible RAB- AMC collaboration	AMC
Two or more English regions	ACE	CC	ACE CC if related to other art and design subject	
N. Ireland	ACNI	ACNI	ACNI/NIMC	NIMC
Scotland	SAC	SAC	SAC/SMC	SMC
Wales	ACW	ACW	ACW/CMW	CMW
England and Wales		CC		
UK				
Exhibitions from overseas (UK venues)	VA	VA CC if related to British craft		

* Painting, print-making, photography, sculpture and architecture. Eligibility of applied art and design and historical art and craft depends on the funder's policy and the context of individual exhibitions.

\+ Excluding conservation crafts.

Sixsmith\bh1332\fig. 10.2 s/s

Figure 10.2 Eligibility chart

Arts Council of Wales (ACW). 9 Museum Place, Cardiff CF1 3NX. Tel 01222 394711. Fax 01222 221447. ACW's Programme Support/Touring Scheme (administered by its three regional offices) helps publicly-funded galleries in Wales make or receive touring exhibitions. Small-scale exhibitions are particularly welcomed. Preference is given to exhibitions of work by living artists/crafts-persons, but non-contemporary work of special interest will be considered. Grants are given towards the costs of exhibition origination and touring. Venues can claim subsidy towards hire fees. Organizers and venues can also obtain grants towards transport, packing and handling of individual works or exhibitions (including to and from abroad) under a new Exhibition Transport Scheme which replaces ACW's directly-provided transport service.

Association for Business Sponsorship of the Arts (ABSA). Head Office: Nutmeg. House, 60 Gainsford Street, Butlers Wharf, London SE1 2NY. Tel 0171 378 8143. Fax 0171 407 7527. There are area offices throughout the UK. The DNH funds ABSA's 'Pairing Scheme', previously known as the Business Sponsorship Incentive Scheme (see 11.6). A business which has never sponsored the arts may have its sponsorship matched on a 1:1 ratio (£1,000 is the minimum amount of sponsorship eligible). Increases in sponsorship are then matched at a 1:2 ratio (for over £2,000 of new money) for second-time sponsors, and at a 1:4 ratio (for over £4,000 of new money) for established sponsors. Prospective applicants should contact the relevant ABSA area office.

Crafts Council (CC). 44a Pentonville Road, Islington, London N1 9BY. Tel 0171 278 7700. Fax 0171 837 6891. CC aims to raise the profile of British contemporary craft activity (i.e. practising 'artist-craftspersons'). Ambitious concepts and showings in prominent venues are welcomed. Exhibitions containing historical material or craft-work from other countries are eligible if presented as relevant to contemporary British practice.

Applications to the Crafts Council must relate to exhibitions taking place in two or more English regions (see 10.7) or in England and Wales. Organizers of exhibitions taking place in Scotland or Northern Ireland should apply to SAC or ACNI. Where an exhibition originating in England or Wales tours to Scotland, CC advises the Scottish venue(s) to apply to SAC for support towards the hire fee, which should be based on the relevant proportion of the full cost. CC will consider joint funding of exhibitions with ACE and SAC.

Scottish Arts Council (SAC). 12 Manor Place, Edinburgh EH3 7DD. Tel 0131 226 6051. Fax 0131 225 9833. SAC supports and promotes the development of contemporary visual arts and crafts in Scotland. It runs numerous schemes, covering research, travel and origination. Venues can apply for hire-fee and transport subsidies and for grants for improving temporary exhibition spaces.

Visiting Arts Office of Great Britain & Northern Ireland (VA). 11 Portland Place, London W1N 4EJ. Tel 0171 389 3019. Fax 0171 389 3016. VA is co-funded by ACE, ACW, SAC, ACNI, CC, British Council (BC) and Foreign Office. It is administered by BC but is an independent organization. VA's purpose is to reinforce cultural relations through the presentation of foreign arts in the UK. It can assist foreign travel for exhibition-related research and development (see 15.6), and can make contributions to the on-shore costs of presenting exhibitions of foreign arts.

Limitations are imposed by VA's policy and overriding diplomatic role. Grants are country-specific, so priority is given to bilateral projects involving one overseas country in preference to international projects involving artists from various countries. Moreover, VA's funding is split into varying allocations for different overseas regions and countries, according to their actual and potential cultural relations with the UK. For example, VA does not give high priority to the USA, because strong cultural relations already exist.

10.6 National bodies (non-arts)

Committee on the Public Understanding of Science (COPUS). c/o The Royal Society, 6 Carlton House Terrace, London SW1Y 5AG. Tel 0171 839 5561. Fax 0171 930 2170. COPUS was established in 1986 to provide a focus for a UK programme to improve awareness and understanding of science and technology (including mathematics and applied aspects, such as engineering and medicine). Its grants are intended primarily to pump-prime new initiatives. Originality and reaching new audiences are top priorities.

Council of Museums in Wales (CMW), The Courtyard, Letty Street, Cathays, Cardiff CF2 4EL. Tel 01222 225432/228238. Fax 01222 668516. CMW's touring exhibition service creates exhibitions in collaboration with Welsh museums; CMW underwrites all production costs. Hire fees (grant-aided at 45 per cent) include transport and installation. There is little scope for collaboration with other regions because of the primary concern with Welsh themes and bilingual presentation. No formal scheme exists to grant aid exhibitions coming into Wales from other countries, but these may be eligible for special project awards.

Northern Ireland Museums Council (NIMC). 181A Stranmillis Road, Belfast BT9 5DU. Tel 01232 661023. Touring is not currently a NIMC priority, but the Council favours networking and collaborative projects as the most cost-effective means of using limited resources. Feasibility grants are available to support developing exhibitions consortia or partnerships.

Scottish Museums Council (SMC). County House, 20–22 Torphichen Street, Edinburgh EH3 8JH. Tel

0131 229 7465. Fax 0131 229 2728. Only museums fully- or provisionally-registered by the Museums and Galleries Commission (MGC) are considered. SMC will grant aid the core research, development and manufacture of object-based touring exhibitions organized as collaborative projects. Exhibitions must incorporate a substantial amount of material from Scottish museum collections and be available for touring for twelve months after the first showing. SMC will also consider subsidizing hire fees for incoming exhibitions. Hire costs for exhibitions for small- and medium-sized venues are given higher priority than those for large venues.

10.7 Regional Arts Boards (RABs)

Each RAB runs schemes to support origination of visual arts and crafts exhibitions, but not all subsidize the additional costs of touring. For example, the London Arts Board advises organizers of exhibitions touring within London to approach the various London boroughs for joint-funding support. ACE's Regional Banding initiative, introduced in 1993/94, has provided additional funding for RABs, combined into Northern, Midlands and Southern 'bands', to support travel, information exchange and touring networks. The ten English RABs are:

- Eastern Arts Board, Cherry Hinton Hall, Cambridge CD1 4DW. Tel 01223 215355. Fax 01223 248075.
- East Midlands Arts Board, Mountfields House, Epinal Way, Loughborough, Leics. LE11 3HU. Tel 01509 218292. Fax 01509 262214.
- London Arts Board, Elme House, 3rd Floor, 133 Long Acre, London WC2E 9AF. Tel 0171 240 1313. Fax 0171 240 4580.
- Northern Arts, 9-10 Osborne Terrace, Jesmond, Newcastle upon Tyne NE2 1NZ. Tel 0191 281 6334. Fax 0191 281 3276.
- North West Arts Board, 4th Floor, 12 Harter Street, Manchester M1 6HY. Tel 0161 228 3062. Fax 0161 236 5361.
- Southern Arts Board, 13 St Clement Street, Winchester, Hants SO23 9DQ. Tel 01962 855099. Fax 01962 861186.
- South East Arts, 10 Mount Ephraim, Tunbridge Wells, Kent TN4 8AS. Tel 01892 515210. Fax 01892 549383.
- South West Arts, Bradninch Place, Gandy Street, Exeter EX4 3LS. Tel 01392 218188. Fax 01392 413554.
- West Midlands Arts, 82 Granville Street, Birmingham B1 2LH. Tel 0121 631 3121. Fax 0121 643 7239.
- Yorkshire and Humberside Arts, 21 Bond Street, Dewsbury, West Yorkshire WF13 1AX. Tel 01924 455555. Fax 01924 466522.

10.8 Area Museum Councils (AMCs)

Following the closure of its Travelling Exhibitions Unit in November 1993, the MGC attempted to devolve its responsibility for supporting touring exhibitions to the English AMCs. Unfortunately, the final sum received by each AMC was too small to make any significant impact on regional provision, which remains fragmented and inconsistent. Of the five AMCs which operated touring exhibitions services in 1994, only the North West Museums Service has not proposed cuts or changes in its touring provision. In theory, with most AMCs opting to wind down their own exhibitions services in favour of an 'enabling' approach, grant-aid will become more readily available to museums generating their own exhibitions. Only the North of England Museums Service does not currently assist touring.

A positive outcome of this change could be greater consistency, with AMCs adopting a concerted approach to facilitating touring both within and between regions, e.g. by pooling resources to set up grant-aid schemes for inter-regional collaborations. At the very least, a clear list of grant criteria relating specifically to touring exhibitions could be compiled by each AMC, preferably in consultation with other AMCs and the relevant RAB. The East Midlands Museums Service's 'non-prescriptive' guidelines for organizers and for venues hiring major shows from outside the region are a useful model.

The seven AMCs in England are:

- Area Museum Council for the South West, Hestercombe House, Cheddon Fitzpaine, Taunton TA2 8LQ. Tel 01823 259696. Fax 01823 413144.
- East Midlands Museums Service, Courtyard Buildings, Wollaton Park, Nottingham NG8 2AE. Tel 0115 985 4534. Fax 0115 928 0338.
- North of England Museums Service, House of Recovery, Bath Lane, Newcastle upon Tyne NE4 5SQ. Tel 0191 222 1661. Fax 0191 261 4725.
- North West Museums Service, Griffin Lodge, Cavendish Place, Blackburn BB2 2PN. Tel 01254 670210. Fax 01254 681995.
- South Eastern Museum Service, Ferroners House, Barbican, London EC2Y 8AA. Tel 0171 600 0219. Fax 0171 600 2581.
- West Midlands Area Museum Service, Hanbury Road, Stoke Prior, Bromsgrove, Worcs B60 4AD. Tel 01527 872258. Fax 01527 576960.
- Yorkshire and Humberside Museums Council, Farnley Hall, Hall Lane, Leeds LS12 5HA. Tel 0113 263 8909. Fax 0113 279 1479.

10.9 The changing landscape

After decades of touring initiatives coming and going (the V&A's Circulation Department, the Science

Museum's exhibitions service, the MGC's Unit), National Touring Exhibitions (NTE), managed by the Hayward Gallery on ACE's behalf, is the sole surviving touring exhibitions agency with a UK-wide remit (arguably now anomalous, as ACE has no residual responsibility for the rest of Great Britain). NTE's recent shift towards partnerships with regional venues reflects the growing interest of UK museums and galleries in initiating exhibitions that tour nationwide. It parallels the more facilitating approach being taken by AMCs (see 10.8).

There is no equivalent to NTE in the non-arts sector, and there is an obvious need for a new agency to fill the gap. Possibly this could encompass all subjects. It could draw together representatives of the various UK quangos and associations involved in promoting and circulating exhibitions, taking particular note of examples in Australia and New Zealand. It could build on foundations laid by the former MGC unit to assist non-national museums and galleries throughout the UK to attract major exhibitions or to undertake exchanges, not least with institutions overseas. Above all, it would at last enable exhibitions to cross boundaries – between regions, countries and subjects – without needing to adapt the exhibition to the widely-varying priorities of the many organizations involved in touring in the UK.

10.10 Further information

The Information Unit of the Crafts Council (see 10.5) will supply listings of current published sources of information and advice on grants covering all arts and museum disciplines. These are also available in CC's Reference Library.

See also Broadbent, A. *The Regional Arts Funding Handbook* (annual publication), Boundtech, London.

11

Sponsorship

ABSA

11.1 Sponsorship for touring exhibitions

Sponsorship is the payment of money (sometimes the supply of goods or services in kind) by a business to an organization, for the purpose of promoting the business name, its products or services. Sponsorship is part of a business's general promotional expenditure. It can encompass a sense of corporate or social responsibility. Sponsorship is not money from a public funding source, whose 'duty' it is to fund exhibitions or venues. Nor is it about making a donation (although a few companies do set aside an amount each year to make charitable donations to good causes which could include a touring exhibition). Sponsorship is a way for businesses to help achieve their business objectives and to help the arts.

Sponsorship has helped galleries, arts centres and museums to put on touring exhibitions. This section does not attempt to provide information on how to find sponsorship in general, nor go into the details of what general benefits organizers and venues can offer to secure sponsorship. Information about this is available in other publications (see 11.2) and is too detailed to repeat here. This section looks at what makes sponsorship of touring exhibitions different from other forms of arts sponsorship.

11.2 Recommended reading

For general guidance on obtaining sponsorship, see the following publications, which are available from ABSA (Association for Business Sponsorship of the Arts):

- *The WH Smith ABSA Sponsorship Manual.*
- *The ABSA Arthur Andersen Guide on Tax on Sponsorship.*
- *Setting Standards for the 1990's.*
- *Evaluating Arts Sponsorship.*

11.3 Why seek business sponsorship for touring?

A touring exhibition brings a new dimension to a venue; it brings a change to the permanent displays and in-house exhibitions, and it needs to be actively promoted if it is to attract visitors. Sponsors are attracted to the new and the newsworthy, and frequently they are seeking opportunities to be associated with the educational activities and the extra publicity, printed or otherwise, which the touring exhibition creates (see 24.2, 25.2, 30.2, 31.16). In short, touring exhibitions offer organizations an easier way into sponsorship than the permanent display and the work of conservation, collection and scholarship; and they offer exhibition galleries in general a special and perhaps more ambitious event that is also attractive to sponsors.

A touring exhibition can be an opportunity for a business to link its customers or operations in different parts of the country. This can be important for business development, e.g. by making presentations to clients at each showing, or by holding receptions and private views which help to give a sense of common identity to employees working in widely-scattered offices (see 30.21).

For the organizer or venue, the principal benefit is more money. More money means more publicity, better displays, outreach programmes, etc. But it's more than just extra money. Sponsorship, and the process of looking for it, means access to a wider audience and often an influential one. It is also proof of a commitment to plural funding, and impresses other funding bodies. Even if the search for sponsorship does not succeed, the organization will have gained some benefits from the process of looking.

11.4 Venues in a sponsored tour

For many venues, touring exhibitions often come with sponsorship attached. Perhaps the best known examples in the UK are the National Touring Exhibitions sponsored by British Telecommunications plc (see 12.3).

If you are a venue taking a sponsored exhibition, ensure that you understand all your contractual commitments to comply with a tailored list of requirements relating to the sponsorship. This list will include detailed requirements about the sponsor's name and logo on publicity materials, in press and advertising, etc. (see 16.4).

Treat such bookings as an opportunity to acquire useful experience of looking after the needs of a sophisticated business sponsor, as well as deriving some kudos from being associated with one of Britain's largest companies. Such experience may prove invaluable later when the venue is seeking sponsorship of its own and/or entertaining these sponsors.

Check whether the contractual arrangements with the sponsor of the tour allow the venue to attract other sponsorship, e.g. for a private view. In practice, most sponsors of touring exhibitions stipulate that they should be the sole sponsor of the exhibition.

Brief staff and take measures with arrangements for access, special decor, complimentary publications, catering, etc to give a good impression to a ready-made sponsor or its local office. The private view of an exhibition which is being used for corporate entertainment will be remembered by the attention given to details like car-parking and cloakrooms, as much as by the exhibition itself. Local business people know each other: news of a disaster will spread quickly, but a success may breed future sponsorship.

Get hold of the names and business addresses of the sponsor's invited guests (see 30.21). The best way to do this is for the venue to offer to send out the invitations, but if this is not possible, then do try to get hold of a list of invitees or, failing that, a checklist of acceptances. It may mean the sponsor's guests become visitors to the venue or they can be approached in the future to become sponsors in their own right.

11.5 Collaborative exhibitions – who does what and how?

The questions of who raises sponsorship, who keeps it and who looks after one or more sponsors need to be thrashed out between the various collaborators before the search begins (see 13.7).

Before these discussions take place, each museum or gallery should give the other collaborators information about each other as it affects sponsorship. This 'development profile' should cover the following points:

- funding status (e.g. funded by local authority, Regional Arts Board);
- any charitable status;
- contact person for potential sponsor;
- policy on sponsorship (and any restrictions on who can be approached);
- any special fund-raising appeals under way;
- any particular agreement/arrangements with an existing sponsor;
- facilities e.g. private rooms;
- catering arrangements;
- licensing arrangements;
- merchandising policies, facilities or restrictions;
- special events of which the collaborator has experience or which it would be prepared to offer to a sponsor;
- names of any locally-based national companies.

The collaborators should delegate one of their number to be responsible for all approaches for sponsorship for the project. This person should prepare and agree with each collaborator a sponsorship proposal for the exhibition and a strategy for fund-raising which takes into account each collaborator's development profile.

The locations of the collaborating galleries and their actual and potential visitors will be important in determining which businesses to approach for sponsorship. The objective is to achieve a perfect 'fit' between what the venues can jointly offer and what a business wants in terms of its operations, markets or customers. It is likely that the value of the sponsorship to the business – and hence the price which the collaborators charge – will be higher if there is a good fit.

Collaborators should agree as best they can in advance how any sponsorship money will be spent. This is particularly important if the business is likely to be less interested in one of the locations. Being prepared to recognize that a single potential sponsor may not be equally interested in all tour venues may be the only way to persuade the business to agree to sponsor at all.

It is often necessary to divide the amount of sponsorship into two parts: the first, to reduce the overall costs of the tour for all the collaborators; the second, to devote to specified areas of extra spending, e.g. on public relations, local advertising as agreed between the sponsor and each collaborator individually. A business may only sponsor if the second facility is available, but this division ensures that the exhibition can be financed in the first place.

Before the sponsorship is agreed, the business will normally want to negotiate with the organizer, but when it comes to implementation of the agreement it will wish to ensure that all venues comply with what was agreed. Sometimes it will be the local office of the sponsor which gets involved with each venue. Frequently this will be its first experience of sponsorship, and so may need hand-holding (see 30.21).

11.6 The Pairing Scheme – how does it work?

Touring exhibitions in the UK have benefited from the Business Sponsorship Incentive Scheme, now renamed the Pairing Scheme (National Heritage Arts Sponsorship Scheme), which ABSA manages on behalf of the Department of National Heritage (see 10.5). The Pairing Scheme is discretionary and there is no guarantee that all applications will be matched. Applications must be received at least eight weeks before the start of the tour.

The Paring Scheme is a tool to enable organizations to persuade businesses to sponsor for the first time or to increase their support. It offers matching money, extra publicity and Government endorsement. The Award money is used by the organization, to provide extra, mutually-acceptable benefits thereby benefiting the organization and the business. Some examples of this are an outreach programme, extra publicity and a full catalogue (see 25.5, 30.2, 32.10).

A sponsor may be eligible to apply jointly for a Pairing Scheme award with one of the organizations involved in a touring exhibition. This applies as much to the sponsor of a venue as to the sponsor for the whole tour. In either case, the organization must be a *bona fide* arts organization, and a registered charity or legally constituted as a not-for-profit company. Guidance on eligibility should be sought from ABSA at an early stage, in writing if possible.

All sponsorship money will need to be paid to the organizer. If ABSA agrees in advance, it may be possible to vary this. Similarly, with the approval of ABSA, it may be possible for the extra benefits which will be given to the sponsor if an award is made, to be provided by another venue which is later in the tour.

11.7 International touring

Sponsorship of international touring is complicated by the different 'cultures' of corporate support. In many countries, there is a greater tradition of philanthropic support for the arts. While this may be attractive in theory, support can dry up in a recession, while sponsorship in the UK has continued. There are differences, too, in corporate income taxes and VAT. Specialist advice and local contacts are necessary. ABSA is a founding member of the European Committee for Business Arts and Culture (CEREC), the association of national sponsorship associations in Europe. CEREC has information about sponsorship relevant to tours which include one or more showings elsewhere in Europe. CEREC is located at 60 Rue de la Concorde, 1050 Brussels.

11.8 What help can ABSA provide?

ABSA cannot find a business sponsor for the whole or part of a touring exhibition, but it is happy to provide advice on all draft sponsorship proposals, and it may have suggestions about possible leads or business sectors to approach. Day-long courses on the basics of arts sponsorship are given by ABSA from time to time in all regions of the country. ABSA may be able to suggest the name of a local fund-raising consultant who can assist in finding sponsorship. However, successful sponsorship is all about establishing a relationship with your local business community, and this is normally best done by staff and trustees, if there are any. For information on the Pairing Scheme, ABSA publications or details of your local ABSA office, contact ABSA head office (see 10.5).

12

Sources of information

Jon Benington

12.1 Introduction

There is no single publication which lists all the different kinds of exhibition that are available for touring in the UK at a given moment. Listings and bulletins do, however, exist for certain types of exhibition, and they do not make a charge for those who submit information. Entries cannot be long for reasons of space, but the inclusion of contact-names and addresses allows enquirers to find out more by getting in touch with the organizer.

What follows is a 'snapshot' of the methods by which touring exhibitions are currently publicized in the UK, together with a note of any geographical restrictions or subject specialisms which may apply. The summary is not exhaustive. It would be impossible, for instance, to list every single organization involved in touring when old ones are being wound down and new ones are emerging all the time. Nor can it be guaranteed that information and/or services will continue to be provided by the same sources.

12.2 Listings published by organizations that are not providing the exhibitions

Arts Council of Wales. Exhibitions From Wales For Tour is an annual bulletin, usually published in the autumn. It gives details of exhibitions of the fine and applied arts organized by museums, galleries, arts centres, colleges and artists' groups in Wales, which are available for further showings in Wales and elsewhere in the UK. Welsh organizations should obtain a standard entry form from the address below; entry is free. The bulletin uses a standard format, giving title, brief description, space required, number of items, publications and publicity material available, related events, hire fee, transport and insurance arrangements, availability and contact address. Potential venues anywhere in the UK can ask to be put on the mailing list, which is free, by contacting Exhibition Services (Bulletin), Art Department, Arts Council of Wales, 9 Museum Place, Cardiff CF1 3NX. Tel 01222 394711. Fax 01222 221447.

Calendar of Art Exhibitions. This is a recent initiative (first published 1993) which lists exhibitions of the fine and applied arts in galleries and museums in the UK. Entries are brief (title, date, organizer, catalogue, tour), and it includes exhibitions that do not travel as well as those which do. It is published annually in December and lists exhibitions taking place over the following 18 months. In most cases, tours have already been established, but the booklet is useful not only for any gaps that do remain but also as a guide for possible contacts and as evidence of the policies and interests of other organizations. The 1995 edition costs £5.95 plus post and packing. Copy is compiled in August, entry is free and forms are available from the Editor, Calendar of Art Exhibitions, Lund Humphries, Park House, 1 Russell Gardens, London NW11 9NN. Tel 0181 458 6314. Fax 0181 905 5245.

Crafts Council. For many years the Crafts Council has published the *Touring Exhibitions Bulletin*, which is circulated free to museums and galleries twice a year. An illustrated brochure, it contains fairly detailed information about exhibitions devoted to crafts, decorative arts and design which are available for hire from museums and galleries in England and Wales. It also provides information on Crafts Council grant schemes (see 10.5) and serves as a catalogue for the exhibitions toured by the Crafts Council itself. There is no charge for including entries, and copy should be sent to the Exhibitions Officer, Crafts Council, 44a Pentonville Road, Islington, London N1 9BY. Tel 0171 278 7700. Fax 0171 837 6891.

Museums Association. Another recent initiative (first published 1994) is a quarterly supplement, *Exhibitions On Offer*, which derived from a joint MGC/TEG listing called 'Net' (no longer available). The supplement is distributed with the March, June, September and December issues of the magazine *Museums Journal* to all subscribing individual and institutional members of the Museums Association. It gives brief information (title, contents, size, hire fee, available dates, contact) about a broad spectrum of exhibitions available in the UK and abroad. There is no charge for including entries, but paid advertisements can also be taken. Details must be submitted on a standard form which can be obtained from the Assistant Editor, Museums Journal, 42 Clerkenwell Close, London WC2H 8EH. Tel 0171 333 1733. Fax 0171 333 1736.

Scottish Arts Council. Guidelines on minimum standards for touring exhibitions have been published by the Scottish Arts Council (SAC), which also gives details of sources and regular organizers of exhibitions in Scotland. During 1995, SAC is developing the range of information it provides about touring exhibitions, to include a sample hire agreement, a condition report, packaging guidelines, advice on promoting exhibitions and a database of venues containing details of hanging facilities and access at each exhibition space. For details, contact Sue Pirnie, Scottish Arts Council, 12 Manor Place, Edinburgh EH3 7DD. Tel 0131 226 6051. Fax 0131 225 9833.

South East Exhibitions Project. In early 1995 is planned the first of a series of annual brochures advertising details of selected exhibitions originated by galleries and visual arts organizations in south-east England. Unlike the Southern Arts service (see 12.5), the Project will not organize exhibitions itself, but exists to facilitate them, not least by providing this brochure. Although the Project is funded by South East Arts and supported by Kent County Council, an important part of its function is to ensure that exhibitions are toured outside the region. To be added to the mailing list, which is free, contact John Gill, Co-ordinator, South East Exhibitions Project, 8 West Hill Street, Brighton, East Sussex BN1 3RR. Tel/fax 01273 325138.

Visiting Arts. For several years, Visiting Arts has produced *VA News* two or three times a year. The listing promotes performing and visual arts from overseas which are touring in the UK over a 12-month period from the date of publication. No charge is made either to subscribers or advertisers. Entries may include up to 50 words of description, and should be made using the standard form available from the Visiting Arts Office of Great Britain & Northern Ireland, 11 Portland Place, London W1N 4EJ. Tel 0171 389 3019. Fax 0171 389 3016.

12.3 National Touring Exhibitions

Touring exhibitions of mainly modern and contemporary art are available from the Hayward Gallery, which operates a touring exhibitions service on behalf of the Arts Council of England. Hire fees vary, depending on the size and complexity of each exhibition, and the security requirements are similarly graded. Two-way transport and insurance are included in the fees, and installation of the two top categories ('A' and 'B') are supervised by the organizer. The service is promoted via an illustrated booklet distributed free twice a year. To be put on the mailing list, contact National Touring Exhibitions, Royal Festival Hall, Belvedere Road, London SE1 8XX. Tel 0171 921 0862. Fax 0171 401 2664.

12.4 Area Museum Councils

Until 1994, subsidised touring exhibition services were available from five of the seven Area Museum Councils (AMCs) in England and from the Council of Museums in Wales (for the names and addresses of AMCs, see 10.6 and 10.8). They have toured mainly object-based (i.e. not visual arts) exhibitions to registered museums and galleries in their own areas. In many cases, they have drawn on the expertise and collections of member museums, enabling the latter to benefit from a centralized case-building, design and crating service.

This range of touring exhibitions was advertised in an annual catalogue, first published in 1992 as a joint venture between the five AMCs. These AMCs offered 'out-of-area' bookings for which most of them charged double the hire fees. A realignment of funding priorities has led to the closure of two of the five AMC touring services and placed another two in jeopardy. Both the South Eastern Museums Service and the Yorkshire and Humberside Museums Council have switched from the role of provider to that of enabler, offering advice as well as grant-aid, and were followed in 1995–96 by the Area Museum Council for the South West (see 10.8). In this changing situation, the fate of the catalogue must be in doubt.

12.5 Regional Arts Boards

In England the ten Regional Arts Boards (RABs, listed in 10.7) provide information, advice and training to arts organizations within their respective areas. Their visual arts and crafts officers in particular will be well placed to provide overviews of trends in regional and national provision. One recent initiative that is likely to be ongoing is a scheme funded by the Arts Council of England to promote development within three consortia or 'bands' of RABs, each of which decides how it wishes to spend its grant allocation. To date, there has been an emphasis on training to promote collaborative working in the South, grant aid for touring and curatorial travel in the North, and the development of a closer working relationship between Derby, Peterborough and Wolverhampton art galleries in the Midlands.

Many of the RABs indirectly support touring through the exhibition programmes of their client galleries, which tour regionally or nationally in order to recoup some of their costs. However, only one RAB is directly involved in the production of touring exhibitions, namely Southern Arts which contracts the Winchester Gallery to run a service on its behalf. It generates about a dozen exhibitions a year focusing on the contemporary visual arts, which are advertised in an annual brochure. Venues in the Southern area benefit from subsidized hire fees, and 'out-of-area' bookings cost at least double, but in all cases the package includes transport, installation and insurance. Further details are available from John Gillett, Winchester Gallery, Park Avenue, Winchester SO23 8DL. Tel 01962 852500. Fax 01962 842496.

12.6 Direct mailings

A glance at the various listings mentioned in 12.2 will give *in toto* a good impression of who are the regular organizers of touring exhibitions, be they museums, commercial galleries, arts centres, heritage bodies or specialized touring agencies. Most will tour on a nationwide basis provided venues cover transportation costs, and some will tour from abroad (see 15.4). One way for a venue to get advance notice of projects while they are still in the planning stage is to study the listings and to make a shortlist of appropriate contact names and addresses. The latter can then be approached to put the venue on their mailing lists for future information on exhibitions they are touring. It is helpful to organizers if venues indicate at the outset the approximate type, size and cost of the exhibition being sought; details of loading facilities and security measures will be useful at a later stage.

Organizers, for their part, can research the range of venues they wish to mail by scanning the *Calendar of Art Exhibitions* or by consulting the *Directory of Exhibitions Spaces* (edited by Richard Padwick. 4th edition 1995, AN Publications; available from Artic Producers Publishing Co Ltd, PO Box 23, Sunderland SR4 6DG. Tel 0191 567 3589). The *Directory* includes details of gallery sizes and policies for more than 2000 venues in the UK, listed by region.

Where a few or even only a single exhibition is being advertised, it will not be viable to produce a printed catalogue. The amount of information and illustrative material that an organizer incorporates into a mail-shot can obviously be more comprehensive than that featured in a listing, but a great deal of time and effort will be saved if the information is structured as clearly and concisely as if it were for a printed catalogue. A simple one-page summary may be sent with a covering letter, and should set out:

- exhibition title;
- size (linear/square metres);
- security (specify requirements rather than give A, B or C grades);
- additional requirements (e.g. environmental controls);
- content (two-line description of the installation);
- transport and insurance arrangements;
- value of exhibition for insurance purposes;
- hire fee (cost for a given period; VAT; what the fee includes/excludes);
- availability;
- turn-round period required (for installation and dismantling);
- publicity material available (with costs);
- publications available (with prices and discounts);
- merchandise available (with prices and discounts);
- organizer's contact, address, phone and fax numbers.

Photographs or slides of exhibits along with installation shots can also help venues to decide whether an exhibition is suitable for their own gallery spaces.

12.7 Networking

Organizers and venues which have successfully shared exhibitions in the past often seek to do so again, targeting their mailings accordingly. A tour may thus be established by bypassing the more democratic channels of information outlined above. An organization which works in this way, even if only on an occasional basis, should acknowledge the fact whenever venues approach it to be included on its mailing list, in order to avoid the possibility of any accusations of bias.

12.8 An eye to the future

The diversity of support for, and information about, touring exhibitions in the UK makes a very fragmented and sometimes confusing picture. Improvements and withdrawals of support are happening continuously, but as yet no one organization has taken on the responsibility of an all-inclusive, nationwide information service. This could take one or more of the following forms:

- A three- or four-monthly bulletin, which had the financial and organizational backing of the current providers of bulletins but without having to adhere to their limited terms of reference.
- The benefits of computer technology could be harnessed, for instance by reviving MagNet, the on-line database of travelling exhibitions developed by the MGC and put on ice in 1993 because of

funding problems.

- Market-places could bring organizers and venues into regular contact and allow them to explain their needs and plans and make bookings or form consortia, according to their specific needs.

13

Collaboration

Linda Theophilus

13.1 'Can the nine-metre boat be shown in all the venues?'

Collaboration is inherent in any exhibition - between lender and borrower, between artist and venue, between visitor and organizer – but this section considers the particular issues surrounding collaborations between all the venues staging an exhibition.

The relationship between the organizations showing an exhibition varies from project to project. In its most simple – or rather undeveloped – format, the exhibition is prepared for a showing at the organizer's own premises and offered for hire to venues on the open market.

The venues need only to give consideration to meeting the requirements established by the organizer, e.g. security and physical conditions, and to paying the hire fee, whether this is a true share of the costs or subsidized by the organizer. A willingness to be flexible over dates and to ensure a logical onward transport schedule is desirable, and any detailed communication may only be concerned with what day and time the van will leave and arrive.

In return, the organizer will expect each venue to meet its responsibilities of packing and checking in a professional manner, to notify the organizer of any damage to, loss of, or change in the conditions of the objects, the exhibition display material and the packing (see 46.1). These are all aspects of what is, in effect, a well-established and mutually-understood process.

This level of collaboration works best for a simple exhibition that contains no surprises, has no large or heavy objects, where all cases and material will go through standard doors or into standard lifts, and that is straightforward to install. It can be supplemented in various ways: the organizer may visit the proposed venue during the planning phase, may request floor plans and route dimensions, and may supervise or assist with the installation and attend the opening, if there is one (see 49.4).

13.2 'Should we have a nine-metre boat in the show?'

What divides this kind of relationship from what might be termed 'real' collaboration is that consideration is only given to the physical aspects of the show, i.e. whether the nine-metre boat will fit in all the venues.

It is only when partners can contribute to the aims and intentions of an exhibition, and are involved in the decisions that carry these through to the content, structure and design, i.e. whether any boat should be included, that the exercise can properly be called a collaboration, or joint venture. It is this element that is essential to a collaboration, rather than equality of financial input or workload (although these aspects will often follow).

There can be an element of cross-over between traditional touring and collaborations. For example, the organizer may bring the proposed venues together to test the thesis for the exhibition; this may be done at a relatively late stage, with a presentation of the type and range of exhibits to be included. The organizer may or may not take the venues' comments on board, because 'ownership' and control of the exhibition is still held only by the organizer. In some cases, venues will not confirm their booking of the show until this stage, which they can do without breaking contracts, but perhaps at the cost of losing friends!

13.3 The characteristics of collaboration

A 'real' collaboration will acknowledge from the first that all parties will:

- have ownership of the exhibition;
- discuss and agree the aims, intentions and outline proposal;
- share resources, responsibilities and benefits.

Within this atmosphere of togetherness, there will need to be a clear division of tasks, and an acceptance that not all aspects can be equally shared: only one organization can be the first or the last venue, or the official borrower; some tasks bring a greater sense of ownership than others, and have a higher profile (see 13.6); and some partners may have more money, staff time or expertise available than others.

13.4 'Collaborations are hell, but you get what you want!'

The advantages and disadvantages of collaborations can be divided into practical and strategic. Practical considerations are usually acknowledged, and include the sharing of resources and workloads.

Funds can be pooled in straited times. Experience and expertise can be shared, as can contacts and add-on services e.g. access to transport, storage, conservators, marketing skills, publicity specialists, education staff. A collaboration can make a larger project feasible, by providing venues with the confidence and resources to tackle more complex projects than they would alone (see 1.5).

Workload can also be shared, although this can also lead to imbalances of workload and resources between the partners. Collaborations are also time-consuming. The need for formal meetings, with time allowed for planning and travel and for a more complex decision-making process will extend the preparation time for the exhibition, and require appropriate consideration when scheduling (see 8.3).

Collaborations offer the possibility of 'getting what you want', instead of receiving the normal toured-in product over which the venue has had little or no influence. This is associated with a greater sense of ownership of the exhibition, rather than as a subsidiary venue of a bought-in touring show. On the other hand, sole ownership will be lost: although one of the co-organizers and owners of the show, a venue may have to accept that it will not have the advantage of the first showing. Press coverage may be spread between several venues (see 30.1).

Strategic advantages are often implicit, but it is important to recognize them (and the corresponding disadvantages). They help shape each party's sense of ownership and pride in the project, as well as providing powerful lobbying tools with colleagues 'up the line' or with outside funders, sponsors, etc.

Strategic considerations include the implied approval of each partner for the other(s). This can increase one party's status within its own management structure e.g. as perceived by local authority councillors or senior management, or extend its reputation into new areas e.g. from the museum sector into independent galleries, or vice versa (see 1.2). On the other hand, there will be a greater possibility of clashes of personality; one partner may not impress the other(s) or cause criticism from other potential partners; and staff changes will have a greater impact.

Other strategic considerations include the possibility of attracting potential sponsors by offering greater geographical access (see 11.3), and a pooling of ideas and avoidance of competition. Often two separate venues will wish to organize a similar show, thus dividing the possible venues, press coverage and potential visitors.

13.5 Avoiding the pitfalls: cooperation

Collaborations present particular difficulties: partners can bring their own priorities, loyalties, ambitions, intolerance, and professional pride, as well as ways of working.

Often collaborations are suggested by those other than the people directly involved, perhaps by a representative of a funding body or a superior. Given the potential for bad feeling and difficulty, those involved must start with the goodwill to succeed. They must 'get on'.

It is imperative that careful exploration of the notion of collaboration is undertaken as openly as possible, and that there is a real opportunity to say 'no', however appropriate the notion may appear to be on the outside.

It is as important to want to collaborate, as to want to organize a particular exhibition: ideally the wish to collaborate should be decided before or concurrently with the subject of the collaboration, so that every stage of the planning can be undertaken and agreed jointly (see 4.6). Otherwise, the sense that the exhibition idea 'belongs' to one partner will be hard to overcome.

It is worthwhile giving considerable time and attention to these initial stages:

- use a 'think tank' technique to reveal as many ambitions and ideas around the project as possible, and to expose and explore differences of intent;
- make full notes of each point, and circulate these for correction, comment and agreement: it may appear that each partner is saying the same thing, but often their subsequent understanding is different; and
- draft a set of aims for the collaboration, as well as for the exhibition.

13.6 Avoiding the pitfalls: ownership

Some tasks bring a higher profile and a greater sense of ownership than others, e.g. the 'selector' may feel it is more their exhibition than the person responsible for the transport.

One way of encouraging a more equable sense of involvement is by the joint commissioning of freelance specialists to work to an agreed brief. They have the advantage of showing equal loyalty to each partner, whereas it is difficult for an employee of one of the partners to maintain this impartiality. They can also bring their ability to dedicate clear and focused time to the project, without the distractions of institutional day-to-day work (see 5.1).

13.7 Avoiding the pitfalls: communication

It is necessary to set clear guidelines for what does and what does not need to be shared by the partners. If the collaboration is to ease workloads, an agreement that allows each partner to make autonomous decisions within their task area is necessary. For approaches to sponsors, see 11.5.

However, some information has a knock-on effect for others. If the 'selector' changes his or her mind about the inclusion of an object, this must be conveyed to the 'loans officer', and the 'transport manager', as well as the designer. In smaller institutions, these roles may of necessity be carried out by the same person. To have to communicate can be unfamiliar, and therefore needs highlighting.

If each partner is to receive appropriate recognition, the form of written credit must be agreed and rigorously carried out. All venues must display this correct information, and do all in their power to ensure that all publicity and press coverage includes it. Again, this is often a new responsibility, and can be overlooked (see 30.13).

13.8 Avoiding the pitfalls: written records

All meetings should be minuted, and the main points of agreement codified into written sets of aims and objectives. A formal agreement will need to be drawn up, setting out the main responsibilities, commitments and rights of each partner (see 16.8).

13.9 Avoiding the pitfalls: end of tour

It is easy for the partners showing the exhibition early in its tour to be otherwise occupied when the tour finally ends. As well as the return of the objects, it is important to include arrangements for the:

- ownership of remaining catalogues;
- responsibility for the exhibition furniture;
- storage or dispersal of packing, graphics, files, etc;
- enquiries after the exhibition has closed;
- final accounts;
- evaluation: report of press coverage, feedback from venues, exhibitors, visitors, etc.

Ideally, one partner should be nominated as the 'archivist', to collect all printed matter, press coverage, feedback reports and files at the end of the project. Opportunity for written comment and feedback from partners will also allow difficult points to be exposed, and assist the planning of future projects (see 6.4).

13.10 Example 1: *Chemistry Set*

A collaboration between the Crafts Council (CC) and Southern Arts Touring Service (SATS), selected by Sara Roberts, this exhibition was initially proposed by the Southern Arts' Crafts Officer as a means of encouraging the Service to undertake more ambitious projects. SATS already had a strong regional reputation for providing small- and medium-scale touring exhibitions. After initial discussions between CC and SAB, the SATS Exhibitions Officer was invited to make a proposal, based on research into the subject.

This was then approved by the CC, which entered into a formal relationship with SATS by means of an agreement that identified the following breakdown of responsibilities. SATS was to be responsible for selection, organization, collections and regional touring, preparation of catalogue text and supervision of design and print, exhibition design and construction. These in-kind contributions were equivalent to 50 per cent of the total cost of the exhibition. The CC covered print, showcases, graphics and photography costs, provided the first venue in London, national touring and return of loans, representing the other 50 per cent of the cost.

13.11 Example 2: *Colour into Cloth*

Colour into Cloth was a collaboration between the Craft Study Centre, Holburne Museum, Bath, and the Crafts Council, selected and organized by Margot Coatts and touring to the Whitworth Art Gallery, Manchester. The idea originated from the CC's wish to make closer links with the Craft Study Centre, based on a study of dyed and printed textiles in the twentieth century. After exploratory discussions with the Museum, it was agreed to appoint a freelance curator to undertake the research.

The Craft Study Centre gave access to its collections and archives, made a commitment to show a large exhibition using all available display space, and allowed items from its collection to tour to an extra venue. The CC was the budget manager, and arranged tour transport, collections and returns, the design of the exhibition and the catalogue. The limited tour was carefully planned to allow each venue the maximum advantage in promotion, interpretation and access: London in April–June, to catch art colleges and schools; Manchester in the summer, with families targeted for workshops etc.; and Bath in September–October targeted at schools and colleges.

13.12 Example 3: *The Woodcarver's Craft*

The Woodcarver's Craft was a collaboration between Cartwright Hall (Bradford), Usher Gallery (Lincoln), Hove Museum and Art Gallery, Glasgow Museums and Art Galleries, and the Crafts Council, organized by Margot Coatts and Jeremy Theophilus.

The original proposal for this exhibition was formulated by its two curators without any specific venues in mind. The collaboration was developed in response to a suggestion from the Museum and Galleries Commission, and taken up by the Crafts Council which had already funded the early research and then acted as broker with the partners in the setting up of the consortium. The format for this collaboration is fully described in its agreement (see 16.8).

14

Working with commercial galleries

Brendan Flynn

14.1 Common aims

Public and private galleries in the UK have tended to plough their own separate furrows apart from occasional examples of collaboration. They appear to be divided by fundamental differences: the public gallery being geared towards interpretation for the general public, and the private gallery towards profit and serving an élite minority of art buyers.

Most private gallery proprietors would dispute this over-simple definition. The majority of them are in the art business because, first and foremost, they are passionately interested in art and committed to promoting it by getting an artist's work seen, appreciated and sold. Only a small proportion of the visitors to their galleries ever buys an exhibit.

Essentially, they offer a massive range of historical and contemporary exhibitions free to the general public. They act as disseminators of information about their special field of interest or the artists on their books. Although it is vital, selling is only part of their activity alongside promoting and enabling artists, documenting their work and cultivating new publics.

And what about public galleries? Given the interest, most of them will sell work from their exhibitions of living artists, and will take their percentage on any such sales. The public gallery network plays an important part in promoting and maintaining artistic reputations. They even follow some of the methods, like the private view and the one-person exhibition, which are techniques par excellence of the commercial gallery.

Public and private galleries have a great deal in common, and the potential for creative and even profitable collaboration is immense. Private galleries are not restricted to London nor are all public galleries located outside London, and the most effective collaborations between the two sectors may not be restricted to London-based dealers and public galleries outside London. Collaborations can range between loans of individual exhibits and jointly-organized exhibitions.

14.2 Benefits for the public gallery

The private gallery can be a point of contact with a network of artists and collectors. It can give the organizer access to a grapevine which is invaluable for tracing the whereabouts of artists and their works.

Commercial galleries often promote the work of their artists as much through publication as through exhibition, and are often willing to enter into co-publishing arrangements with public galleries that wish to show these artists, e.g. making it possible to include colour illustrations in a catalogue by buying an agreed quantity of the print-run (see 32.4).

An association between a public gallery outside London and a private gallery with premises in London, which leads to an exhibition on both sites, can act as a lure for corporate sponsorship.

Many private galleries have good contacts with the art press and media, which can be of great help to an organizer working on a collaborative project.

A private gallery can be a reservoir of information and a useful resource for the organizer and the researcher, with its access to catalogues, reviews, reproductions, etc. Many proprietors of private galleries are acknowledged experts in their field and may make excellent guest curators (see 5.1).

Retailing works of art is becoming more and more important to public galleries as a source of income. Private galleries can offer expertise on the marketing of exhibits, the way that they are presented and priced, and how to target potential buyers.

Many dealers and proprietors of private galleries who deal in works by living artists want to promote the artist's work more widely. As a way of promoting contemporary art from premises that may be small or only open by appointment, a private gallery may have a deliberate policy of touring its exhibitions, often providing public galleries with exhibitions just at the moment when that artist is beginning to attract critical attention.

Private galleries can often arrange the loan of exhibits at relatively short notice, compared with many public galleries which can insist on up to six months' notice for the approval of loan applications. This can be a great advantage to an organizer who is required to arrange or research an exhibition urgently.

14.3 Benefits for the private gallery

Private galleries are often small because they are in high rent and rate areas in city centres, and can show only a small sample of an artist's work. There is little space for adventurous installation pieces or full retrospective surveys, and the spaces, facilities and the professional and financial resources offered by the public sector can give the opportunity to artists to exhibit at crucial stages in their careers.

An exhibition with a reputable public gallery can enhance the saleability of exhibits. Buyers can feel reassured by the endorsement of the work by a public and independent institution. A collaboration between the dealer and a public gallery can be good for the artist. The prospect of a major one-person show can inject new inspiration and urgency into the artist's work and allow ambitious projects to be brought to fruition. A major one-person show can also be an opportunity to attract an informed critical response to an artist's work.

The artist can take advantage of opportunities arising from the active education programmes which public galleries administer but which might not be available in the private sector. The opportunities range from single lectures and workshops to residencies in the gallery or in the local community (schools, colleges, etc.).

Sharing production costs with the public gallery can enable the private gallery to improve its own image/public profile, as sponsors of the project, through more substantial catalogues and/or more striking posters, and through notice by the press.

Public galleries have their own networks of contacts which could be of use to a private gallery for finding and cultivating potential buyers.

Exhibiting important works from public collections can enhance the reputation and prestige of a commercial gallery, and enable it to show its current stock in context, thus improving saleability.

Partnership with a public gallery can mean that a private gallery and its artists can benefit indirectly from grants from the national arts councils and regional arts boards, for which they would normally be ineligible (see 10.4).

Storage is a major headache for many commercial galleries. Public galleries would often welcome the chance to borrow high-quality exhibits on long loan. A potential buyer might be more inclined to purchase a work which is on attachment to a public collection, rather than one that has been in store. The same body of work cannot be shown again in a dealer's gallery. Loans to public galleries or collaborative exhibitions can extend the 'shelf life' of an artist's work and introduce it to a new public.

14.4 Some 'Dos' and 'Don'ts' for the organizer

When contacting artists for the first time, establish whether they are represented by a dealer. Ensure that the dealer is aware of/involved in all discussions about a possible exhibition. Negotiating with an artist without the dealer's knowledge could be a recipe for problems later on. Make the studio visit early on, if possible with the dealer. Conversely, always involve the artists in any negotiations with their dealers about collaborative projects which involve their work. Do not assume that an artist's motives and expectations are the same as the gallery proprietor's.

Get onto the mailing lists of private galleries, and put them on yours. Find out what they specialize in, and which artists are on their books. Go to their exhibitions and introduce yourself. Meet the proprietors, and let them know your area of interest. Make an appointment. Don't just drop in. Make it clear from the start whether or not you are a potential buyer. This can prevent misunderstandings.

Invite proprietors of private galleries to your gallery to view the spaces and facilities. Give them some idea of your track record. If possible, offer to pay their expenses. If the exhibition under discussion will tour to other galleries, then involve the relevant people in the venues. Invite them to the discussion, have the details of their spaces and facilities, including storage capacity and technical support, and send them a report of the meeting. Agree between the private gallery and the venues a provisional timetable for the delivery and onward transport of exhibits, allowing sufficient turnround time (see 8.2).

A contract is essential for any collaboration between two or more parties. It can take the form of a simple written agreement which outlines the commitments of the parties concerned, the time frame, the financial input. AN Publications provide excellent model contracts which apply to most projects. Again, make sure that the artist and the galleries participating in the tour are fully involved. Copies of the draft contract should be sent to the respective parties for their comments before signing. Highlight any sections of particular relevance to that party.

Establish what work is available for including in the exhibition. Beware of work that may be sold or needed at an art fair or under negotiation. The organizer could end up with the rump of unsold work from a previous show. As far as possible, list in the agreement (or attach as a schedule to the contract) the actual exhibits required. Subsequent to the contract, the dealer will inform any buyers of the proposed exhibition, which may help the organizer to borrow the purchased work all the same.

Clarify the question of sales of exhibits, the terms of sale and percentages due to each party. Terms of sale include payment details, such as deposits and the timing of the payment of the balance, and collection. Where deposits are forfeit upon default of payment of the balance, the division of such deposits between each party must be negotiated and specified in the contract. The contract should specify the percentages due to the dealer, to the organizer and, where appropriate, to the venue from which a work is actually sold (see 35.6).

Remember that the commercial art world is subject to change without a great deal of notice. Many proprietors of private galleries live on the edge of financial viability and are affected by unpredictable fluctuations in the market. The organizer should keep plans under regular review and try to be flexible when required. While doing the utmost to accommodate the interests of the private gallery, the public gallery must adhere to establishing accounting procedures, making payment for goods and services actually received.

15

International touring

Janet Moore

15.1 Introduction

Taking part in an international tour, whether as the organizer or as a venue, can be exciting and rewarding. Apart from extending the life of an exhibition and giving it an international audience, an overseas tour may increase the profile and reputation of an organization and/or of its permanent collection, and the extra finance generated may allow a larger project to be realized. However, an international tour can be complex, costly and take much preparation, and it is essential to have an infrastructure in place to support it. Early planning is the key, and it is crucial to be methodical and keep comprehensive documentation of information, procedures and agreements.

15.2 'Packages'

As with a tour within the UK, an international tour may take the form of an organizer hiring out a 'packaged' exhibition to venues in other countries (see 13.1). The organizer will be responsible for the exhibition's initiation and have complete curatorial control. It will most likely show the exhibition first before touring it overseas. It may be that venues are secured after this first showing, so the exhibition has to be designed to be flexible.

For the organizer, an overseas tour will mean a heavy administrative workload; for a venue, it may mean a lighter workload. It might give the venue the opportunity to show an exhibition that it may not have the time or resources to work on, and to work on other projects or to use the exhibition to focus on aspects of its own collection. However, 'buying-in' from overseas is rarely a cheap option, not only because of increased transport and insurance costs, but also because of larger hire fees and more complex administration (which often includes translation).

15.3 Collaborations

The 'packaged' exhibition can carry considerable financial risk for the organizer, despite having hire fees as income to set directly against exhibition expenditure. A collaboration spreads the financial risk, and is becoming increasingly common for touring even within the UK (see 13.2).

A collaboration takes the form of two or more institutions working closely together on the initiation and organization of an exhibition, or organizing an agreed exchange of exhibitions. Collaborations usually stem from contacts already made and interest in a specific area or project already established. Regular meetings and deadlines are set up in advance. Compromises will be made. Work will be done collectively or delegated, and formal agreements will be drawn up as to who is responsible for what. Costs are increased when working internationally, but the budget should be discussed between the collaborators and the costs shared between them.

15.4 Directories

As with national tours, information exchange and keeping records of other institutions and touring bodies is crucial, whether to an organizer who intends to regularly tour overseas or a venue looking for exhibitions from abroad. Published directories can be useful for finding potential venues or collaborators. These include:

Artyear. The *Annual Exhibition Guide*. Published by Hopefulmonster Editore, Milan. A diary of art institutions and what they are showing as temporary exhibitions in that year. This is a good indication of the interests of the institutions represented, useful for those organizing international tours or looking for collaborators. UK distributor: Shaunagh Heneage

Distribution, 1 Stewarts Road, London SW8 4UD.

Informationen zur Ausstellungsplanung. Published by the Institut für Auslandsbeziehungen (the German equivalent to the British Council) and IKT (see 15.5). Consists of a simple list of exhibitions planned by the Kunstverein/Kunsthalle circuit in northern Europe, seeking collaborators and venues. Exhibitions can be advertised as well as sought. Contact Institut für Auslandsbeziehungen, Charlottenplatz 17, D-7000 Stuttgart.

International Directory of Arts. Published annually in Germany by Art Address. Gives up-to-date names of directors and curators of museums, galleries, academies, universities, etc. UK distributor: Hilmarton Manor Press, Calne, Wiltshire SN11 8SB.

Visiting Arts News. Lists events including overseas exhibitions that are available to UK venues. Also, will list touring exhibitions organized in the UK but featuring non-UK artists. Does not usually give details or information about potential collaborations. For the address, see 12.2.

15.5 Organizations involved in touring internationally

Government/funding bodies hold useful information, particularly Visiting Arts (see 12.2). The British Council's Fine Arts Department (11 Portland Place, London W1N 4EJ) will provide British Council contacts in specific countries who can give information on potential venues. Also it is useful to look for organizations from other countries that have offices in the UK, e.g. the Goethe-Institut which promotes German exhibitions and is a good source of information.

The International Committee on Exhibition Exchange (ICEE) is a sub-committee of the International Council of Museums (ICOM) and can be contacted via ICOM's current UK committee (see the annual Museums Yearbook).

Other touring institutions and groups include the International Kunstausstellungsleitertagung (IKT), literally the 'international art exhibition organizer's conference', which is a membership organization that meets twice a year for the Kunstverein/Kunsthalle circuit. Contact Peter Weiermair, Frankfurter Kunstverein, Steinernes Haus, am Römerberg, Markt 44, D-6000 Frankfurt (Main) 1. This is very much a German-led organization.

15.6 Networking

Networking is essential for finding an exhibition or a venue overseas. In general, every opportunity should be taken to make overseas contacts, whether it be through visits abroad, through the British Council or at conferences. Organizers and venues should keep themselves up-to-date on current policies for travel grants from the Arts Councils, the Museums and Galleries Commission and Visiting Arts (see 10.5).

Contact names, addresses and relevant information (collections, sizes of galleries, budgets for buying in exhibitions etc.) should be kept, preferably on a database that can be used as a mailing list. If this is not possible then a simple record card system will suffice.

Different countries have distinct ways of circulating exhibitions. Some only work on a collaborative basis, while others are serviced by sophisticated touring agencies which are government-run (e.g. the Rijksdienst Beeldende Kunst in the Netherlands) or by independent or semi-commercial agencies (e.g. the Australian Exhibitions Touring Agency). If an agency tours an exhibition on behalf of the organizer, it will usually want to negotiate the hire fee in order to cover its costs.

15.7 Direct mailings

The most productive method is to target individual venues by letter, signed by the organizer's director. This will usually ensure a reply, even if it is negative. If possible, translate the letter into the language of the recipient.

If there is interest, the organizer should send a standard pack of information, again translated into the language of the recipient, if possible. Unsolicited proposals are often not returned from overseas venues, so establish firm interest before sending a large pack.
The pack should include:

- a description of the concept of the exhibition;
- some illustrations;
- details of the size, availability, costs of the exhibition;
- a list of exhibits (confirmed or unconfirmed);
- details of catalogue;
- details of educational and other supporting material.

State if the exhibition is sponsored and whether the venue will be expected to credit the sponsor(s). The pack must be professional and comprehensive without being complicated or expensive.

It is imperative that sufficient time is given to finding venues in other countries, whether for a 'packaged' exhibition or for a collaboration. The more firm the tour, the easier it is to get agreements from lenders and funders.

The following are considerations additional to the information given in other sections of this manual.

15.8 Concept

Compromises may be necessary as with a collaboration within the UK (see 4.6). The gallery space and the resources of each institution will be taken into account when exhibits are selected. However, negotiations may be more complex, as overseas institutions may have different cultural emphases (e.g. a non-Western view of the history of art) or different exhibition policies (e.g. a wish to include or exclude certain artists for political reasons). The integrity of the exhibition can also be affected if there are exhibits that lenders will not allow overseas (see 15.11).

15.9 Schedules

All meetings between the partners in a collaboration will need to be scheduled much further in advance than for a collaboration within the UK (see 13.4). Agendas should be well prepared, since meetings will entail greater travel and expense. An overseas venue may have to go through an organizational process or bureaucratic structure (e.g. it may need to seek the approval of its Ministry of Culture). Extra time should be allowed, if the exhibition texts, publicity material and catalogue have to be translated. All of these factors will extend the lead-time for organizing the exhibition (see 8.2). In addition, showing dates should be carefully calculated to take into account the time it takes to transfer the exhibition. Storage should be organized if necessary.

15.10 Agreements

Responsibilities should be clearly apportioned between the partners in a collaboration and agreements put in writing. Hire agreement should be as comprehensive as possible (see 16.7). The terms used should be straightforward, to avoid the misunderstandings which may occur through language differences. Information should be laid out so that it is easy to see what is required of the other party. Telephone conversations should always be confirmed in writing; a fax is invaluable here.

An organizer should be realistic about costs and what a venue is likely to be able to pay. An international hire fee is usually higher than a UK hire fee, reflecting the additional time and resources spent and different systems of subsidy. In the UK, there is a tradition of subsidizing tours at source (e.g. National Touring Exhibitions, see 12.3) which is quite different from other countries where venues may be subsidized direct.

The organizer should be aware of VAT regulations. For a showing outside Europe, VAT does not have to be charged on a hire fee; inside the European Union, it does, although a venue can claim this back if it is registered for VAT. Tax now has to be paid on insurance, a cost which the organizer will need to pass on to the venues if they agreed to pay for insurance. Agreements should state how payments are to be made: usually made in sterling drawn on a London bank, if the organizer is in the UK.

15.11 Borrowing exhibits

As with a national tour, both the safety of the exhibit and the integrity of the exhibition must be considered carefully when exhibits are being selected for an overseas tour. The lender will decide whether there are any restrictions (e.g. number and types of venues, countries and climates, etc). This stage may take much longer than for borrowing for a national tour, if the lender has to obtain information from, or even arrange a visit to, venues with which they are not already familiar (see 37.4).

Most exhibitions that travel overseas will be accompanied by a courier from the organizer and one or more representatives of different lenders. The cost of a courier is usually additional to the hire fee, and the venue will be required to cover flights, accommodation and expenses, charged at a daily rate (see 51.6). If several couriers are required, it may make costs prohibitive for a particular venue. In a country where English is not the first language, it is advisable to have a translator close at hand who can relay instructions.

15.12 Funding

A larger contingency should be allowed for unexpected costs, e.g. extra travel, additional shipping. Often there will be more than one currency in use, and the cost implications of this should be addressed. Recent fluctuations in exchange rates between the countries in the tour may affect the cost of goods or services paid by the organizer or a venue.

Clearly, it is sensible to apply to grant-giving trusts or organizations that support international touring or promote relations between the collaborating countries. An exhibition organized by the Museum of Modern Art Oxford of an established French photographer was supported not only by Visiting Arts (see 10.5) but also by the cultural department of the French Embassy in London and by a French brandy company which wanted to promote itself in Britain and the rest of Europe. There are several directories that are useful in the search for trusts which support international touring in general or certain countries in particular (see 11.7).

The prestige of being involved in an exhibition touring overseas can be a major attraction to sponsors. It is important to be realistic about the sponsor's demands and the likelihood that an overseas venue can meet them. The venue may not want to meet these requirements unless it can see an obvious benefit. The collaborators should decide whether they should all look for separate sponsorship in their own countries or whether one will co-ordinate it all and approach multi-national companies (see 11.5). Different institutions may target different aspects of the exhibition, e.g. transport or catalogue. Whatever is agreed, it is important that there are no conflicts of sponsors.

15.13 Transport

The type of transportation required will be dictated by the lenders' requirements and the type, value and condition of the exhibits. Whether the exhibition is air-freighted will depend on how quick the 'turn around' time is between showings.

For overseas travel, a higher standard of crates is often required. The type of packing and specification for crates will depend on whether the exhibition can be delivered straight to a venue or will be transferred between different modes of transport (see 54.4, 55.6). It may be possible to commission a specialist transport company to act as agent and as carrier (see 52.1). Building up a relationship with a reliable carrier is of utmost importance and can save much time and work. They will usually work direct with the agent on your behalf. They can also investigate storage, should it not be possible to store the exhibition or its packing at the venues.

The weight of cases, plinths and other elements of an installation may make it cheaper for each venue to construct their own, if the exhibition is to be air-freighted. Where possible, Perspex should be used as it is lighter and safer than glass.

15.14 Text panels and labels

Multiple sets of labels can be printed in one language to be supplied to the venues, but it is more usual and practical for the organizer to provide (perhaps on disk) a list of exhibits and the copy for text panels, so that they can be translated. Such information must be supplied as soon as possible: not only may it need to be translated into another language, but it may also have to be adapted for the particular cultural context in which the exhibition is to be shown. No organizer should expect a text to be translated literally, and venues must expect to devote time and expense to necessary contextualisation. However, the organizer should approve the proofs, in order to check credits and acknowledgements.

15.15 Catalogue

Sales of a catalogue produced for an international readership can be substantial and contribute towards the exhibition's costs. Production of the catalogue and other printed material will depend on the requirements of each venue and their budgets (see 32.3). Often text will have to be translated, and it should be decided whether to publish one edition or separate language editions. If the catalogue is printed in another country, checking proofs or shipping copies to the venues can add significantly to its cost price.

15.16 Publicity material

Posters, private view cards, etc. can be printed with each venue's details, as for a national tour (see 27.12). However, it can be more straightforward, if not all venues are English-speaking or if there are different sponsors or funding bodies to be credited, to supply blanks for each venue to overprint.

16

Hire agreements and fees

Jeremy Theophilus

16.1 Purpose

The purpose of a hire agreement is to identify as clearly and precisely as possible the essential elements of transferring an exhibition between venues. It should be appropriate to the nature of the exhibition, the material it includes, and the size and scale of the venue(s) to which it travels.

There are two basic types of relationship that such an agreement needs to describe: the traditional hire and the collaboration. In the first, the organizer offers the exhibition to interested venues as a ready-made package, for a fee that reflects a proportion of the production costs (see 9.9).

The second is a much closer partnership between organizer and participating venues, starting at a much earlier stage in the production process and sharing areas of responsibility, in return for a much larger contribution to the costs of the exhibition (see 13.4).

While every exhibition is unique, there are basic elements that apply to all, and the agreement must identify these elements to the appropriate degree of detail. It is for the organizer to define the scale of the project and to draw up an agreement to suit. However, this need not reflect the physical size of the exhibition, as one with few exhibits could just as easily contain a whole 'shopping list' of display, transport and conservation requirements.

16.2 Timing

The agreement acts as a marker in the development of the touring exhibition, and is an important 'milestone' as far as scheduling is concerned (see 8.1). The agreement cannot be implemented until a certain stage in the creation of the exhibition, yet a relationship with venues must be confirmed before further planning can be undertaken.

The agreement should be created as early as possible, as soon as the exhibition's concept, educational aims, contents and display implications can be adequately described (see 4.4, 22.1). This should be sufficient for the venue to plan its reception of the exhibition with confidence. Ideally this should be at a stage when the approximate number of exhibits, their size, value and conservation and display requirements can be identified and matched with the spaces offered by venues.

More specific information relating to photography, crating, transport, display, etc. can be provided in a supplement to the agreement, which should be confirmed in writing (see 17.2).

16.3 Format

Taking the basic elements of an exhibition and its production as the starting point, it is usual to test a draft agreement against the facilities and requirements of the organizer's own exhibition space, before passing it through to venues or collaborators for approval, final draft and signature.

In the case of a traditional exhibition hire, the agreement will focus on physical arrangements (see 16.4), whereas a collaboration will identify those areas where each participant has to contribute a share of the duties involved in the exhibition (see 16.7). A crucial difference between these two is the timing of their confirmation: the involvement of collaborators needs to be agreed at a sufficiently early stage to allow for the research to proceed, backed by their financial contributions; whereas hire agreements assume that the exhibition has already reached such a stage.

16.4 Example 1: National Touring Exhibitions

A traditional hire agreement is represented here by the standard contract issued by National Touring

South Bank Centre Touring Exhibitions – Terms and Conditions of Hire
This document is a contract between the South Bank Centre and
*
relating to the exhibition *
for a booking period from *
Loans of South Bank Centre exhibitions are made subject to the hirer's agreement to the following conditions.

1 *Acceptance of Offer*
Acceptance of an offer to take a SBC Touring Exhibition is by return of this contract, appropriately signed, to the Exhibition Bookings and Transport Co-ordinator within four weeks of the date of the offer letter. If it is not received the offer will be considered void and the exhibition will be available for booking elsewhere.

2 *Booking Period*
The booking period shown is the maximum length of time for each showing. It excludes the time needed for installation and dismantling. Under certain circumstances, e.g., a long transport move or a difficult installation, the South Bank Centre will advise if an exhibition should open later or close earlier. The hirer may decide to shorten the showing period provided that
2.1 the exhibits are safely stored by the hirer for the time they are not on show;
2.2 the total showing period is not less than an average of five hours per day over the booking period;
2.3 any changes are communicated to and approved by the South Bank Centre before publicity material is printed.

3 *Insurance*
The South Bank Centre takes responsibility for the insurance of all works in touring exhibitions. In most cases these will be covered by British Government indemnity.

4 *Transport*
Unless otherwise stated the transport of exhibitions is arranged and paid for by the South Bank Centre.

5 *Security*
The hirer must satisfy the South Bank Centre that all necessary steps are taken to protect the exhibition against the risk of accidental or wilful damage or loss due to extremes of temperature, humidity or lighting, or due to theft, fire or vandalism. The hirer must not permit any act which would vitiate the indemnity arranged by the South Bank Centre. Any loss or damage occurring while the exhibition is in the hirer's custody must be reported immediately by telephone to the Director of Exhibitions. Wilful damage and thefts must also be immediately reported to the police. No press or other public statement about loss or damage should be made without prior reference to the Director of Exhibitions. Repairs must not be undertaken by the hirer until a report has been made to the Director of Exhibitions and such repair authorized. Protective glass or perspex must not be removed without South Bank Centre approval.
Security must be provided to at least the minimum levels required for each category of exhibition from the time of delivery to the time of collection, including periods of installation and dismantling.
5.1 *Category C* exhibitions must be under regular supervision during opening hours and the premises securely locked at night.
5.2 *Category B* exhibitions require constant patrolling while open to the public and a comprehensive alarm system and secure premises for silent hours.
5.3 *Category A* exhibitions require round-the-clock invigilation: during opening hours, a warder must be stationed permanently in each exhibition area so that all exhibits are under constant surveillance. Shift changes must take place in the gallery, at which point the installation should be checked against a diagram of the layout. During the silent hours an alarm system may be used instead of silent hours patrolling only with South Bank Centre approval.

6 *Delivery and collection*
The hirer must be prepared for the delivery and collection of the exhibition on the specified dates, even

Figure 16.1 National Touring Exhibitions – terms and conditions of hire

though the showing may open later or close earlier than the offered booking period. Adequate help must be provided for unloading on delivery and for re-loading on collection. Unless otherwise advised by the SBC Exhibition Organizer, the hirer is responsible for unpacking and re-packing the exhibits and must ensure that they are handled only by trained members of staff. The condition of each item must be checked immediately after unwrapping and before re-wrapping. During the showing all packing material, cases, crates, etc., must be stored safely and wrappings replaced with new and clean packing material when necessary.

7 *Installation and dismantling*
The exhibition must be shown complete with nothing added, and separate from other exhibitions taking place at the same time, except by special arrangement with the South Bank Centre Exhibition Organizer. The suitability of the galleries for the exhibition must be confirmed with the SBC at the time of booking. Installation and dismantling of the exhibition is normally the hirer's responsibility. The hirer will be advised if the South Bank Centre is to provide assistance and/or if the installation is to be supervised by the South Bank Centre Exhibition Organizer. The South Bank Centre reserves the right to arrange the hang of the exhibition in consultation with the gallery's staff. Unless informed otherwise by the SBC, mirror-plates or other fittings for installing the exhibition must be provided by the hirer for 'A' and 'B' category exhibitions. Such fixings are usually provided by the SBC for 'C' category cased exhibitions. Labels or numbers must not be attached to the exhibits.

8 *Publicity*
8.1 A certain amount of publicity material is supplied free of charge by the SBC. Publicity proposals for the exhibition must be developed in consultation with the SBC Visual Arts Promotions Officer. The hirer must ensure that the exhibition and related events and educational activities are effectively publicized and promoted using the material supplied by the South Bank Centre., and that the South Bank Centre and its sponsor is credited in any publicity material produced by the hirer.
8.2 *An Exchange of Information Form* will be forwarded to the hirer after receipt of the signed contract. This form must be returned to the South Bank Centre by the date shown on the form to allow the South Bank Centre to prepare educational and publicity materials.
8.3 At the close of the exhibition, the *Exhibition Returns Form* must be completed and returned to the South Bank Centre with details of attendances, sales, educational activities, publicity and press coverage, by *
Unused posters, cards and other material must not be made available for sale.

9 *Publications*
9.1 A catalogue is available for most exhibitions. A minimum number of catalogues are to be purchased at a discount of *% from the SBC by the hiring venue. The minimum purchase order for the exhibition referred to by this contract is *. Further catalogues are available for purchase, or can be supplied on a sale-or-return basis (both at a discount). The cost of the catalogue for this exhibition is *.
9.2 Delivery of the first order of catalogues will be free, with costs of delivery for re-orders during the run of the exhibition charged to the hirer.
9.3 During the showing, catalogues and any other material for sale must be clearly displayed and available for purchase in, or en route to, the exhibition area and must be re-ordered before the stocks are exhausted or minimum holding reached. An agreed minimum number of catalogues are to be held by the hirer for the duration of the exhibition.
9.4 A maximum of *% of unsold catalogues taken on sale-or-return may be returned to the SBC (in multiples of ten). It is the responsibility of the hirer to return unsold catalogues to the Publications Warehouse properly packaged to ensure they arrive in mint condition. The hirer will be charged for lost or damaged returns.

10 *Education and supporting activities*
The hirer is expected to take responsibility for the provision and promotion of supporting activities for the general public and the formal education sector. Such provision, appropriate to the hirer's resources, is a

Figure 16.1 National Touring Exhibitions – terms and conditions of hire (*continued*) central requirement of these terms and conditions of hire.

In some cases additional support up to a maximum of 20% of the exhibition hire fee is available from the South Bank Centre on a matching pound-for-pound basis. Details of this are included in the Educational Guidelines enclosed with this contract.

11 Sponsorship

The sponsor of National Touring Exhibitions holds exclusive sponsorships rights. The terms of the South Bank Centre's agreement with its sponsor require the hirer to use all reasonable endeavours to ensure the fulfilment of certain sponsorship benefits. Assistance will be given by the South Bank Centre's Development Department to enable hirers to fulfil the below with the help of the sponsor's local representative.

11.1 The sponsor shall be granted the right to host a Private View organized and administered by them, after the host gallery's own Private View. The venue hire, additional staff costs and catering costs shall be borne by the sponsor. One or more of the following options shall also be made available to the sponsor where appropriate:

- an opening private view jointly organized and jointly funded by the sponsor and the host gallery;
- an agreed number of invitations for the sponsor to attend the host gallery's opening private view;
- a press view for the sponsor, organized by them in consultation with the South Bank Centre's Press Office and in conjunction with the host gallery, before the opening private view.

11.2 The host gallery shall credit the sponsor on gallery-generated printed material, gallery signage and in verbal statements relating to the relevant exhibition.

12 Cancellations

The hirer must advise the South Bank Centre of any change in the circumstances of the exhibiting gallery which could adversely affect the showing. Cancellations must be made in writing to the Exhibition Bookings and Transport Co-ordinator accompanied by an explanation. If a cancellation is made less than six months before the opening date at the venue referred to in this contract the hirer will be required to pay the hiring fee. The costs of overprinting posters and cards will be charged to the hirer cancelling the showing or otherwise changing publicity details if this has already been undertaken.

13 Invoice

An invoice for the hire fee and publicity material in excess of the free allowance will be sent to the hirer at the end of the showing. Publications provided for sale will be accounted for separately, during the exhibition for purchase orders and after receipt of the invoice. All prices are shown exclusive of VAT, which will be charged if applicable.

The South Bank Centre reserves the right to apply further conditions to particular exhibitions as and when the need arises.

I agree to the terms and conditions detailed above

....

(signature of responsible officer at the hiring venue)

....

Roger Malbert (Head of National Touring Exhibitions)

Figure 16.1 National Touring Exhibitions – terms and conditions of hire (*continued*)

Exhibitions (see 12.3). The following comments refer to different paragraphs of the 'Terms and Conditions of Hire' (see Figure 16.1).

Paragraph 1. A major point of frustration in fixing tours can be the inability of venues to commit themselves to dates. This clause stresses the importance in making a decision by a given date.

Paragraph 2. It is important to differentiate between actual showing dates and the time needed for delivery, installation, dismantling and removal.

Paragraph 3. Where insurance or indemnity cover is not provided as part of the package, this section will need to identify where responsibilities are divided between venues and organizer (see 40.6, 41.3).

Paragraph 4. Similarly, where transport is not provided as part of the package, this section will need to identify where responsibilities are divided between venues and organizer (see 49.5, 53.5).

Paragraph 5. Note the ways in which this issue is addressed here, establishing codes of good practice in describing the process by which problems can be resolved. The categories in sub-paragraphs 1–3 are a shorthand which refer only to broad security requirements for exhibitions. They do not include environmental requirements. They are often used, wrongly, to define the status of galleries and museums (see 42.1).

Paragraph 6. It is important to ensure that venues can provide adequate assistance in dismantling and installing exhibitions, particularly if the exhibits are bulky or complex to pack. Note also that not only care of exhibits but also their packing materials are covered here (see 45.1, 48.2, 49.7).

Paragraph 7. If the exhibits demand specific care and consistency in the way they are displayed at each venue, it is important that the organizer is able to retain control over these elements, particularly if they are representing the originator of the work (see 34.4).

Paragraph 8.3. In order to evaluate the success of the exhibition at each venue, any way in which the organizer can obtain relevant information should be implemented within the terms of the agreement (see 6.3).

Paragraph 9.1. Note the value to the organizer in making each venue purchase a fixed number of catalogues, in addition to the hire fee, as part of the agreement. Not only does this ensure accuracy in estimating the print-run, but it also establishes a guaranteed income at an early stage of the exhibition (see 32.3).

Paragraph 10. By making educational activities a part of the agreement, the organizer can ensure that the exhibition will be taken more seriously by each venue (see 25.2). National Touring Exhibitions is in an unique position to be able to offer matching funding (up to a maximum figure) for these activities, but this could also be taken up by other organizers where funding has been raised for this purpose: indeed this could form part of the sponsorship package (see 11.5).

Paragraph 11. This is a good example of the ways in which sponsors can maximize on their support for an exhibition, by taking advantage of an exhibition tour to promote its own activities country-wide (see 11.4).

Paragraph 12. It is vital that all terms relating to cancellations should be well identified, both to reinforce the agreement, but also to safeguard and forestall any future conflict.

16.5 Sales

In cases where exhibits can be sold from touring exhibitions, it will be necessary to clarify the procedure for handling and accounting for any sales (see 35.7). The following is an extract from a standard hire agreement used by the Crafts Council:

> 15% of the sale price of any work will be paid to the venue responsible for the sale on receipt of an invoice. Sold work cannot be collected until the end of a tour, when it will be returned by the Crafts Council to the point of sale. The venue is responsible for contacting the purchaser about payment and collection. Purchasers should make cheques payable to the Crafts Council. No work can be collected until payment is received and cheques cleared. The venue must send details of sales including the name and address of purchasers and date of sale to the Crafts Council as soon as possible.

16.6 Hire fees

There is no doubt that resolving the hire fee for an exhibition can be the most vexing part of the whole process. It should:

- reflect an appropriate proportion of the income generated for the exhibition (taking into account grants and sponsorship);
- reflect as accurately as possible, and proportionately, the 'value' of the exhibition;
- reflect the 'going rate' in the market for touring exhibitions and fix the level of the exhibition within it.

Issues that need to be taken into account when arriving at a hire fee include the size and value of the exhibition, its relevance to other exhibitions that might have addressed the same theme, or any limitations on the extent of the tour (for conservation or security reasons). The size of target venues, both in physical and operational terms will also have a bearing on the level of the fee.

For some originators, the fee is directly related to the need to raise income, for others the need to have the exhibition seen as widely as possible is much more important; it is clear that these two divergent motives alone can affect the nature of the 'market place' for touring exhibitions.

Furthermore, some exhibitions, particularly those

Exhibition Consortium agreement between: the Crafts Council of Great Britain; City of Bradford Metropolitan Council Arts, Museums and Libraries Division; Usher Gallery, Lincoln County Council Recreational Services; Hove Museum and Art Gallery, Hove Borough Council; and the City of Glasgow District Council, Department of Museums and Art Galleries.

IT IS AGREED THAT:

1. Title of exhibition
The Woodcarver's Craft

2. Exhibition content
The exhibition will compromise the exhibits listed in the catalogue.

3. Dates
The exhibition will be held at:

The Crafts Council	18 November 1993–16 January 1994
The Usher Gallery, Lincoln	30 January 1994–5 April 1994
Cartwright Hall, Bradford	16 April 1994–3 July 1994
Art Gallery and Museum, Kelvingrove, Glasgow	15 July 1994–25 September 1994
Hove Museum and Art Gallery	9 October 1994–4 December 1994

4. Credits
The following credit will appear on all posters, press releases, and all printed material:

The Crafts Council in collaboration with Bradford Art Galleries and Museums, Glasgow Museums, Hove Museum and Art Gallery, and Lincolnshire County Council – Usher Gallery, Lincoln.

5. Participation fee
The participation fee is £4000 + VAT. This is payable by City of Bradford Metropolitan Council Arts, Museums and Libraries Division, Usher Gallery, Hove Museum and Glasgow Museums. (See appendix 1.) These consortium galleries will each remit this amount to the Crafts Council within thirty days of receipt of their Invoices. The participation fee paid to the Crafts Council covers the costs of the undernoted items:

(i) The exhibition as defined in paragraph 2 above.
(ii) All exhibition display equipment, graphics and signage.
(iii) 400 A3 posters overprinted with venue details.

6. Finance
The individual consortium venues are each responsible for all costs relating to their own staff time in organizing and administering the exhibition. They are responsible for their own local costs including, but not limited to, loading and unloading, unpacking and repacking, installation and dismantling, local publicity, opening events and security.

7. Admission fees
If an admission fee is charged, such funds will accrue to the benefit of the institution charging the fee.

8. Catalogues
Catalogues will be supplied at wholesale price. Sales proceeds will accrue to each venue.

9. Administration
The Crafts Council will be responsible for the financial administration of the exhibition and will act as budget

Figure 16.2 Collaboration agreement

officer, transfer officer, and exhibition design supervisor. Hove Museum and Art Gallery undertakes to handle all relevant correspondence with lenders and to provide copies of all relevant correspondence to the other consortium members. The Usher Gallery is responsible for all print supervision. Glasgow Museums are responsible for all conservation supervision and the provision of contracts. Cartwright Hall, Bradford is responsible for the organization of transport.

10, Packing and transportation
The Crafts Council will supervise the preparation and packing of all works arriving from lenders to London. Each consortium venue in consultation with Cartwright Hall, Bradford is responsible for the supervision of the preparation and packing of all works following the close of the exhibition at their venue. Each consortium venue is responsible for the cost and replacement of any packing material needed for repacking at their venue.

All consortium members will agree to a single transportation company for the transportation of all work for the duration of the exhibition period. Following such agreement, they will each be given an estimate of costs for their transport liability as defined below.

Cartwright Hall, Bradford will administer all transport.

On receipt of the final account for transport the Crafts Council will invoice each venue for their liability in the transport costs. Each venue will be responsible for the cost of one fifth of any transport costs in excess of the costs already included in the main exhibition budget. Each venue will settle the invoice for transport costs within thirty days of receipt of invoice from the Crafts Council.

Each venue will maintain packing and crates in good condition and will preserve any packing materials in the crate to which they belong.

11. Insurance and indemnity
Valuation of work will be agreed on the basis of the values indicated by Hove Museum and Art Gallery and lenders.

Each venue is responsible for insuring all loans during their storage and exhibition at that venue and insurance during transit to the next venue. Hove Museum and Art Gallery is responsible for insurance cover during transit of returns. Each venue will be responsible for the handling of any insurance claims that arise from any damage that occurs while the works are in its care under the coverage it has arranged.

12. Care and supervision
Each venue will be responsible for the care of works in the exhibition and during the transport for which it is responsible. It will make all necessary arrangements to ensure the safe keeping and security of the works in the exhibition, including the observation of any serious environmental requirements that may be specified by the Crafts Council.

13. Condition reports
A condition report, with photographic documentation, will accompany each exhibit. This condition report must be annotated and signed at each unpacking and packing by a qualified member of staff. All condition reports should be returned to the Crafts Council following the completion of the packing of the exhibition at the final venue.

14. Procedure in the event of mishap
Each venue will inform the Crafts Council in writing of any loss, damage, destruction, or theft which occurs while the exhibition is in its charge. Any damage or change in condition shall be photographed immediately it is discovered, and the photograph included in the return report if the damage appears to have occurred during shipment. The institution unpacking the work shall preserve all packing materials for inspection and shall photograph the packing case and material upon discovery of the damage.

The institution responsible for the transport shall give written notes to the transporter and the institution in receipt of the exhibits at that point shall inform the insurers as applicable and will also be responsible for informing the Crafts Council and the owner of the work.

Figure 16.2 Collaboration agreement (*continued*)

15. Conservation
No conservation or restoration work or unframing shall be performed without authorization of Glasgow Museums and, where applicable, the owner of the work. The person treating any object shall fully document any treatment and append the documentation to the condition report together with a copy of the provision for treatment.

This agreement is made in Scotland and is subject to Scottish law.

Signed.. Date..................................
(Crafts Council)

Signed.. Date..................................
(City of Bradford Metropolitan Council Arts, Museums & Libraries Division)

Signed.. Date..................................
(Usher Gallery, Lincoln County Council Recreational Services)

Signed.. Date..................................
(Hove Museum and Art Gallery, Hove Borough Council)

Signed.. Date..................................
(The City of Glasgow District Council, Department of Museums and Art Galleries)

Appendix 1

Participation fee

This will be paid in installments by the venues listed.
(As agreed in the minutes of the meeting of 15 December 1992)

Lincoln	1993/94	£4 000 (when show opens)
Bradford	1993/94	£2 000
	1994/95	£2 000
Glasgow	1994/95	£4 000
Hove	1993/94	£1 000
	1994/95	£3 000

Figure 16.2 Collaboration agreement (*continued*)

that are smaller in scale and with the potential for a much longer life on the road, can continue to generate income over a number of years: this will inevitably affect financial planning, in that forecasting can be difficult to predict (see 9.9).

The gallery and museum sectors have each been influenced by the provision of subsidized touring exhibitions, not least through National Touring Exhibitions (see 12.3). The latter has lost something of its dominant position, as individual galleries have become more involved in providing their own touring product and have consequently influenced the market values for such exhibitions. Accordingly there is now much greater freedom to offer shows at a level that is more appropriate to the true costs of their production than has been the case in the past. For an impression of the 'going rates' in the market for different types and sizes of touring exhibitions, see the listings in 12.2.

In most cases, fees will be negotiable, and regular users of the networks of touring exhibitions will often find ways to accommodate each others' particular difficulties. However, the necessity remains for a fixed price to be established, from which any variance can be agreed.

16.7 Collaboration agreement

The agreement for a collaboration will require much more careful wording in order to clarify the greater involvement of members of the group, in which there will be varying levels of responsibility and (possibly) financial contribution (see 9.9).

This can be most effectively resolved by producing a draft agreement collectively, meeting to work out the various elements of the project and agreeing on respective allocation of tasks, together with each shareholders' stake (see 13.4). Inevitably there will be some areas where the true nature of a particular aspect of the exhibition might not be apparent at this stage. A degree of flexibility will need to be allowed for in anticipating such changes.

16.8 Example 2: *The Woodcarver's Craft*

An agreement for a collaboration is represented here by the Exhibition Consortium agreement drawn up for the exhibition, *'The Woodcarver's Craft'* (see 13.12). The following comments refer to different paragraphs of this agreement (see Figure 16.2).

Paragraph 4. In order to avoid any potential rivalry between participants, it is essential that the billing for the exhibition shareholders is clearly described without losing sight of the collective ownership (see 30.13).

Paragraph 5. Note the terminology: 'participation fee' clearly implies the purchase of a share in the exhibition (see 16.9). It is also useful to be able to plot and agree the points at which each participant pays their contribution to the costs of the exhibition, bearing in mind the time at which it will show in the gallery, and its impact upon respective financial years and cash-flow (see 9.6).

Paragraphs 6, 7 and 8. A common cause of dissent between collaborators is the definition of areas covered (or not) by the participation fee. This must be sorted out at a very early stage. Areas where staff time can (or cannot) be set against financial contribution should be agreed.

Paragraph 9. This follows on from the preceding points, and clearly states the degree of commitment of resources to the production and management of the tour. It is very important to base this allocation upon each venue's realistic ability to provide such services, in the recognition that this will strengthen their sense of ownership of the exhibition.

16.9 Participation fees

Participation fees can be defined in two ways: either as a percentage of the core costs, divided equally amongst the collaborators, or in proportion to their respective involvement in the exhibition.

As with the hire fee, participation fees can be difficult to establish, but it is all the more important to do so, particularly where there are variations between each participant in terms of size of operation, galleries, staff, annual turnover etc.

Likewise, the contribution needs to be defined by mutual consent. Because of the longer relationship with the exhibition, payments can be stretched over two or more financial years to accommodate the cash flow within participants' organizations (see 9.6).

17

Advance information

Valmai Ward

17.1 Two-way information

A touring exhibition belongs as much to the venue as to the organizer, and a fundamental principle of touring is that organizer and venue should exchange relevant information as soon as it is available and should update each other as and when there is any new information or any alteration to details previously supplied.

In one direction, this information is a way for the organizer to keep the venues informed about the development of the exhibition. It will cover all the necessary details which a venue will need to know before the arrival of the exhibition itself.

In the other direction, it will comprise information from the venue, about the space and facilities available and its requirements for publicity and educational materials, which the organizer will need in order to prepare the exhibition. In some cases, this information will be included in a facilities report (see 38.1).

17.2 The checklist

The following checklist (17.3–17.20) is an *aide-mémoire* of the information most commonly exchanged. It is up to the organizer and venue to use what is relevant to the project. Some of this information will be available at the booking stage, and will form part of the hire agreement (see 16.2).

The checklist can be set up on a word-processor and then adapted to suit each exhibition. It can be designed as a standard pre-printed form or be freshly amended for each issue. In either case, it will provide, at a glance, a record for both organizer and venue of what is jointly known about the exhibition. By the gaps that still remain, the checklist also serves as a reminder for both parties of what information may need to be exchanged in the future.

If it is used as a form, the organizer should add a standard headline, e.g. 'Please note/supply the following/attached information'. The direction and purpose of the information would then be clear by the sender circling or underlining either 'note' or 'supply'. Information can be printed out for each issue or typed on the form or attached to the form as supporting pages. Again, the purpose should be clearly indicated by circling or underlining either 'following' or 'attached'.

With an appropriate headline ('on offer/state quantity required/herewith'), the checklist can also be used by the organizer to list the materials available for publicity and educational use, by the venue to place an order for such material, and by the organizer again when this material is actually supplied to the venue.

17.3 Date of issue

It is important to date each issue, so that both parties know which is the latest information.

At what stages information is exchanged will depend on the size and complexity of the exhibition and the amount of time that a venue will need to devote to preparing for its arrival. An organizer should give some indication at the booking stage when information will be available, and the venue should indicate if it requires information earlier.

At the beginning of a tour, it is rare for an organizer to know all the details. For the first one or two venues at least, advance information may be updated and reissued several times, with each issue confirming, building on or amending the previous one.

17.4 Title

To avoid confusion, always give any working title by which the venue knew or booked the exhibition, then add the current title by which the exhibition will be publicized and, where appropriate, any sub-title:

- working title;
- official title for publicity purposes;
- sub-title.

17.5 Contact names

Name, address, phone and fax numbers of:

- the organizer;
- external curator (see 5.1);
- the person responsible at each venue;
- their staff responsible for education, publicity, installation, etc.

17.6 Sponsorship and fund-raising

Documentation should include:

- development profile for each partner in a collaboration (see 11.5);
- responsibilities for fund-raising (see 11.5, 15.12);
- any restrictions on fund-raising (see 11.4).

Logos (see 30.13), and wording of credits and acknowledgements, to:

- organizer (or organizers in a collaboration, see 13.7);
- external curator (see 5.13);
- sponsor (15.12, 30.2);
- and funder (10.4).

Check any translated text (see 15.14).

17.7 Dates

Dates available (see 16.4):

- actual showing period;
- plus installation time; and
- dismantling time.

17.8 Contents

Information on content should contain:

- description of theme, message (see 4.1);
- inventory of exhibits (see 7.3);
- environmental profile of each exhibit, where appropriate (see 43.2);
- draft Condition Check Docket (CCD, see 46.2);
- texts of panels, captions, labels (see 15.14);
- photographs/slides;
- display cases, panels, plinths, etc provided by the organizer (see 7.9);
- equipment provided by the organizer (see 27.4), plus repair kit, spare bulbs, replacement cassettes, etc (see 21.3, 21.6, 21.8, 23.7, 24.5, 26.13);
- list of materials with their fire retardancy (see 27.3).

17.9 Gallery requirements:

The facilities the exhibition will require at each gallery will include the following:

- wall-space required: total length in metres, plus unusual height requirements and/or notes on display of particular exhibits (see 34.4);
- floor-space required in square metres, for display cases, plinths, equipment etc;
- possible exhibition layout (see 27.9, 49.7);
- venue floor plan (see 38.6, 38.7, 38.18)
- any unusual sizes or weights of exhibits;
- lighting: height of system and fittings available (20.7);
- power supplies required (see 20.10);
- maintenance required (see 23.10, 24.5);
- display cases, plinths, etc to be supplied by the venue (see 38.12);
- equipment to be supplied by the venue (see 26.13);
- skilled staff needed (see 23.8);
- security (see 38.14–38.17);
- environment (see 38.9–38.12).

17.10 Transport

Paperwork for the transportation of the exhibition consists of:

- transport manifest (see 53.10);
- delivery: date and time, name of carrier (see 53.12), cost (see 49.5);
- collection: date and time, name of carrier (see 53.11), cost (see 49.5);
- vehicle requirements: size, weight, timing, staff, suspension, environmental control, security, etc (see 52.5);
- access for vehicles (see 38.7);
- handling equipment to be provided by carrier and/or venue (see 53.11).

17.11 Installation and dismantling

For the installation and dismantling of the exhibition, the following documentation will be required:

- Crate contents and packing instructions (see 46.9);

- condition check dockets and handling guidelines (see 46.2);
- instructions, diagrams and photographs for installing and dismantling display cases, plinths, equipment (see 9.4, 21.3, 23.5, 24.5, 27.4);
- labour required: number, when (see 48.4);
- handling equipment required: what, when required;
- dates and times when the organizer and/or couriers will be available to supervise; cost of couriers (see 51.6);
- dates and times when exhibition area needs to be ready (see 53.6).

- Unpacking: date and time; who should be present (see 46.8);
- condition check: date and time, and who should do it (see 46.10);
- installation: date and time, and who should do it (see 49.7, 51.4).

- Dismantling: date and time, and who should do it (see 49.7, 51.4);
- condition check: date and time, and who should do it (see 46.10);
- packing: date and time; who should be present (see 46.8).

Further documentation will be required relating to storage:

- storage of the complete exhibition, after delivery and/or before collection and between showings: location, space, security & environmental conditions required (see 43.3, 50.1);
- storage of unused exhibits: lenders' permissions obtained, space, security & environmental conditions required (see 50.5);
- storage of crates and packing: location; space, security and environmental conditions required (50.6);
- storage of equipment, replacement bulbs, etc (see 50.7).

17.12 Insurance and indemnity

Documentation relating to insurance and indemnity falls into three categories.

- List of valuations and owners' details (see 40.3);
- advice on GIS applications (see 41.3);
- whose responsibility – organizer's or venue's – for insuring the exhibition: on display; in storage;
- whose responsibility – organizer's, the last venue's or this venue's – for insuring the inward transit (see 40.6, 41.4);
- whose responsibility – organizer's, this venue's or the next venue's – for insuring the onward transit (see 40.6, 41.4).

- Fire certification (see 27.5);
- fire alarm/smoke detection system (see 27.6);
- copy of Fire Officer's report (see 27.13);
- confirmation of Fire Officer's approval (see 27.16);
- summary of fire precautions during the showing (see 27.5);
- recommendations for fire extinguishers (see 27.7);
- priorities for emergency rescue of exhibits (see 27.8).

- Public liability (see 29.3).

17.13 Hire fee

Information relating to the hire fee should include:

- basic hire or participation fee (see 16.6, 16.9);
- Valued Added Tax;
- what the fee includes;
- what the fee excludes or other costs (see 32.3, 51.6);
- when payable;
- cancellation procedure (see 16.4).

17.14 Publicity

Information concerning publicity is divided into origination and usage.

- overprinting details;
- posters: format, cost, quantity required, overprinted or blank (see 30.9);
- cards for private views/other publicity purposes: format, cost, quantity required, overprinted or blank (see 30.20);
- press release: format, cost, quantity required, overprinted or blank (see 31.8), or text of press release;
- press photographs: format, cost, quantity required (see 31.9)
- number of complimentary catalogues: available/required;
- logos to be used (see 17.6).

- Names and contact numbers of press officers (see 30.3, 31.4);
- names and addresses (on labels?) of exhibitors, lenders, sponsors and other persons to be invited to formal openings (see 11.4, 30.20, 31.6, 34.7);
- responsibility for booking advertisements (see 30.6);
- list of photographic restrictions (see 31.10, 33.12);
- restrictions on TV filming;
- photographs and written details of any controversial exhibits (see 34.3).

17.15 Publications

Publications relating to an exhibition include:

- merchandise offered directly by the organizer: cost and price, quantities required, whether overprinted or blank (as appropriate):
- catalogue (see 32.5);
- other material (see 32.8);
- posters for sale (i.e. not publicity, see 32.7);
- cards for sale (i.e. not publicity, see 32.6);
- information sheets;
- work sheets.

Thought should also be given to whether there will be any complimentary copies, and disposition instructions for unsold stock.

17.16 Sales and trading

Information should relate to:

- average turnover per exhibition visitor (see 32.3);
- location of sales point (see 32.3);
- merchandise display policy (see 32.3).

Suggestions for sales items other than those directly supplied by the organizer (see 32.2): stock name and description, where available, cost and price, procedure for orders, invoicing and return of stock.

17.18 Sale of exhibits

The following information relating to the sale of exhibits should be circulated:

- sales record (see 35.7);
- procedure for sales (see 35.7);
- when available to purchaser (see 35.1, 35.2);
- division of commission (see 35.6).

17.19 Related events, education, interpretation and special needs

Information required will include:

- visitor profile (see 3.5);
- target visitors (see 6.7);
- number of active visitors anticipated (see 32.3);
- education policy (see 25.2);
- prospectus of educational materials, people and other information (see 25.3);
- legal requirements, licences, etc (see 26.1);
- chart for estimating audiences at audio–visual displays (see 23.4).

17.20 Reports

The following reports should be generated at the appropriate times and circulated:

- receipt on delivery;
- contents checked on unpacking (see 46.10);
- any exhibits not displayed (see 34.4);
- any loss, damage, hazards, inability to meet loan conditions or changes in temperature/humidity agreed (see 7.16, 43.5);
- contents checked on packing;
- receipt on collection;
- attendance figures: exhibition, private view, workshop(s), lecture(s), etc.;
- sales figures for catalogues, posters, cards, etc.
- sales information on exhibits sold (see 35.7);
- press cuttings (see 31.17);
- evaluation: formal surveys, visitors' comments, venue's comments (see 6.3).

18

Designing exhibition galleries

Elizabeth Goodall

18.1 A good brief and a close working relationship

> We finish the building feeling so proud of its look, the way we have resolved all the complex issues of making services invisible etc., all the major things, and then the client complains the doors open the wrong way! (Architect).

Whether it is a new building, or a conversion of an existing building, it is the seemingly small elements of the design which are capable of having the major positive or negative impact. For this reason, a good clear brief from the client is essential. So is a continual and close working relationship with the architect during the design and construction. The architect's work will only be as good as the information that has been provided in the brief and in the ongoing discussion and exchange of information.

18.2 Writing the brief

Prior to writing the brief, it is helpful for the client to consult widely with all the 'stake-holders' in the project, including future users, to gather information. Standards and guidelines are available (e.g. from the Arts Council of England and the Museums and Galleries Commission) for security, environmental control, disabled people's access and other aspects of the design of museum and gallery buildings (see 28.7, 42.1).

The brief for the architect should be in writing. It is important that the future user of the building should specify the results he/she is seeking and what the organization hopes to achieve, in terms of the exhibitions it plans to organize or hopes to attract and the ambience provided for visitors. A successful result will depend on the commissioning body's representations of what is to be achieved and its ability to convey this to the architect.

Changes that need to be made to designs at a later stage, because the brief was imprecise or poorly-researched, can have dramatic consequences in terms of delays and extra cost. In some cases, it may even be too late or too expensive to effect the necessary changes. Once the building is finished, it may be convenient to blame the architect for any inadequacies, but the client will have to work with them. It is therefore imperative that the client does as much work as possible on preparing a clear and detailed brief.

18.3 What should be in the brief?

Although not exhaustive, the following list identifies requirements that a client may wish to include in the brief. Organizations of different sizes and policies should be able to extract the parts relevant to themselves. At the very least, it should provide a checklist to ensure that most factors in gallery design are taken into account when the brief is written – not added later when the building is half-completed.

- overall impact and ambience;
- external access routes, for exhibits and visitors;
- description of the building/facility in use, e.g. a sequence of its normal or anticipated activities;
- guidelines for access for people with disabilities;
- maximum sizes of exhibits, crates and display cases;
- maximum weights of exhibits, crates and display cases;
- total length of surfaces (including partitions) for displaying two-dimensional exhibits;
- height of display surfaces (including partitions);
- composition of display surfaces (e.g. wood/board to take screws); decorative appearance of display surfaces (e.g. no pipes, switches, decorative features);
- hanging system for two-dimensional exhibits;
- frequency of maintenance/ease of colour change for display surfaces (walls and partitions);

- total area of exhibition space for three-dimensional exhibits and display-cases;
- appearance of floor surfaces for display purposes, visitor comfort and ease of maintenance;
- floor loading;
- power sockets;
- telephone sockets;
- signing (permanent, emergency, poster sites, provision for banners, etc.)
- delivery area (size of vehicles, weather protection, security);
- storage area (size, facilities, access);
- packing area (size, facilities, access);
- security system and procedures for display, storage and packing areas;
- environmental control of lighting, temperature, humidity and pollutants for display, storage and packing areas;
- public facilities (e.g. air-handling, ventilation, seating, shops, catering, cloakroom, toilets, etc.);
- staff facilities;
- access to lighting and plant for maintenance.

18.4 The brief in detail

For example, when considering the overall impact and ambience of the building, the client should address the following questions:

- What atmosphere is wanted?
- If a listed building, what original features will be retained?
- What features would be in keeping with the building?
- Will the interior detract from, or hide, the exhibits?
- Have sufficient resources been put aside to upgrade all furniture, fittings, display cases, etc.?
- If a new building, is it to be a 'landmark' or are cheaper building materials sufficient?

18.5 After the brief has been written

The client's role is not only to convey to the architect the practical needs and aesthetics of the exhibition galleries, but also to ensure that any decisions made by the architect will not compromise those needs.

The selection of architects is critical. Previous work should be taken into account, to ensure that the architects are sympathetic to the aspirations and aesthetic beliefs of those commissioning the work.

A continual and close working relationship between the client and the architect is essential during design and construction. It is helpful to outline to the architect the role envisaged for the client, who should:

- insist on a programme of regular meetings with the architect to discuss all aspects of the design;
- ask the architect to provide a written record of all decisions made at any such meeting;
- require that all details (wall- and floor-finishes, fixtures and fittings) be agreed with the client;
- insist on being involved in any discussion with fire officer, licensing officer, safety officer, security advisor, planning officer, listed building consent officer, English Heritage officer, etc;
- specify the percentage to be spent on artist/craftspersons;
- determine the procedure for the selection of artists and their involvement in the consultation and planning process.

18.6 Working with the architect

If the client has done as much work as necessary for the initial brief, then the number of changes to be made to designs after building work starts should be limited. Where changes are necessary, their cost should be determined before a decision is made to vary the instructions.

It is essential that the client checks all details from the moment that the architect produces outline plans and as the designs progress. For example, it is important that the placing of electric sockets, telephone sockets, switches, sensors, signing, decorative features, service pipes, heating units, etc is discussed and agreed. Often, these details are put in at a late stage and are capable of ruining a display area.

Plans and scale drawings may be checked by asking for paper patterns to be made at actual size, to help visualise narrow spaces, low passages, obtrusive reception desks, etc. As much as possible – and as early as possible – the client needs to be able to envisage how the building would be used, and how varying numbers of staff and visitors would use its spaces.

Future maintenance should be discussed, including the exterior as well as the interior of the building, how frequent maintenance should be and whether access is easy and safe. The client should see and test all samples of furniture, furnishings, etc before agreeing them. Appropriate technical advice should be sought on all specialist equipment proposed.

18.7 Managing the project

Following the compilation of the brief, the project needs to be planned and timetabled. The following points may seem obvious, but these are the areas where mistakes or misunderstandings often arise.

It is important to check exactly what is included in the budget. A building works budget will rarely cover more than major fixtures and fittings. There should be a separate allocation for telephones, furniture, computer cabling, signing, etc.

A quantity surveyor or building project manager should provide a detailed timetable for the project. The client should check that sufficient time has been allowed for planning permission, tendering the work, building work, employment of sub-contractors, etc.

A hand-over period should be allowed for problems to be put right between builders and architects. Because the opening date may be critical to planned exhibitions, it is worth considering whether a penalty clause should be inserted in the contract for any delay in completion, although this may increase the price that is initially quoted.

19

Commissioning a designer

Giles Velarde

19.1 The design brief

The design brief is the organizer's description of a problem that needs solving, whether it be presenting a quantity of text in an attractive and legible manner or displaying a number of exhibits safely and conveying a series of ideas effectively. The brief should not be confused with the design concept (see 19.4) and the specification (see 19.5).

A brief for designing the installation or graphic material may consist of:

- a statement of the aims and aspirations of the organizer (and the venues), with the numbers and types of visitors anticipated (see 4.1, 4.6, 22.3);
- an outline script (see 22.1);
- a provisional list of exhibits, with any special needs, e.g. conservation or interpretation (see 7.3);
- an overall schedule: opening date, length of tour and details of venues if known, or general parameters if not available (see 8.6);
- the budget available (see 9.2).

Clearly the outline script and the list of exhibits is less important if the designer is only dealing with the publicity material (see 30.8). A different set of requirements will be important for any publication (see 32.9), but the following procedures should still be relevant.

The outline script will evolve alongside the design itself into the final story-line, text and exhibit list, i.e. the content that will be supported by the physical structure described in the specification. Both design and script will be influenced by the availability of exhibits and the choice of techniques to interpret them. Conversely, the practical considerations that emerge during the design process may preclude some elements of the story or require extra sections to be written in and exhibits to be found. Although the design brief should be prepared by the organizer, it is best if it is finalized in discussion with the designer.

It should also be clear from the outset how long the tour is expected to last and who are likely to be the main handlers. An exhibition on a limited tour handled by the same expert team need not be so robustly constructed as one expected to tour for several years, travelling the length and breadth of the country and handled by different people in each venue.

The organizer should state the budget and ensure that financial constraints are an integral part of the brief. Often a designer is asked to produce a scheme which is then costed competitively against other designers' schemes. This is unethical when it is done without a fee.

19.2 Choosing a designer

Designers who work for or with museums and galleries will generally have been trained either in graphic design (in which case their strength will be two-dimensional work) or in museum and exhibition design, interior-, furniture- or three-dimensional design (in which case they will be stronger in three dimensions). Designers from other fields (e.g. theatre, product or textile design) may move into exhibition work, as might architects.

Graphic design is such a specific skill that every exhibition which includes text and images to supplement the exhibits should involve such a specialist, even if the three-dimensional work is done by others. Some graphic designers have become highly-proficient 3-D designers and can look after the whole project.

Where there is no designer on the staff, or where such a person is not available or suitable for the work, the organizer can turn to freelance designers. For a discussion of the advantages and disadvantages of using in-house and freelance designers, see the present author's article in the *Museums Journal*, 1988, vol 87, no. 4, p. 181.

The organizer can draw up a shortlist, and invite each designer to give a short (maximum 30 minutes) presentation on solving the design problems. This is known as a 'credentials pitch', where the designers show examples of their previous work and discuss the brief. The Chartered Society of Designers regards as unethical the practice of asking designers to do free 'creative pitches', i.e. asking for a sketch design without payment.

Alternatively, the organizer can arrange a limited competition, in which three or four designers are selected and offered a fee for a creative solution, from which is selected the designer. Although the other shortlisted designs belong to the organizer, copyright remains vested in their designers and using elements from these designs can be an infringement of copyright.

A successful exhibition will be the result of a friendly and trusting relationship between the organizer and a designer. Adequate time must be given to selecting a designer with whom the organizer will be able to work, sometimes under considerable stress, for a long period of time.

19.3 Fees

A designer, like any other professional who contributes to an exhibition, should be properly reimbursed for work done. Museums often have in-house designers and, before cost-centre budgeting was widely accepted, design was often a hidden expense which may have fostered the idea that design was not a real cost (see 9.7). Until the Department of Trade declared them illegal, the Chartered Society of Designers regularly produced a scale of charges, but a set of common practices has evolved and has been generally accepted.

Fees should be agreed between organizer and designer at the outset. There are three basic methods of calculating fees: as a percentage, as a fixed amount or as a daily or hourly rate.

A percentage, varying between 12 per cent and 18 per cent (the lower the overall cost, the higher the percentage) can be agreed on the cost of anything made as a result of the designer's work. The advantage is that the relationship between construction, design fees, VAT, and expenses can be easily defined in the exhibition budget. The disadvantage of this method is that the budget can be exceeded if not watched very carefully. Penalty clauses are rare, largely because of the imprecise nature of the evolution of an exhibition. It would be wise to allow a 12–15 per cent contingency sum as a reserve against unforeseen events.

The advantage of the fixed amount is that both parties know exactly where they stand, but it must be worked out with great care and specified precisely in the contract to ensure fairness. A fee can be calculated as a proportion of the estimated cost of the exhibition, but will not increase if the cost overruns or decrease if savings are made.

With a daily or hourly rate, the organizer and designer estimate the probable number of days' work and review this carefully as the project progresses. This method depends on the designer being well known to the organizer and there being an established relationship of trust. Some designers are, quite understandably, more expensive than others, and rates should be weighed in relation to reputation, overheads, expenses, etc.

Whatever method is chosen, the organizer's budget should also allow for Valued Added Tax (as many designers are registered for VAT), plus expenses (fares, subsistence, printing, photography, etc.), which can amount to 10 per cent of the designer's fee.

With the first two methods in particular, it is normal practice to pay a third of the fee when commissioning the designer. The timing of further payments during the progress of the job should be agreed at the same time. Normally, the organizer will retain the final payment until the designer's work is completed to everyone's satisfaction (see also 5.12).

Many design practices have a standard contract designed to define the task to be carried out as well as to protect both parties. The organizer and designer should adapt this standard contract to the specific task. Where the organizer works in local or central government, there may be a different standard contract, and it may be necessary to make the two forms of agreement compatible. A standard form of agreement, including conditions of engagement, is available from the Chartered Society of Designers, 29 Bedford Square, London WC1B 3EG. Tel 0171 631 1510. Fax 0171 580 2338.

19.4 The design concept

The design concept is the general philosophical and practical description of the designer's solution to the brief, with the reasons for doing it in that way but without details. It is the earliest creative stage in the design process.

The purposes of the design concept are:

- to test how far the designer's vision of the proposed exhibition matches the requirements of the organizer: at this stage, the concept can be discussed and tweaked, amended, torn up and started again;
- to outline the overall interpretive scheme, defining the methods to be used to ensure that visitors understand the meanings conveyed by the exhibits (see 22.1): these methods can be many and varied, and include the relationship of exhibits to other exhibits, to labels, captions and text panels, as well as to audio-visual and interactive devices;

- to enable the designer to make a preliminary estimate of the cost of implementing the design.

The design concept will consist of an oral or written description, drawings, sketches, perspectives, plans and/or sections, and possibly a model. The designer must present his/her solutions in ways intelligible to the organizer and not expect or assume specialist knowledge or experience of reading drawings and plans.

At the same time, the organizer must give time and attention to the design concept in order to ensure that it meets all the requirements in the brief, and to consider the cost implications. Alterations become time-consuming and expensive once detailed design has begun.

19.5 Detailed design

Once the organizer has agreed in writing the design concept, the designer can move on to detailed design. Detailed design covers both written specification and detailed drawings. This stage involves the production of working drawings and specifications, to a level of accuracy and detail sufficient to communicate exact details of the design to the technicians contracted to build any components of the exhibition structure. A specification is a written description of the method to be used, but drawings can contain all the specification that is needed, depending on the methods of the chosen designer. The organizer should not need to supervise this process, but should be given a set of the relevant documents and be briefed as to their content.

19.6 Construction

Ideally, the designer and the client should work together as a team, so that they arrive at the point of seeking competitive prices for the work, with a mutually-produced and -agreed solution to the problem described in the brief. Once the detailed design is ready, the organizer should leave the designer to deal with any contractor. Complicated and detailed designs presume a great deal of shared knowledge between designer and contractor, and can be confusing and incomprehensible to the non-specialist.

Some designers offer a 'design and build' package, within which they will undertake the handling and contracting, supervision and payment of all sub-contractors. The designer will naturally charge a handling fee for all contracting and invoicing, usually on a percentage basis (up to 20 per cent of the cost of each item handled). The advantage for the organizer is that it obviates all day-to-day management of the construction. The disadvantage is that it denies the organizer ready access to the work, and a relationship based on total trust needs to be established at the outset. In times of financial uncertainty, another danger is that the design company can go into liquidation while holding a large part of the exhibition budget.

For public liability, see 29.5.

20

Lighting

John Johnson

20.1 Introduction

Although widely recognized as a crucial element in exhibition design, lighting is often left until the last minute simply because it is one of the final aspects to be set up and adjusted before the public comes through the doors. Last-minute arrangements will be at best unsatisfactory and at worst disastrous. It is essential to plan for lighting alongside other aspects of design and installation.

As with other aspects of incoming exhibitions, lighting may be a learning experience which will reduce the requirement for assistance on future exhibitions. Venues that do not have the practical experience will need the help of someone who has, possibly the organizer of the exhibition or one of the other venues. Alternatively, advice can be obtained from manufacturers (although their advice will be biased towards their products) or from a lighting consultant, particularly one experienced in exhibitions.

Don't panic! Lighting may seem a complicated business, but common sense and practical experience are the best tools to tackle the problems.

20.2 Display requirements

There is no correct formula for lighting an exhibition. An artist's requirements can be as varied as 'the light equivalent to the North Yorkshire Moors on an overcast day in February' (Henry Moore), or 'bright and perhaps a bit brighter' (Bridget Riley), or 'subliminally dark' (James Turrell). In addition to such requirements, lighting will be a combination of the preferences of other lenders, their conservators, the organizer and the lighting designer and curators and technicians at the venues.

The basic exhibition requirement for a particular show should be constant for all venues. What will vary will be the installation conditions and the available hardware to achieve the desired result. The budgets available will also have a role in narrowing the choice of possible approaches.

20.3 Levels

Exhibits that have no restrictions placed on them are now far rarer than those with limits. Detailed conservation practice is explained in other publications (see 20.12), but a simple summary of the maximum light levels for different materials is as follows:

Material	Maximum level
Textiles, works on paper, organic materials	50 lux
Oils, acrylics	200 lux
Unpainted metal and stone, other untreated inorganic materials	Unlimited

Lux is a measure of illuminance, i.e. the light reaching a particular surface.

In addition, the ultraviolet (UV) content of the light must be controlled to a level less than 75 microwatts per lumen. A lumen is a measure of luminous flux, i.e. the quantity of light emitted by fittings. Since the UV content is a proportion of visible light, UV will be reduced at lower illuminance levels.

The contribution of any daylight must be included in these measurements. Since both the overall and UV levels of daylight are very high, most sensitive exhibitions will require very tight control or the total exclusion of daylight.

Lux and UV are measured separately, using different instruments which exhibition galleries are expected to have (see 38.11). Couriers often carry their own light meters and UV monitors when accompanying exhibits, and there should not be disparities between readings by different meters if the equipment is well-maintained (see 51.4).

20.4 Dosage

Increasingly, the principle of dosage is becoming important, since the duration that an exhibit is exposed to light is as critical as the level (see 38.11). Organizers will increasingly face a maximum permitted dosage – expressed in lux-hours – for the period of the loan, and they in turn will require each venue to keep within an appropriate proportion of this total. However, this change in practice is slow, and fixed levels are still the most common stipulation.

20.5 Light sources

In practical terms, differences of approach between venues vary mainly in the distribution of light from the fittings (formally known as 'luminaires'). Broadly, these are spot(light)s or flood(light)s, each with narrow, medium or wide variants. Spots will tend to give pools of light which may or may not merge to give wider areas of coverage (see Figure 20.1). Floods will almost always give a more even spread but may cause problems with excessive light to the sides of objects or on floors or ceilings. 'Wallwashers' are specially designed floods that can produce wide coverage of walls with good uniformity from top to bottom given the correct installation conditions (see Figure 20.2).

The most widely used light source for exhibitions is tungsten halogen. Many different types are available but all should give the same colour of 'white' light (approximately 2900°K in colour temperature) with good colour rendering. Dimming lowers the colour temperature and shifts the colour rendering towards the red end of the spectrum, so it is better to change lamps to a lower wattage to reduce light levels, than to rely entirely on dimming circuits.

Most modern lamps or fittings are 'glass enclosed' i.e. with some sort of front glass cover. This acts as a shield in the unlikely event of a lamp explosion, but more usefully it filters out UV radiation, taking tungsten-halogen lamps below the level of 75 microwatts per lumen usually specified for conservation purposes. For sensitive material, extra filters may be necessary. Fluorescent lamps emit much higher levels of UV radiation. This can be filtered by special sleeves which fit over the tubes and which should be replaced as soon as they cease to be effective.

In all cases, good quality lamps from known manufacturers should be specified. There are many cheap unbranded, imported lamps on the market. While the latter may be quite acceptable on building sites or even shops, their inconsistency in performance and physical dimensions will give very poor results in exhibitions.

Figure 20.1 Controlled soft-edged spotlighting gives calm serene results. (Courtesy of John Johnson)

20.6 Common types of lamp

Capsule lamps (10–100 w) operate at low voltage, so require transformers. They are used in specially-designed reflectors. They can give good-quality light distribution, with low replacement cost and long lamp life.

Dichroic lamps (20–75 w) are low voltage lamps with built-in reflectors. They are designed mainly for retail use, so beam quality is not always acceptable, and back-light effects are also a problem. Beam width of fitting can be altered by changing lamp. Colour can change through life, and many users complain of short lamp life.

Metal reflector lamps (20–75 w) are rarer and more expensive than dichroics, but usually with better beam performance and life. They have a good range of beam width and easier lamp changing with bayonet caps.

Linear mains voltage lamps (100–2000 w) are usually double-ended, with the smaller sizes used in floods and wallwashers. They have a long life and high output.

Mains voltage reflector lamps – PAR 30, PAR 20, etc. – (50–120 w) are the latest additions to the halogen range. They do not require transformers, but ragged beam control so far limits acceptability in museums and galleries.

Compact fluorescent lamps are strongly promoted for energy-saving reasons, and they are very effective in some wall-washing functions. Because of their size, they cannot be focused into precise beams, so spot-lighting and large-scale wallwashing is not possible. They may be useful inside display cases or behind diffusing panels, where low heat output is also an advantage.

20.7 Installation conditions

For directional light sources, the colour of walls and other surfaces will not normally affect the light directly reaching exhibits. In older galleries where the lighting is general, fluorescent lighting will often illuminate an area of wall high above the exhibition, and a large proportion of the light falling on the exhibits is reflected from the walls. However, the colour of walls and other surfaces will affect the perception of brightness in a space. Dark colours can make the space feel gloomy and thus necessitate extra fittings.

One of the most important variables in lighting is the length of throw of the beam. Often this is dictated by the ceiling height of the exhibition space. Light spreads from a luminaire in the form of a cone and thus with greater distance spreads over a wider area and is consequently less bright. The crucial importance of the mounting height of the fittings is illustrated by the mathematical relationship that the light reduces proportionally with the square of the distance.

Because of variations between venues, it will be essential for the organizer to obtain from each venue the plan and the height of the lighting system and a complete list of the available lighting to see if a consistent lighting design can be achieved for the entire tour (see 17.9). It will be impossible to re-create exactly any particular design in the changing surroundings of the touring show, but knowledge of the types of lighting available will determine whether each arrangement will be within an acceptable tolerance.

If the equipment available is unsuitable or installation conditions vary too widely, then consideration must be given to taking a lighting rig with the exhibition. Except where the exhibition comprises a series of display cases which can include integral lighting, this is not an easy option, and has its own problems (see 20.9).

20.8 Evaluating available equipment and conditions

In the overall plan, the concept of the lighting design must be clear: individual spots or wallwashing or perhaps a band of light may be preferred for wall-hung exhibits; for three-dimensional objects, individual spot-lighting, directional pools or general overall lighting may be options. When looking at each showing, organizer and venue must agree how or whether this can be achieved.

For example, a painting one metre square may require a pool of light to cover the canvas and then fade out gently at the edges. The equipment to produce this on a ceiling that is 2.5 m high will be very different from fittings that are mounted twice as high. For the lower ceiling, a low-voltage spot with perhaps a 30- or 40-degree beam may be used, or even a simple reflector lamp with similar beam spread. On the higher ceiling, this same lamp would produce a much larger and rather dim pool of light, and a 15- or 20-degree lamp would therefore be more appropriate.

The venue must check its equipment to see if it can achieve the organizer's specifications, not just for levels of light but also for the quality and type of illumination. With experience, this checking may be done from knowledge of lamp type or evaluation of the technical (photometric) data, but the simplest way to check is to see a fitting working, at the correct height, aimed at a typical display surface. Allowance must be made for the combined effects of several fittings, but the general effect should be discernible.

If the effect is judged to be satisfactory, then the task is relatively simple. Make sure the gallery has plenty of spare lamps and a lighting crew, or at least willing hands, and try to allow sufficient time between installation and opening to install and adjust the fittings. Five minutes before the Royal guest arrives is not ideal!

If the equipment available at a venue does not meet the organizer's requirements, then the problems and the costs start to increase. Light fittings can be hired,

Figure 20.2 Wallwashing on large walls, spotlighting on small. (Courtesy of John Johnson).

although purchasing will be cheaper for any showing over three months.

20.9 Integral lighting

The fixing of light fittings is completely unstandardized, but some types (e.g. Concord Lytespan) are more common than others, and it may be possible to find a common system for the various venues. A travelling set of luminaires, ideally with adjustable beam angles, will then cover the need, assuming tracks or other mounting positions are in suitable places.

If no compatible systems, or any systems at all, are available, then one solution is to take a complete travelling rig which, with some ingenuity perhaps, can be installed at a constant mounting height to give consistent lighting for the whole tour. The easiest method of providing such integral lighting is where the exhibition consists of exhibits in display cases.

For a screen-type exhibition, it may be possible to fit luminaires on arms to the screen system, although this can be visually obtrusive (see Figure 20.3). Alternatively, a track system could be suspended from the ceiling or other lighting system, assuming that the venue does not have restrictions on this. Suspended track will probably give the best results, but may be difficult to install or have other problems (see 29.2).

20.10 Loadings

It is important to add up the total number of luminaires and to determine the total electrical loads. This is usually done in watts or kilowatts, and each venue should be able to tell whether sufficient power is available. It will normally be possible to provide extra power from other circuits, but further costs may be incurred (see 27.15).

20.11 Positioning of fittings

It is critical that fittings are positioned in such a way as to give the best effect on exhibits. The objective is to throw light on to them without causing glare, reflection or shadows. This means establishing the best angle in relation to the display surface.

For paintings, lighting that is too close to the display surface will narrow the beam, cause shadows in deep picture frames and pick up texture on the display surface. Too far away will cause reflections or shadows of heads. Recommendations vary from 30 to 45 degrees from the vertical, with 40–42 degrees being most practical (see Figure 20.4). A light fitting at a height of 3 m would need to be approximately 1.3 m from the display surface, in order to light a picture centred at 1.5 m. For a height of 5 m, the fitting would be 2.9 m from the display surface.

Three-dimensional objects are often more tolerant than paintings, in that they do not have flat surfaces to cast reflections. On the other hand, objects in display cases can suffer from similar problems of glare and reflection on the glazing. If external lighting is used, shadows can be cast by the frame of the display case or by visitors. Three-dimensional objects will often have different lighting requirements, in terms of emphasizing texture or volume, or adequately illuminating all sides.

Fittings should always be positioned and aimed to avoid the visitor having direct sight of the lamp. Similarly, the final aiming should be checked to ensure shadows are not thrown onto exhibits or around the structure of the exhibition.

20.12 Further reading

Thomson, G. *The Museum Environment*, 1986, Butterworth, London. This is the book for conservation requirements, not how to do it.

Turner, J. *Lighting – An Introduction to Light, Lighting and Light Use*, 1994, Batsford. This is biased towards Concord Lighting, but still has very useful information.

Figure 20.3 Low voltage luminaires on arms overcome the lack of mounting positions. (Courtesy of John Johnson)

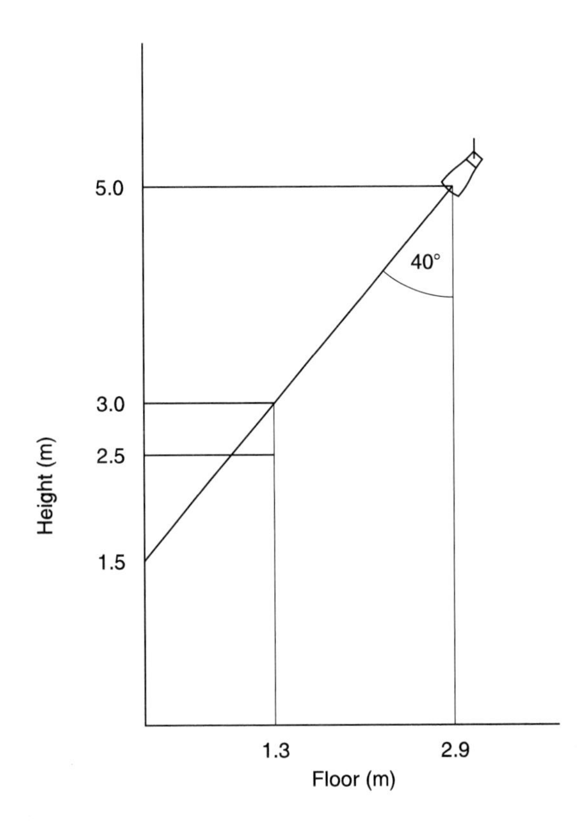

Figure 20.4 Relationship of offset to height of fittings.

21

Display cases

Josie Adams

21.1 Specifications for display cases

This section discusses a range of characteristics – portability, durability, cost, versatility, appearance, interpretation, protection and neutrality – normally required in display cases. The same factors apply whether the 'display case' is a frame which supports and protects a single two-dimensional exhibit such as a drawing, or whether it is a micro-climate for costumes on mannequins.

In most instances, a display case will involve a combination of these factors. Frequently there are compromises between the different needs, but designers are usually able to satisfy several needs at once. Two panels hinged together can serve, when open, to display a number of exhibits. When closed, and with appropriate packing, these panels might become a transit frame for the same items, which do not have to be handled as a result. Closed like a suitcase, the panels might even serve as a crate for moving the exhibits between venues.

The following factors are not in any order of priority, because new priorities will have to be set virtually for each exhibition, although factors such as portability, durability and cost have a special significance for touring. The organizer should define these priorities, whether for briefing a designer for a purpose-built system or for buying (or borrowing) the structure that supports and/or protects exhibits while on display. The following checklist can be used equally to assess whether existing cases should be used, if an off-the-shelf system will be satisfactory or what criteria a designer should work to for making a completely new system (see 19.1).

21.2 Portability

Display cases are often the bulkiest and heaviest items to travel with an exhibition, but with foresight can be designed to suit the smallest dimension in any of the venues. As for exhibits of unusual size or weight, the organizer should ask the venue for plans showing the exhibition area and the route from the delivery area (see 38.6, 38.7, 38.18). The organizer should inform the venue how many people are required to move the case or its component parts, and what lifting gear and other equipment may be required (see 48.2).

Glass is the heaviest part of a display case, especially where 11.5 mm laminated or 18 mm anti-bandit glass is used for security purposes. Sheets of glass should be of a size that can be handled by the technical help available and within current Health and Safety guidelines (see 48.7–48.10). If glass is to be handled without a supporting frame, glass clamps should be provided. For other components, there should be lifting positions, handles, cut-outs, etc according to the weight, bulk, access routes and equipment available.

21.3 Durability

As with the crates containing the exhibits, durability is related to portability. Something that is very heavy or too big to go easily through doors, into lifts or up stairs will get damaged. Exhibits will be given more care because they are irreplaceable, so the structure should be designed to survive without glazing being replaced or other repairs being necessary at every showing. Added strength or extra packing can mean further weight, bulk, difficulty and risk of further damage, so it should be possible to dismantle display cases to a minium number of easily-handled components.

Each venue should be informed how many people and how much time is required to unpack and assemble – and subsequently to dismantle and repack the case(s) (see 17.11). A display case should be easy to assemble and dismantle, and the organizer should provide a checklist of components, instructions and assembly diagrams, a repair kit, plus any special tools and equipment needed to install and dismantle. Components should be given a unique code or number, marked on under-surfaces or attached as removable labels as appropriate. The code or number and description of the component should be recorded in the particulars of components and equipment (see 7.9), as well as used in assembly and packing instructions. Parts to be joined together should be coded at their junctures with letters or symbols.

21.4 Cost

The initial price for designing and building new display cases can be the single highest cost for a touring exhibition of small, three-dimensional items.

Ongoing costs should also be considered, e.g. the costs of transport and maintenance. Venues may not agree to pay the increased costs for onward transport of a structure that has proved heavier and bulkier than originally estimated. Display cases that are easily damaged will incur expense in maintenance or replacement of parts.

21.5 Versatility

The choice of existing display cases or the design of new ones will be affected by the exhibition areas in each of the venues, e.g. whether there is a series of small rooms or whether there are other obstacles such as radiators or fixed seats in the centre of a gallery. Individual display cases might be designed either to be combined to make larger display containers or to be physically linked to make an installation which is more stable and sequential.

The organizer should provide an outline layout, showing how the cases can be arranged to maintain any desired sequence (see 49.7). However, each venue should make the final decision on layout, based on its experience of visitor-flow, the need for emergency egress, and the provision of lighting and power (see 27.9).

21.6 Appearance

Although there may be a temptation to provide plinths and bases which are also crates, the organizer must consider how well they will look after several transits and installations, if their primary purpose is to protect. Suitable protective packing, the provision of lifting positions and ease of assembly will help to prevent the cases from becoming shabby, but there should also be instructions and a repair kit for renovating the appearance of a display case. Venues should be provided with instructions on how to clean finger-marks on glass, scuffs on carcass, etc. before and during the showing.

Ideally a display case will establish a scale which balances what is appropriate for each venue's exhibition gallery and what is appropriate for the size of the exhibits.

A display case should not obstruct the visitor's view in any way that will make it difficult to see any significant part of the exhibit. It should not distract attention by causing glare. If children or people in wheelchairs are expected to visit the exhibition, will they be able to see the exhibits (see 28.2)? How many people will be able to examine an exhibit at any one time, and how many angles will be visible?

Where display cases depend on the venues' normal lighting system, careful positioning of the cases and subsequent directing of the lights will be necessary to ensure lighting is satisfactory, avoiding shadows, from the case's own frame as much as from visitors, on exhibits and on labels (see 20.11). It should also avoid a build-up of heat (see 43.5).

Lighting that is a part of the display case should be in a compartment that is separated from the display chamber by transparent barrier, usually tempered glass or heat-reflecting glass, often with a diffuser and/or light-directing louvres, and provided with a UV filter where required. The lighting compartment should be vented, to reduce the amount of heat radiated into the display chamber. There should be separate access to the lighting compartment, i.e. not through the display chamber, so that equipment can be maintained and lamps changed without risk to the exhibits. The choice of system, e.g. fibre-optic, low-voltage, fluorescent, etc., will depend on whether accented or diffused lighting is required. The organizer should specify what the power needs are (see 20.9), and should ensure that the repair kit is re-stocked with lamps and other consumable items.

21.7 Interpretation

A display case mediates between the visitor and an exhibit by providing the immediate physical context within which the exhibit is experienced. Scale and mounting should be appropriate: the type of shelf or mount should support the exhibit safely, in a manner that enables it to be experienced or understood. The case should allow two or more exhibits to be shown together if juxtaposition is part of the brief. Colours or shapes may be used to distinguish different aspects or themes of the exhibition.

How is information to be placed? Labels or captions which might be satisfactory alongside large objects may look disproportionate and obtrusive by smaller ones. Numbers or letters referring to a key takes the attention away from the exhibits. As with the exhibits themselves, labels should not be placed where the reader's shadow will fall on them or where they will be illegible to most visitors (see 20.10). Once the labels are in position, will they stay there? They have a tendency to come adrift almost as soon as the last courier has departed, with instructions that the case is not to be opened until she returns.

21.8 Protection: security

The display case is a key element in protecting exhibits from external threats, not least from theft and accidental damage. It is a way of distancing visitors, to prevent them from touching a fragile exhibit or from removing something that is valuable.

Period frames may need to be protected within a suitable container (see 39.14). Display structures in a touring exhibition must be stable, as there is little possibility of fixing to floors. Where possible, self-levelling devices should be incorporated to improve stability on uneven floors, partly to avoid displacing the exhibits, but also to prevent distortion of the carcass which might prevent doors from shutting.

The method of construction should not be obvious from the outside. All parts should be locked in place, and the case should preferably be assembled and dismantled from the inside.

Door locks should be to the appropriate British Standard, or should be hidden, e.g. by magnetic plates (see 42.5). Keys for display cases in a touring exhibition should be kept in the venue's key cabinet during the showing, and included in its Disaster Plan (see 7.16). There should be ease of access for people who are permitted. The mechanism should allow the door to open away from the exhibit, but should not overbalance the case or distort the frame. Sharp edges and corners should be avoided, to reduce the risk of injury to staff. If the case is constructed so that a final panel must be added after the exhibits are installed, then fitting and removal must be easy and smooth, so that exhibits are not displaced by vibration or shock.

Cases in a touring exhibition can be fitted with stand-alone, battery-operated alarm units to react either to the opening of the access door or to vibration as the case is moved or disturbed (see 42.5).

21.9 Protection: environment

The display case can also be a key element in protecting exhibits from pollutants, dust and environmental fluctuations, by reducing the exchange of air with the gallery environment (see 43.3). This may be particularly important to a touring exhibition if any of the exhibits are used to stable conditions and if conditions vary between venues or if conditions are unstable within one of the venues. With good seals, a case can slow down the rate of change. It can also provide a closed circuit if air in the display chamber is recycled over a conditioning material (e.g. silica-gel to control humidity or activated carbon to absorb pollutants) concealed in the base unit, which should be accessible without opening the display chamber. Monitoring devices, e.g. dial hygrometers, can be placed discreetly inside the case.

If one or more of the venues does not filter UV radiation from its artificial lighting and from any natural lighting, then it may be necessary to include UV-filters on the case glazing. Any lighting integral to the case may also need to be filtered.

Any transformers in the lighting compartment will generate heat which must be vented away from the display compartment (see 21.6). Unless cold light sources are used, lighting will radiate heat, which will put exhibits under stress and raise the temperature of the display chamber. Higher temperatures mean lower relative humidity and speeded-up chemical reactions (see 21.10). When lighting is switched off, air will contract as it cools down, and room air (with particulates, pollutants, humidity) will be sucked into the case.

21.10 Neutrality

Both the carcass and the dressing should be made of fire-resistant materials. Details of the constituent materials should be sent to each venue for its Fire Officer to approve (see 27.3).

The better the seal, the better the protection that the case offers against external threats, but the better also to seal in internal pollution. In principle, only passive materials like stainless steel and glass should be used. In practice, active materials like wood, adhesives and paints are used, which may expose exhibits to harmful emissions unless they are given time and ventilation to get rid of all solvents. Wood releases organic acids, and formaldehyde is released by adhesives used in some wood products. Normal practice is to paint wood to create a vapour barrier, but paint does not give total protection.

Paint is also a source of volatile emissions when freshly applied. The water released by emulsion paints is not dangerous, but other emissions, e.g. the formic acid released by alkyd paints, are corrosive. The nature of the material will dictate whether a few days or a few months are necessary before emissions reach an acceptable level, and sufficient time should be given before exhibits are placed in the same environment as high-emission materials.

For lists of safe or stable materials see Green, L.R. *Selection of Materials and Methods for Display*, 1990, The British Museum report, 1990/91, pp. 1–10, and Brooke Craddock, A. 'Construction materials for storage and exhibition', in *Conservation Concerns. A guide for collectors and curators*, 1992, Cooper-Hewitt Museum and Smithsonian Institute, New York.

22

Interpretation

Sally Rousham

22.1 The overall interpretive scheme

Interpretation is the process of communicating the significance of a place or object. In an exhibition, it can be broadly considered to encompass the whole subject or 'story' of the exhibition, or it can be more narrowly defined as interpreting specific exhibits (see 4.5).

The aims and objectives of the exhibition should be set out in the exhibition brief, which should encompass the overall message and the techniques of the exhibition. Three fundamental questions should be addressed at the outset:

- Why is this exhibition being organized?
- What is the overall message or story-line?
- Who is it for?

Interpretation might take the form of text panels (the script), exhibit labels and captions, interactive devices, live demonstrations or performances, and publications. All should be part of an overall scheme which is the package or – in marketing terms – the 'product' which the visitor experiences. Which techniques are chosen will reflect:

- the sub-themes to be developed within the story-line;
- the most effective means of communicating these themes;
- the knowledge and reading age to be presumed of visitors;
- how the exhibition will vary from one venue to another;
- who will have overall responsibility, and who will implement the various elements.

22.2 Who should be responsible for interpretation?

Interpretation should be an integral part of the whole planning process. It can be compared to the functions of the editor of a newspaper, who is responsible for the content and presentation of the final result, but who relies on the skills of many individuals to provide the parts which make up the whole. It is unlikely that an 'interpreter' would be part of the project team, but the organizer, researcher, scriptwriter or education officer should be given the responsibility for interpretation. This may mean that this person will need to rethink their normal role and take a wider view than their particular specialism. It is important that the person responsible should be given the authority to ensure that the interpretive scheme/message of the exhibition is conveyed in a cohesive and stimulating experience for the visitor.

The message and the interpretive scheme chosen should be kept in focus by everyone involved in the planning and design of the exhibition. The interpretive element should be coordinated between curatorial, education, design, research, scripting and marketing functions. If these functions are represented by different members of staff, a project team will be necessary, and should be put together as quickly as possible. The end result will be better if everyone has the chance to contribute at an early stage.

An artist, researcher or selector may have an important role to play in providing raw material for interpretation (see 5.4, 34.8), but this material should be selected and edited by a trained scriptwriter to suit the knowledge, reading age and stamina of visitors. The presence on the team of a specialist in video or CD-ROM or in live interpretation should not commit the project to these techniques. It may be advisable to buy a day of an expert's time to get advice on possibilities and costs rather than undertaking to use a particular technique before its interpretive implications are understood.

The team must be assembled as quickly as possible because sufficient time must be allowed for planning and implementing a satisfactory presentation of the message or specific themes within an exhibition. If insufficient time has been allowed, for example, an interactive video may not be ready until the eve of the first showing, when it will be too late to discuss and develop the content to ensure that it meshes with the story-line. Where possible, interpretation should be developed and tested before the exhibition is finally assembled (see 6.2). Time and patience is required to coordinate different technologies of communication, to ensure that they play a constructive role within the overall interpretive scheme, and contribute to a positive experience for the visitor.

Ideally, each venue should also be involved on the team; at the very least, it should be able to contribute to the evolution of the overall interpretive scheme (see 13.2). Each venue will be interested to know how far the story or sub-themes can be exploited or added to or adapted to take account of its visitors. How does the subject matter relate to the local socio-economic or physical environment? Are there exhibits in the venue's own collection or available on loan which will give the exhibition more local impact? Photographs, press reports and oral history tapes are some of the resources which might be available at each venue to bring out the local angle. Shops, businesses, industries, clubs and societies might be able to contribute with loans, advice or an account of relevant local experience. Following up these possibilities takes time, tact and patience, and is only possible if it has been allowed for at the planning stage (see 8.3, 25.4).

22.3 The visitors

Interpretation is about making connections between exhibits and people, so it is important to have a clear idea of the target market (see 6.7). For some exhibitions, the target audience is 'everyone we can get'. Other exhibitions may be geared to children, which may mean striking a balance between the formal (National Curriculum) content of the exhibition and the informal (family/holiday visitor) content. This may mean re-thinking how a touring exhibition will be used during the school holidays.

For a touring exhibition, the target market may differ between one venue and another, and there may be completely different requirements, even different languages, leading to a different solution for each venue. Labels and panels and other 'fixed' methods can be pitched at an average level agreed by all the venues, and optional methods (special leaflets, demonstrations, lectures, etc.) can be developed by each venue, using information supplied by the organizer (see 25.5). Printed material for school children can be tailored to the National Curriculum. This is more effective than trying to make captions and other information fit school-related topics at the same time as appealing to the general public.

Organizers should bear in mind what it is like for people coming to the exhibition for the first time. Visitors have not spent weeks or months thinking about the subject. Exhibition titles are frequently clever rather than descriptive. Every effort should be made to ensure that visitors are able to grasp what the exhibition is about. The layout and context will vary from one showing to the next, so each venue might provide a simple leaflet setting out the scope and arrangement of the exhibition. If so, how will the leaflet be dispensed? The important thing is to make visitors feel welcome and comfortable (see 28.1).

An exhibition should be led by the exhibits and their messages rather than by techniques and technology, although it is often easier to raise funds and enthusiasm for an exhibition that includes new gimmicks than for a purely exhibit-based display. Touring exhibitions are ephemeral events and it is appropriate that they should take account of current fashion in modes of communication (CD-ROM at the moment), but the babble and physical involvement of 'hands-on' should not necessarily be equated with really effective communication and 'brains-on'.

22.4 The words

Interpretation should use the minimum number of words, which is easy to say but difficult to achieve without being condescending, boring or banal, particularly when the target audience is as wide as the 'general public'. It is received wisdom that written words are the enemy of a popular exhibition, but this is nonsense. Text panels and exhibit labels have turned off many a half-hearted visitor, because the wrong words have been chosen or because there are too many of them. Words are invaluable: they make our ideas communicable, but they should be treated like gold.

On the one hand, it is easy to assume that an exhibit speaks for itself and everyone knows what it is and does. On the other hand, curators have a tendency to want to tell everything they know or to write for their peer group. These two extremes – symbolized by the artist who wants no interpretation at all and the researcher who wants a book on the wall – can be avoided if there is a well-written brief which takes full account of the presumed knowledge and reading age of visitors.

It is usual for text panels to carry the main story-line or message of the exhibition, and for labels to relate the specific exhibits or images to the overall context of the exhibition. However, the text and the labels should be written so that they can be read at random: it should not be assumed that the visitor has dutifully read through everything in the 'correct' order.

Curator, designer and scriptwriter should work together to decide if it is appropriate to group the text panels or to spread them evenly through the exhibition. It is often useful to have a hierarchy of text: heading, introduction, main copy and captions/labels. If so, the brief introductory sentence should be larger and bolder than the main text, so the visitor can read it without stopping. Type should be large and easily legible from where the visitor will be standing. It is helpful if headings, introductions and main copy are to be found at the same level throughout the exhibition. For adult visitors, it is important to consider how easy the script is to read for people who wear bifocals or reading glasses.

Brevity is essential but there are no hard and fast rules about the number of words. Two hundred words on one panel is rather long, but if there are only half a dozen text panels in an exhibition, this is quite acceptable. Sentences should be short and simple: it is very difficult to follow a literary style in an exhibition context, and something nearer the patterns of spoken language is more appropriate. Paragraphs should also be short. Complex words, jargon and foreign expressions should be avoided. The people asked to vet the script should be required to read it through standing up without pause for refreshment, so that they appreciate what is expected of the visitor. Exhibit labels and captions should also be as concise as possible and should include only information that is of interest to visitors: provenance is not usually relevant, and accession numbers are a deterrent to reading; however, donor's names are sometimes required.

Bilingual scripts are sometimes desirable or essential; they present a special problem because the number of words is immediately doubled. If a second language is used, consider printing it in a different colour – people catch on very quickly and edit their vision accordingly. If it is desirable to have two or three languages or different age levels and interests, it might be worth going to the expense of multi-channel sound commentaries (see 23.4, 28.3).

For further information, see:

Belcher, M. *Exhibitions in Museums*, 1991, Leicester University Press, Leicester.

Brooklyn Children's Museum. *Doing it right: a guide to improving exhibit labels*, 1989, Washington (DC), American Association of Museums.

Kavanagh, G. *Museum Languages: Objects and Texts*, 1991, Leicester University Press, Leicester.

Kentley, E and Negus, D. *Writing on the Wall: a guide for presenting exhibition text*, 1989, National Maritime Museum, London.

Royal National Institute for the Blind. *Making Museums Accessible*, RNIB Arts Information Pack A5.

Royal National Institute for the Blind, *Making Print Legible*.

Rouard-Snowman, M. *Museum Graphics*, 1992, Thames and Hudson, London.

Royal Ontario Museum. *Communicating with the Museum Visitor*, 1976, Royal Ontario Museum, Toronto.

Serrell, B. *Making Exhibit Labels: a step-by-step guide*, 1983, American Association for State and Local History, Nashville (Tennessee).

22.5 Interpretive design

The designer has a crucial role to play in interpretation, as the design function involves a great deal more than making things look good (see 19.1). The juxtaposition of exhibits and the style of the exhibition play an important part in the interpretive messages. The practicalities of space, circulation and the need to adapt the exhibition from one venue to another can impose daunting constraints. For a popular exhibition or a venue with limited space, a one-way visitor route may be necessary for managing visitors, but in most cases a choice about visitor flow can be made at the conceptual planning stage.

Many exhibitions have strong narrative story-lines or themes, but the linear organization of material may be neither necessary nor desirable. Even if visitors are compelled to follow a set route through an exhibition with numbered text panels, they do not necessarily look at everything in order, as they tend to skip to more attractive or less crowded displays. A large degree of flexibility may be required if, at busy times at some venues, there are to be live interpreters or demonstrators (see 26.12). Again, this should be considered before the final brief is written.

22.6 Take-home interpretation

If an exhibition is to offer more than a transitory experience, some form of take-home interpretation is required. Any printed information sheet, leaflet or booklet should be part of the overall interpretive scheme of the exhibition.

A publication can be – and usually is – read elsewhere so, although the message will be the same, the organization of the material and the words used may be different. Whereas an exhibition script is designed to be read in one place with a known relation to exhibits and other display devices, a publication can be read anywhere and at any time. An exhibition script is conceived to be read standing up, whereas publications are usually read sitting down, and this affects content, layout and sentence structure.

Catalogues or hand-lists of exhibits consisting merely of information on identification and provenance have no interpretive content. At the other extreme, catalogues can be major works of scholarship which contain learned introductions and expositions which go way above the heads of many visitors and can be very expensive. An interpretive publication should be aimed at the same target visitors as the exhibition. It should contain pointers which would enable anyone whose interest has been aroused to follow up with further reading, and probably an indication where other relevant material can be seen (see 32.5).

23

Audio–visual media

Helen Luckett and Jem Legh

23.1 What are audio–visual media?

There are many forms of audio–visual (A–V) media, and technology is developing rapidly. For the purposes of exhibition, the main tried and tested types are tape-slide and video (High- or Low-band U-Matic, VHS). 16 mm film is not very practical, since film-loop is notoriously prone to breaking and scratching, and reel-to-reel film requires a projectionist. CD-ROM and Photo-CD will no doubt increasingly replace tape-slide and video, not least because they are interactive. In the case of CD-ROM, programs can be designed so that visitors can produce their own guides, find contexts for the exhibits, find out about equivalents to be seen elsewhere, design an object or their own exhibition, etc. (see 24.2).

Tape-slide combines the use of slide projectors with an audio cassette to provide sound and pictures. Images from two (or more) slide projectors can be dissolved from one to another using synchronized pulses encoded onto the audio cassette alongside the sound track. These pulses are fed to the projectors using cables via a dissolve unit, and the sound track is fed to speakers via an amplifier. Once set up correctly, many presentations can run all day, resetting themselves automatically and starting again. There are many manufacturers of this specialist equipment, and not much compatibility, so the organizer should ensure that the correct equipment is available.

Projected media are ideal for audiences larger than five people. Because of the amount of equipment and the complexity of installation, they are also more suitable for permanent installations. For a touring exhibition it can be more convenient to use a self-contained back-projection unit which uses a TV-sized screen, or increasingly to transfer a tape-slide presentation to video tape. Video uses a pre-recorded programme on a video-cassette or laser disc and plays it back via a monitor (television) or via a video projector if audiences larger than five people are anticipated. Most playback decks have a facility for the programme to cycle all day. If the programme has come from abroad, it may have been recorded using a different broadcast standard (PAL, NTSC, SECAM) and the venue should ensure that it has the correct equipment.

23.2 Why use audio–visual media?

Audio–visual media can be used for various purposes in exhibitions: to enhance and enliven displays, as exhibits in their own right, as a substitute for exhibits or as a means of interpretation or orientation.

In consultation with the venues, the organizer should determine the purpose and content of the programme, the audience it is intended for, and overall design implications for the exhibition (see 22.2). Its format (tape-slide, video, CD-ROM etc.) and the length of programme can then be decided.

23.3 Is audio–visual necessary as a means of interpretation?

The programme should be an integral part of the overall interpretive scheme for the exhibition (see 22.1). If a programme can be left out at a venue where space or technical assistance is lacking, then it may not be worth the effort and cost to produce it in the first place.

A programme should complement the exhibits and other forms of interpretation. It might present a context or an aspect of the exhibition which cannot be shown through the exhibits or through static images, e.g. where a manufacturing process is being demonstrated or a site described. It might take the place of written information where the voice-over can point out features and explore details, e.g. a documentary survey of an artist's life might include illustrations of important stages in that person's career.

The programme should be a subsidiary part of the exhibition, i.e. its showings should not dominate the installation, and its final effect should be to re-direct the audience's attention with fresh eyes to the exhibits themselves. Above all, it should not duplicate any other aspect of the exhibition, unless this is done so consciously for deliberate reasons, e.g. to address a target group of visitors.

23.4 Who is the intended audience?

The organizer and venues should agree whether an A–V programme is intended for all visitors to the exhibition or will be designed for a particular section of visitors.

If the programme is to be used by children, what age-group is envisaged – under 7, 8–11, 12–15, 16–18? If it will be used by people with special needs, will they be people for whom English is a second language? Bilingual scripts are sometimes desirable or essential; they present a special problem for printed information because the number of words is immediately doubled. If it is desirable to have two or three languages or different age levels and interests, it might be worth going to the expense of multi-channel sound commentaries.

Audio-visual materials might help people with learning or physical disabilities. Tape-slide, projected on a large scale, can help people with visual impairments. Disability organizations may be able to advise on recent equipment and technologies (see 28.6, 28.7). Audio guides combined with thermoforms (tactile diagrams) or models of objects in the exhibition may help people who are partially sighted or blind.

When designing an A–V programme, it is important to define whether it is for people with a high, medium or low degree of interest. Similarly, it is important to define whether the programme is for people with a high, medium or low level of knowledge.

For planning the type and format of the programme, and for siting it at each venue, prepare a chart to estimate how many people each venue expects to watch the programme at any one time. The same format of chart can be used during the showing to record actual usage, which can eventually be amalgamated into an overall summary as part of the evaluation of an A–V programme. Such a chart would divide the day into convenient periods, one or two hours long, and the venue would insert the number of people estimated for each period. Saturdays and Sundays should be distinguished from weekdays.

23.5 Where is it to be sited?

Organizer and venues will need to agree whether the programme must be shown in or near the exhibition. If it can be shown away from the exhibition, in the same building or even outside the venue, it may form part of an outreach programme and require its own publicity arrangements (see 25.5, 25.9). If the programme can be shown at more than one site, the venue should consider how many copies will be required. If the programme is to be shown in the exhibition, how frequently will it be shown? A presentation of a few minutes can be left to cycle. Longer presentations (twenty minutes or more) should have fixed starting times, e.g. on the hour every hour.

Seating should be provided, for any programme over five minutes' duration, for a target audience of the young or the elderly, and for numbers which might make it difficult for people at the back to see the programme.

If a programme is on continuously, a sound-track delivered through loudspeakers may annoy visitors not using the programme, and invigilating staff may be tempted to turn the volume down to a level inaudible even to those wanting to hear it. Headphones can cut down sound overspill and help to cater for the needs of people who are deaf or hard of hearing.

The organizer should inform the venues if the equipment requires special installation, e.g. walls or partitions built, space for projection, mounting or boxing, and how much of this installation will be provided as part of the exhibition package.

Ideally, the programme should stop, rewind and restart automatically. If it requires human intervention, the venues must be advised how frequently, so that they can plan and brief their staff (see 17.11).

23.6 Production

The choice of medium and format, and the type of production, will almost invariably be conditioned by the budget available. As the cost of A–V will fluctuate according to the general financial climate and technological developments, it is impossible to give accurate indications of the cost of typical programmes. The best course is to ask for estimates, well in advance of programme preparation.

The 'Suppliers and Services' section of the *Museums Yearbook* includes details of various specialist production houses. Commercial production houses and media studies departments of universities or colleges have sophisticated equipment and expertise, but are often commercially assertive and therefore not to be considered a particularly cheap option.

Be sure to emphasize when the programme is to be completed, and also ask for an indication of production schedules. Many production houses expect to have ownership over all aspects of production, from concept and script to final installation. While this can sometimes be an advantage, it can also be obstructive to the organizer who expects to retain creative control.

Some budgetary implications worth bearing in mind are:

- fee for writing the script;
- fee/s for narration;
- translation fees;
- production of slides and other source material;
- copyright, for images (including thermoform illustrations), text and sound (see 26.11 and 33.2);
- studio costs;
- pulsing (tape-slide);
- video transfer from tape-slide;
- hardware (and is this to tour?).

23.7 How will the programme and equipment travel?

For logging the movement of equipment, see 27.4.

For tape slide, the organizer should provide at least two spare audio cassettes and at least one spare set of slides. The slides should be in glass mounts, as slides not mounted in this way have a tendency to pop in or out of focus as they warm up. Instructions and appropriate cleaning materials should be provided by the organizer.

Small compromises may be necessary on the image size when projection equipment is installed, but the organizer should provide lenses of appropriate focal lengths to compensate for variations between venues. The phenomenon known as 'keystoning' which is the result of projecting at an angle to the screen, is more exaggerated when using wide-angle lenses over a short distance, and lenses with keystone correction should be used when necessary.

23.8 Responsibility for the A–V programme at the venues

Each venue should designate a member of staff to take responsibility for the equipment, including supervising installation and removal, maintenance, cleaning and replacement of any faulty components, where authorized.

23.9 Installation

The first requirement is a power source which does not involve trailing leads that staff or the public can trip over. For the installation of electrical equipment, see 27.15.

As far as visibility is concerned, a video monitor can be placed more or less anywhere in a gallery, but the venue should ensure that lights do not reflect on the screen, and should adjust the brightness, contrast and colour controls to suit the conditions.

Video projection and tape slide presentations, on the other hand, should be put in a darkened (ideally blacked out) space. Particularly in a blacked-out space, equipment should be out of reach of the public but easily accessible to the technical staff. The positioning of the projectors and the screen depends on the desired image size and the space available. Beware of positioning the equipment in such a way that the audience casts shadows on the screen. A wall painted matt white works perfectly well in a darkened space, but glass-beaded screens give a brighter picture. The latter should be considered where total black-out cannot be achieved, although this type of screen works best with narrow-angle lenses. A suitable screen must be used for back projection.

23.10 During the showing

Signs, leaflets and other information should include the running time of the presentation, so that someone watching has some idea of how long they need to stay to see a complete programme. Longer presentations with fixed starting times should have these times stated on signs, leaflets and other information.

The designated member of staff in each venue should view a complete cycle of the programme daily, to ensure everything is running satisfactorily. Slides should be cleaned once a week, using a camera lens blower brush. The tape heads in the cassette player should be cleaned at least once a week. Video heads should be cleaned when necessary (a snowy picture indicates the need for cleaning). Electrical equipment attracts dust very quickly, and monitor screens should be cleaned daily. At the same time, check the brightness, contrast and colour, because visitors like to fiddle with the controls!

Before turning the power off at the end of the day (see 27.17), the designated member of staff should ensure that:

- a tape slide programme is allowed to re-set to be ready for the next day;
- a video cassette is ejected, and replaced in its box;
- a laser disc player is 'parked'.

23.11 Further information

For further information and advice contact:

Jem Legh, The Arts Council of England, 14 Great Peter Street, London SW1P 3NQ. Tel 0171 973 6456.

MITES (Moving Image Touring Exhibition Service), 45–46 Bluecoat Chambers, School Lane, Liverpool L1 3BX. Tel 0151 707 2881.

LEA (London Electronic Arts), 5-7 Buck Street, London NW1 8NJ. Tel 0171 284 4588.

Butterworth-Heinemann Ltd publishes under the name of Focal Press a whole series of very good guides on all aspects of the audio–visual medium. A list can be obtained from the marketing department on 01865 310366.

Finally as the world of IT seems for ever to be launching new products and digital technologies a subscription to *Audio Visual* magazine would enable you to at least keep abreast of these changes. Tel 0181 688 7788.

24

Interactive exhibits

Nick Winterbotham

24.1 Why use interactive exhibits?

Interactive exhibits can enhance the impact of many exhibitions. They act as a focal point, give rise to interaction between visitors and frequently result in conversations which explore the nature of the display and of the principles behind it. They may also distract attention from exhibits that are near them, and their use must be carefully controlled.

24.2 'High-tech' exhibits

High-technology exhibits can now include: devices triggered by press-button, pressure-pad or PIR (passive infra-red) sensors; video-tape, laser-disk video, film and tape-slide; projection of video, planetarium or microscope; 'talking heads'; fibre-optic display, laser projection; CD-ROM video and sound; tape, disc or digital sound-store audio presentations . . . in fact this list will be out of date by the time it is published!

The array is almost limitless. The equipment tends towards high cost, although the more tried and tested a technique becomes, the more reasonably priced it becomes. Each brings with it a new technology that staff have to learn to use and to maintain.

For these reasons, these items are worth exploring only if the budget is fairly substantial. For example, an off-the-shelf, low-maintenance sound store system is unlikely to be available for much less than £3000; a low-maintenance, three-projector tape-slide show will cost £2000 for the equipment alone. In both cases, the initiating costs of the programme will be additional.

High-tech exhibits tend to be spectacular, and will have an impact well beyond the space they occupy in any exhibition – provided they are kept working. Few things spoil the tone of an exhibition as much as interactives that are 'on the blink'. If they break down, and this is more often the case than not, it is worth making sure that they can be removed or disguised. If this is not possible, then a suitably-whimsical and properly-printed notice should be immediately applied. It should suggest a very brief repair-time and perhaps offer alternative attractions. In a touring exhibition, such a sign should be provided by the organizer as a standard element in the back-up kit of parts.

A persistent snag with high-tech exhibits is that they can get in the way of the message the exhibition is trying to communicate. Including such exhibits for their own sake will not make that message clearer or more accessible.

24.3 'Low-tech' exhibits

Low-technology exhibits now comprise: objects to identify or verbal questions, with lift-up flaps or sliding doors for the answers; tools and an enormous array of scientific 'test-bench' experiments (as perfected by Launchpad in London, Xperiment in Manchester, the Exploratory in Bristol and in many other similar establishments); 'feely boxes' or environments to go inside; 'Please Touch' exhibitions (particularly in the art realm); historical technology (printing, writing, milling, ship's rigging, etc.); period costume and body ornaments; drawing, writing and modelling materials; handling objects, especially 2D and 3D equivalents for touching and remaking.

This field is becoming more and more inventive as time goes on, with much use of magnets, velcro, melamine, stainless steel, nylon and many other modern materials unknown to previous generations. 'Low-tech' exhibits are not necessarily cheaper than their high-technology counterparts, but if properly tested before being displayed, they may be more reliable.

24.4 Testing

Whether interactive exhibits are high- or low-tech, testing is crucial (see 6.2).

Test for durability. Any handles, buttons, controls or levers will be tested to destruction by the visiting public, and it is probably better that the exhibition team beats the public to it. All switches should be given military-grade specifications and should have a repair back-up readily available. Any exhibit that must be dismantled and reassembled several times in a tour must be robust enough to withstand this treatment.

Test for safety, for the immediate user and beyond. All electrical equipment should be easily isolated, and should have circuit-breaker systems fitted as standard. By law, all systems should be tested as soon as they are brought into a new 'work-place' prior to use (see 27.15, 29.1).

Test for impact. If testing the mechanism is crucial, then so is testing the impact of the exhibit within the context of the exhibition (see 6.8). Any display should be 'paced' so that visitors do not spend an inordinate amount of time and energy on a few 'hot-spots' at the expense of other items. The interactive should be operable without any written cue being necessary. After all, the public loses patience with anything that requires the prior acquisition of a particular expertise or concept.

The best testing probably involves letting a socially-mixed focus group have a go with the prototype exhibit and, if possible, the whole exhibition. This salutary process will throw up likely areas of confusion, disaffection and misuse, such as:

- confusing language;
- inexact operating process;
- plodding technology;
- excessive operating time (thus excluding others);
- fragility;
- excessive complexity of technique;
- excessive sophistication of message;
- dull outcomes
- inaccessibility.

If two or more of these problems are identified at the testing stage, it is probably worth scrubbing the idea and thinking again.

The most persistent 'front-end' evaluation of exhibits in the UK has probably taken place in the British Museum of Natural History. Where interactive exhibits failed to deliver, they were scratched and other solutions found. One overriding philosophical change in planning such exhibits has been the shift from 'teaching' theory with its listing of intended display goals, to 'learning' theory where far more emphasis is placed on the impact of individual experiences on the visitor. This altogether more heuristic approach has paid greater attention to the context of exhibitions, the threshold of understanding of visitors and the summative evaluation of all likely impacts.

The message for the organizer may be put fairly simply as 'don't hypothesize and then try to make the outcome fit; instead, watch what really happens and ring the changes if you don't like what you observe . . .'

24.5 Some dos . . .

- Write a synopsis which makes clear what the interactive exhibits are intended to achieve within the overall interpretive scheme (see 21.1).
- For each exhibit, think of a budget and double it.
- Design for ease of unpacking, assembly, dismantling and re-packing, and provide instructions and diagrams (see 7.15, 49.7).
- Test for impact, safety and durability (see 24.4).
- If the exhibit falls into two or more of the traps in 24.4, ditch it.
- Make maintenance as simple as possible, and provide clear instructions to the staff who will have to maintain the exhibit(s).
- Always budget for repair and maintenance.
- Be prepared for breakdowns with a printed notice and a repair kit.

24.6 . . . and some don'ts

- Never take anyone else's word for an exhibit's efficacy – go and check it for yourself.
- Don't place interactives immediately adjacent to an exhibit which requires contemplation.
- Never use high-tech if low-tech will do.
- Don't use exhibits which only have one outcome if multiple outcomes are possible.
- Don't use exhibits which are operated only by one person if group interactions are possible.
- Don't use too many of the same types of interactives. Anything becomes stale and predictable after a while, especially video.
- Don't use any interactives which attempt to engage for too long – ten minutes should be the absolute maximum, even where film, A–V and video are involved.
- Above all, never use interactives gratuitously. The 'real thing' is always more culturally valuable than the means to interpret it . . . !

25

Education programmes

Sue Clive

25.1 Definitions

In this section, 'education' is used to refer to the wide variety of materials and activities that are used to interpret exhibitions. It is not restricted to work with schools or to teaching in a formal sense. It can embrace events for adults and/or children, for individual visitors and/or groups, for formal and/or informal education sectors, and for special- and/or minority-interest groups.

'Materials and activities' are used to denote what an organizer might devise or provide for the venues. These can include written, audio-visual and interactive materials, workshops and other events, longer-term projects and outreach activities. They are concerned with the different ways in which the exhibition might be perceived by different visitors, in both formal and informal contexts, and with enriching the visitors' experience during and after their visit.

'Programme' is used for the selection and arrangement of these materials and activities by each venue, for a series of events that is actually carried out. For a venue in a tour, an education programme is a way of interpreting an exhibition that is designed to be seen in several places and by a general public. The education programme is also designed for the specific needs of particular groups of visitors that the venue may be attracting or wish to attract. It provides a bridge between organizational and curatorial decisions and the reception by visitors at each showing in a tour.

'Prospectus' is used for the list of materials and activities that summarizes the possibilities for each venue to consider, to avoid confusion with another possible use of the word 'programme'.

'Recording' is used to denote the collection of evidence about workshops and other events. It is used in preference to 'documentation', which is used by educationalists to denote this activity but might be confused with the more general museum use of the word in connection with information on collections.

25.2 Planning materials and activities

The potential for education programmes should be considered right at the conception of a touring exhibition (see 4.5). If left until later, venues will have less chance to be involved and their use of educational materials and activities will be less effective (see 22.2).

At the booking stage, the organizer should provide venues with information so that they are conversant with the research and concepts behind the exhibition and with the organizer's general educational aims (see 16.2). These aims might make reference to:

- promoting appreciation and understanding of the exhibits, especially key ones;
- getting across specific items of information;
- communicating key concepts or themes;
- demonstrating a relevance or relationship to contemporary cultures and concerns;
- informing and engaging an identifiable sector of the general public, e.g. schools;
- stimulating debate amongst a committed public;
- providing intellectual or psychological access to a sector that might be disenfranchised in some way;
- allowing venues to approach interpretation in their own ways.

The organizer should ask each venue for a statement of its overall education policy (if available), its general aims for the showing, the education budget and other resources it might be able to make available for this showing, and its existing and target visitors (see 6.7). Ideally, this statement will coincide with many of the organizer's aims, and might set out specific objectives in terms of the numbers and types of visitors each venue hopes to attract.

With these aims in mind, the organizer will be able to devise educational materials and activities for the tour, where applicable making reference to:

- the nature of the exhibition, its design and scale;
- target visitors and the marketing potential of the exhibition;
- the appeal and accessibility of the exhibition to people with special needs and interests;
- the exhibition's relevance to the National Curriculum, GCSE, A Levels, NVQs, university and college modules, etc.
- the exhibition's relationship with other exhibitions, collections, public art, architecture, popular culture, retailers, the natural environment, performances, etc beyond the venues;
- the resources and funding the organizer can provide;
- materials and activities that can tour with the exhibition;
- possible activities developed by one or more venues to complement the touring package.

The exhibition budget should provide for planning, commissioning and making educational materials and activities (see 9.2). If possible, and especially where there is sponsorship, it should also provide for help with the programmes planned by venues, which might include these materials but which might equally involve different activities (see 11.3).

The organizer should consult educationalists or other professionals about the nature and content of all materials and activities to be provided with the exhibition. These materials will complement the labels and information panels which are a fixed part of the exhibition. For other sorts of materials provided by the organizer, see 23.1, 24.2 and 24.3.

25.3 Prospectus

The organizer should provide a prospectus or menu informing venues about the materials and activities that will be available and giving advice on aspects to be carried out by the venues. Materials devised or proposed by the organizer might include:

- leaflets, illustrated guides and guides looking at specific exhibits;
- work sheets, quiz sheets, discovery trails and other suggestions for activities to be carried out in the exhibition;
- teachers' packs and other suggestions for activities at home or school as preparation or follow-up;
- specially-commissioned children's books;
- reading lists;
- labels and guides written and designed in collaboration with people who are visually impaired or have other special needs;
- translated labels and guides.

In addition, the organizer might circulate information about:

- live guides trained by the organizer;
- workshop leaders, lecturers or speakers selected and briefed by the organizer.

The prospectus should also contain supporting information, which will complement the package of materials included in the tour. This information will help venues to devise their own programmes, and might include:

- information about the exhibition's concept, theme and content;
- the historical, social, cultural or artistic context within which the exhibits were found or made;
- information about makers or other people associated with exhibits;
- a reading list;
- contact list of specialists known to work with exhibitions or whose work is related to the exhibition, e.g. artists, crafts-persons, researchers, educationalists, speakers, performers;
- contact list of relevant national organizations, especially those with regional centres or personnel;
- information about the ways in which venues might research local groups and organizations which might have a special interest in the exhibition;
- information about related National Curriculum subjects' Attainment Targets and Programmes of Study.

25.4 Briefing the venues

The organizer should budget for and arrange meetings with venues, both to explain the exhibition and stimulate interest in interpretation, and to pool ideas so that venues benefit from each other's experience (see 49.3).

To make the best use of materials and activities that are provided with the exhibition, the venue should, if at all possible, visit a previous showing in the tour to see how materials and activities are used and publicized. This will allow plans to be based on direct experience of what has been seen at other showings of the exhibition as well as on discussion with those venues.

As well as general lessons for the installation of the exhibition and its signposting outside and inside the building, a visit can help to decide what materials and activities should be included in the education programme. This might include considerations such as:

- priorities for spending, e.g. the cost-effectiveness of lecturers, guides or seminars arranged by the organizer;
- how to publicize and market lectures, talks, videos and films to target visitors;
- how to arrange evaluation, e.g. by invigilators or by

questionnaires if these are not provided by the organizer (see 6.3);
- advertising the presence of educational materials in the gallery, in the rest of the building and on publicity material (see 25.9).

In terms of the allocation of space, a visit can help to determine more precisely than any description at second hand:

- the elements of an education programme which can or must be delivered in the gallery, and which can be located in a foyer or elsewhere;
- appropriate spaces in or near the exhibition for audio–visual and interactive materials, and whether or not it is important that this kind of interpretation is seen and heard in close proximity to the exhibits (see 23.5, 24.6);
- arrangements for seating or blackout for screenings or performances, and their timing and frequency (see 23.9).

A visit can help to establish whether or not the venue's staff can service and deliver the events:

- will they be able to answer questions?
- what training is necessary, in relation to the concept and theme of the exhibition, the nature of the exhibits and the proposed education programme?
- have the staff the necessary technical expertise?
- are there the resources for photocopying and replacing leaflets?
- are they able to distribute or sell guides, leaflets, work-sheets or audio-guides?
- are they available for extra invigilation e.g. for reading-areas and spaces where there are interactive materials, or for events after normal hours?

A visit can also ascertain whether written materials need to be adapted to suit the venue and its target visitors. Adaptations might include:

- translations;
- changes in style and size of typeface;
- reference to the venue's collection, the building and its immediate environment;
- local and regional references, e.g. other exhibitions, collections, buildings and sites to visit, festivals and events, craft workshops, artists' studios, etc.

25.5 Devising an education programme

Venues should use the organizer's prospectus and the experience of any prior showings of the exhibition to devise programmes relevant to their institutions and visitors. A venue's education programme should be based on – but not necessarily restricted to – what the organizer proposes to provide. Like the exhibition itself, these materials and activities are not only a resource for the visitors to the exhibition, but also a learning tool for the staff in the venue, who should take full advantage of different perspectives or techniques with which they might not be familiar.

As well as each venue's overall education policy, its education budget and its existing and target visitors, a venue's aims and objectives for its showing will be conditioned by:

- the timing of each showing in relation to the academic year, examinations, National Curriculum tests, public holidays, religious and local festivals, etc.;
- opening hours and admission charges;
- the potential for relationships between the exhibition and any permanent collections, the building and other departments within it (library, loan collections, shop, theatre, etc.);
- the resources available in-house, including the skills, knowledge and interests of the staff;
- any existing regular educational programmes and traditions;
- the facilities other than the exhibition and the education programme that the venue can provide, e.g. toilet arrangements, child care, catering, lunch room, transport, lifts, etc.;
- the potential for raising additional resources;
- the space available for educational events and activities in or near the exhibition and elsewhere in the building.

It is more effective to organize really well a small programme which gives ample attention to planning, organization, monitoring and evaluation than to plan a large programme which does not. The programme might consist of:

- In-house workshops, which might be led by artists or other professionals, and will probably include discussion and practical work, taking place in the exhibition gallery.
- Remote workshops, similar to the above, but taking place in schools, colleges, community centres, hospitals, etc.
- Projects of longer duration than workshops which might link different institutions and disciplines with the resulting exhibitions and/or performances.
- Residencies, demonstrations or commissions in the venue or elsewhere.
- Visits to sites relevant to the subject of the exhibition e.g. artists' studios, archaeological sites, natural history locations, etc.
- A lecture or a lecture series, courses, gallery talks, guided tours.
- Seminars and conferences.
- Performances.

- Outreach projects, which draw attention to aspects of an exhibition, often before its showing. For example, before the opening of an exhibition on Roman glass, a group might work with a professional to look at Roman remains in the area, and might produce a leaflet about their findings; this project might also receive coverage in the local newspaper and so provide useful advance publicity.

25.6 Implementing the programme

The venue should prepare a budget for the planned programme, using its own education budget and other resources available to it. It should identify other sources of funding, resources and expertise, e.g. local education authority, regional arts board, youth and community leaders, local authority officers, retailers.

It should consider the potential for raising additional resources and for setting up partnerships with museums and galleries, local education authorities or privatized advisory services, local authority offices, schools and colleges, youth and community services, WEA, University of the Third Age, etc. The venue should:

- consult community leaders about the appropriateness of aspects of any programme intended for the groups they represent (see 2.5);
- inform in writing and arrange meetings when appropriate with group leaders and temporary staff to ensure that everyone is fully briefed and knows what to expect, especially with regard to the provision of staff and other resources for long-term and outreach projects;
- book the required spaces and equipment, whether in-house or from outside (see 26.12, 26.13);
- use the evidence of visitor research, to select the most appropriate days and time for live guides to be in the gallery (see 3.5);
- use research on visitor behaviour in the gallery to determine the most appropriate pick-up points for materials (see 6.8);
- consider events at which materials can be delivered, e.g. a teachers' evening to launch teachers' packs or a children's event to launch discovery trails;
- identify and order the materials needed for practical events that the venue has agreed to provide;
- make appropriate catering arrangements;
- ensure that visitors will be made welcome.

25.7 Staffing implications

The skills, knowledge and interests of in-house staff, including voluntary staff, are a key resource which will be available in the period leading up to – as well as during – the exhibition's showing and which should help to ensure an effective and consistent programme.

When planning the delivery of the education programme, the venue should make an audit of the skills and knowledge of in-house staff and, having ascertained their potential for the programme, allocate and clearly define their responsibilities with respect to the programme itself, to any temporary staff and to recording and evaluation. Time should be allowed for day-to-day management of the programme, and targets should be set for tasks to be completed.

The venue should decide which staff will take bookings, brief them thoroughly about the nature and content of events and activities, and make arrangements for confirming bookings and issuing receipts.

A contact person should be chosen and briefed to liaise with incoming groups and any temporary staff, to act as a trouble-shooter should any difficulties occur, and to liaise with other departments (marketing, publicity, development, curatorial).

Appropriate staffing, e.g. technicians, child-minders, signers, caretakers, invigilators, should be identified and arranged (see 26.14, 28.5). All front-of-house staff should be briefed about events and activities taking place in the building, and should ensure that visitors are made welcome.

25.8 Temporary staff

If in-house staff cannot deliver the programme, the venue should look for local experts, celebrities, community leaders and professional and amateur groups who might contribute their knowledge, insights and cultural perspectives, to suggest people and approaches.

The venue should decide what knowledge, skills and experience are required for effective delivery of the programme by artists, freelance educationalists and other professionals (see 34.10). These might include:

- skills in communication, demonstration, performance, enthusing an audience and devising interpretive materials and activities;
- experience in gallery and museum education and awareness of curatorial practice and conservation needs;
- experience of working with certain age-groups and/or special needs;
- knowledge of the statutory and non-statutory education sectors;
- quality of artistic practice or knowledge of the history of art and design, social history or other discipline relevant to the subject of the exhibition;
- record of working collaboratively and in outreach;
- record of teaching, lecturing, teacher training or multicultural education;
- administrative skills;

Temporary staff should be appointed to supervise or carry out a series of events where the venue has neither the capacity nor the expertise: this will be usually done informally, on the basis of curriculum vitae, recommendations and meetings, except in the case of long-term projects and residencies which should be advertised and applicants selected and interviewed. For other temporary staff, see 5.8–5.12. For public liability, see 29.5 and 29.6.

Individual work-plans should be devised, particularly for temporary staff, relating to the aims and objectives of the exhibition and the education programme, the proposed participants, the location and timing of the event or activity, the materials and equipment needed and how they will be organized, and the allocation of responsibilities, especially with regard to any servicing that may need to be provided by full-time staff.

All arrangements with temporary staff should be confirmed in written contracts or letters, setting out procedures for fees (including preparation time), expenses, areas of responsibility, cancellation (by visitors, venue or temporary staff), aims, work-plans, duration of project, number and nature of participants, and arrangements for recording and evaluation.

Work-plans should be updated after planning meetings with school teachers, college tutors, community group leaders or other people organizing the proposed participants.

For arrangements by a venue, see also 26.14.

25.9 Publicity

The education programme should not only be marketed to target visitors, but should also be publicized with the exhibition and given a high profile, so that other groups and sponsors are aware of the venue's work (see 30.1). Publicity should ensure that:

- the language, content and tone used is welcoming and persuasive to target visitors;
- the relevance of the exhibition and the education programme to different education sectors is highlighted;
- printed material is designed for the partially-sighted and translations made, where needed;
- information is given about access to the exhibition as well as to the building, including access outside opening hours if needed for special occasions;
- contact names and procedures for booking and payment are given clearly;
- information about facilities – parking, catering, cloakroom, lunchroom, toilets, child care, lifts – is given prominence.

25.10 Recording and evaluating an education programme

Recording an education programme, by collating all published material with photographs, reviews and other records of the actual events provides material for raising an organization's profile and for future fundraising (see 6.1). This information should be collated and disseminated to all involved, including the organizer, who should have a complete set of all educational materials produced independently by a venue.

Evaluation indicates successes and failures and informs future programmes. It should be based on the aims and objectives of the exhibition, including its education programme. The organizer should budget for expenses and personnel to monitor and evaluate venues' educational programmes, and should arrange for evaluation to be carried out by venues, organizer or an outside assessor, and for its dissemination (see 9.2). The venue's budget for the showing and its education programme should include items for recording and evaluating the programme. The venue should appoint and brief in-house or temporary staff, or ask participants, to record and evaluate the programme (see 6.4).

25.11 Further reading

Hooper-Greenhill, E. *Museum and Gallery Education*, 1991, University of Leicester Press, Leicester.

Selwood, S. Clive, S. and Irving, D. *Cabinets of Curiosity*, 1995, Art & Society, for the Arts Council of England and the Calouste Gulbenkian Foundation, London.

26

Live events

Louise Karlsen and Tracy Teasdale

26.1 Planning events

A touring exhibition will often include lectures, guided tours, residencies, demonstrations, performances or workshops (see 25.5). All such live events, however informal, should be high-quality and memorable experiences for visitors. The safety of visitors, staff, performers and exhibits should be ensured at all times, and several practical and legal considerations need to be taken into account.

When offering lectures, guided tours, residencies, demonstrations, performances, workshops or other events to a venue, the organizer should draw attention to these considerations. Each venue is then responsible for ensuring that it meets the relevant requirements. See also 29.5 and 29.6 for public liability.

Venues should seek advice at the earliest opportunity from appropriate local authority officers, as regulations are complex and can involve physical adaptations of spaces and/or the payment of fees, which will have to be timetabled and budgeted. Performances of drama, dance, singing or music, whether involving ticket sales or not, are covered by a wide range of licences and regulating bodies.

26.2 Building Control Officer

Local authorities have such officials in their Planning and Design or Architects' Departments. Many Building Control Officers produce published information about required or desirable standards of provision in public buildings for both the able-bodied and people with disabilities.

26.3 Health and Safety Officer

Local authorities may have one or more Health and Safety Officers covering a number of departments or the authority as a whole. They can advise on all aspects of Health and Safety provision and on procedures, as well as provide copies of publications dealing with employers' and employees' responsibilities and current European and British legislation.

26.4 Fire Officer

The local Fire Authority must be consulted and will advise on safe means of egress from public buildings for both the able-bodied and people with mobility problems. The Fire Officer will also advise on safe occupancy figures for particular spaces and how to reconcile emergency evacuation procedures with security of exhibits (see 27.13). Buildings used for the purposes of public entertainments and related activities are usually equipped with automatic door releases, fire alarms and fire and smoke exclusion or containment systems. These are covered by a fire certificate monitored regularly by the local Fire Authority.

26.5 Public entertainment licence

The local authority's Environmental Health Department approves, provides and monitors such licences, which cover issues such as occupancy figures, adequate toilet and sanitary facilities, events involving special risk, structural alterations to premises, times of performances and electrical inspections.

26.6 Liquor licence

These are again approved, provided and monitored by the local authority's Environmental Health Department. A liquor licence must be held by any establishment selling alcoholic beverages of any kind in an interval, for a reception or before or after an event. The licensing authority may reject applications for liquor licensing on the grounds of inadequate toilet and sanitary provision, or unsuitable occupancy figures or unsafe means of egress in emergencies. Occasional liquor licences, which cover one event at a time, may be arranged through the local authority's own catering services or, alternatively, by the proprietor of a nearby licensed establishment. The latter costs at present (1995) a nominal fee of £4.00 to arrange through the local magistrates court. In both cases, the licensee or their named representatives (often the gallery or museum staff) must be on the premises and have the licence ready for inspection by the police or licensing authorities. Stock usually has to be provided by the licensee, although this is not always the case.

The local authority will also provide information on the regulations governing food preparation and premises in which food is prepared for public consumption.

26.7 Temporary stage play licence

The local authority will advise on the circumstances in which such a licence is required. Living History projects could come under its remit, which defines a play as

> any dramatic piece, whether involving improvisation or not, which is given wholly or in part by one or more persons actually present and performing and in which the whole or major proportion of what is done by the person or persons performing, whether by way of speech, singing or action involves the playing of a role (Theatres Act, 1968).

It is important here not to confuse 'Living History' (which involves costumed actors) with 'Live Art' (which is a branch of contemporary visual arts). The latter involves performance artists as distinct from performing artists practising the traditional performing arts of music, dance and theatre. Live Art can combine any or all of these art forms with other visual art forms such as sculpture, photography and/or video etc. Live Art would more usually be covered by public entertainments and cinematic licensing.

26.8 Cinematic licence

Performances or screenings of film (including video) to a paying audience must be covered by a cinematic licence. Events presented without the intention to make profit, and defined for the purpose as being for public exhibition, are usually exempt. The Home Office will provide guidelines and advice.

26.9 Performing Rights Society

Information about public performances (either free or ticketed) of any type of music, live or recorded (and this includes background music for any type of event) must be returned to the Performing Rights Society, which concerns itself with the rights of composers or publishers and levies a charge based on the principle of royalties. A local authority often makes an annual overall return for all establishments under its control undertaking musical performances or presentations. Venues may seek advice from the local authority in the first instance.

26.10 Phonographic Performance Limited

This organization follows much the same principles as the Performing Rights Society, but deals exclusively with record and compact disk companies where recorded sound is used either for background music or for dance or other activities.

26.11 Mechanical Copyright Protection Society

This Society deals with the rights of composers and publishers when copying onto tape in the form of compilations is involved. Copyright permission must be sought from them.

Information about the last three bodies is available from Phonographic Performance Ltd on 0171 437 0311.

26.12 Choosing and preparing a space

The venue should establish well in advance the precise space requirements for an event. The space allocated should be big enough to accommodate staff, equipment and anticipated audience. Emergency exits must be kept clear at all times (see 27.11). Is there enough room for visitors to circulate without damaging exhibits (see 28.2)? The venue may need to consider moving exhibits or introducing protective barriers or covers during an event. If the risk to exhibits cannot be reduced to an acceptable minimum, the venue should re-consider or relocate the event.

If black-out is required, make sure this is achievable in the space at the relevant time of day and year. If an event occurs during opening hours, consider conflicting noise from other spaces in the venue.

If necessary, arrange alternative routes to toilets, cafes and offices during an event. If an event occurs outside normal opening hours, those areas of the building not being used should be secured to prevent visitors wandering into unsupervised spaces (see 42.6). This must not interfere with emergency exits, and staff may need to cover access points to areas that cannot be blocked off. Routes to the event and toilet and refreshment facilities should be clearly signed and supervised. A stock of temporary signs should be maintained for this purpose.

If possible, allocate a supervised space for visitors' coats and umbrellas. This will contribute to their comfort and avoid cluttering up the event area.

If an event lasts all day, identify an area in which visitors may eat packed lunches. If there is a cafe, tables should be reserved if possible for people choosing to eat there.

26.13 Equipment

The venue should establish well in advance the precise requirements of an event in terms of equipment. Deadlines for hiring or purchasing equipment not available in-house should be set. A schedule should be drawn up for installation, and adequate staff made available. Visitors have the right to expect an exhibition to be open at all the advertised times during its showing at a venue. If any installation requires a gallery to be closed to visitors, this should be stated in all publicity relating to the exhibition.

All equipment should be checked prior to each event. Electrical items should be tested to ensure that they work and that they meet safety requirements (see 27.15). Always have a supply of spare parts available and know how to fit them – projector bulbs can blow at the most inconvenient moments! Ensure the safety of equipment and visitors when the former is not in use by providing secure storage or arranging supervision.

After the event, equipment should be dismantled as soon as possible, checked for damage and returned to its owner or storage place.

26.14 Staff

All staff, permanent and temporary, should be familiar with the timing and nature of the event. Make sure that temporary staff arrive at the venue in time to familiarize themselves with the space, check layout and equipment, and make final adjustments.

Make sure they understand the venue's procedures regarding access to spaces and the security of visitors and exhibits, including emergency procedures. Introduce temporary staff to as many permanent staff as possible. Organize a final briefing session with all those involved in the event to check that everyone is clear about the overall plan and their specific areas of responsibility (see 25.7).

If preparations have been thorough, the event should run smoothly. However, people are unpredictable, so be prepared for the unexpected! Make sure a contact person is always available to temporary staff, just in case.

Note which aspects of the event worked well and which areas can be improved. Work on recording and evaluating the event should be completed after the event, and a report sent to all involved (see 25.10).

After the event, remember to thank everyone who has helped.

27

Fire precautions

John Bevin

27.1 General principles

Successful fire prevention starts with a low fire risk, excluding as much easily combustible material as possible. Fire risks and regulations should be carefully considered when complex exhibition installations are planned. It is essential that galleries are equipped for early fire detection and action, to keep damage to the minimum. The fire brigade's hoses should be required only as a last resort, as water can add considerably to the damage caused by fire (see 44.4).

27.2 The organizer's responsibilities

As far as fire precautions are concerned, the organizer's task divides into two main areas:

- to design the exhibition to ensure it meets the expected and required standards for fire prevention, so that it is not itself a fire hazard; and
- to provide sufficient instruction, guidance and information to the venues to enable them to discharge their duties in fire prevention.

27.3 Materials

The designer commissioned by the organizer should endeavour to ensure that all materials used in the exhibition conform to class '0' of BS 476. Class '1' materials should only be used where there is no alternative. Class '0' is defined as a material of limited combustibility which restricts both the spread of flame across a surface and also the rate at which heat is released from it, with a more strict control than class '1'.

The easiest and most effective method for a designer to meet this requirement is to ask manufacturers or suppliers to provide the relevant information. Suppliers are obliged by the Health & Safety at Work Act to provide this information. All reputable suppliers will have this information readily available and will be happy to provide information on the fire retardancy of their products and in particular whether a product meets the class '0' standard.

The organizer should supply the venues with information on the fire retardancy of all materials within the exhibition. A simple list should be compiled of all material with their fire retardancy classification (hopefully all class '0') and with the suppliers supporting information as necessary.

27.4 Electrical equipment

To ensure that 'off the shelf' equipment ordered from a manufacturer is satisfactory, the organizer should confirm that the equipment meets the British Standard by checking the suppliers' literature and seeing if the equipment bears a kite mark, or if the equipment is from abroad that it meets the European equivalent (see Figure 27.1).

If the equipment is specifically designed and constructed for the exhibition, then the organizer must stipulate to the designer that it meets the correct IEE regulations. In return, the organizer should receive from the designer a statement which stipulates that the equipment does meet the IEE regulations as well as a completed proforma with particulars of the equipment (see Figure 27.2). A similar statement should also be received from the person who constructs the equipment.

Prior to the arrival of the exhibition (see 17.11), the organizer should supply each venue with:

- a list of equipment which identifies each item by a unique number or code; and
- 'particulars of equipment' or relevant manufacturer's information for each item.

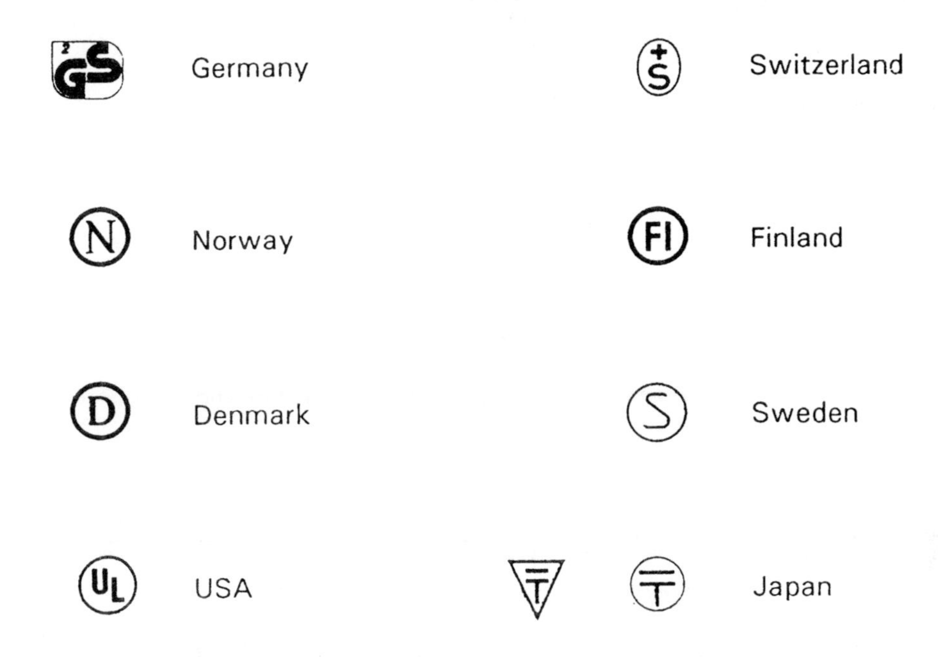

Figure 27.1 Equivalent electrical safety standards to the British safety mark

27.5 Suitability of venue

The organizer will need to be satisfied that each venue can meet the expected requirements for fire precautions, initially by requesting general information and thereafter receiving regular updates from the venue. If this information is not provided on a Facilities Report (see 38.4), the organizer should request the following information from a prospective venue:

- details of fire certification;
- details of fire alarm and smoke detection system (see 27.6);
- copy of venue's disaster plan and other related information (see 27.8).

This information will provide an indication of the prospective venue's fire precautions. If the organizer feels unable to assess this information, it can turn to the local fire brigade or an accredited fire consultant. It may be necessary for the organizer to visit the venue (possibly with their own expert), if there are any doubts arising from the information supplied.

Thereafter, the venue should be required to keep the organizer fully informed on fire precautions, by providing:

- a copy of any report plus supporting drawings from the preliminary visit to the venue by the Fire Officer (see 27.13);
- when the exhibition arrives on site, confirmation that the installation has received the approval of the Fire Officer (see 27.16);
- a summary of arrangements for fire prevention which have been and will be carried out during the exhibition's stay (see 27.17).

27.6 Fire/smoke detection system

The organizer should stipulate the level of fire detection required of the venues. If a touring exhibition contains irreplaceable exhibits, the organizer may insist on a fire detection system which meets the 'PI' standard (protection of the building) as set out in BS 5839. Otherwise, it may be sufficient to have local fire detection in the exhibition area. There is no golden rule, and the organizer must make a judgement commensurate to the content of the exhibition.

An automatic fire detector system will depend on heat and/or smoke sensors. The planning of such a system is a task for a specialist, but points to bear in mind are:

- the system must cover the whole building, as a partial installation may not comply with the relevant British Standard;
- the system can be constantly monitored together with the intruder alarm, e.g. by British Telecom's RedCARE equipment (see 42.4).

PARTICULARS FOR INSTALLATION

(Delete or complete items as appropriate)

Type of installation New/alteration/addition/to existing installation/maintenance

Type of Earthing (312–03): TN–C TN–S TN–C–S TT IT

Earth Electrode: Resistance............................ohms

Method of Measurement...............................

Type (542–02–01) and Location...................

Characteristics of the supply at the origin of the installation (313–01):

Nominal voltage....................volts

Frequency.............................Hz

Number of phases.......................

Prospect short-circuit current.......................(ascertained by enquiry/ determined by calculation/

Earth fault loop impedance (Zf).......................measured

Maximum demand...............A per phase

Overcurrent protective device. Type BS..............Rating...................

Main switch or circuit breaker (460–01–02): Type BS................Rating...................

Number of poles...

(if an r.c.d. rated residual operating current I..mA

Method of protection against indirect contact:

1. Earthed equipotential bonding and automatic disconnection of supply

or 2. Other (describe)..

Main equipotential bonding conductors (413–02–01/02.547–02–01) Size ....mm

Schedule of Test Results: Continuation...pages

Details of departures (if any) from the Wiring Regulations (120–04, 120–05)

....

Comments of existing installation, where applicable (743–01–01)..............

Figure 27.2 Particulars of installation

If an intruder alarm system is also being installed, it will be cost-effective to use the same installer for both systems and to use a single communication module (see 42.4).

27.7 Fire fighting equipment

The organizer must recommend to the venues the type of fire extinguishers which will be effective in extinguishing a fire occurring in the exhibition (see 17.12). The choice of extinguisher is dependent on the contents and structure of the exhibition, as different extinguishers are appropriate for different types of fire. Types of fire are classified in BS 4547. A large number of reference sources describe the properties and effectiveness of fire extinguishers, to help the organizer decide which to choose, e.g. Guide to Fire Precautions in Existing Places of Entertainment and like Premises, HMSO. In cases of doubt, the organizer should seek advice from an expert such as the local fire brigade, Fire Officer or from a recognized national organization such as the Fire Protection Association. The venue should be informed of the recommended type(s) and the minimum number necessary for the exhibition itself.

27.8 Rescue of exhibits

The organizer should be satisfied that each venue has a contingency plan for what to do in the event of an emergency. The venue should be asked to provide a copy of its Disaster Plan. The organizer should confirm that this contains satisfactory contingencies for the rescue of exhibits in the event of a fire, and should stipulate any priorities for exhibits from the touring exhibition that the venue should attempt to rescue. The organizer should supply a photograph of each of the exhibits to be rescued, and request the venue to identify them in the same way as its own material is identified in its Disaster Plan (see 7.16).

27.9 Exhibition layout

The organizer should prepare a drawing showing the preferred layout of the exhibition, particularly if it consists of a number of display units (see 49.7). There are no definitive guidelines on the layout of an exhibition and the question of means of escape. It is an area which is often left open to the interpretation of the Fire Officer, who will take into consideration the number of fire exits and clear escape routes from the display area, expected number of people visiting the exhibition and other factors.

For its own showing, the organizer should devise a layout to allow sufficient space between display cases for the expected number of visitors and to provide visible and unobstructed exits from the display area. The local Fire Officer can then be invited to give his/her views on the proposed layout, which should then be revised on the basis of any recommendations from the Fire Officer.

An acceptable layout can then be given to each venue, with the recommendation that it be adapted to suit the intended exhibition area, and that the approval of its Fire Officer be sought for its proposed layout.

27.10 The venue's responsibilities

In preparing to receive a touring exhibition, the venue has to ensure it is able to meet the standards required for fire precautions. Indeed an acceptable level must be achieved to obtain approval to hold the exhibition from the statutory enforcing authorities.

27.11 Means of escape

Although there are many factors in choosing the area where the exhibition is to be staged, one essential aspect to consider is whether the area chosen is suitable for fire precautions and likely to meet the approval of the Fire Officer. The venue's first task is to decide whether the preferred location will provide an adequate means of escape. In the UK, there are two basic principles to bear in mind when considering means of escape which appear in the 1991 Building Regulations, Approved Document B, Means of Escape. These principles are:

- There should be alternative means of escape from most situations.
- Where direct escape to a place of safety is not possible, it should be possible to reach a place of relative safety, such as a protected stairway, which is on a route to an exit, within a reasonable travel distance. In such cases the means of escape will consist of two parts, the first being unprotected in accommodation and circulation areas, and the second in protected stairways (and in some circumstances protected corridors). The ultimate place of safety is the open air clear of the effects of the fire.

A simple but practical exercise is to imagine that a first-time visitor has to leave the exhibition in an emergency. Charting the routes to safety will confirm if there is adequate means of escape. Walking the route will help to determine where additional signs or emergency lighting could be provided.

27.12 Means of escape for visitors with disabilities

Envisaging how a disabled visitor would escape in an emergency can help in identifying management arrangements to provide assistance. However to ensure there is adequate provision for visitors with disabilities, advice should be sought from an experienced disability adviser, who can be contacted via the local authority or via one of the following national organizations:

- Access Committee for Wales/Cyngor Cymru I'r Anabl, Llys Ifor, Crescent Road, Caerphilly, Mid Glamorgan CF8 1XL.
- Centre for Accessible Environments, Nutmeg. House, 60 Gainsford Street, London SE1 2NY.
- Centre on Environment for the Handicapped/ Access Committee for England, 35 Great Smith Street, London SW1P 3BJ.
- Disabled Living Foundation, 380-384 Harrow Road, London W9 2HU.
- Joint Committee on Mobility for the Disabled, 9 Moss Close, Pinner, Middlesex HA5 3AY.
- National Federation of the Blind of the UK, Unity House, Smyth Street, Westgate, Wakefield, West Yorkshire WF1 1ER.
- Royal Association for Disability and Rehabilitation, 25 Mortimer Street, London W1N 8AB.
- Royal National Institute for the Blind, 224 Great Portland Street, London W1N 6AA.
- Royal National Institute for the Deaf, 105 Gower Street, London WC1E 6AH.
- Scottish Council on Disability, Princes House, 5 Shandwick Place, Edinburgh EH2 4RG.

There is considerable legislation and guidance on the subject of means of escape and this must be considered in conjunction with the building and its use. However, the ultimate responsibility for ensuring a public building such as a museum or gallery meets the requirements for means of escape will fall to the local authority's Fire Officer (see 26.4). He/she often has considerable experience and knowledge and is best equipped to decide on interpretation of legislation.

27.13 Preliminary visit by the Fire Officer

After selecting the area to be used for the exhibition, the venue should contact the local authority and ask for a visit from the Fire Officer to establish whether the means of escape are adequate. Regular contact with the Fire Officer should already exist, but it is advisable for the venue to have a meeting at the earliest opportunity specifically to discuss the exhibition. For this meeting, the venue should:

Plan the proposed layout, using the suggested layout received from the organizer, transposed and adapted to suit the building. The Fire Officer will need to be satisfied that the proposed location and layout are acceptable.

Prepare a list of the materials. Those to be used in the exhibition will be supplied by the organizer, and any additional materials used by the venue should be chosen to conform to class '0' of BS 476 (see 27.3). The Fire Officer will then be able to confirm that the choice of materials is acceptable.

Propose the number and type of fire-fighting appliances to be in position when the exhibition arrives. The organizer will have provided advice on the type of extinguisher required by the exhibition (see 27.7). The above procedure should be used to determine whether further extinguishers are required. This exercise should also give the Fire Officer the opportunity to advise on the location and number of extinguishers.

Identify fire exit signs on the drawing and then walk the routes with the Fire Officer to confirm there is acceptable signage.

Check the emergency lighting, using the same procedure as above.

Be prepared to provide details of the smoke detection system, to confirm that it meets requirements.

On completion of the meeting, the venue should compile a note of the Fire Officer's requirements and circulate to all concerned within the organization and to the organizer, so that the requirements are known, understood and implemented. Finally, the venue should arrange for the Fire Officer to visit again when the exhibition arrives, to give formal approval that it meets fire precaution requirements.

27.14 Preparation of site

The preparation of the site with regard to fire precautions will mainly be governed by the requirements laid down by the Fire Officer, e.g. additional signs, emergency lighting, etc. In addition, the following aspects should be addressed.

Any extra display material which the venue is to provide in support of the touring exhibition should be fire retardant and meet the standards as set out in BS 476 and meet class '0' standard (see 27.3).

Routine maintenance and testing is a requirement of BS 5839, so it is advisable to arrange for a test of the fire detection system serving the display area before the exhibition arrives. This will confirm that the system is operating effectively or allow for its repair in good time, should a fault be identified.

All contractual works need to be carried out with due regard to fire precautions. The venue must ensure that all contractors arriving on site are familiar with these precautions which should be presented to them in writing. If the venue does not have a written statement prepared, then the contractor should be informed

CERTIFICATE OF TEST

Address ....

....

....

The item listed below has been inspected and tested with the following results recorded at the time of test:

Item ....

Test No .... Serial No ....

Date of Test .... Code No ....

Tested By ....

Earth Bond Test: PASS/FAIL

Insulation Test: PASS/FAIL

Flash Test: PASS/FAIL

Load Test: PASS/FAIL/NOT TESTED

Leakage Test: PASS/FAIL

Signed ....

Name of Company ....

Figure 27.3 Certificate of test

that they must meet with the DOE booklet, Standard Fire Precautions P5, HMSO. All 'hot-work' must only be carried out with a 'permit to work'. Appropriate and adequate supervision must be carried out by the venue, by persons who have been trained and are aware of the requirements for fire protection. See also 29.4.

27.15 Installation

All electrical equipment which forms part of the exhibition must be tested before installation. Not only is this a necessary precaution against the risk of fire, but it is also a requirement under the Health and Safety at Work Act and Electricity at Work Regulations 1989. Only companies registered with either the Electrical Contractors Association or the National Inspection Council for Electrical Installation Contracting should be employed to carry out the work of installing electrical equipment.

On arrival of the exhibition, the venue must establish the electrical equipment to be tested, by reference to the equipment checklist previously supplied by the organizer (see 27.4). This checklist should provide a unique identification number/code for each item, and should be accompanied by particulars of each piece of equipment or manufacturer's or designer's information. The venue must ensure that this information is given to a qualified electrician who must be Joint Industrial Board approved and who will be responsible for carrying out the relevant testing. The electrician should be present when the exhibition is being installed, and should on behalf of the venue check the equipment. The results of the tests must be recorded, preferably on a prepared proforma (see Figure 27.3).

If a piece of equipment fails during testing, it must not be connected to the venue's low voltage supply system. The organizer must be notified immediately, so that it can authorize the venue's electrician to carry out the repair or can make arrangements to repair or replace the equipment.

On satisfactory completion of the testing, the electrical equipment can be connected to the low voltage system. A sensible precaution is to protect the power supply to the exhibition by the use of Residual Circuit Breakers, so that in the event of a fault, which may or may not lead to an electrical fire, the electrical supply will be disconnected. The venue should instruct the electrician to carry this out using his judgement as to the most practical and effective way.

27.16 Approval by the Fire Officer

On completion of the electrical installation, a visual inspection should be carried out to ensure the display is consistent with the information provided by the organizer and that the layout conforms with the Fire Officer's requirements for means of escape.

The venue should receive the Fire Officer and summarize the preparations carried out since the preliminary meeting. The Fire Officer should, all being well, give formal approval to allow the exhibition to be opened to the public.

27.17 Ongoing precautions

From the opening of the exhibition until it departs, the venue must set out procedures outlining what fire precautions are required.

Once a fire starts, it is essential to have fire-fighting equipment immediately to hand. All staff should be briefed on how to use the various extinguishers to be found in the display area, particularly any new extinguishers brought in as a consequence of the exhibition. Short training sessions should be arranged in-house, to demonstrate how to use the extinguishers and to specify which extinguisher to use on a type of fire (e.g. CO_2 to combat an electrical fire). Where a venue does not have a member of staff who can carry out this demonstration, it should contact the local fire brigade, many of which run courses on the use and operation of fire extinguishers. It may be helpful to have 'safety signs' showing which extinguishers to use on a given type of fire displayed next to the extinguishers in the gallery. These signs are readily available from safety sign suppliers.

The venue must ensure a good state of housekeeping and vigilance is carried out for the exhibition area. This is often met by effective invigilation (see 42.6).

The most common causes of fire are electrical installation or equipment, cigarette smoking and heating installations, so regular inspection and maintenance of equipment and systems, together with rigorous enforcement of smoking rules will pay dividends. Venues should adopt a daily checking routine at opening and closing times:

- *Electrical equipment*: is it on or off; is it working properly with no warning lights illuminated; is the flex worn? See also 23.10.
- *Heating system*: is it on or off; is it working properly; are there combustibles in close proximity?
- *Smoking*: are notices displayed if it is not permitted; are ashtrays provided and is debris extinguished where smoking is permitted?
- *Waste, flammable liquids and stores*: are they properly stowed away and clear of sources of ignition?
- *Contractors elsewhere on the premises*: is 'hot' work being safely carried out; are work areas checked before closing; are hazardous materials correctly and safely stored in the agreed location?
- *Means of escape*: are they unlocked and unobstructed on opening; are they locked on closing?

28

Care of visitors

James Shea

28.1 Exhibitions with disabilities

There are two sorts of barriers which visitors may encounter when approaching an exhibition and which the organizer and the venues alike must take action to remove or otherwise neutralize.

Physical barriers are often easy to recognize, e.g. steps that hinder access for wheelchair-users, although they can be expensive to put right.

Attitudinal barriers may not involve any significant changes to the fabric of a building but can be harder for the people concerned to accept and rectify, e.g. unsuitable interpretation in the exhibition or a lack of sympathy for the hesitation of children and other people perhaps unused to the venue and what it represents.

Physical and attitudinal barriers can occur quite inadvertently. Such barriers will result in lower attendances at exhibitions, and may cause animosity between venues and groups of potential visitors. This can be compounded in the case of a touring exhibition if the organizer and the venues do not consult each other about physical and attitudinal accessibility to the exhibition.

People with disabilities, children and their carers, elderly people and visitors whose first language is not English all have specific needs which must be addressed. By consulting representatives of these sections of the population on what services should be provided for them, and then by appropriate marketing to draw attention to these services, exhibitions can be made accessible to visitors who traditionally do not visit them.

In the short term, such attention should increase attendances, but a greater sensitivity to the needs of visitors (and the publicity which often accompanies these efforts) should also attract and enhance the experience of existing visitors, improving satisfaction generally.

28.2 Some considerations for the design of exhibitions

There should be adequate space between displays for people in wheelchairs and people with prams to move easily around the exhibition space.

Exhibits displayed on walls should be hung with a mid point of 137 cm (54") where the dimensions of works allow; this is an optimum height, allowing easy viewing by all. Plinths and showcases should be at a height where exhibits are visible to people of all heights and wheelchair-users (see 21.6). All tables used for workshops and interactive activities should be high enough to accommodate wheelchair-users (see 24.4).

Display cases should be internally lit where possible, to reduce the likelihood of glare or reflection when children or people in wheelchairs are looking at the exhibits (see 20.10, 21.6).

28.3 Some considerations concerning interpretation

Labels for individual exhibits should have the main information (e.g. the name of the maker of a work of art) no smaller than 24 point text, and any secondary information (e.g. title and medium and other information) no smaller than 18 point. Lettering on information boards should have a point size between 14 and 24, depending on display space available. Labels and information boards should be positioned so that they can easily be read by all visitors (see 22.4).

The text in catalogue, leaflets, posters, private view cards, education packs and information sheets should have a minimum point size of 12.

Large-text versions of catalogues, leaflets, education packs and information sheets for people with visual disabilities can be available for reference within the exhibition space. An inexpensive way of producing these is by enlarging existing text on a photocopier. Black text on yellow paper enhances visibility in these enlarged versions.

Posters, private view cards, gallery calendars and all other publicity material should contain information about access (see 30.12). Appropriate disability symbols can be used on publicity material. SHAPE and Artlink organizations can advise on symbols and sources of supply (see 28.6).

An audio guide or taped version of the catalogue or leaflet for people with visual disabilities can be provided within the exhibition space. The RNIB operates a service for providing this (see 28.7). These may be played in standard portable cassette players such as the Sony Walkman. By using a double adaptor in the headphone socket and an extra pair of headphones, a visually-impaired person can listen to the tape simultaneously with a guide person.

Gallery talks and lectures can be interpreted in sign language for hearing-impaired people (see 25.7). The RNIB offers this service. If an induction loop is not already fitted in rooms where talks take place, a portable induction loop would be useful. Details of systems may be obtained from the RNIB (see 28.7). Always check that the induction loop is turned on and operating.

28.4 Removing the barriers from venues

Venues should carry out regular access reviews in consultation with local or national disability arts organizations. Such a review may help a venue to make a better case for a showing of a particular exhibition. As with other requirements (e.g. for security and environmental controls), there are advantages in anticipating the organizer's needs, rather than having to arrange a review from scratch when the organizer may be in a hurry to finalize the tour. Appropriate measures should be taken by individual venues to ensure accessibility. All venues should consult local SHAPE and Artlink organizations in order to target their marketing campaigns (see 28.6).

Many venues may fear that they are inaccessible because main entrances, exhibition galleries or lavatories are approached by steps, because the building has heavy fire doors throughout, or because control buttons on lifts are out of reach of people in wheelchairs. The Centre for Accessible Environments (see 28.7) has details of sources of funding for improving access.

Even if funding is not forthcoming, it may be possible to use inexpensively-constructed wooden ramps for spanning shallow flights of stairs, to provide illumination, signposting and attendants for secondary entrance doors for wheelchair users (although venues should preferably be accessible via the main entrance), and to train staff to assist people with disabilities in opening doors and operating lifts.

28.5 Some simple practical measures for venues

All staff can receive Disability Equality Training and Sympathetic Hearing Training. Attendant staff should be trained to recognize and approach people who may need assistance. Trainers can be contacted through local SHAPE or Artlink organizations (see 28.6).

Adequate parking should be made available for visitors. Where coach or mini-bus parties are expected, arrangements can usually be made in advance with the local constabulary to allow them to park close to the museum or gallery entrance in areas normally restricted to parking.

Adequate seating should be supplied within the building, preferably in the form of chairs with arms.

Public telephones can be fitted with induction loops so that they can be used by people with hearing aids.

A drinking bowl for guide dogs can be made available in the entrance to the building, advertised by an appropriate sign.

Museum and gallery cafes can make available lightweight eating utensils (obtainable from large chemist stores) and drinking straws. Tables should be capable of accommodating people in wheelchairs, and adequate spaces should be available for wheelchair users. Adequate seating furniture for children can be supplied, including high chairs.

Goods within art gallery and museum shops should be displayed within the easy reach of people in wheelchairs. There should be adequate floor space around displays to allow easy negotiation by wheelchair users and people with prams.

For emergency egress, see 27.12.

28.6 The SHAPE and Artlink Network

Artability South East, St James Centre, Quarry Road, Tunbridge Wells, Kent TN1 2EY. Tel 01892 5515478.

Artlink Central, The Norman MacEwan Centre, Cameronian Street, Stirling FK8 2DX. Tel 01786 50971.

Artlink East, Unit 2, Peterborough Arts Centre, Orton Goldhay, Peterborough PE2 0JQ. Tel 01733 237073.

Artlink Edinburgh and the Lothians, 13a Spittal Street, Edinburgh EH3 9DY. Tel 0131 229 3555.

Artlink for Lincolnshire and Humberside, c/o Humberside Leisure Service, Central Library, Albion Street, Hull HU1 3TF. Tel 01482 224040.

Artlink West Midlands, The Garage and Media Centre, 1 Hatherton Street, Walsall WS1 1HG. Tel 01922

616566.

Artlink West Yorkshire (previously Shape Up North), 191 Bellevue Road, Leeds LS3 1HG. Tel 0113 2431005.

Arts Connection (previously Solent Artlink), Cumberland Centre, Reginald Road, Portsmouth, Hampshire PO4 9HN. Tel 01705 828392.

Artshare South West, c/o South West Arts, Bradninch Place, Gandy Street, Exeter EX4 3HA. Tel 01392 218923.

Arts Integration Merseyside, Mount Vernon Green, Hall Lane, Liverpool L7 8TF. Tel 0151 709 0990.

East Midlands Shape, 27a Belvoir Street, Leicester LE1 6SL. 0116 255 2933.

Ithaca (previously Southern Artlink), Unit 4, St John Fisher School, Sandy Lane West, Oxford OX4 5LD. Tel 01865 714652.

Northern Shape, Todd's Nook Centre, Monday Crescent, Newcastle-upon-Tyne NE1 1PG. Tel 0191 226 0701.

North West Shape, The Green Prefab, Back of Shawgrove School, Cavendish Road, West Didsbury, Manchester M20 8JR. Tel 0161 434 8666.

Shape Buckinghamshire, 38B Prices Estate, Summerleys Road, Princes Risborough, Buckinghamshire HP17 9PX. Tel 01844 274493.

Shape London, 1 Thorpe Close, London W10 5XL. Tel 0181 960 9245.

28.7 Other sources of information

Access Committee for England, 35 Great Smith Street, London SW1P 3BJ. Tel 0171 233 2566. Lists local/regional Access groups; *Access Action* newsletter.

Arts Council of England, 14 Great Peter Street, London SW1P 3NQ. Tel 0171 333 0100. The Access Unit promotes and advises on access, and publishes a resource pack, including a 'Code of good practice'.

Artsline, 5 Crowndale Road, London NW1 1TU. Tel 0171 388 2272 (voice and Minicom). London's information and advice service on arts and entertainment for disabled people.

Centre for Accessible Environments, 35 Great Smith Street, London SW1P 3BJ. Tel 0171 222 7980. Advises on accessible design.

William Kirby, Consultant in Art and Design for Blind and Partially Sighted People, 11 Eastgate Street, Winchester SO23 8EB. Tel 01962 854003. Advises museums and galleries on physical, tactile and visual access.

London Disability Arts Forum (LDAF), 34 Osnaburgh Street, London NW1 3DN. Tel 0171 916 5419/5484 (voice and Minicom). Fax 0171 916 5396.

MAGDA (Museums and Galleries Disability Association), Secretary: Kathy Niblett, City Museum and Art Gallery, Bethseda Street, Hanley, Stoke on Trent ST1 3DW. Organization of museum professionals with and without disabilities which promotes access.

Museums & Galleries Commission, 16 Queen Anne's Gate, London SW1H 9AA. Tel 0171 233 4200. Provides a resource pack on access for disabled people, including an extensive bibliography.

Partially Sighted Society, Queen's Road, Doncaster, South Yorkshire. Tel 01302 323132. Provides information on partial sight, including a booklet *Lighting and low vision.*

Royal National Institute for the Blind (RNIB), 224 Great Portland Street, London W1A 6AA. Tel 0171 388 1266. Provides a range of services including Community Education, Publications Unit, Reference Library, Leisure Service (arts information and advisory service) and customer services. For transcription of braille, tapes etc., phone 01733 370777.

Royal National Institute for Deaf People, 105 Gower Street, London WC1E 6AH. Tel 0171 387 8033. Minicom 0171 3833154.

29

Public liability insurance

Steve Brake

29.1 Liability

It is the responsibility of the organizer and the venue to ensure that, at all times, all exhibits, associated display systems and exhibition areas are suitably covered by an insurance policy in respect of 'public liability'.

In an increasingly-litigious society, it is imperative that suitable insurance protection is in place. Any museum or gallery can be subject to a possible claim in respect of any hurt or harm that may befall any member of the public or visitor, whether legally entitled to be on the premises or in the exhibition, or otherwise. The most likely problem areas are:

- when exhibitions are put into non-gallery spaces;
- when exhibition areas are public thoroughfares and fire exits;
- when workshops, public demonstrations or interactive displays are part of the exhibition.

Bearing in mind that, amongst other things, insurance companies will try to offset any claims either against other insurance companies or against individuals, the organizer and venue should try to anticipate all problems that might arise. Do not be afraid to consult the Health and Safety Officer and colleagues in other museums and galleries, or even to ask the insurance company to visit and assess possible areas of risk.

29.2 Consider everything

Because of their temporary nature and moveable character, exhibitions can lead to particular problems. Adequate physical protection must be provided for the public from the exhibits and their means of display.

- Barriers should be placed to keep people away from unstable exhibits or exhibits with sharp points.
- Display cases and screens should be adequately anchored.
- Suspended exhibits must be secure, and the area below isolated.
- An exhibit on a plinth should be able to withstand the force of a child running into the plinth without dislodging the exhibit.
- Exhibits containing water, fire, chemicals or other harmful materials (e.g. lead) must be protected.
- Any exhibit using electricity must be earthed with approved earth-leakage protection (see 27.15).
- Suspended clear displays of Perspex or glass must be clearly identified.
- Displays must not be installed in positions where people may easily fall or trip into them, e.g. at the bottom of stairs or even below a single step.

The above examples are just a few of the more common areas of risk. Try to think of everything – if you do not, it is more likely to happen!

29.3 Touring Exhibitions

The organizer must either provide, or ensure that the venue provides, adequate physical protection for the public from the exhibits and their means of display.

If the organizer is responsible for the installation of an exhibition in another venue, it is important that the organizer's employers have cover for public liability that is adequate for both the organizer and the exhibition while on the venue's premises.

Where a venue takes full responsibility for installing an exhibition, it is still incumbent upon the organizer to notify the venue of all possible aspects of the exhibition that may comprise a danger to the public (17.12).

Venues should bear in mind that an organizer may have a very different space and facilities, or even no exhibition area at all, and may have a very different clientele. It is therefore very important for the venue to assess the safety of the public in relation to the incoming exhibition, using the venue's own criteria and experience of visitors in its own space.

If the venue does not normally show exhibitions, e.g. if it is a park, shopping mall, pedestrian precinct, bank or railway station, its public liability insurance cover must be thoroughly checked by the organizer. Specific cover may have to be arranged for such non-gallery venues.

29.4 Contractors

While it may not be the responsibility of the organizer and the venue to provide cover for work by external contractors, it is their duty to use bona fide contractors and to ensure that the company has the necessary cover in respect of exhibitions in public spaces. This should apply to all contractors, whether they be designers, electricians, builders or other trades.

29.5 Freelance staff

Any self-employed person working in an institution – whether a technician installing an exhibit or an educationalist leading a workshop – must have public liability insurance cover. Only in the case of such persons carrying out detailed specific orders which allow no interpretation, will liability for any harm or injury rest with the institution. For example, liability rests with a self-employed person who is simply told to put a three-pin plug on a lead; it rests with the institution if its staff specify which coloured wire goes to which screw.

Should such persons not have suitable insurance cover, it is normal practice for the institution to take them on to the staff in an employed capacity – even if only for half a day – so that they will then be covered by the institution's own policy. In the case of a claim and subsequent discovery that such self-employed persons have no insurance cover, liability may fall on either the organizer or the venue. It is therefore essential that such provision is checked by both parties at the outset.

29.6 Workshops/classes

It is the responsibility of the venue to ensure that all leaders or workers engaged in workshops, demonstrations and classes are properly protected against claims of liability, both third party and public indemnity. This protection must be ascertained even if the event is provided by the organizer. If there is any doubt about insurance status, put the workers concerned on the venue's payroll, so that they are employed and consequently covered by the venue's policy.

In the case of leaders or workers for activities for children and young people, it is essential that:

(i) a police check is carried out, to certify that the workers have no convictions deeming them unsuitable to work with children or young persons; and
(ii) all appropriate steps are taken to conform to the regulations of the Childrens Act, 1989 which states the qualifications workers need, ratios of workers to children, time-limits on activitites, infrastructure needs such as toilets, etc (see Shaws Annotated Acts, Childrens Act 1989).

Non-compliance with either (i) or (ii) will render both the venue and the organizer of the activity liable to prosecution.

29.7 Extent of cover

The insurance companies themselves will determine the cover limitations needed according to the most recently negotiated settlements and awards being made through the courts.

30

Publicity

Joan Asquith

30.1 The marketing strategy

The marketing of an exhibition may be sophisticated or simple, but the main objective remains the same – to generate publicity in order to attract visitors. To meet the needs and exploit the strengths of the organizer and venues, publicity tactics should be coordinated in an overall marketing strategy, which the organizer agrees with venues, their press or marketing officers and sponsors.

The strategy should reflect:

- the nature and relative importance of the exhibition, e.g. is it a long-awaited exhibition on Impressionism with a national tour or a small environmental exhibition of appeal to local school children and 'green' enthusiasts;
- each venue's estimate for admissions and the organizer's overall target numbers;
- the range and type of visitors targeted, e.g. children/adults, social groups, local/national, and how to reach them;
- the total publicity budget, including input from venues and sponsors, e.g. will the latter contribute financially or in kind, by donating editorial or advertising space;
- the availability of human resources at each stage of the exhibition, e.g. can an under-funded venue cope with a press launch or sponsor's reception;
- the assigning of responsibilities, e.g. for mailings and overprintings;
- time of year and seasonal factors that help or hinder, e.g. will people turn out in freezing February or will summer tourists boost admissions;
- tour length, e.g. a short tour needs early press coverage, while a longer one will need more servicing, press photographs and a budget spread over a longer period;
- the organizer's print production schedule and timetable for venues to receive all publicity materials;
- a timetable when organizer and venue can expect the various elements to be available.

The strategy might be fairly basic, relying on word of mouth, good editorials and a simple poster campaign or it might be comprehensive and costly, using every possible means of promotional activity. It may be useful to engage a marketing consultant, to advise on all aspects of marketing for an important exhibition or reopening of a gallery.

30.2 Sponsorship

The exhibition or one of its showings may attract one or more sponsors, whose benefits will be agreed in their contracts with the organizer and/or the venues (see 11.3). Sponsorship may result in an unusually large publicity budget input, in which case it may be worthwhile to engage a marketing consultant or an agency or media-buying company (see 30.7).

Often sponsors will be seeking to raise their profile by publicity from participation in the event or alternatively they may wish to be totally discreet and unobtrusive. They will usually be credited on all publicity material as well as inside the exhibition itself, in a size and style which is agreed between organizer and sponsor. Credits are rarely big enough for the sponsor, and a prominence that is appropriate is often the subject of much careful negotiation. It is important that all print, press and advertising is checked with sponsors, and the exhibition's production schedule may be extended by several days to allow time for such approval (see 8.3).

30.3 The tour umbrella

Some touring exhibitions will have their own 'publicity machine' i.e. specialized staff in the organizer's marketing department, responsible for the press and publicity at each stage of the tour. The organizer will usually administer and fund that part of the advertising campaign which is most appropriate and cost-effective for a central operation. Venues should notify the organizer of names and contact numbers of their own press officers, so that the latter can liaise with any central publicity machine and avoid duplication (see 17.14).

30.4 Publicity materials

Publicity materials include posters, press and private view invitations, advertisements, leaflets, merchandising, road signs, banners, special offers and promotions, and advance ticketing. Some or all of these materials will be useful to each venue.

30.5 Banners

A large colourful banner hung vertically or horizontally outside the venue clearly announces the exhibition to the entire neighbourhood. A banner can be part of the overall publicity for the tour, but because of the variety of buildings and locations in a touring exhibition it is often produced locally by each venue using artwork provided by or derived from the organizer.

30.6 Advertising

The organizer may arrange advertising in national newspapers and magazines at least for the first venue, and preferably at intervals during the tour, which may be complemented by local advertising arranged by each venue in their events magazine or newspaper. Local advertising should relate in style and content to national advertising to reinforce the latter and to act as a reminder to the potential audience which may have seen earlier advertising in the national press.

The organizer and the venue should agree who is responsible for booking space for national and local advertisements, poster sites, etc. The person responsible should check the notice required for the type of advertising wanted, and make a booking as soon as possible. Several months' notice are necessary for prime poster sites or advertisement positions. Copy dates for print/artwork vary from a few days for a newspaper to several weeks for a magazine. Most publications provide an advertising rate card, although rates can often be negotiated. Advertising space in newspapers and magazines is sold in units of the single column centimetre (scc) and costs vary according to position and circulation.

BRAD (British Rates & Data) is a useful publication for anyone booking space direct, as it contains details of specifications – costs, dimensions, printing methods, screen sizes and copy dates for all advertising media. BRAD is sold by subscription or by the single copy, 1995 prices from £100, from BRAD, 1A Chalk Lane, Cockfosters EN4 DBU. Tel 0181 242 3105.

30.7 Advertising agents and media-buying companies

Whether they regularly place advertising or have not the time or the expertise, the organizer or the venue might employ an advertising agent or media-buying company. Either can advise on all manner of advertising and publicity and plan a specific campaign. The main difference between them is that an agency provides more creative services, e.g. design of advertisements, posters and leaflets, copywriting and production of radio and TV advertising.

Both charge commission varying from 10 per cent to 15 per cent on space booked, but will none the less negotiate the most economical rates and deals. Occasionally, they will charge a fee as well, especially for creative services. They can be engaged for a one-off exhibition or by contract until further notice. If the budget is unusually large, due to a sponsor's input, then it may be worthwhile engaging an agency or media-buying company.

Preferably the advertising agent or media-buying company should have experience in the cultural or heritage area. A small agency might be able to provide a better service than a large one more used to working on huge campaigns. Recommendation is the best way to find an agency, or by asking the marketing or market research manager of a regional arts board or national arts council. Performance can be measured over a period of time using criteria including the following:

- Is the publicity producing more visitors, i.e. are the media correctly chosen and the timing right?
- Is the day-to-day service efficient?
- Is the creative material satisfactory?
- Is the expense justified?

A marketing consultant does not buy advertising space or provide creative services, but could arrange them.

30.8 Design

Design and artwork for exhibition advertisements is usually provided centrally by the organizer. The graphic designer who designs the text for the exhibition may also be responsible for publicity materials, such as poster, leaflet, advertisements and banners. This can prove too much work for one freelance designer or small firm, resulting in serious delays, so often two or more designers may be involved. An advertising agency may also design publicity material, but this may be more expensive. When commissioning design services, the organizer should:

- set out the design brief clearly (see 19.1);
- request an estimate of costs;
- agree copy deadlines and quantities;
- supply copy, logos, photographs and credits;
- check and approve proofs for all designs;
- agree appropriate specifications for printing, e.g. weight and type of paper, waterproof/non-fade inks for outdoor posters, printing method, correction and proofing charges, run-on costs, production schedule, colour separation charges, etc.
- agree who is responsible for obtaining comparative quotations from printers.

30.9 Posters

Posters are the normal vehicle for advertising exhibitions, and if available for sale they sometimes become much collected and sought after. Their visual impact effectiveness depend on the organizer's vital choice of image and how efficiently they are displayed and distributed, nationally and locally. A poster should:

- have immediate visual impact;
- be able to convey the essence of an exhibition at a glance, especially if a famous or striking image is used;
- give a brief, informative message: exhibition title and sub-title, the venue, its address and telephone number, transport details, opening hours and dates (including the year), admission prices, national and local credits and logos;
- have clear graphics, legible at some distance and in poor light.

Normally, the organizer commissions the poster according to the agreed marketing strategy, as it is more economic in time and money for a single poster to be produced centrally and customised for each venue. The number of posters required by a venue will be conditioned by the target number of visitors, size of mailing list, number of available sites and whether the poster is primary publicity or reinforcing a wider campaign. Posters for selling may have a simpler message, probably on heavier paper, and several may be produced using different images if a large volume of sales is forecast (see 32.7).

An advertising agency or market research company (see Millward Brown below) could arrange the testing of several different images amongst targeted visitors. Otherwise, images simply could be tested in-house. Research on the effectiveness of exhibition posters, including the Visual Arts and Exhibitions Research Digest, is available in the library at the Arts Council of England. Much of this information has been researched at various venues by Millward Brown International, Olympus Avenue, Tachbrook Park, Warwick CV34 6RJ. Tel 01926 452233.

30.10 Poster sizes and sites

Exhibition posters come in a variety of shapes and sizes to suit all budgets and advertising sites, ranging from the humble but useful handbill to giant 48-sheet billboards. Preferred sizes in the regions are A2 or A3 to suit outdoor municipal sites, which vary in size and cost from city to city. London is perhaps an extreme example of the considerations that need to be borne in mind when deciding sizes.

In London, sizes are affected by London Underground's single-sheet Double Crown sites (76 cm x 51 cm/30" x 20") and four-sheet Double Crown sites (152 cm x 102 cm/60" x 40"), the latter also being used for Adshell bus shelters. Hence, London museums and galleries tend to use Double Crown for display and mailings. London bus sites are different again, as bus sides are banner-like and the front and back differ from each other. Posters are also sold on the sides of London taxis, but these are extremely costly. London Underground Advertising has recently been privatized, as have the bus companies, so changes are to be expected. Public transport sites are sold directly by the company or through an advertising agency which can sometimes arrange a discount. Sites are sold in packages of 50, 100 or more, usually by the month. The very large or back-lit variety are sold individually. It is possible to specify positions and/or stations.

30.11 Poster mailings and deliveries

Traditionally, posters are mailed free to the venue's own basic list, consisting of sites in schools, colleges, libraries, arts centres, museums, hospitals, citizen's advice bureaux, job centres, theatres, local societies, Friends organizations and special groups identified as the target visitors or busy public places with a notice board or display site and someone to put them up.

If the list is not suitable for a particular exhibition, then another must be acquired. This can be arranged with a friendly local venue, either on a reciprocal basis or by paying for an insertion in its mailing at the appropriate time.

Alternatively, the distribution companies that deliver leaflets also deliver posters (see 30.15). The cost of mailings depends on quantity, postage, packing and weight: each envelope may cost between 50p and £1.00.

Hand delivery is a useful alternative to consider, especially if the venue has volunteer or casual labour. It is best to go out provided with posters and fixing materials (drawing pins, adhesive tape, etc.) so that posters can actually be put up in local shops, cafes, pubs, hotels, tourist information centres, etc., always by kind permission of the manager. A note of each location is useful for any future deliveries.

30.12 Overprinting

Wherever possible, overprinting of posters and cards should be arranged by the organizer as part of its umbrella publicity. This ensures consistency of style, and avoids the unprofessional appearance of cheap stick-on labels. It should also be more economic for this to be done centrally and at one time, although overprinting may be done at a later stage if the tour is very long, bookings are late or a venue has to change its details. Overprinting should contain precise details of each showing:

- correct title, address and logo;
- opening hours/dates with exclusions (e.g. Bank Holidays);
- any admission charges;
- information about access (see 28.3);
- any local credits or logos.

30.13 Logos

It is normal practice to include the logo or corporate identity symbol of every organization involved in a touring exhibition on national and local publicity material. This may include the logo of the organizer (or each of the partners in a collaboration, see 13.7), its local authority, sponsor (see 30.2) and/or national funding body, each of whom regards such information as a matter of legitimate interest even to people who may not visit the exhibition. Logos should be modest in size but clearly visible. If they are made too small, the funders may be irritated, but fortunately designers are becoming adept at arranging many logos on a leaflet or poster.

30.14 Leaflets

Occasionally an organizer will produce a leaflet, colour-printed and folded to one-third A4, which typically describes the exhibition, its education programme and the tour; if produced centrally, the required quantity is dispatched to each venue for local distribution, possibly with its forthcoming events leaflet. More often, the organizer agrees with the venues that they incorporate details provided by the organizer about the exhibition in their forthcoming events leaflets.

30.15 Leaflet distribution

A venue may use postal or hand delivery, to the same outlets as for posters (see 30.11). Alternatively, local distribution can be done by engaging a professional distribution company, which will ensure that leaflets are displayed in their special display stands. For example, Brochure Display Ltd (Wye Estate, London Road, High Wycombe, Bucks, HP11 1LH. Tel 01494 444967) distribute arts and entertainment leaflets to several thousand tourist, academic or business sites in London, the Midlands and the South (but excluding Dorset and the West Country). Costs depend on the number of outlets chosen and for how long, with a minimum contract of four weeks.

In addition, there are 20 consortia of publicly-funded arts and leisure marketing organizations in mainland Britain, which provide subscribers and non-members with a variety of useful services, including leaflet and poster distribution. Each consortium operates in a different way: some are non-profit making, and each provides services appropriate to its region, whether urban or rural. For current details of the nearest consortium, consult the Marketing and Market Research Manager at the Arts Council of England, or the publicity department of the appropriate regional arts board, tourist board, local theatre, etc.

30.16 Proof-reading of publicity material

Proof-reading is vital. Whenever possible, material should be sent to all the parties involved, for proof-reading their own material.

30.17 Print quantities

The organizer calculates print quantities for posters, invitation cards, leaflets, etc. by asking each venue for the numbers required of each item (see 17.14). A certain number of each is usually provided free in the exhibition hire fee, after which they are charged at a standard run-on cost.

30.18 Road signs

Road signs provided either by the AA (Automobile Association Tel 0800 393808) or the RAC (Royal Automobile Club Tel 0800 234810) are a relatively cheap and effective method of advertising an exhibition locally.

Both motoring organizations, which now have centralized sales operations, need a minimum of six weeks' notice for arranging road signs. They work closely with the transport departments of local authorities, which decide how many signs are necessary for signposting each venue, depending on convenient parking, one-way systems, etc. The organizer may arrange signs for the whole tour, or ask each venue to do this locally. Unless it is a large complex, a venue can normally only be signed for one event at a time.

Yellow AA signs are more eye-catching but blue RAC signs are currently more economical. Costs are variable, and both organizations do a free survey of the area before producing firm quotations. The RAC's minimum charge (1995) is £169 plus VAT for 10 signs for 10 days, though usually more signs are required for a longer period. The AA has no minimum charge, but an average cost for 10 signs is £250 for a week or £400–£500 for a month. Even if a quotation is not acted upon, a record should be kept for future reference, once a venue has been surveyed.

30.19 Private views

Private views are a vital part of exhibition publicity, as even the arrival of an attractive invitation can set off the word of mouth – as people clamour to be invited – so important to the successful exhibition. It is rare not to hold some kind of celebration of the opening of the exhibition, and this usually only happens when funding is very restricted.

A private view will normally be held in the evening, from 6 pm to 8 pm, when refreshments are served either free or at a pay bar (depending on licensing arrangements). It is either preceded by or combined with the press view, depending on local conditions and convenience (see 31.12). Sometimes a celebrity will open the exhibition, in which case the press officer may need to be involved in order to arrange media coverage (see 31.13). If speeches are to be made, a dais and microphone may be necessary if the private view is held in a large space. Speeches should be kept to a few minutes' duration if guests are standing.

30.20 Invitations and distribution

A private view arranged by each venue may be part of the overall marketing strategy, in which case economies of scale will normally lead the organizer to arrange the design and printing of invitation cards, with matching envelopes if necessary, and the overprinting (see 30.12). The same card, with appropriate overprinting can be used for the press view and for entertaining by sponsors (see 30.21).

Each venue usually has a private view list, increasingly on database, consisting of the Friends organization, local dignitaries and politicians, societies, artists, writers, designers, teachers, etc. to which should be added special names for the exhibition concerned. This is supplied by the organizer, and typically consists of funders, sponsors, selectors, committee members, exhibitors, lenders and catalogue contributors (see 11.4, 34.7). Invitations are normally sent out two or three weeks in advance, or four to six weeks in advance for a special event.

30.21 Sponsors' receptions

Sponsors may wish to entertain at each venue's press and private views, or to hold their own private receptions, dinners, etc (see 11.4, 11.5). This may involve the sponsor's local manager making contact with each venue to negotiate the special arrangements, which might include:

- invitation cards, e.g. number required, information to be overprinted, envelopes;
- practical details, e.g. catering, cloakroom, parking, extra security, etc.;
- number of guests and – eventually – a guest list;
- location of drinks and food as permitted by insurance and indemnity;
- financial arrangements.

30.22 Advance ticketing

Advance ticketing is normally only undertaken for larger exhibitions at major venues with an admission charge and the expectation of a large number of visitors. It is arranged through a ticket agency, such as First Call or Keith Prowse, which charge commission to the purchaser.

30.23 Evaluation

It is important to evaluate the cost-effectiveness of the marketing strategy, locally and nationally. A brief report should be produced, which the sponsor may also be interested in seeing (see 6.1). Admission figures should be recorded, to trace the effect of publicity measures. Market research or a visitor survey can be commissioned (see 3.13), particularly if the sponsor wishes to evaluate the effectiveness of participation and is willing to fund it. Voucher copies of display advertisements will be provided by the advertising agency or by the newspaper if booked direct.

31

Press coverage

Joan Asquith

31.1 The press campaign

A press campaign should be an integral part of the marketing strategy (see 30.1).

How much press coverage an exhibition gets depends on sheer hard work, persistence and timing. Results are not achieved by merely sending out a press release or leaflet or by placing an advertisement in a local paper. It is most important to follow up all press releases and invitations to the media by telephone and personal contact. At the same time, luck and certain qualities help: for example, if the exhibition involves a famous and articulate living person, who likes publicity, has local connections, is willing to give interviews and is photogenic; or if the exhibits are also photogenic and have never been seen before.

The news media will need some specific local or national interest to justify a claim on space. The following guidelines may be helpful in getting exhibitions featured in the editorial (i.e. not the advertising) columns of the local, national and international media, the broadcast news and the arts, diary or events sections of newspapers or magazines.

31.2 Planning a press campaign

The more important the exhibition, the earlier the press campaign should be planned.

Up to two years' notice may be necessary in order to interest BBC TV's *Omnibus*, LWT's *South Bank Show* or Channel 4's Commissioning Arts Editor. Less notice, two or three weeks, is needed for local news programmes. Major features with national newspapers' weekend magazines should be arranged up to a year ahead. As competition becomes fiercer, so they will demand exclusivity. They may not get total exclusivity, but it is important that each magazine is offered a different angle and different illustrations, or it may prove impossible to work with them again.

Three to six months' notice of an event should be given to the 'glossy' monthly magazines such as *Vogue* which plan well ahead. Usually the features editor is the best person to approach first, or the arts editor for an art exhibition. Deadlines vary a good deal and can only be established by asking the particular journalist or editor. Names change frequently but are listed on the 'mast-head' of a magazine or as a 'byline' beside an article, or can be obtained from a press directory or by ringing the publication or programme. At least three weeks' notice should be given to daily and weekly newspapers.

31.3 Press consultants

A specialist press or PR firm can be engaged either for the first venue or preferably the entire tour. The best way to find one is either by recommendation or by consulting the press and marketing departments of an arts or heritage funding body or of a major museum or gallery.

The consultant will require a clear brief on the marketing strategy and the objectives of the press campaign well in advance of the opening date, in order to meet deadlines and to take account of any competition from other events.

After being briefed, most consultants will draft a proposal containing their recommendations for action and realistic objectives. Typical tasks to be proposed could include writing the press release, choosing press photographs and collating press packs, and organizing an advance press conference, photocall, press trip and/or press launch.

Typical objectives could include obtaining an agreed amount of editorial coverage in the national press: the arts or features pages of the broadsheet newspapers, glossy magazines such as *Vogue* or *Tatler*, educational, tourist or specialist magazines, inclusion on BBC

Radio 4's *Kaleidoscope* or Radio 3 talks, on BBC TV's *Newsnight*, or on a radio or TV Breakfast programme; or, if it is agreed with the venue that this will be done centrally, obtaining local press coverage.

The consultant will also submit an estimate of the fee or daily rate and normal disbursements, unless asked to work within a specified budget. A regular reporting system should be set up, as convenient. A final report should be submitted including the evidence of coverage achieved.

31.4 In-house press officers

Venues with their own press officers should be in touch with the press person appointed for the tour, and with the sponsor's press officer, if appropriate, so they can all work together to agree individual priorities and to avoid duplication.

31.5 Overseas showings

For major international touring exhibitions, an overseas press officer will need to be in touch with the UK equivalent at the first venue, or vice versa, depending on who originates the exhibition. Occasionally, journalists who have seen an exhibition abroad may place articles in the UK press unknown to the UK press officer. This can be useful, but it may also upset any exclusive arrangements for major features.

Agreements for major features should mention that the organizer's press officer will take all reasonable steps to maintain exclusivity.

31.6 Press lists

Normally, each venue will expect to distribute any press release, invitations, press packs and photographs to its own press list or database of contacts in local radio and television, local newspapers, events and listings magazines. This list will include the names, addresses, telephone and fax numbers of contacts known personally to the venue, who will be invited to events on the basis of their personal interest as well as corporate policy, and who should be identified and personally welcomed at press views.

The organizer should expect to complement this local coverage by arranging distribution of press information for national and/or specialist coverage as part of its umbrella publicity (see 2.5). Because of their detailed knowledge of the field, press consultants will be able to circulate this information to their own local or national contacts that are appropriate to the subject or nature of the exhibition.

A useful contact list for the arts press in England, Scotland and Wales is obtainable from the Press Office of the Arts Council of England (0171 333 0100), price £25 (1995) including postage and a half-yearly update. This includes the names and addresses of the national media, their various section editors and critics, and a list of useful freelance arts writers and their interests.

Comprehensive media directories with optional updates are published (1994 prices) by:

Pims: Complete Media Directory is available annually with optional monthly updates, price from £80 (£40 for back-issues), from Pims, Pims House, Mildmay Avenue, London N1 4RS. Tel 0171 226 1000. Towns (media listed by town), European and US press directories are also available.

PR Newslink: Editors in six separate volumes published annually covering national and provincial newspapers, consumer press, business and professional, broadcast media, freelance writers, price from £110 to £335, some with regular updates, from PR Newslink, 9/10 Great Sutton Street, London EC1 0BX. Tel 0171 251 9000.

PR Planner: Complete UK Media Directory is available annually, price from £155, from PR Planner, Hale House, 290-296 Green Lanes, London N13 5TP. Tel 0181 882 0155. European, US and Australian directories are also available.

Pims and PR Newslink also provide full media services, which include printing and mailing, faxing or hand-delivering press releases, press cuttings, photographic reproduction and captioning, collection/delivery, media evaluation and presentation, maintenance of media databases, media labels, press kit assembly, etc.

If overseas coverage is required for a major exhibition, the annual list of UK members of the Foreign Press Association can be obtained price £42.50 from the Secretary, Foreign Press Association, 11 Carlton House Terrace, London SW1Y 5AJ. Tel 0171 930 0445. Alternatively, a press release can be sent for the members' notice board.

31.7 Press packs

A specified number of press packs should be sent by the organizer to the venue well in advance of the latter's showing. A press pack can be an A4 folder, plastic sleeve or even a specially-designed folder with inside pockets, in which are placed all press releases, a leaflet/guide, a couple of postcards and/or press photographs. It is best kept as simple and lightweight as possible. Its purposes are:

- to hand out at a press view;
- to post to the press who have not attended the press view;
- to hand out to a journalist who arrives unexpectedly during the showing, e.g. at a weekend.

31.8 Press release

The organizer should provide each venue with a press release, either in a final form or as a draft that the venue can adapt to its own format. In either case, the press release should include the wording of any acknowledgements to the organizer(s) and sponsor(s). The letterhead to be used should also be agreed between organizer and venue.

Although one press release is the norm, different press releases can be provided for a major touring exhibition. The organizer may provide press releases on the exhibition itself, the sponsor, details of prizewinners, catalogue and other merchandise, to which the venue could add any appropriate local angles or stories.

Attractive merchandise may get editorial coverage in the national or local press, if specially promoted by the organizer or the venue in a press release circulated to shopping or women's page editors (see 32.11). An important catalogue may be reviewed in the books pages, if circulated with the press release to literary editors or the appropriate critic.

The following guidelines on drafting a press release include extracts from 'How to Write a Press Release', courtesy of Sue Rose, Arts Council of England:

- use A4 letter-headed paper, 1½-line spacing, one side only;
- give the day of distribution or the date and time of any embargo, e.g. 'Embargo: morning papers or 12 noon, Friday 14 April 1995';
- include the Press Officer's name and telephone number;
- state PRESS RELEASE;
- provide a non-gimmicky heading that states what the press release is about;
- number each page, add catchlines and put 'Ends' at the end of the text;
- place important facts at the beginning;
- give brief details (WHO, WHAT, WHEN and WHERE) in the first paragraph, including details of the venue for which the press release is being issued;
- subsequent paragraphs can include details of artist(s) or creator(s), the importance or context of the exhibition, a brief description of the exhibits and anything newsworthy or unusual;
- keep to a minimum the details of catalogue, education programme, selector, organizer and sponsor;
- a half-tone photograph can be incorporated, if desired;
- put tour details on a separate sheet if they are very long.

31.9 Press photographs

The organizer should obtain or commission photographs of the exhibits, artists, originators, lenders and any other relevant subject, and clear all uses for publicity purposes with any copyright owners (see 33.2). Original photographs should not be sent to the press, except by arrangement if they are required for a very special feature or cover story. Instead, duplicate photographs should be made: they should be good-quality 25 cm x 20 cm (10" x 8") glossy black-and-white prints or 35 mm or 13 cm x 10 cm (5" x 4") colour transparencies. They should be fully captioned with all necessary information and credits, including:

- the title of exhibition;
- any credit to a sponsor;
- description/title of the subject of the photograph, with name of artist where relevant;
- acknowledgement to lender;
- acknowledgement to the owner of copyright in the exhibit, if different;
- credit to photographer;
- the address for the return of the photograph.

Some photographers can incorporate captions into the duplicated prints.

Press photographs should be available several months in advance. This is particularly important for a major exhibition, which might attract national newspapers, magazines and television. However, it is equally important that venues have photographs sufficiently in advance for insertion in their own listings or to take advantage of local events and listings magazines (see 17.14).

Sufficient photographs should be ordered for the needs of the initial press campaign and the tour, although they can be recycled. Total quantity required can be estimated from the different requirements of each venue. The organizer should have original photographs of at least 10 per cent of the exhibits ready for duplication. It is increasingly necessary to have a good choice of sharp transparencies of the choice exhibits – famous or long-lost items or those not previously exhibited – because of new events magazines and TV stations and because of the improvements in colour printing.

Where it is necessary to commission photographs of the entire exhibition's works, e.g. for touring a large contemporary art show, it is a good idea to have at least three sets of originals – typically one for illustrating the catalogue, one for duplication by the publicity/press department for advertising and press use, and one for the organizer to retain as a back-up set and for checking the condition of exhibits (see 46.3).

31.10 Permitted reproductions

At the beginning of the tour, the organizer should circulate to each venue a list of exhibits and the photographic restrictions that apply to them for different purposes e.g. education, television or film, and newspapers (see 17.14). It is essential that each venue receives and adheres to this list, which should be handed to any photographer or TV crew covering the exhibition.

31.11 Press catalogues and/or exhibition guides

Catalogues and/or guides should be provided free and in advance, whenever possible, for the specialist press who might be writing in depth, and for radio and television producers making programmes. The media should be advised to use the press photographs supplied, not images from the catalogue which are not necessarily cleared for reproduction by the press (see 31.10).

31.12 Press views

The following guidelines on organizing a press view include extracts from 'How to Organize a Press Conference', courtesy of Sue Rose, Arts Council of England.

Like the private view (see 30.19), a press view arranged by each venue may be part of the overall marketing strategy for the exhibition. Organizer and venue should agree who arranges the mailing and who should be invited. The same invitation card may be used as for the private view (see 30.20) with appropriate overprinting, or more economically a personal letter if the local press is very limited. Check that the day of the week and the date correspond on the invitation.

When planning a date for an important press view, press conference or press trip from London to a regional showing, Mondays and Fridays should be avoided if possible. Journalists may not show up to a Monday press view because the venue has not been able to contact them to remind them the day before. Saturday papers may have limited news space (excluding weekend sections which may go to press ten days before) and a Friday opening is often too late for the Sunday papers.

It is worth finding out what other events may conflict, by ringing the press office of the Arts Council of England (which maintains a 'clash chart' for all London arts press events) or of a national museum. Outside London, a phone call to a friendly arts reporter or editor on the local newspaper will be sufficient. If an exhibition is very important, the press will come anyway, but it is worth checking in case attendance is poor: at least you – and more importantly, the sponsor – will know why.

Generally the best time to invite the Press to view an exhibition is between 11 am and 1 pm, or failing that at the evening Private View. Hospitality should be provided, and entertaining can be more elaborate if a sponsor is involved. If the aim of the press view or press conference is to get coverage in the following day's papers, then it should take place in the morning, as newspapers (certainly the nationals) tend to go to press about 5 pm.

The organizer, and the curator and/or director of the venue and the press officer should be present if an exhibition opening warrants a press view. If possible, the artists/creators, the selector and a sponsor's representative should also be present. All should wear lapel badges which clearly identify their role in the exhibition. They should be prepared to answer press questions of all kinds, especially about how much the exhibition cost and the value of the sponsorship, the nature of any special or controversial exhibits, expected admissions, etc.

The press officer should be present to give out the press material and catalogues at a press desk, where journalists are asked to sign in and receive the press pack (see 31.7). Signing in is essential both as a record and as a way of identifying and welcoming new faces, but it also ensures that those who did not attend can be sent further information, e.g. the press pack.

31.13 Celebrity opening

If royalty or a celebrity is present at the press view or opening the exhibition at the private view, the chances for news coverage are much improved, particularly if the event is in the earlier part of the day, to catch the deadlines for the following day's papers. When the royal rota (which strictly limits the number of press) is in operation, the press officer or curator should liaise with the appropriate royal press office for advice. Security is increasingly important on these occasions.

31.14 Filming and photocalls

For a major exhibition, it is sometimes necessary to arrange a special time for TV crews to film, e.g. earlier in the morning, but normally it is within the press view. TV crews may comprise between two and ten people. The list of photographic restrictions (see 31.10) should be given to each TV crew on arrival. If possible, a member of staff should always stay with a TV crew, for reasons of security, conservation and practical help. A TV crew will need access to power points for lighting, unless hand-held lights are specified by the venue.

A photocall is held to obtain publicity by inviting photographers or TV companies to photograph an exhibition in the making or a specially-staged event which is eye-catching or newsworthy, e.g. unpacking or hanging a rarely-seen exhibit or a visit by a distinguished guest or elusive artist. It is possible to arrange an 'exclusive' with the picture desks of one or two newspapers or TV channels before the press view, for useful advance publicity. Again, the earlier part of the day is more appropriate.

Photocalls are arranged by faxing an invitation entitled 'PHOTOCALL' to the picture desks of national papers or press agencies, freelance photographers and to forward planning in TV news. The invitation should include:

- date, time and place;
- description of the event;
- contact name and telephone number.

The exhibition press release should be faxed with it, for background information. The fax should be followed by a phone call to ascertain receipt (as they often get mislaid), their interest and acceptance and to discuss practical arrangements for parking, admission, lighting, etc.

It is useful for the organizer or sponsor to engage a photographer for publicity photographs for the monthly magazines or for the sponsor's house magazine or annual report. This is also an insurance, in case no-one turns up.

31.15 Hospitality and advance visits

Journalists are used to being wined and dined, especially if they make time to travel out of London. A sandwich and a coffee is not considered adequate hospitality for travelling several hours, often with a very early start and a late finish.

For a major exhibition, critics and journalists from the national and/or regional press can be invited to travel to the opening or to visit a site associated with the subject of the exhibition, e.g. the home town of the artist represented in a retrospective. Travel and hospitality is normally provided, with costs shared between the organizer, the venue and a sponsor. A good deal of 'chasing up' is necessary to fill the places, especially if the event is more than an hour's journey from London or if it clashes with something else. A press officer should accompany the journalists, providing press packs, catalogues and photographs on the journey and organizing refreshments, taxis, etc.

31.16 Sponsorship

Sponsors will be looking for acknowledgement in any editorial coverage, which should be sought by the press officer at every possible occasion. Some publications willingly credit a sponsor, space permitting. Others will not, under any circumstances.

ABSA, the Association for Business Sponsorship of the Arts, publishes guidelines on media crediting of sponsors and actively campaigns to persuade the media to credit them (see 11.8). It suggests that the sponsor should be credited in a stand-alone paragraph at the end of the piece, which should be additional to – and not at the expense of – the review of the exhibition.

If in doubt – and to avoid what could be a difficult situation if a sponsor is not mentioned – the press officer may do a special 'ring round' the media expected to be reviewing the exhibition, to ascertain the current situation. The response from this exercise should be retained for the publicity report.

A sponsor may offer help in kind from its own marketing or press department or advertising agency. Such expertise and advice can be very useful if it is tailored to the needs of publicizing the exhibition.

31.17 Evaluation

The cost-effectiveness of the press campaign should be assessed as part of the evaluation of the marketing strategy (see 30.23). Press cuttings from national newspapers and magazines can be obtained via a subscription with one of the following press cuttings agencies at costs starting from £50 for three months or 100 cuttings (1995 prices):

Romeike & Curtice: Hale House, 290–296 Green Lanes, London N13 5TP. Tel 0181 882 0155.

Durrants Press Cuttings Ltd: 103 Whitecross Street, London EC1 8QT. Tel 0171 588 3671.

The International Press Cuttings Bureau: 224 Walworth Road, London SE17 1JE. Tel 0171 708 2113.

Tellex Monitors: 210 Old Street, London EC1V 9UN. Tel 0171 490 8018. This company also records broadcasts.

32

Publishing and retailing

David Breuer

32.1 The gallery supermarket

> You only have to walk into any art gallery these days to see that the real action is in the shop. Most people want to like art . . . but face to face with a great painting they feel like gate-crashers at a Mayfair reception. Back in the gallery supermarket, they can happily check out the product like so many pin-ups, wallet in hand, the big spender in control again (Michael Dibdin, Dirty Tricks)

What applies to art galleries and permanent displays also applies to museums and temporary exhibitions. Organizers have no excuse for ignoring the 'gallery supermarket'. It helps to pay for their exhibitions. It should also reassure them, if the experience of the exhibition has made visitors want a souvenir to recall their visit or information to learn more about what they have seen.

Merchandising for exhibitions should be relatively straightforward. That it is not, is attested by the large stocks of unsold and forgotten exhibition catalogues and related material that nestle in the store-rooms of most museums and galleries. Not only does it cost money to store this material, but also the income-earning potential of the exhibition has been miscalculated. Even for the disappearing breed of galleries that treat publications as part of expenditure on exhibitions, from which any income is a bonus, it must be a disappointment that many visitors have gone away without the souvenirs or information that the organizer has spent valuable time and money on preparing.

32.2 Existing merchandise

For permanent collections, related merchandise has a long period of commercial viability. In contrast, exhibitions are temporary and purely ephemeral high points in a venue's year, and merchandise reflecting an exhibition will have a similarly ephemeral viability at this location. A tour extends the period of viability and puts the merchandise in front of the diversity of visitors that different venues attract, but it also brings its own problems in gearing up each venue in turn to promote and sell unfamiliar material.

Books and other items that are concerned with or reflect similar periods, styles or subject areas can all be introduced as merchandise. There should be a range of items and prices predicated on the visitor profile for the exhibition (see 6.7). The organizer can locate and order such stock via publishers' catalogues, book and gift fairs and wholesalers, but will normally come across a wide variety of published material while researching an exhibition. As a matter of course, loan forms should ask the lender where any reproduction can be obtained, if the exhibit has been reproduced in poster, postcard, video or other published format (see 36.7). All this information should be carefully logged, so that venues can be provided with full details of existing publications and other merchandise (see 17.5).

Actual arrangements for the supply and return of merchandise must be made directly between suppliers and venues. With sufficient warning – two months is adequate in most cases – publishers and distributors are generally happy to supply such material at normal discount rates (generally about 35 per cent for books) on a sale-or-return or consignment basis for the duration of the exhibition, since it enhances the possibility of sales for publisher and gallery at no extra financial risk for either party.

Sale-or-return is the preferred option for temporary exhibitions where maximum impact has to be achieved from the outset. A supplier provides an agreed quantity free of charge at the outset, takes back any unsold stock within an agreed period and invoices the gallery only for the amount sold. Operating on a consignment basis means that the institution must pay up-front and only afterwards does the supplier reimburse it for any unsold stock. An exhibition already represents a significant capital outlay, and an organizer may find it impossible to spend more on stock, especially where there may be commercial risk.

32.3 Material produced specially for the exhibition

Such general merchandise can act as support material for items specially produced for the exhibition. Researching such material should prevent the unwitting duplication of similar material that already exists, and will help to identify the new items that the market can sustain. However, creating merchandise for a temporary exhibition is a risk, and such merchandise must be undertaken with the same rationale for a return on investment that lies behind, say, calendars in which there is a highly proscribed period when the product will sell. The cost of merchandising for an exhibition frequently exceeds the cost of mounting the exhibition, and therefore requires a sophisticated investigation into the exhibition's marketability and potential visitors.

The first stage of merchandising is to establish the style of the proposed exhibition, the type of visitors it is intending to attract and what these people will expect in terms of supporting material they can take home (see 3.6). Organizer and venues must be ruthlessly aware of the commercial limits to any exhibition's potential and seek to generate maximum revenue out of merchandise created within those limitations. They should share their intentions and ambitions with the shop staff, and take advantage of their perspectives and experience. To take an extreme example, producing without grant-assistance an expensive catalogue raisonnée of an unknown local artist who has an exhibition in your gallery may be nice for the artist but may also be commercial suicide because the market and the expectations of visitors to the exhibition will not be matched or satisfied by the product on offer.

In producing a substantial publication, the organizer should bear in mind that no more than 5–10 per cent of active visitors are likely to purchase. 'Active' means those that, of their own volition, visit the exhibition, i.e. not school-children or other visitors who come as members of an organized group. If the expected active profile for the exhibition is less than 20 000 visitors, a catalogue in traditional book form is unlikely to be economically viable. To make such a calculation for a touring exhibition, the organizer should ask each venue the following questions (see 17.16):

- what number of active visitors do you anticipate for your showing?
- what is your average turnover per visitor when you have a temporary exhibition?
- do you have a sales point in the exhibition gallery?
- if no, would you be prepared to provide one?
- are visitors able to browse through stock, without asking to see it?

It is possible to establish a contractual obligation with participating galleries, whereby they guarantee to purchase an agreed quantity of catalogues with the exhibition (see 16.4). This spreads the financial load and the relative risk amongst all the venues. However, this is not popular amongst venues which may be cash-starved and reluctant to fill their own stores with unsaleable merchandise.

32.4 Co-publishing

If the expected number of active visitors is too low to make a catalogue economically viable, one option is to sell the concept to a commercial publisher. Generally, the organizer will underwrite the financial risk of the venture, and the publisher will increase the print run to enable the book to have a general trade presence. This reduces the unit cost and allows the book to be sold at a price that is acceptable to both general bookshop and exhibition purchasers. The publisher will generally control all trade distribution and pay the organizer and/or copyright holder a royalty on sales realized.

A commercial publisher will tend to alter the fabric of a catalogue to make it more appealing to a general readership. When negotiating with commercial publishers, the organizer must ensure that their publishing styles are appropriate to the subject and that the final product has not been commercialized too much to alienate the more highly-defined buying public at the exhibition itself, from whom the gallery will generate the majority of its revenue.

A suitable publisher will have a publishing profile which enables the proposed publication to fit within its existing list in a way which will not surprise the general trade. Negotiations must commence at least a year before publication. Since publishers generally produce two catalogues a year of forthcoming titles, the contracts and at least a proposed cover design must be finalized at least six months before publication. Royalty arrangements can be complicated by many variables, and expert advice may be necessary.

If the organizer is publishing a catalogue itself, a commercial distributor will normally be contracted to sell the book to the trade. A distributor will not pay royalties on their sales, but will generally buy an agreed number of copies and pay up-front at an agreed discount. The size of the discount will depend on the quantity purchased, and will generally be 50–60 per cent on the retail price, which is set by the organizer.

Especially with a one-person exhibition, a catalogue is often co-published with the artist or the dealer or commercial gallery. This might be in the form of a contribution in cost or in kind to part of the publication, notably colour illustrations. The artist or dealer will then take a proportion of the print-run to sell or distribute as part of their promotional materials. Agreement on pricing is as important as with a commercial publisher: in this case, the catalogue may be sold below cost price or, if artist or dealer is aiming at a targeted distribution, then it may be even given away free (see 14.2).

32.5 The exhibition catalogue

The traditional purpose of the catalogue is to list and describe all works included in an exhibition. The extent to which this basic function is extended and elaborated will depend on the overall aims of the exhibition and the expected size and commitment of the exhibition's visitors. For a major scholarly exhibition, the catalogue has always been regarded as of first importance, providing a detailed commentary on all the exhibits and an illustrated record which will be of interest even to those who have not visited the exhibition. Contributing to the research on individual objects in this way can often be an important factor in a lender's decision to make exhibits available, and will be emphasized in the request for the loan (see 37.1).

However, the chief purpose of the publication has increasingly become to continue or extend the discussion of the subject of the exhibition, as the 'book of the exhibition' rather than a simple catalogue of exhibits. For many exhibitions, a short introduction with selected illustrations are all that is required to supplement the simple list of works. For exhibitions of this kind, the catalogue and poster have very occasionally been combined to provide an attractive broadsheet. Any further expenditure will not be justified, unless costs can be shared and sales guaranteed by a number of venues.

32.6 Postcards

If the production of a catalogue is problematic or commercially unjustifiable, there is a temptation to support the exhibition with a selection of two-dimensional merchandise such as posters or postcards. Such a temptation is entirely understandable given the relative ease and cheapness of production of these items and the high profit margins that can be achieved through sales. A card is often produced for private view use. However, this too can be dangerous. The minimum quantity for economically viable postcard production is 2000 units. A selection of just six images will therefore leave the gallery with 12 000 units for sale which in themselves will not constitute a sufficiently impressive use of the exhibition's content to engage a buying public.

Production of large-volume items such as postcards should therefore also be entered into with a potential distributor in mind. There are many specialist postcard publishers and distributors around who will assess the potential of the exhibition images available and will buy at trade price a quantity of the print-run for sale to other shops. If the images are not interesting enough for a distributor to purchase, it is unlikely that they will engage a museum or gallery's public sufficiently to justify the level of purchaser volume required by the postcard's print-run for the duration of the exhibition.

If the image reproduced remains in copyright, then royalty arrangements for all merchandise have to be entered into and included in costing the viability of any merchandising project (see 33.7). Permissions and approvals must also be obtained for use of the image in the proposed selling format. Some artists, for example, do not take kindly to the idea of their work being used in a merchandising context (see 34.9). Since it is not cost-effective to regularly audit individual postcard sales, royalties are in this case generally paid in advance on an agreed print-run. Although permission and royalty rates differ and are all negotiable, the benchmark figure is generally 7.5 per cent of the maximum possible gross income from the print-run. So, for 2000 units of a postcard selling at 40p, the copyright holder will receive £60 in advance of production and a further amount on any reprint.

32.7 Posters

A poster should obviously contain an immediately arresting image to draw the public's attention. For publicity purposes, it will be produced relatively cheaply on minimum grade paper (see 30.9). However, it is easy to run-on on high-grade art paper as many or as few copies of the poster as are required for re-sale during the exhibition. If the strength of the poster in sales terms lies in the image it shows rather than the information it imparts, it is also a simple process to remove at the run-on stage the printer's plate containing the extraneous wording. In this way, support material can be produced at low unit cost in quantities satisfactory to the sales potential of the exhibition.

32.8 Other material

Books, posters, postcards are the minimum one can acceptably produce to support an exhibition and, in the case of the commercial potential of many exhibitions, they will suffice. To move from two-dimensional to three-dimensional material is more problematic in view of the different production strictures involved, but the same contingencies apply as in the production of a single postcard: can the necessary investment be recouped sufficiently quickly either through sales at the exhibition venue or through other outlets, to justify production. In producing unusual but sympathetically appropriate items to support an exhibition – clothing, masks, furniture or whatever – one is limited only by one's imagination and by the parameters of the commercial potential of the exhibition.

32.9 Production checklist

Print costs will be affected by quantities, paper quality and general design and make-up, number of illustrations in colour and black-and-white, etc. Because of the high cost of print and paper, it is essential to plan printing to meet likely demand and avoid wastage. Competitive quotations should always be sought.

Once the shape and contents of the exhibition have been established, it will be possible to consider the detailed make-up of the catalogue: number of illustrations, approximate length of preliminary sections (i.e. acknowledgements, introduction, chronology, bibliography) and catalogue entries, index, etc. Heavy cover papers, high quality paper for inside pages and colour reproductions will all increase costs. Unusual page sizes are likely to prove expensive in paper, and an outsize publication will not in any case sit easily on most book shelves. Unusual design solutions, boxed sheets, envelopes of individual cards or special bindings can be very attractive, but are seldom commercially successful.

Designer and printer should be chosen at least six months before the required publication date (see 8.5 for a sample publishing schedule). General content and design of the catalogue should be decided with the designer (see 19.1). A specification should be drawn up, giving size, number of pages or approximate number of words, number of illustrations (black and white or colour), paper quality, cover paper and print, and binding. It can be useful to base the specification on an existing publication similar to the proposed catalogue. This first specification will be used to obtain comparative quotations from printers, and changes in the make-up of the catalogue may be made later. Printers are then invited to submit quotations. Several quotations should always be sought.

The size of the print order will depend on estimated sales at the exhibition, on tour and with an allowance for free copies to lenders, sponsors, selector or author.

An ISBN (International Standard Book Numbering) number should be printed on the back of the title page or, if this is not possible, at the foot of the page itself. It should also appear at the foot of the outside back cover if practicable, and at the foot of the back of the jacket if the book has one; if neither of these alternatives is possible, the number should be printed in some other prominent position on the outside of the publication. A leaflet describing the ISBN procedure is available from the ISBN Agency, Whitakers, 12 Dyott Street, London WC1A 1DF.

32.10 Pricing

The trade or wholesale price is usually calculated as follows: a basic unit cost is calculated from all preparation (author's fees, reproduction fees, design, printing) costs divided by the number of copies printed. Beware the common practice of keeping the unit cost down by printing a longer run than the market justifies.

This unit cost can be reduced as a matter of policy, if the organization is willing to subsidize the item to make it more attractive to buyers or to make its educational content more generally available. Sponsorship or grant-assistance can also be specifically targeted to reduce the unit cost.

The unit cost can equally be increased as a matter of policy, if the organizer feels that the product is sufficiently commercial to realize a profit on every copy sold.

The retail or sale price will depend on the following: a commercial publisher will mark up unit costs by a factor of five, in order to cover its costs and to provide a reasonable profit margin for the bookshops to which it is selling on. The retail price of a commercial publication will probably break down as follows: trade discount 50 per cent, manufacturing cost 17 per cent, royalties 10 per cent, overheads 10 per cent, and marketing/distribution 8 per cent, leaving a net profit of 5 per cent to the publisher. Museums and galleries may not have to mark up to quite the same extent, if their overheads and other expenses are not attributed to the publication, or if royalties are not paid (see 9.9).

Libraries will often place standing orders which can be a regular and useful source of income, but they will expect a discount of at least 40 per cent on the normal retail price in the shops. Post and package will be added to the discounted price. Any publisher or distributor should be aware of such standing orders and the discounts offered.

A special exhibition price is normally offered during the period of the exhibition and its tour, which should include any mark-up that each venue is able to retain as an incentive for it to sell the publication. Even if the venue's percentage on income from sales disappears into the general coffers of the venue or its local authority, the record of sales can still be used to reduce the apparent cost of the exhibition in any report to a governing body.

32.11 Retailing

The main thrust of a product's commercial potential lies in its sale at the exhibition venue. Estimates may be realistic in relation to the numbers of visitors, but actual sales may be lower because no effort is made to sell. The exhibition sales point must therefore be designed or arranged in a manner that maximizes the associational appeal of the product available. As far as possible, the exhibition should be installed so that visitors leave by way of the shop. Ideally, an exhibition should be designed to incorporate a sales outlet to be part of the overall exhibition installation.

Much revenue is lost through the integration of exhibition-specific merchandise with the general products on sale in a museum or gallery shop. The organizer will often take great care in the design and layout of an exhibition to maximize the impact of the presentation of its content. The same care should also apply to the shop, for which a context for exhibition merchandise must be established to enable the presentation of the product to be perceived as an extension of the exhibition. If the exhibition is of, say, surrealist art, then an entertaining shop design and product presentation can be created that is as idiosyncratic and subversive as that of the exhibition, thereby creating a retail environment for visitors that engages through association and invites the same level of interaction as does the exhibition. For less obvious subjects, the extension is more difficult, but with a bit of imagination a defining link can be formed between exhibition and exhibition shop. Imagination is the key to all successful merchandising and exhibition retailing and is crucial in maximizing potential revenue from whatever material is produced for sale.

Merchandise should be marketed in a way that enables the exhibition's visitors and any other potential buyers to be aware of its existence, e.g. ensuring that any press release about the exhibition will also list its merchandise (see 31.8). A catalogue that is truly an important reference document with sales potential after the exhibition has closed, should be sufficiently commercial to exist independently of the exhibition it has been designed for. It can be marketed through more subject-specific areas of the media than the arts pages that the exhibition publicity will be aimed at. Shopping pages, book reviews, lifestyle colour supplements can be targeted in order to safeguard the merchandise from relying exclusively on the exhibition venue for generating sales. If co-publishing or distribution agreements have been entered into, then they will provide a link into trade awareness and purchase of the product thereby allowing its dissemination into a public sales space away from the site of the exhibition itself.

33

Reproduction and copyright

Nicholas Sharp

33.1 General principles

For most exhibitions, some agreed reproduction will be involved, most commonly for publicity or promotion, often for catalogues and postcards, and occasionally for merchandise connected with the exhibition. For touring exhibitions, it is important that the organizer's obligations and legal responsibilities towards the lender, owner or copyright-holder are not compromised by any shortcoming of the venues; equally, it is important that venues are not placed in a difficult position because of any failure on the organizer's side.

In all cases, the written consent of the lender will be needed. This includes exhibits where copyright never existed or has expired or where the proposed reproduction is a 'permitted act' in copyright legislation.

Where the lender is not the owner of the exhibit (e.g. if the lender is a museum which has the exhibit on loan from the owner), the consent of the owner will also be needed if the owner has imposed restrictions on reproductions as a condition of its loan.

In cases where the exhibit, or photograph of the exhibit, is protected by copyright, the written consent of the copyright owner must normally be obtained before any reproduction is made.

Any statutory moral rights of artist/creator must be respected.

Credits/acknowledgements to lender, artist/creator and photographer must be agreed. Contracts will be required to formalize agreements with lender, owner and/or photographers on the one hand and publishers and/or venues on the other.

33.2 Copyright

Copyright prevents original literary, artistic, dramatic and musical works and published typographical editions from being reproduced or issued to the public without the consent of the copyright owner.

Copyright is normally first owned by the artist/creator even where the work is commissioned by someone else. The exception is work created in the course of employment, where the employer will own the copyright.

The copyright owner may transfer or assign copyright to someone else, in writing.

In the UK, copyright normally lasts for 50 years after the death of the artist/creator. It will soon change to 70 years because of an EC Directive.

Ownership of copyright is distinct from ownership or possession of the exhibit itself. A gallery or a museum will rarely own the copyright of the objects on display. Photographs of exhibits are separate copyright works distinct from the exhibits themselves.

Certain 'permitted acts' of reproduction are permitted without infringing copyright, eg:

- photographs of sculpture and other craft works on permanent public display;
- fair dealing for criticism or review or for reporting current events, if acknowledgement is given;
- photographs of artistic works for the purpose of advertising the sale of the work.

The Copyright, Designs and Patents Act 1988 changed the law in the UK, but the old law will still be relevant for earlier works, e.g. the commissioner will be the owner of the copyright for commissioned photographs taken before 1st August 1989. Specialist advice may be needed in cases of doubt.

33.3 Moral rights

Moral rights were introduced by the 1988 Act, and exist independently of copyright. They are retained by the artist/creator (or his/her heirs) and cannot be assigned or transferred. They normally last for the same term as copyright.

Under the right of 'paternity', artists/creators have the right to be identified when the work is publicly exhibited or commercially published. Paternity right must be asserted by the artist/creator, usually by including appropriate wording in contracts with galleries, publishers, etc. Assertion normally only affects the person to whom it is given or to whose notice it is brought.

The right of 'integrity' gives artists/creators the right to object to 'derogatory treatment' of their work. This might include altering the work, e.g. cropping an image or reproducing it in a different context in an advertisement.

These statutory rights can be supplemented or varied by contract wording.

33.4 The organizer's responsibilities

Identify any exhibits which are to be reproduced and to which copyright might apply, e.g. where the artist/creator is still alive or has been dead for less than 50/70 years, or where photographs are supplied by the lender.

Obtain the consent of the copyright owner(s) to any reproduction(s) (if the lender is the copyright owner, see 33.9; otherwise, see 33.10).

If the lender is not the owner of the exhibit, ensure that the lender is free to authorize the requested reproduction(s); if the lender cannot authorize, agree with the lender who should contact the owner to obtain consent.

Agree with the lender the extent of permitted reproduction(s) and embody this in the loan agreement (see 33.9).

Request photographs from the lender or if agreed make arrangements for new photographs to be taken. This should normally include ensuring that the copyright of any new photographs is assigned to the lender (see 33.11).

Agree credits/acknowledgements to artist/creator, lender, owner and photographer as appropriate.

Advise venues of any restrictions on reproduction, any special requirements and any assertion of moral rights. Embody these in the hire agreement or advance information (see 33.12).

Label all new photographs with the copyright symbol, name of copyright owner and date of first publication.

Return photographs to the lender at the end of the tour, unless otherwise agreed.

33.5 The lender's responsibilities

Notify the organizer of the copyright in the exhibit and in any photographs to be supplied.

If the lender is not the owner of the exhibit, ensure that the lender is not restricted by its contract with the owner from authorizing reproductions. If there are restrictions, agree with the organizer who should contact the owner for consent.

Agree with the organizer the extent of permitted reproduction(s) of an exhibit and any photograph supplied (see 33.9).

Specify wording for credits and acknowledgements to accompany reproductions.

Supply existing or new photographs to the lender. If new photographs are to be taken, ensure that the copyright is assigned to the lender (see 33.11).

Label all new photographs with the copyright symbol, name of copyright owner and date of first publication.

33.6 The venues' responsibilities

Observe any restrictions on reproduction or any special requirements imposed by the organizer (see 33.12).

Ensure that, if any new photographs are permitted, the copyright is assigned to the lender (see 33.11).

Label all new photographs with the copyright symbol, name of copyright owner and date of first publication.

Ensure that proper credits and acknowledgements are given, and statutory moral rights are respected.

33.7 Obtaining copyright clearances

Where the consent, or licence, of the copyright owner is needed in order to permit reproduction, this should be in writing signed by the copyright owner and the organizer. No particular form is required, and a clearly-expressed exchange of letters will suffice, dealing with:

- form of reproduction;
- number of copies (if restricted);
- duration of permission;
- any quality requirements, e.g. approval of colour quality;
- ownership of copyright in any new photographs; and
- any fees or royalties (if appropriate).

Example 2, Copyright consent (see 33.10) contains a suggested form of words which can be adapted as necessary, including where the exhibit or photograph is out of copyright but the owner's consent to the reproduction is still needed.

33.8 Dealing with photographers and publishers

If any new photographs are required, suitable contractual arrangements will need to be made with photographers, to ensure that there is no doubt as to the ownership of the copyright.

If the photographer is an employee of the lender, then the lender will own the copyright, and nothing more need be done. If not, the copyright should normally be assigned by the photographer to the lender. Example 3, Copyright assignment (see 33.11) can be adapted as necessary.

If reproductions are to be published by a publisher as a third party, a publishing contract will be needed, including suitable wording on copyright (see 32.4).

33.9 Example 1: Loan agreement

The following comprise some possible clauses to be inserted into the contract between lender and organizer, see 37.5):

1 Name of Organizer
2 Name of Exhibit
3 Name of Lender
4 Name(s) of the Copyright Owner(s)
5 Subject to the Organizer obtaining the written approval of the Copyright Owner(s), the Organizer may reproduce the Exhibit and any photographs supplied by the Lender for the following purposes (the 'permitted reproductions'):
  (a) illustration in catalogue;
  (b) reproduction in the following publicity material: (here state poster/invitation card/press release as applicable);
  (c) reproduction in the following sales material: (here state posters/reproductions/postcards/other merchandise as applicable);
  (d) reviews;
  (e) archive providing a record of the exhibition and consisting of a non-lending and non-income-generating reference and research resource.
6 The Organizer will pay the Lender the following fees/royalties for permission to reproduce the Exhibit as above (here state fees/royalties, how calculated, when payable, etc).
7 The Lender will supply on loan to the Organizer the following photographs (here state which photographs, identified by names of photographers, negative numbers, etc.), which the Organizer will use only for producing the permitted reproduction(s), and the Organizer will ensure that all photographs are returned to the Lender as soon as practicable after the end of the exhibition.
  and/or
  The Organizer may arrange for the Exhibit to be photographed in connection with the permitted reproduction(s), provided that the Organizer ensures that the copyright in any new photographs is owned by the Lender.
8 The Organizer will ensure that any permitted reproduction(s) are of good quality, and will supply the Lender with a copy for approval prior to printing.
9 The Lender warrants to the Organizer that, unless otherwise specified in clause 4 above, the Lender is the owner of the copyright in the Exhibit and any photographs to be supplied by the Lender, or is otherwise authorized to grant the right to make the permitted reproductions.
10 The Lender agrees that the Exhibit may/may not be photographed by the public using existing ambient lighting.
11 The Organizer will ensure that all permitted reproductions will bear the copyright notice/credit as follows (here state wording of credit).
12 The Lender hereby notifies the Organizer that the artist/creator of the Exhibit has asserted his/her right to be identified as such whenever the Exhibit is exhibited in public or whenever the permitted reproductions are published. The Organizer agrees to bring this assertion to the attention of the Venues.

33.10 Example 2: Copyright consent

The following is an example of a document for use when the lender is not the copyright owner.

I the undersigned confirm that I am the owner of the copyright in the Copyright Work specified below ('the Work') and HEREBY CONSENT to the following reproduction of the Work:

1 the Copyright Work
2 permitted reproduction
3 manner of reproduction
4 number of copies
5 territory
6 duration
7 credits
8 fees or royalties
9 description of any photographs to be supplied
10 special terms (if any).

The above is to be governed by English (or Scots) laws. The above consents are given to you personally and may not be assigned or transferred by you to any other person without my written approval.

It is a condition of the above consent that the copyright in any photographs or other permitted reproductions shall belong to me absolutely.

Please confirm your acceptance of the above terms by signing and returning the enclosed copy.

The organizer should sign a copy and return it to the

copyright owner. Note that this form can be adapted for use when the exhibit or photograph is out of copyright but the owner's consent is needed.

33.11 Example 3: Copyright assignment

The following is a sample form for use when new photographs are taken.

In consideration for the fee(s) to be paid to me for the Work summarized in the Schedule below, I the undersigned hereby assign and transfer to the Assignee named below the copyright (including where relevant the present grant of future copyright) and all rights derived therefrom in the Work throughout the world and in all languages for the full period of the copyright and all renewals and extensions thereto.

I warrant and confirm that I am the owner of the copyright in the Work, that the Work is original to me and has not previously been published; and that I have not made any assignment or purported assignment to any third party of any of the rights hereby assigned.

I hereby assert my moral right to be identified as the creator of the Work whenever the Work is published in any catalogue, publicity material, postcard or other material:

Schedule

The Work:..
Assignee [name and address of the person to whom the copyright is assigned]
Signed:...
Name:...
Address:..
Date:..

33.12 Example 4: Permitted reproductions

The following possible clauses may be inserted into the hire agreement between organizer and venue or subsequent advance information, (see 16.2, 17.14, 31.10).

1 Name of Venue
2 Name of Organizer
3 Name of Exhibit
4 Name of Exhibition
5 The Venue may use any photographs of the Exhibit supplied by the Organizer for the following purposes (the 'permitted reproductions'):
   (a) reproduction in the following publicity material: (here state poster/invitation card/press release as applicable);
   (b) reproduction in the following sales material: (here state posters/reproductions/postcards/other merchandise as applicable);
   (c) reviews of the Exhibition:
   (d) archive providing a record of the exhibition and consisting of a non-lending and non-income-generating reference and research resource.
6 The Venue will pay the Organizer or, at the Organizer's request in writing, the Lender or Owner direct the following fees/royalties (if any) for permission to reproduce the Exhibit (here state fees/royalties, how calculated, when payable, etc).
7 The Organizer will supply on loan to the Venue the following photographs (here state which photographs, identified by names of photographers, negative numbers, etc.), which the Venue will use only for producing the permitted reproduction(s), and the Venue will ensure that all photographs are returned to the Organizer as soon as practicable after the end of the showing.
   and/or
   The Venue may arrange for the Exhibit to be photographed in connection with the permitted reproduction(s), provided that the Venue ensures that the copyright in any new photograph is owned by the Lender.
8 The Organizer warrants to the Venue that the Organizer is authorized to grant the reproduction rights as above.
9 The Organizer agrees that the Exhibit may/may not be photographed by the public using existing ambient lighting.
10 The Venue will ensure that all permitted reproductions will bear the copyright notice/credit as follows (here state wording of credit).
11 The Organizer hereby notifies the Venue that the artist/creator of the Exhibit has asserted his/her right to be identified as such whenever the Exhibit is exhibited in public or whenever the permitted reproductions are published.

34

Working with artists

Hilary Lane

34.1 The artist as exhibitor

This section follows the normal convention of using the term 'artist' to mean also crafts-people, photographers and other exhibitors who regard exhibits as in some way representative of their *oeuvre* or working practice.

There are important distinctions between the work of living artists and objects in museum collections, which directly affect how artists and curators regard exhibitions and the exhibits in them.

Exhibits by living artists are usually for sale, and the artist may expect, realistically or otherwise, that efforts will be made to sell.

Artists may be interested in an exhibition's impact on their careers in the immediate future, while a public collection may be more concerned about the effect of the tour on the safety of objects in their possession.

Exhibits in an exhibition of the work of living artists may not exist at the time that the exhibition is negotiated. In some instances, exhibits may be commissioned directly for the exhibition; in many others, the exhibition will be expected to contain work created as part of the artist's normal practice over the period leading up to the opening of the exhibition. This may lead to the unexpected.

34.2 The contract

All arrangements regarding the selection of the exhibit(s), insurance and transport should be confirmed in writing. The NAA Public Exhibition Contract published by AN Publications (PO Box 23, Sunderland SR4 6DG. Tel 0191 514 3600) provides a basis for an agreement between organizer and artist, and includes a section devoted to touring. The agreement should set out the artists' responsibilities too. The exhibit(s) selected should be available at the date and time agreed in advance, as should other information, photographs, biographical material, artists' statements, titles, dimensions, hanging instructions which the artists have agreed to provide. The Exhibition Payment Right should be paid where appropriate, and should be quite separate from expenses, framing costs and fees for workshops and other activities.

If the artist is represented by a dealer or commercial gallery, arrangements for borrowing material may be made through that gallery (see 14.4). The arrangements for sales should be worked out in detail in advance (see 35.7). The price for each exhibit should remain the same at each gallery, so commission and VAT arrangements should be brought into line, and the division of commission between the various parties (dealer, organizer and venue) should be worked out in advance (see 35.6).

34.3 Selection of exhibits

Artists will need to know well in advance if their work is going to be used, especially if a lengthy tour is envisaged. Eighteen months' notice will allow time to consider other commitments.

When borrowing from artists, and especially when working with them on a touring exhibition, it is important to predict areas where there may be concern or difficulty and to involve the artist(s) in their resolution. This is best done face to face, after an initial letter, and then confirmed in writing.

It is wholly reasonable for an artist to be working in areas as yet unfamiliar or uncomfortable to the general public, but galleries will know from experience how far such work can be shown in public, and it remains illegal to show some images. Difficulties should be anticipated well in advance and discussed fully between the artist, the organizer and the venues if an exhibit is likely to be controversial or to contravene regulations governing public exhibition. Sensitivity is necessary on all sides: the artist should anticipate any problems to be faced by those exhibiting and caring for the exhibit; the organizer should agree a strategy with the artist to help the venues to respond to comment and controversy, and the venues should be fully briefed and ready to defend the artist's intentions.

34.4 Display considerations

Artists will also be concerned to see that their work is physically presented in the best possible way. How an exhibit is to be displayed should be discussed in detail and confirmed in writing, with instructions for hanging and presentation prepared where necessary to help the venues to show it as far as possible as the artist intended.

It may not be possible, where a number of venues are concerned, for artists to be present. If it is not possible to hang or place an exhibit precisely as indicated, the artist should be consulted at the earliest possible stage. The artist is usually best able to solve problems of this kind, and will agree to modifications and compromises if the facts are given. They may wish to see gallery plans and display arrangements.

If, for reasons of space, any exhibit will not be shown at a venue, the artist must be informed in advance and the exhibit packed and stored carefully.

34.5 Packing

Artists should be asked to provide detailed handling and packing instructions. For a touring exhibition with a number of transits where the cost of insurance is to be met by the organizer and/or the venues, the organizer should provide and pay for suitable packing. Artists may prefer to do this themselves, but it is preferable that they advise the organizer on suitable arrangements, especially if specialist crate-making is required (see 45.2).

34.6 Insurance

The organizer is the intermediary between artists and venues, and has a duty of care for the exhibits borrowed, not only to the artist for the safety of the exhibits, but also to the venues to ensure that exhibits are packed, transported, stored and displayed to professional standards. The organizer should arrange to collect the exhibit from the artist and to return it after the tour. The exhibit should be insured 'nail-to-nail' by the organizer and/or venues. In some instances, it may be more convenient for the artist to deliver and collect the exhibit, but care should be taken that this does not invalidate the terms of the insurance or indemnity cover (see 40.3). Any damage should be reported to the artist as soon as possible, and not be mended or restored without prior permission from the artist and the insurer or indemnifier.

34.7 Publicity

The organizer should give the artist a list of the venues with dates, contact name and phone/fax numbers. Similarly, the organizer should give the venues a list of all the artists whose work is in the exhibition, with addresses and phone/fax numbers.

The organizer should ask each artist to provide a mailing list of people they would like to be invited to previews, lectures, workshops or to be informed that the exhibition is on (or to be sent a catalogue, if an overseas address). This list should be given to each venue (see 30.20).

Artists will be concerned that their work is seen by critics, collectors and purchasers for public collections. As far as possible, the organizer and the venues should try to attract such people: it will not always be possible, but the attempt should be made (see 31.6).

Local radio stations are often willing to interview artists, which can help to publicize the exhibition. Such opportunities should be discussed beforehand with the artist and arrangements made with the radio station for an interview during a private view or subsequently if the artist visits the venue for a lecture or a workshop.

34.8 Interpretation

Artists will be concerned to see that their work is shown in the best possible way, including the context in which it is to be shown. Early discussion should include details of the exhibition, size, scope and rationale. An artist will be interested to know which other artists' work will be shown. Their view of their own work may be different from that of the selector, particularly if a category informs the selection. For example, some artists may need to be persuaded of the reason for including them in an exhibition of 'pop art' or 'outsider art', if they have never viewed their work in that light.

Artists will be interested to know who is going to be writing about their work, and may, if appropriate, be able to recommend a writer, poet, critic or collector who knows their work and could write about it. Where artists do not wish to write about their own work or may not be the best people to do so, it may be worth considering an interview. The organizer must ensure that all written material is intelligible to the intended visitors at all the venues, and the agreement with the artist may include the possibility of the organizer or a scriptwriter re-drafting, simplifying or expanding on a text, without losing the essential content or message (see 22.2).

34.9 Copyright and reproduction

As with any other lender, artists should be consulted about the use of reproductions of their exhibits in the catalogue or on cards or posters (see 32.6). They will usually own the copyright on the images, with legal protection against unlicensed use (see 33.2). They also have moral rights (see 33.3).

34.10 Education programmes

The organizer and each venue should consider the possibilities for commissions, lectures, workshops within the exhibition or at a nearby college or university. However, not all artists wish to speak or run workshops. Time away from the studio must be paid for. Arrange fees and expenses in advance, so that they can be included in the exhibition budget (see 25.8).

35

Selling exhibitions

Philip Hughes

35.1 The fixed type of selling exhibition

Touring exhibitions which offer work for sale generally divide into two main types. The 'fixed' type allows exhibits to be purchased during the tour, but they are not available for collection until the tour has ended, which might be a disincentive for the buyer. The range of exhibits and the catalogue list remains fixed throughout the tour, but later venues may be left with less saleable work.

35.2 The replenishable type of selling exhibition

The other main type of selling exhibition allows exhibits to be bought and taken away immediately or at the end of the showing. Whole or part of the exhibition may consist of work for sale, in which case the appearance of the exhibition may change considerably over the period of the tour. Alternatively, saleable works may be provided in a discrete selection separate from the core exhibition. The organizer supplies new exhibits to restore the displays at the end of each showing.

35.3 Features of a selling exhibition

As with all touring exhibitions, a selling exhibition needs to be flexible in order to adapt to different venues. However, display systems and installation have to take into account supplementary requirements.

Exhibits must be easy of access, so that they can be removed without difficulty or damage to the exhibit that is being sold or to those that remain (e.g. in a display case from which the work sold is being removed). Installation and lighting should also take into account an extra need for visibility, if invigilating staff are distracted from their security role by the procedures of selling, with which they might be unfamiliar.

At the outset, the organizer must assess the feasibility of selling, according to the expectations of the exhibitor(s), the type of exhibits, their prices and the likely venues for the show. A selling exhibition will appeal to venues which have to generate an income from their exhibition programme. In turn the organizer will be more likely to contact and give preference to venues with a good record of selling. The organizer may need sales to generate income to support the exhibition, and the likelihood of sales may also have been one of the main reasons for an artist agreeing to lend work for a long tour. Venues that do not normally sell from exhibitions may have difficulties in promoting and processing sales, and their visitors may not expect exhibits to be for sale.

Innovative work can and does sell, and price often reflects an existing demand elsewhere which has been created by the quality of the work.

35.4 Promoting purchasing

Design and finish of all printed material should be to the same high quality for any other touring exhibition. How forthright the sales message should or can be will depend on the circumstances of individual venues. A venue which does not normally sell will need to spell out to the visitors to the exhibition that some or all of the work is for sale.

Evidence of selling and purchasing can stimulate interest in buying. For sales, a printed sticker which spells out that the exhibit has been sold can be attached to the label of any sold items which remain on display for even a short period.

For purchasing, the wording of interpretive material can be specially geared towards this possibility. With the owner's permission, exhibits borrowed from a long-standing owner can carry the phrase, 'in the collection of . . .' or 'purchased by . . .', especially where the person concerned is well-known. There may be occasions when a caption by a borrowed exhibit may set out, in that person's own words, why she bought the exhibit, what it means to her, the pleasure of owning, etc.

Signs, information panels and exhibit labels are vitally important for reinforcing the sales message, especially where jargon can be avoided. The organizer should provide signs appropriate to the exhibition and to the venues, e.g. 'Some of these works are for sale. Please ask at the desk', 'Enquiries with regard to purchasing exhibits should be directed to . . .', 'All items are for sale and may taken away immediately', etc.

It is important to state when purchases can be collected by the buyer. It is also important to agree what methods of payment can be accepted. Credit card facilities may be necessary where it is possible for a buyer to take away a purchase immediately. The limits of cheque guarantee cards mean that payment by cheque can be a problem at weekends. The Arts Council of Wales' Collector Plan offers interest-free credit for purchases over a certain amount at many galleries in Wales, and many Regional Arts Boards in England (see 10.7) now run similar schemes as an incentive to buying.

In a one-person exhibition, an information panel can include a curriculum vitae, a statement of ideas and other introductory or background material, to stimulate interest in the artist and an appreciation of the work. Smaller captions on specific exhibits – or individual exhibitors in the case of a mixed exhibition can be placed alongside the works on display. People buy for many different reasons, and may buy not only the object but also its story, e.g. its significance in the production of a person who makes a living doing this sort of thing. Detailed information can help to justify or provide reasons for buying.

As an alternative to panels and captions, high-quality portable information (in colour where possible and appropriate) is also good for sales. Leaflets on exhibitors or on selected key pieces can be drafted, as above, to promote the idea of buying.

35.5 Prices

In addition to the name of artist/maker, title, catalogue number and other information normally placed there, the label must clearly identify each exhibit that is for sale. Preferably, the price shown on the label should be that which a buyer would pay, i.e. it should not have 'plus VAT' in small letters! In an exhibition where some exhibits are for sale and others are not, the latter should carry the phrase 'Not For Sale'. When an exhibit is sold during the course of the tour, the old label with its 'sold' sticker can be left for subsequent showings, in order to encourage sales.

If the price is not given on the label, a printed price list should be designed and displayed to the same standard as the rest of the exhibition. If the price list is only available at the desk, this should be clearly visible, so that visitors do not have to ask to see it.

As part of the contract with each artist, the organizer will normally agree with the artist and/or dealer a selling price for each work that is for sale. This price should remain in force for the entire tour, but it is not unknown for values to increase over a tour. If a price has to be increased, the new price should come into effect only after adequate notice and on a date agreed between the organizer and the artist and/or dealer. Preferably the new price should not come into effect before the end of the current showing, so that the organizer has time to change the labels and other documentation, and advise the venues and the insurers.

35.6 Commission

The organizer should agree an overall rate of commission for the tour with the artist and/or dealer, based on standard practice for exhibitions of a similar nature (a percentage ranging from 30 per cent to 50 per cent of selling price excluding VAT is normal). Because a venue does not own the exhibits it is selling, it is in effect handling sales arrangements on behalf of the artist (or dealer). The commission is therefore a charge to the artist or dealer and is defined as a percentage of the selling price, e.g. a 30 per cent commission on an exhibit selling at £300 would give the organizer's gallery £90.

For the position on Value Added Tax, it is best to take advice direct from Customs and Excise, but the notes on the NAA Public Exhibition Contract are also useful (see 34.2). Either VAT will be paid on the total selling price (i.e. similar to a retail operation) or VAT on the commission only (i.e. the organizer acts as agent for the exhibitor). In the latter case, the prior agreement of Customs and Excise is necessary.

As part of the hire agreement, the organizer should agree a sub-division of this overall rate of commission for the tour with the venues participating in the tour (see 16.5). There are varying practices for these split commission agreements, and many are on an *ad hoc* basis and by individual negotiation. The most common arrangements are:

- a 50/50 split: for example, on an overall rate of commission of 30 per cent, 15 per cent would be retained by (or returned to) the venue and 15 per cent by the organizer; or
- a set percentage for the venue: for example, where the rate is set at 10 per cent of the selling price, this percentage would be retained by (or returned to) the venue, which would leave 20 per cent to the organizer if the overall rate of commission was 30 per cent.

In the 'fixed' type of selling exhibition (see 35.1), later venues may have little chance of selling, because the more attractive exhibits have already been sold. They may therefore expect a higher proportion of the commission, and the organizer should consider a sliding scale. Sales at an early showing might divide commission equally (e.g. 15 per cent to the organizer and 15 per cent to the venue), whereas a later showing might give a larger proportion to the venue (e.g. 5 per cent to the organizer and 25 per cent to the final venue).

The organizer's budget and accounts will include sales income based on the full commission rate for sales if the exhibition is shown at the organizer's premises. For sales at the other venues, income will instead be based on the split rate. In both cases, due allowance must be made for VAT.

35.7 Administering sales

Even where the primary aim may not be sales (e.g. an exhibition which is designed as an educational event and from which sales are a by-product) or even where only some of the exhibits are for sale, procedures must be clear so that venues know what to do if a visitor expresses an interest in buying.

A unique number is essential for the purposes of identification and for easy sales administration. No two exhibits should have an identical reference number. Where exhibits are available in several versions or in limited editions, an extended identification number will be necessary, e.g. number 95.b will indicate that it replaces 95.a which has been sold. Such numbering should be as clear and accessible as possible.

Contracts of sale vary, but they should include matters such as terms of sale (payment details, deposits and the timing of the payment of the balance) and collection.

The organizer should maintain throughout the tour a master list of all exhibits that are for sale, with their numbers and financial details (i.e. artist's price, commission, VAT and selling price).

Each venue should be sent an adapted copy of this list, in order to record details of sales. As sales occur, the venue should enter details onto its copy of this Sales Record, and the organizer should be notified immediately, so that it can update its master list and revise the insurance list (see 40.3). At the end of a showing, the organizer will use its master copy as the basis for calculating and issuing an invoice to the venue, for exhibition sales less the venue's agreed commission. The organizer should inform each exhibitor of any sales and ask at the same time for an invoice requesting payment for the selling price of the exhibit, less the commission agreed for the organizer and the venue.

With the replenishable type (see 35.2), the organizer should inform exhibitors of sales as they occur, either by letter or by telephone followed by written confirmation, in order that speedy replacement may be made. All replacement exhibits must be supplied to the organizer, so that they can be checked and added to the master list before joining the exhibition at the next showing.

36

Borrowing exhibits

Margot Coatts

36.1 The organizer as borrower

It is now a well-established practice for exhibitions that are organized within the public sector to tour to several venues after their initial showing. This initial showing normally takes place at the premises of the organizer, i.e. the institution directly responsible for all aspects of borrowing exhibits and subsequently returning them.

In the case of exhibitions organized by National Touring Exhibitions, an area museum council or other providers of touring exhibitions (see 12.3, 12.4), borrowing exhibits is still the responsibility of these organizations, even though they may not show the exhibition on their own premises.

Both types of organizer are the official borrowers for the purposes of a loan. The organizer will liaise with any lenders to the exhibition and will be responsible for the safety of the exhibits.

36.2 Borrowing from museums

It is also well established that public collections and academic institutions lend works of art and other objects to each other, nationally and internationally, on a reciprocal basis without charging administrative fees or expenses, although transport costs for the loan and travelling expenses for any courier *are* charged to the organizer.

In most cases, reciprocation will not be immediate or formally defined. However there will be a willingness to lend when approached, partly because of the possibility of needing to borrow in the future, and partly because loans to exhibitions help public collections to meet their obligations to provide access to their holdings.

Within the museum profession, organizers can therefore take for granted a fair amount of co-operation and common interest. Museums will often have a well-developed and formal lending procedure (see 37.1).

36.3 Sources other than museums

The same level of co-operation, or formality of procedure, will not necessarily exist when organizers approach corporate or private collectors, specialist archives and libraries, churches, colleges, universities, manufacturing companies, or even artists and craftsworkers.

Individuals in these groups are less conversant with loan procedures and the considerable obligations they can place upon the lender as well as on the organizer. An organizer should approach such lenders with proper respect and understanding, and not with the attitude that it is imperative for them to 'hand over the goods' for the sake of cultural projects. Extra attention should be given to infrequent lenders to help them to understand the organizer's plans, procedures and methods.

Negotiating loans outside the formal museum and gallery network can be costly. More staff time is used on visits and for follow-up work and cataloguing. Phone and fax costs can be higher, and all details concerned with insuring, packing and transporting exhibits from non-museum locations can prove time-consuming (see 39.1, 40.4, 45.2, 46.2). In addition, some lenders may wish to levy a charge or may request a donation for their time and trouble.

Artists, craftsmen and designers, along with manufacturers, might appear to be more easy-going at the outset, but in practice they rarely turn out to be so. They are, in fact, the group with which the organizer often needs to be most precise in relation to the final selection of exhibits, and most clear in respect of the dates and duration of the loan under negotiation (see

M	A	R	G	O	T
C	O	A	T	T	S
Exhibition curator Writer		13 Evelyn Road Ham	Richmond Surrey TW10 7HU	Phone and Fax	081 948 5897

J. K. Elward, Esq.
Managing Director
Best Museum Products Ltd
20-30 Gallery Road
Manchester M15 6HU

12 August 1994

Dear Mr Elward

I have been commissioned by Cheltenham Art Gallery & Museums to curate a retrospective exhibition entitled **'Robert Welch - Designer-Silversmith';** it spans Robert Welch's interesting 40-year-long career from 1955 to the present day. The exhibition will include examples of metalwork in silver, stainless steel and cast iron, industrial products including lights, plus their prototypes, designs and sketches. The project is supported financially by the Crafts Council and by private donations.

We are seeking loans from public and private sources, and I am writing to ask if I may visit to see the silver wine and water flagons commissioned from Robert Welch in 1975 for use in your company's boardroom. I would like to consider these items for exhibition, if the proposal is viable.

The exhibition will open at Cheltenham Art Gallery in June 1995, and transfers to the Holburne Museum, Bath, Manchester City Art Gallery and Birmingham Museum and Art Gallery in 1995-6. There will be an accompanying, fully illustrated, catalogue and associated educational events. Formal loan arrangements will be carried out by Mary Greensted, Keeper of Museums, and her staff at Cheltenham, who will supervise handling throughout.

I look forward to hearing from you at my office address above.

Yours sincerely

MARGOT COATTS
Curator: Robert Welch - Designer-Silversmith

Figure 36.1 Sample initial letter to lender(s)

34.2). Lenders who wish suddenly to withdraw items (usually for well-argued reasons) are hard to dissuade, even though such action would prejudice the integrity of the exhibition and catalogue and would require alterations to the packing and insurance inventories and arrangements.

36.4 Research

A written outline or brief (if not a drawn plan of the various sections of the exhibition) should be held on file and periodically updated (see 4.4). This outline or brief should be accompanied by a 'wish list' of key exhibits and their locations. Working in this way will define the priorities for visits and avoid wasting too much time on irrelevant quests. The organizer's job is to build an exhibition by primary research and accumulated knowledge, both of which progress in tandem with each visit to view potential exhibits.

Despite having to pay attention to plans, dates and budgets, the organizer should remain endlessly curious and tenacious in the search for exhibits. Prize exhibits are still to be found in the unsuspecting hands of the descendants of artists, in country churches, in factory storerooms, in craftsmen's garages and in county archives. Few exhibits come ready catalogued and 'squeaky clean' from a modern museum environment, and securing unusual loans for public exhibition presents a series of diverse but worthwhile challenges.

Where potential exhibits are identified from published sources, the organizer should make every effort to see them in person. Each object seen will need to be considered for:

- its contribution to the organizer's research on the subject;
- its part in the story that the exhibition will tell;
- its visual appeal, individually and in combination with other exhibits;
- its condition, and whether it is fit for exhibition and robust enough for a tour;
- its availability for loan;
- packing requirements, and any access restrictions for packers and shippers.

The organizer must be fairly confident about the historical and aesthetic significance of a potential exhibit before making a visit in order to assess its condition and availability for loan. The exhibitable condition of a potential exhibit can often be improved by professionals, if the organizer has the lender's permission and the budget to carry out conservation, cleaning, mounting or framing (see 39.2). A final decision will depend on the importance of the loan to the exhibition, as well as cost factors, and cannot be taken until most of the potential exhibits have been surveyed.

As the official borrower, it is also the organizer's role to be aware of physical aspects of the show and relate these to potential lenders. These matters include:

- the exhibition's size and the space required to show it;
- the sequence and context of the exhibits;
- security arrangements;
- mounting and design arrangements.

36.5 The initial enquiry

Draw up a 'long list' of suitable exhibits. Mark this list with categories of preference, and amend as research progresses.

Check the locations of each exhibit on the 'long list'. Check that all contact names and addresses are correct and up-to-date, by telephoning and writing to colleagues, publishers, salerooms, etc. Treat all private names and addresses in confidence.

Send an initial letter of enquiry to potential lenders (see Figure 36.1). This letter should include the following points:

- the name and nature of the exhibition;
- the specific exhibit(s) or class of exhibits for which the loan is sought;
- the dates and venues;
- the immediate request, e.g. to arrange a meeting to view, to examine a specific item, to survey a number of potential exhibits or to ask for reference photographs or slides;
- the role of the person signing the letter.

If there is no reply, send a second letter by recorded delivery, telephone for the information, and/or seek other contacts.

36.6 Visit

Telephone for an appointment after receiving a positive response. The appointment should be made at the convenience of the lender, but the organizer should be sure to ask for sufficient time to examine the item, make notes and take photographs. Obtain permission in advance for taking photographs, stating that they are for research or record purposes only.

Check research references and be well briefed. When meeting a potential lender, take photocopies of any published references and illustrations, which may prove invaluable in finding an exhibit in store, especially when dealing with an individual who is unfamiliar with your request.

Visit and view the exhibit(s). Preferably using a standard format (see 46.2), record on the spot as many of the following details as may be relevant, and photograph items as necessary:

- medium and support;
- dimensions;
- signature or maker's mark;
- physical condition;
- environmental conditions (see 43.2);
- display requirements, e.g. new mounts, frames, fixings, etc;
- packing requirements;
- any access stipulations, for packers and their vehicles.

Report on the visit. Write and file a report under the name of the potential lender. The report should include details of each exhibit, any recommendations for remedial conservation, an assessment of its relevance to the exhibition, and any verbal agreement made with the owner/lender. File with the report any photographs, plus outline cataloguing data (see 7.2).

36.7 Requesting loans

Draw up a shortlist of loans to be requested. When approximately three-quarters of the 'long list' has been seen, the organizer should decide, usually in a planning meeting with colleagues, on the allocation of budgets for transport and insurance, conservation, mounting and design, with reference to specific loans (see 19.1, 39.2, 40.1, 53.4). This will effectively confirm, or alternatively rule out, the viability of applying to borrow specific exhibits.

Draft the loan form (see Figure 36.3). It is often necessary for organizers to revise their institution's standard loan form to suit each new exhibition subject. The data required for silver, for example, is very different from that for paintings. Of the many details normally included on the standard loan form, it is imperative that a question be included asking who is the legal owner of the exhibit, as this information is essential in the event of an insurance claim (see 40.3). It might ask whether the exhibit has been reproduced, and where (see 32.2); it might request consent for reproduction (see 33.9). See also 37.3 and the 'Loans In, Loans Out' in Museum Documentation Association, *Spectrum*. MDA, 1994.

Draft a letter of request. The letter should act as a covering note for the loan form, setting out in plain language the exhibit that is being requested, for what reason and for what period. It should include any requests to photograph, clean or mount the exhibit. It should also give assurances regarding insurance and transport (see Figure 36.2).

36.8 When loans are agreed

Check returned loan forms. The returned loan forms provide the basis for the following:

- list of valuations;
- requirements for mounting and display, to be conveyed to designer, technical staff and venues (see 19.1, 43.3);
- acknowledgements in catalogue and on labels;
- ordering of photographs or arranging new photography for catalogue or publicity purposes (see 33.1);
- precise addresses for collections and returns, for preparing transport lists, which are used for arranging transport and/or obtaining quotations (see 53.2);
- updating cataloguing entries, e.g. new information on materials, provenance, dimensions, dating, signature, etc (see 7.6).

Inform lenders of insurance arrangements. Valuations taken from the loan forms are used for preparing lists which are passed to insurers. In some cases, lenders will ask for advice on valuations, and the organizer may be able to help with obtaining valuations from salerooms. Lenders should be supplied with copies of insurance documents as necessary (see 40.5).

Inform lenders of transport arrangements. The organizer should notify them well in advance of the dates and times when collections and, in due course, returns are planned (see 53.11). Alternatively, the organizer should notify lenders of the names of the carriers who will be doing this work, in which case, the carriers will normally make the final appointments with lenders to collect and return exhibits.

36.9 Once exhibits have been collected

Acknowledge safe delivery. This can be either a simple signed receipt or, more commonly nowadays, a photocopy of a completed and signed condition check docket (see 46.1).

Invite lenders to the first private view and supply them with catalogues (see 30.20). Some lenders, even anonymous ones, require additional invitations, leaflets and complimentary catalogues; the organizer should order enough of each to meet this eventuality. Keeping a log of catalogues given or sent to lenders is essential.

Send 'thank you' letters and a tour schedule. Shortly before the close of the first showing, the lenders should be sent letters of thanks stating the week the exhibits will be returned. The letter should include a list of where and when the exhibition is showing, together with the forthcoming private view dates. The address labels used for this mailing can be run off and sent to the venues, to ensure that cards for each private view reach all concerned (see 30.20).

2 February 1995

Dear

Robert Welch Designer Silversmith: Letter of Request.

Thank you for the help you have given to Margot Coatts in the research for this exhibition. I enclose loans forms for the object/objects we would like to borrow. I do hope you will be able to lend to this major retrospective of Robert Welch's work.

The exhibition opens in Cheltenham on 10 June 1995. It will then tour till March 1996 to the Holburne Museum, Bath, City Art Galleries, Manchester and Birmingham Museum and Art Gallery.

The loans will be fully covered by insurance at all venues and in transit. Transport will be by a fine art carrier approved by our insurers and items will be handled only by trained museum staff. All loans will be displayed behind glass unless otherwise indicated and security at all tour venues meets standards laid down by the National Security Adviser for the Museum and Galleries Commission. Environmental conditions at all tour venues are regularly monitored and come up to the standards laid down by the Victoria & Albert Museum.

There are two copies of each form; one should be returned to me, the other is for your records. Please let me know if you have any queries.

With many thanks

Yours sincerely

Mary Greensted

Mary Greensted
Keeper of Museums

Figure 36.2

LOAN REQUEST FORM

EXHIBITION: Robert Welch, Designer - Silversmith

TOUR DATES AND VENUES:

LENDER

Name:

Address:

Telephone: Fax:

Contact name:

EXHIBIT

Title/description:

Marks/Inscriptions:

Date of design:

Date of making:

Other exhibitions/literary references:

Dimensions (in mm)

Insurance value:

I am willing to lend the above work in accordance with the conditions outlined in the original letter of request.

Signature ....

Date ....

Signature ....
(For Cheltenham Art Gallery & Museums)

Date ....

Figure 36.3 Loan request form

37

Larger museums as lenders

Hilary Bracegirdle

37.1 Introduction

Most large museums, including the national museums and galleries (NMGs, i.e. those funded by central government, see 41.1), are active lenders, with lending policies which ensure that their exhibits are seen in new contexts or by different publics, with the added benefit of encouraging new research.

However, the work involved in preparing and administering the loans must be integrated with their own programme of exhibitions and gallery displays. Likewise, the benefit of increased public access to the exhibit must be offset against the risks involved in packing, transportation, handling, installation and display.

Loan requests are usually subject to a more formal approval procedure, and more stringent conditions may be attached, than may be the case with other lenders. Exhibition organizers should therefore plan well in advance, contact the lenders for advice as soon as possible, and be aware of the implications for the exhibition budget.

37.2 Preliminary enquiries

Most major museums need at least six months' notice in order to complete the necessary stages in agreeing and preparing a loan. However, discussions should start far earlier.

The first stage should be to contact the Registrar (if there is one) or the curators concerned, in order to discover the application procedure and the general conditions that are attached to loans. There may be a policy of not lending certain categories of exhibits, for example, or to touring exhibitions with more than a certain number of venues. The organizer must also establish whether all the potential venues are likely to meet the security, environmental and display conditions.

Even though the plans for the exhibition may still be fairly fluid, the next stage is to contact curatorial staff for advice about the selection and general availability of exhibits for loan. There may be reasons which rule out a particular exhibit from the outset: it may be promised elsewhere, be too large to dismantle or be too fragile to travel; conservation costs (which are usually borne by the lender) may be prohibitive; there may be a restriction placed by the donor on whether the exhibit can be lent; the exhibit may be central to the lender's own display or even an advertising campaign.

Early discussions should mean that the organizer will know if exhibits are available that are central to an exhibition and, if not, give the organizer an opportunity to find an alternative source. Loans from large museums, and particularly NMGs, can take longer to arrange and be more costly to both lender and organizer than loans from smaller museums. Alternative lenders should be considered even before a major museum is contacted, so that it is not approached for an item which a smaller and nearer museum would be happy to lend.

A third stage is to visit to inspect any exhibits under consideration, ideally with the exhibition designer. This will give an idea of their packing and display requirements as well as how they fit into the exhibition (see 36.6). Display methods (stands, cradles for books, etc.) may need to be discussed with the lender, who may wish to supply these or to approve the organizer's design.

Unless all the intended venues are regular borrowers, the organizer should also contact the Museums Security Adviser (MSA) at an early stage (see 42.1).

37.3 Formal request

The lender's literature should indicate the deadline for receiving requests and the form that these should take.

Some museums expect requests to be addressed to the director, others to the curators concerned, and others to the registrar. A formal request should include:

- the title of the exhibition;
- venues and dates;
- the organizer's name, address and telephone and fax numbers;
- the name, address and telephone and fax numbers of a contact at each venue;
- scope of the exhibition;
- list of exhibits requested, quoting museum numbers;
- reason for inclusion of the exhibits;
- who is responsible for preparing the exhibition and its costs;
- who is responsible for transport between venues and its costs;
- whether a catalogue will be published.

In many larger museums, the supply of photographs and purchase of reproduction rights is handled by another department, which should be contacted as soon as possible (see 33.4). It can take time to schedule photography along with other work on the exhibit, and often payment is required before work can proceed.

37.4 Consideration of request

There may be a delay of several weeks before the organizer hears whether the museum is prepared to lend.

A condition check will be carried out on each exhibit, and curators and conservators will decide whether it is fit to travel or if a reasonable amount of conservation will make it so (see 39.1). The lender will also need to consider the request in the light of existing commitments and the resources available to conserve, pack and administer the loan.

The approval procedure for many large museums may include submitting all recommendations for approvals or refusals to lend to one or more committees. High-value exhibits or exhibits with restrictive covenants may need to be referred to a meeting of trustees, which may only take place infrequently.

Many large museums will send a facilities report to each venue (see 38.2). In other ways, lenders may ask venues to indicate the environmental conditions which they can provide, and will subsequently specify requirements in relation to light, temperature, humidity, etc., for each exhibit (see 20.3, 43.3).

NMGs submit details of all potential loans to the MSA, who will visit each venue or send a questionnaire, in order to confirm that reasonable measures are in place to protect the exhibits from fire or breaches of security. If any arrangements are insufficient, the MSA will usually recommend measures which will allow the loan to proceed. For NMG loans, the organizer must arrange transport which meets the criteria specified in the Government Indemnity guidelines. When loan conditions have been met and when a venue has been approved by the MSA, an NMG is empowered to grant an indemnity (see 41.2).

37.5 The loan agreement

When curatorial, conservation and security checks have been satisfactorily completed, the lender will send a formal agreement to lend, which should set out the organizer's responsibilities and indicate the likely costs. Any problems should be discussed as soon as possible, as most difficulties can be resolved by negotiation. The lender may attach specific requirements at this stage, concerning security or environmental conditions (see 41.4, 53.6).

The organizer must ensure that all the venues meet the conditions of loan, and must inform the lender immediately should a venue drop out or another be added. Lenders should be advised of any changes in dates, temporary closures or other alteration to the tour arrangements. If there is a delay between two showings, the organizer should agree with the lender whether the exhibits should be returned to the lender or whether they should be stored securely.

During the approval process, the lender will decide whether the complexity of the arrangements or the value or fragility of the exhibits means that one or more couriers will be required to accompany the exhibits in transit and to oversee condition checking and installation and dismantling at the venue (see 51.4). Depending on the nature of the risks which might reasonably be anticipated, the courier may be a curator, conservator, member of the registrarial staff or an object technician. Large museums will routinely share a courier to accompany loans from different departments within the same museum or from different museums. For some touring exhibitions, a courier may be sent on the first leg only and the exhibition may then continue unaccompanied if no problems are encountered.

37.6 Costs covered by the organizer

The organizer must include in the exhibition budget adequate provision for the costs of borrowing exhibits, and decide in advance how these costs might be allocated between venues. Costs may include some or all of the following:

- mounting of prints or paintings;
- framing;
- cradles for books and other supports for other exhibits;
- packing;

- transport/shipping agent;
- photographs/transparencies and reproduction fees;
- travel, accommodation and expenses for couriers;
- insurance or minimum liability.

Lenders usually cover the costs of conserving the exhibits and administering the loans. However, where an exhibit requires considerable conservation in order to travel, and where a lender cannot absorb these costs, the organizer may have to include these costs in the exhibition budget (see 39.2). The lender should inform the organizer immediately if this is the case.

Because lenders will be incurring significant costs, they must be informed as soon as possible should any exhibit be withdrawn from the list of exhibits or the whole loan be withdrawn. In such an eventuality, the organizer should be prepared to pay a contribution towards actual costs incurred by a lender.

38

Facilities reports

David McNeff

38.1 What are facilities reports?

Facilities reports are documents which conveniently gather together practical information relating to aspects of proposed loans. Their purpose is:

- to facilitate the processing of loan requests by curatorial, conservation and security staff at the lending institution;
- to replace lengthy exchanges of correspondence between a lender, an organizer and the venues;
- to avoid expensive and impractical site-visits to the venues.

They represent an important element in the consideration of loan requests (see 37.4). Lenders that issue facilities reports normally regard the return of the questionnaires as essential for the further review of the loan request. A venue that is slow to complete and return its form may hold up a final decision for the whole tour until the lender has received and reviewed the details of every venue.

38.2 Alternative procedures

Facilities reports can be issued in two ways: by lenders or by the organizer.

As part of their established standard procedure for the review of loan requests, lenders may issue facilities reports when they acknowledge receipt of loan requests. A lender will send the forms via the organizer or direct to the venues, for the venues to complete and return. The advantage of this method is that lenders sometimes feel happier using their own forms. Its disadvantages are that venues may have to complete many different forms and that the loan review process may take longer.

As soon as possible in the loan review process, the lender can issue facilities reports directly to each of the venues, or the lender can give the facilities reports to the organizer, asking for them to be distributed to each of the venues. The organizer should forward any facilities reports received from the lender to each of the venues as quickly as possible, and relay to the venues the information given by the lenders as to the completion and purpose of the facilities report.

Alternatively, facilities reports can be produced by the organizer. In anticipation of lenders' demands for further detailed information, an organizer may ask its venues to complete or compile facilities reports, which can then be sent with the request to borrow exhibits. The advantage of this alternative is that the venues can complete the facilities report as soon as the booking is confirmed, so speeding up the process of asking for loans. Its disadvantage is that the lender may require additional information, although this should be avoided if a standard format is used (see 38.3).

The organizer should devise a form for the tour and send it to each of the venues as soon as possible. The lender should refer in the first instance to the facilities report prepared by the organizer, and send its own facilities report to the organizer and/or venues only if the organizer's form lacks information vital to the review of the loan request.

38.3 Standard format

Facilities reports generally take the form of a questionnaire. Individual institutions may prefer to devise their own facilities reports to address particular concerns, or they may choose to use an existing standard format. This second option has the following advantages:

- it uses a document which is recognized and accepted by many museums, and familiar to all parties in loan arrangements;

- it helps to avoid confusion, misunderstandings and delay; and enables an organizer to prepare in advance a single document which venues can complete and which can then be used with all loan requests connected with a particular exhibition.

Standard formats include that produced by the American Association of Museums Registrars' Committee Standard Facilities Report and that published in 1995 by the United Kingdom Registrars' Group (UKRG). The following checklist summarizes points to be covered in a facilities report.

38.4 Content

Facilities reports are specific to a location rather than to an event. They relate to each venue, concerning themselves with the environments in which exhibits will be stored or displayed, or through which they will pass, and with the handling arrangements being proposed for those exhibits. The actual use within the exhibition of each exhibit requested will instead be explained and justified in the formal request to borrow (see 37.3).

A facilities report will generally take the form of a questionnaire in which simple yes or no answers lead on to requests for further details. Some of the more complicated requests have been left in the following, but most of the simpler prompts have been omitted, to save space.

38.5 The building

- Are the premises a purpose-built gallery or museum?
- At what date were the premises originally completed?
- What is the main construction material/method (see 42.2)?
- Is there any ongoing construction work?
- Is any construction work planned during the period of the proposed loan?
- Are there routine inspections for rodent, insect and micro-organism problems: in the building as a whole; in the exhibition areas; and in display cases (see 47.2)?
- Are plants or cut flowers used on the premises?
- Have the premises ever been assessed by the Museums Security Adviser; if so when (see 37.4)?
- Does the institution have a disaster plan (see 7.16)?
- In the event of an emergency, who would be authorized to remove items from danger (see 27.8, 44.5)?
- Is smoking permitted anywhere in the building? If yes, state where and how this is controlled (see 27.17, 48.4).

38.6 For each exhibition area used

- What are the dimensions?
- When was this exhibition area opened or last refurbished?
- What methods are used to secure framed works to walls and partitions?
- Are there weight restrictions for this type of hanging system?
- What is the maximum load capacity of the floor?
- How is the number of visitors monitored?
- Is the consumption of food or drink ever permitted?
- Is smoking ever permitted (see 27.17)?
- Are events (concerts, dance, etc.) ever staged (see 26.12)?
- Are barriers or other methods of physical protection used for material on display (see 42.5)?
- Please supply details of how the exhibition area is managed during an exhibition with regard to routine lamp replacement, cleaning procedures, checking of equipment, etc.

38.7 Access

- Are there restrictions to vehicle access to the premises (low archways, tight corners etc.)?
- Is there a loading bay? If no, where are loans delivered? If yes, is it covered?
- Are there restrictions on the size and weight of vehicles?
- Are access, loading, storage and exhibition areas on the same level/floor?
- Is there a goods lift? If yes, what are its interior dimensions and load capacity? If yes, does it serve all access, loading, storage and exhibition areas? If there is no goods lift, or if the lift does not serve all areas, how are loans moved between different floor levels?
- What is the maximum size of object/packing case that can be brought into the exhibition area by the normal route (see 48.5)?

38.8 Handling

- Where are loans unpacked and repacked prior to and after display?
- Who is responsible for making out incoming/outgoing condition reports?
- Where are loans stored prior to and after display?
- Are these areas adjacent to the exhibition areas? If no, where are they in relation to the exhibition areas?
- Are there specialist packers/handlers on the staff? If no, who carries out the packing/handling of loans?
- Are regular checks made for dust and damage? By

whom and how often? Who dusts loans on open display?
- What arrangements are made for the storage of packing cases, packing materials etc?
- Has it ever been necessary to make alternative arrangements for the storage of large packing cases, etc.?

38.9 Environmental monitoring

This section (and 38.10 and 38.11) covers conditions in the exhibition areas and in display cases, and the form will therefore duplicate many of the questions to cover both the larger and the smaller spaces.

- Are temperature and relative humidity monitored on a regular basis?
- Please supply details of instruments used and frequency of calibration and servicing.
- What range of temperature and relative humidity do you attempt to maintain throughout the year (maximum and minimum readings for each season see 43.1)?
- What times of year are these conditions most difficult to maintain?

38.10 Environmental control

- How are temperature and relative humidity controlled (in exhibition areas and display cases, see 38.9)?
- Are these methods in operation 24 hours per day (see 43.1)?
- Are the same environmental conditions maintained in your storage and unpacking/packing areas as in the proposed exhibition area? If no, please supply details.
- Are there dust filters on the air intakes? If yes, please state particle size.
- Are there activated carbon filters on the air intakes?
- Please supply details of instruments used and frequency of calibration and servicing.

38.11 Lighting

- What type of light will be used to illuminate the loans (in exhibition areas and display cases, see 38.9)? For daylight, please state skylights, windows, etc. For artificial lighting, please state type of lamps used, etc.
- How many hours per week will the items be exposed to light, including the period when closed to public?
- How is artificial light controlled?
- Are there ultraviolet (UV) filters: on lights; on windows; in display cases. If yes, please state type used.
- Do you have a light meter?
- Do you have a UV monitor?
- Are light and UV levels monitored and controlled when an exhibition is being installed and dismantled?
- Are spot-checks made and daily records kept throughout the exhibition period?
- What range of visible and UV light can be maintained during exhibition?
- Is direct sunlight excluded from exhibition area?
- If daylight comes from a variable daylight source, how is the light falling on objects controlled (see 48.11)? If louvres or blinds are used, are these manually or automatically controlled? Are these louvres or blinds closed completely when the exhibition is closed to the public?

38.12 Display cases

- Please supply details of display cases to be used (construction materials, display materials, types of seal etc.).

38.13 Confidentiality

Many venues will be justifiably reluctant to divulge details of their security measures. It may be possible to avoid this by returning the security information separately from all other identifying information other than a reference code known only to the two institutions. In the same way that the NMGs seek approval, many lenders may be satisfied that a venue has been approved by the Museums Security Adviser and the date of that approval (see 37.4). Museums devising their own facilities reports might wish to address the following points.

38.14 Physical security

- Which floor levels are used for exhibitions?
- Do doors from the exterior open directly into display areas? If yes, describe the doors and locking mechanisms (see 42.3).
- Are there windows and/or roof-lights in the display area? If yes, describe the physical and alarm security defences used (see 42.3).
- Are the exhibition areas secured independently of the rest of the building?
- Have there been any incidents of theft or damage during the last three years? If yes, please supply details of both the incidents and subsequent precautions to avoid further such incidents.

38.15 Invigilation

- Is there a 24-hour human guard security? If no, are you willing to provide 24-hour guards?
- Are the attendants: security employees of your own institution; contracted from an outside service company; students; volunteers; other (see 42.6). Are the attendants equipped with radio? If no, please supply details of communication method used.
- Please indicate the number of attendants on duty in the exhibition areas: patrolling/stationary; during public hours/when closed to public but open to staff/when closed to both public and staff.
- How many rooms/galleries are assigned to each attendant (see 42.6)?
- Is an attendant deployed during installation and removal of exhibits (see 42.5)?
- Are attendants supported by equipment such as CCTV?
- Is a secure storage area provided for loan objects? If no, what security measures are taken during storage?

38.16 Intruder alarm system

- Is there an intruder alarm system in operation currently throughout the building (see 42.4)? If yes, please give year of installation, specify types of sensors (magnetic control, microwave, photoelectric ray, pressure, ultrasonic, sound, infra-red, CCTV, other) in use.
- Who does the alarm system alert?
- Who responds to an alarm condition?
- What is the average response time?
- Has the police response to the alarm system ever been withdrawn? If yes, give details.

38.17 Fire detection

- Is there a smoke/fire detection alarm system in operation currently throughout the building (see 27.6)? If yes, please indicate type and extent.
- Who does the fire detector system alert?
- Who responds to a fire alarm?
- What is the average response time?
- Is any part of the building fitted with an automatic fire repression system (water sprinklers, halon gas etc.)?
- Is fire fighting equipment provided for immediate use?
- Is any part of the building fitted with a flood alarm system?

38.18 Additional information

The answers on a facilities report may need to be supplemented with supporting documentation that is specifically requested. This might include a floor plan of each exhibition area, clearly showing the position of routinely opened doors and windows, unshaded glazing, sources of heat or draughts etc (see 38.6) and for a plan of the normal route from delivery point to the exhibition area (see 38.7). It might include copies of readings for temperature and relative humidity for the exhibition areas, specifying that these should be continuous, that they should cover the period of the previous year equivalent to that of the loan period, and that they should show the rate of change on the most regular basis available, preferably daily (see 38.9).

38.19 Advice on completing the form

Whether it is the organizer or the lender who issues facilities reports, the venues should be advised:

- who should complete the form;
- to whom the form is to be returned;
- what additional or supporting information is required;
- that the return of the form and the information contained in it is important to the consideration of loans; and
- to contact the appropriate person should they have any difficulty in completing the facilities report.

38.20 Completing a facilities report

The form should be completed by the staff at, or directly responsible for, each venue, liaising with those best qualified in the individual areas of expertise, i.e. conservators for the environmental questions, security staff for the security questions. Only as a second resort should reports be completed by the organizer of the touring exhibition, if that person is not directly responsible for the venue described.

Venues should complete and return as quickly as possible the facilities report in line with the advice and instructions, and supply any additional information which may have been specified to support the facilities report. They should contact the appropriate person should they experience any difficulty in completing the facilities report.

It is important for venues and organizers to remember that facilities reports are intended to help both lender and organizer to consider – or, in the case of the organizer, to consider again – the individual needs of the exhibits requested in terms of the capabilities of the venue, its resources and its other uses.

Facilities reports are also intended to identify potential problem areas connected with the proposed loan in sufficient time to allow the lender, the organizer and the venue to devise solutions. Facilities reports should NOT be seen as some form of simplistic examination to which there are 'right' or 'wrong' answers. If a venue has difficulty in understanding a question, whoever issued the form (lender or organizer) should be contacted for clarification. If a venue has difficulty in providing an answer, this may mean that the facilities report has highlighted a potential problem. The return of the form with that question unanswered allows lender, organizer and/or venue to begin to address that problem.

38.21 After the return of the facilities report

Each venue should update the organizer about any changes either in the arrangements for the exhibition or in the building which will affect or alter information contained in returned facilities reports.

The organizer should update the lenders as to any changes to the tour or addition to existing venues or any intermediate locations (transit storage warehouses, etc.) in which exhibits may be housed for any time. This information may affect or alter information contained in returned facilities reports or require additional forms to be completed.

39

Conservation

Birthe Kruse Christensen

39.1 The conservator's role

This section has been written to help organizers and venues that do not have a conservator on their staff to appreciate why and what conservation may be necessary before an exhibit is lent or goes on tour, and to set out how to go about commissioning a conservator.

Lenders should thoroughly examine and assess the condition of an object before agreeing a loan. It is usually the responsibility of the owner to assess the suitability of an object for lending to a touring exhibition. Where the owner does not have any conservators readily available to examine the object or carry out any necessary remedial conservation work, the organizer must be prepared to arrange for this work to be done.

In an ideal world, every exhibit would visit a conservation workshop before it goes on tour. Handling, transport, previous conservation treatments, display conditions and construction of the object all contribute to the deterioration of the object. The conservator will take all these factors into consideration and present the observations in a report to the owner, outlining the remedial and the preventive conservation work required. See also 41.3.

These observations usually form part of the basic loan agreement (see 37.4). They will form part of the initial status report in the condition check procedure (see 46.4). The conservator should also recommend an appropriate and reversible method of attaching a label to the exhibit or otherwise identifying it during handling and installation; this recommendation should be passed to the organizer.

39.2 Budgeting for conservation

Conservation treatment, whether preventive or remedial, can be costly, and the organizer must allow for this in the exhibition budget (see 9.4). The organizer may have to balance the importance of individual exhibits to the exhibition versus conservation work for which appropriate funding should be available. Loan applications may have to be withdrawn, where there is no budget for advice and subsequent treatment.

Most public collections have an ongoing programme of conservation work. Any objects requested and agreed for loan will usually be slotted into an already-prioritized programme. A late loan application for an exhibit which requires remedial conservation work could be turned down due to internal workloads. In this situation, the lender may agree to conservation being undertaken by an external conservation agency at a cost to the organizer.

Collections without direct access to a conservation agency and without an ongoing conservation programme may find it difficult to finance the remedial conservation work required. The organizer should be prepared to pick up this cost also in this instance.

Preventive conservation work required as part of the loan agreement will usually be charged to the exhibition organizer. Measures such as hard backing and glazing of paintings or remounting of prints and drawings may not be necessary for displaying the works at the lender's premises, but will help to maintain a stable environment throughout a tour.

39.3 Scheduling for conservation

Conservation treatment also takes time, and the organizer must allow for this when scheduling the exhibition (see 8.2). The materials used for constructing the object and its intended function are crucial elements in establishing the conservation time required, e.g. the time it takes cleaning a ceramic jug will be different from the time needed for cleaning a marble life-size statue, although the same method and materials may be used. Additional factors – the condition of the object, any special mounting or other display requirements, and the environmental conditions at the venues – can also add to the time required. On the other hand, an African ceremonial costume may require less conservation time than a historic coronation robe, because minimal intervention is preferred for objects from Oceania, Africa and the Americas.

39.4 How to choose a conservator

The conservator or curator at a local museum may be able to carry out the conservation assessment or suggest a local conservation agency. The relevant Area Museums Service will also be able to supply names of conservators in the area. The Conservation Unit of the Museum and Galleries Commission maintains a register of qualified and experienced conservators. The Unit publishes a leaflet detailing this service, 'How to Choose a Conservator'. A similar service is also offered by the Scottish Conservation Bureau of Historic Scotland.

39.5 Writing the brief for the conservator

When writing a brief for the conservator, the organizer should ensure that the conservator:

- outlines the proposed treatment, including other options considered, with the cost and the timing implications;
- divides the proposed treatment into essential and desired work;
- provides details of any proposed conservation materials to be used;
- writes a report on completion including any recommendations on labelling, handling, packing, storage and display conditions.

The organizer should send the brief to at least two conservation agencies. The returned tenders should be compared and the quality versus the cost should be carefully examined. Under no circumstances should the lowest tender be accepted as a matter of principle. However, the exhibition organizer must ensure value for money is achieved.

The chosen conservator should be given as much information as possible. Details of the different venues (including facility reports, transport method, storage between venues and preferred display method) all help the conservator to accurately assess the suitability and to write appropriate recommendations for the loan (see 38.1, 50.2, 53.1).

39.6 Why conservation is needed

Conservation is a discipline dedicated to preserving exhibits for the future and to ensuring that they can be displayed in a visually stimulating manner. The construction of the exhibit and the choice of materials can render it susceptible to deterioration. Other factors such as light, temperature, moisture and handling speed up the natural deterioration process.

The following is a brief summary of the many different indicators of deterioration for which a conservator will look during the detailed examination of the object. Particular emphasis is paid to damages attributed to physical, chemical, biological or environmental causes. The overall aesthetic appearance is also considered.

39.7 Physical damage

Incorrect and excessive handling may have caused physical damage to both two- and three-dimensional objects. A composite object (e.g. a mixture of wood and metal) requires thoroughly checking for loose metal pieces and their subsequent securing before it goes on tour. Canvases may have relaxed over the years, and the stretcher frames will need re-tensioning. Ceramic and glass objects may have been repaired in the past using adhesives susceptible to breaking down in high relative humidities and as a result will have to be re-conserved before the tour.

39.8 Insect infestation

Although no live insects can be found on the object, there can be many signs of previous infestation. Insect eggs can be dormant for several years and will hatch given a change in environment or an increase in temperatures. Mould and micro-organisms are usually easy to identify and can be effectively dealt with in the conservation laboratory. Suspected insect infestations in objects are equally easy to deal with, although the time-scale is somewhat longer. Not all chemical treatments are without damage to the objects, and each case needs to be individually assessed. The exhibit may have to be kept under close observation for some time. Treatment for insect infestation is not permanent (i.e. no chemical is deposited in the object to prevent re-infestation), so the exhibition organizer should be aware of any tell-tale signs of active infestations and seek appropriate assistance from a conservator as necessary (see 47.3).

39.9 Dirt

The exhibit may have accumulated much dirt over the years. This can vary from loose dust to ingrained dirt including flyspecks. Again long-term planning is important for the organizer. Depending on the size of the exhibit and the amount of dirt, the time involved in cleaning for display could be considerable. Often dirt can conceal serious physical damage (e.g. lifting paint or loose gilding) and the original estimated time and cost for cleaning the object could be severely increased. A yellowed varnish layer on a painting may need removing and the painting subsequently revarnished. Metal work may need to be polished. Sacred dirt may need to be secured on objects from Oceania, Africa and the Americas.

39.10 Chemical damage

Particular metals are susceptible to chemical damage (e.g. corrosion). Humidities over 40 per cent generally encourage corrosion. The presence of some pollutants will cause corrosion. The conservator may insist that all display materials are tested for pollutants and found acceptable. The science departments of a national museum or gallery (see 41.1) may be able to recommend non-harmful materials for display or to test intended display materials at a cost. Glue containing formaldehyde used in the construction of display cases will cause lead to corrode very rapidly. Other metals such as brass and silver will start to tarnish with the slightest amount of sulphide present.

39.11 Light

Even in small doses, light will cause permanent damage to objects. This will eventually be noticeable as fading, changing of colours or weakening of materials. The conservator will assess the light damage that has already taken place and will recommend lighting levels and dosage for the period of loan (see 20.3, 20.4). This is a compromise between deterioration, visibility and colour rendering.

Similar damage (fading, weakening of fibres, etc.) is caused by ultraviolet radiation. Paintings, prints and drawings can all be glazed using glass or Perspex with incorporated ultraviolet filter to limit the damage.

39.12 Relative humidity

A change in relative humidity (moisture level) causes changes in size and shape of moisture containing materials such as wood and ivory. High moisture levels are favourable growth conditions for mould and microorganisms. Low moisture levels cause embrittlement of paper, textile and leather and could lead to physical damage. Materials such as wood and ivory will split and warp. Warped or split wood cannot easily be rectified, and certainly this cannot be done without serious interference. The conservator will specify a stable environment and possibly try to create a micro-environment for the display of the exhibit (see 43.3). There are various organizations that hire out humidifiers and dehumidifiers. Most industrial units do not have humidistat controls and are not suitable for controlling relative humidity in exhibition galleries.

39.13 Temperature

High temperatures can dry out objects leading to cracking and shrinkage. Low temperatures may mean the dew point is reached and condensation can occur on the exhibits.

39.14 Accidental or wilful damage

Damage caused by disasters, acts of vandalism or accidents can very rarely be anticipated. The conservator will try to protect the exhibit by ensuring it is displayed behind glass or Perspex. Paintings are usually protected with a hard backing board, and period frames may need to be built up to take the depth of protective glazing, or the frames themselves may need to be protected within a suitable container (see 21.8). Often a courier is used to see the object safely installed in the exhibition gallery (see 51.4).

39.15 In the event of an accident

Should an accident occur, it is as a general rule better to leave everything as it is and call a conservator to inspect the damage. Consult the venue's disaster plan (see 7.16). Precious fragments or paint may be lost forever if the debris is cleared away. Glass fragments from picture framing could easily scratch or puncture the surface of the object.

However, there may be situations where it is advisable to remove or protect the object from the source of damage. For example, with water damage, the exhibit should be moved away from the source of damage or covered with polythene. Never attempt to wipe liquids off exhibits, as the area of damage might be increased. Try to position the exhibit in such a way that the liquid does not run further down it (see 44.6).

39.17 Sources of information:

The Conservation Unit, Museums and Galleries Commission, 16 Queen Anne's Gate, London SW1H 9AA. Tel 0171 233 4200. Fax 0171 233 3686.

Scottish Conservation Bureau of Historic Scotland,

Stenhouse Conservation Centre, 3 Stenhouse, Mill Lane, Edinburgh EH11 3LR. Tel 0131 443 1666. Fax 0131 445 8260.

Cassar, M. *Environmental Management: Guidelines for Museums and Galleries*, 1994, Routledge, London.

Mecklenburg, M.F (ed). *Art in Transit: Studies in the Transport of Paintings*, 1991, National Gallery of Art, Washington.

Thomson, G. *The Museum Environment*, 1986, Butterworths, London.

40

Insurance

Scot Blyth

40.1 Introduction

This section concerns insurance cover for exhibits. The organiser should also ensure that there is adequate legal and public liability insurance cover in place at each venue (see 29.1). In many cases, owner and lender will be the same person or institution, but in other cases the lender may not be the owner. Both terms are used in this section, according to the context..

The subject of insurance inevitably involves other aspects of exhibition organizing, all of which influence one another. It is important to treat the tasks in planning and preparing an exhibition as interrelated and not as a list of discrete areas which can be ticked off item by item. Establishing whether an exhibit is fit to travel, identifying the various risks to which it might be subjected from the moment it is collected from the lender to the moment it is returned, and minimizing these risks must be of paramount importance. Any insurance cover or policy merely offers financial protection to the organizer against the unforeseen, within certain specified conditions and with detailed exclusions.

Accurate estimates can only be prepared once the location, size, age, fragility and approximate value of each potential exhibit has been established. Before loan forms have been returned, the organizer can ascertain market values, through dealers' lists, auction catalogues, independent valuation and other resources or through Christie's, Sotheby's and other bureau services.

As with other aspects of budgeting, items may be deleted from the provisional list where overall values and/or particular stay or transit risks are likely to lead to a high insurance premium. Budgetary constraints will always be a restricting factor, but limited funds should not be allowed either to lower the level of care by which exhibits are handled, stored or displayed, or to influence the level of insurance cover. The Government Indemnity Scheme in the UK demands certain conditions to ensure the safety of the exhibits (see 41.4, 41.5), and these same demands should be used as guidelines where commercial insurance is effected.

40.2 Obtaining cover

Insurance may be arranged through any reputable company, and competitive quotations should always be sought. Where an exhibition is being arranged by a local authority gallery, the insurance company usually employed by the authority may be able to offer favourable terms. However, it is recommended that the organiser approach a specialist fine art insurance broker who will be able to give appropriate advice and will also be able to offer competitive rates. Specialist insurance brokers can be located through the trade press, by personal recommendation or by asking the advice of the British Insurance and Investment Association. A copy of their claims policy and procedures should be requested, and their information requirements should be noted. At this point in the planning of a touring exhibition, venues may not be known, and it is worth establishing, in consultation with the broker, the minimum requirements and standards of care for venues to maintain. The organizer should chose a broker not only on price but also on the level of service and the all-round cover required. In consultation with the broker, the organizer should then establish the loan form or contract, or agree any necessary changes to an existing one.

The role of the broker is to ensure that the liability of an organizer (or a venue where appropriate) is well covered and to set up an acceptable claims procedure. In the past, the insurance market has tended to take an average view of museums and galleries. However, a growing trend is for brokers and underwriters alike to be more aware of each venues' procedures and controls and of its competence in administering and handling exhibitions, as well as to know the level of care and professionalism to be expected from individual carriers. They will take these factors into account when determining the strictures of the insurance policy and the premium which will be attached. The past claims history of the Insured will always count for much in the underwriters' assessment of the risk to be covered, but even a first-time buyer will find that professionalism will attract a lower premium.

Brokers should be provided with the following details:

- number of items in the exhibition and the nature of individual exhibits (size, weight, physical condition);
- full itinerary and schedule for transit and storage;
- carrier(s) responsible for packing and shipping;
- specifications of any packing cases/crates;
- the minimum vehicle specification requested of a carrier;
- method of each transit (air, sea, road, etc.);
- highest value single item, average value of the items, total sum to be insured, and the maximum aggregate value per transit or load at any one time;
- all conditions required by a lender as part of the loan agreement;
- condition checking and reporting procedures;
- presence of couriers;
- any previous history of loss or damage;
- security arrangements at each venue and while in transit.

40.3 The insurance list

Insurance premiums will be determined by the value of the exhibits, by 'transit' risks (i.e. route, distance, the number of moves and type of transport) and by 'stay' risks (i.e length of exhibition and security and environmental conditions of each venue). Before cover can be arranged, a detailed insurance list will be required, setting out for each exhibit:

- owner;
- title (with artist or common name);
- medium, dimensions (and weight if appropriate);
- value;
- any remarks about condition, e.g. fragility.

Information for this list can be extracted from the completed loan forms returned by lenders. Insurance should be arranged on a 'value agreed and admitted' basis. This means that the value agreed between the owner and organizer is accepted by the insurance company, and should not therefore be subject to arbitration in the event of a loss. Values submitted by owners should be carefully checked against current market values. If an owner's valuation is too low, the organizer should discuss a re-valuation with the owner. An insurance company may refuse to insure an exhibit of which the value given is grossly unrealistic. Where the value of an exhibit is given in a foreign currency on the loan form, the insurance cover should be expressed in exactly the same way and should not be converted into a sterling equivalent. Any claim in respect of this exhibit would then be discussed and met in that currency.

40.4 Risks

In insurance, risks or perils are divided into two broad categories: the catastrophic, over which no-one has any control, and the particular, against which preventive measures can be taken. Underwriters give these various potential risks different 'weightings' in calculating the premium, e.g. the exhibit will be more at risk from vandalism while on display, but more at risk from accidental damage or theft while in transit.

'All Risks – Nail to Nail' with full stay cover on an agreed and admitted liability with absolutely no exclusions is the ideal. 'All Risks' includes fire, theft, loss, accidental and malicious damage. 'Nail to nail' (or 'shelf to shelf') means cover from the moment an exhibit is collected from the lender to the moment it is returned. 'Full stay cover' means that the cover is fully effective throughout the exhibit's stay at a venue.

Insurance provides financial protection against specified contingencies. In the case of exhibits, loss or damage is the most obvious risk, although there are other contingencies such as seizure (e.g. for repatriation) or toxic contamination and consequential loss. The latter may be detailed as exclusions to the cover offered (as may be loss or damage due to terrorist activity), and may need renegotiation if it is decided that cover should be effected for these specific risks. It is as important to consider the exclusions within a policy as to look at what is actually covered. In fact the exclusions will say more about the cover offered than the 'inclusion' section.

Even the ideal policy will not be worth the paper it is printed upon, if the conditions of cover imposed by the underwriter are not met in full by the organizer and the organizer's contractors. Mindful of the constraints within which the organizer may be operating, an owner may offer to deliver an exhibit personally. Financial compensation may not be forthcoming in the event of damage or loss during this transit, if the conditions of insurance stated that a professional fine art handler and transporter be used. Methods of working with known lenders which may have been satisfactory in previous circumstances may not be acceptable to the underwriters insuring the risk of a full-scale exhibition. A loss assessor may not view historical practice as acceptable or standard in the event of a claim.

40.5 Negotiating loans

An owner will understandably expect the best all risks cover nail to nail. The owner will also expect one point of contact – the organizer – even though the exhibition may be travelling to several venues. Any exclusions under a policy and the procedures by which any claims are settled, including arbitration in the event of dispute, must be clearly advised and agreed in advance. The owner should be advised if insurance cover is to be effected separately for the various venues of a touring exhibition, and when and how each policy kicks in and out (see 40.6).

It is important for owners to understand that, in the event of a claim, the broker or a loss adjuster appointed by the underwriters will need to establish, firstly, whether a claim is admissable under the policy, and secondly, liability. In the event of damage, the broker or loss adjuster would appraise the level of damage, agree the cost of restoration and possible depreciation and decide the level of compensation due to the owner.

Damage, however slight, may render an exhibit irretrievably sullied in the eyes of a private collector who may then expect to receive compensation for total loss. The general rules a loss adjuster might employ to assess depreciation for an Old Master with many layers of paint and with previous restoration will be different from a more modern painting consisting of a thin wash of acrylic which is essentially impossible to restore.

Where a loan consists of a pair of candlesticks or a set of chairs, an owner should be satisfied how a 'pairs and sets' clause will operate in the event of one of the items being lost or damaged. The organizer should be prepared to increase the valuation on a particular exhibit during the course of a tour, e.g. in the event of a similar piece attaining a record sales price at auction.

The organizer should forward certificates of insurance to the lenders when insurance arrangements have been completed.

An owner may wish to insure the exhibit on his/her own policy. A common practice in such situations is for the organiser to ask to be shown in the policy as co-insured. However, the underwriters could well refuse to do this, firstly because the organiser does have an 'interest' in the exhibit, and secondly because the owner would not have legal recourse against a co-insured party in the event of a claim or dispute. If shown as co-insured on the lender's policy, the organiser should ask that a waiver of subrogation clause be included, renouncing recourse against carriers and packers and the gallery's agents and representatives. If the owner and/or insurance company will not agree to showing the organiser as co-insured, a waiver of subrogation must be requested not only against packers, carriers, agents and representatives but also against the organizer. If this is not possible, the organizer will need to take out legal liability cover to protect it against a claim which could be made against it. The organizer's insurance list should record brief details of the owner's insurance arrangements, with the name and address of the broker or insurance company.

40.6 Single v. multiple policies

A single policy to cover the whole tour can be simpler to administer than several consecutive policies, and the premium may be lower than the aggregate of the separate premiums paid by the different venues. There is also no confusion as to where and how a claim should be made in the event of loss or damage. However, there may be a perception of reduced accountability and responsibility (see 41.4). The organizer, its brokers and underwriters may also lack detailed knowledge of conditions at the venue, which could mean a higher or inappropriate premium.

The process of checking and recording the condition of each exhibit at the time of collection from the lender and at the time of the return of the lender is important for insurance purposes because it documents the state of each exhibit at the moment of transfer from one insurance cover to the next (see 46.4).

When a tour is covered by several consecutive policies, it is imperative that a detailed condition report is made out every time an exhibit is handed over from one cover to the next, and signed as being a true and correct representation of the state of the exhibit at that moment (see 46.10). Timing will be known in the event of total loss following a theft or catastrophic incident, but the condition check docket (CCD) can be used to pinpoint when less dramatic damage or deterioration occurred, and will therefore assist any loss adjuster in establishing under which cover a claim should be made.

40.7 Third parties

Those participating in the organization of an exhibition take on responsibilities and a duty of care not only to the owner of a particular exhibit but more specifically and importantly to the exhibit itself. This responsibility is invested by proxy in the various sub-contractors, whether they be carriers or venues. Due care may be difficult to define, and is not necessarily the level of care exercised by the owner, e.g. a national museum may give a higher level of care than can be afforded by the commercial gallery lending the exhibits.

Delegation of responsibility to third parties should be based on an objective analysis of how best to reduce the risks to the exhibits while they are away from the organizer's immediate care. This involves not just trust in the third party but also a realistic appraisal of the competence of the third party. Specialists in packing, handling or transport may appear expensive at the outset. However, their expertise will help to reduce the risks to the exhibits, give peace of mind to the lender, reduce the insurance premium that the organizer or venue has to pay, and enhance the reputation of the organizer or venue in the eyes of the lenders and the underwriters.

40.8 In the event of loss or damage

Organizer and venues should have a formal plan for emergencies, to minimize damage, provide a rapid response to any emergency and to inform the relevant people, including owners/lenders (see 7.16).

Make written notes immediately, detailing: when the loss or damage was discovered, and by whom; how the loss or damage occurred; when the exhibit was last seen in good condition, and by whom; and any other relevant information regarding the circumstances of the incident, before it is forgotten.

Telephone/contact the insurance broker as soon as these notes are ready. If possible, send a fax, detailing: the extent of the damage; the circumstances in which the incident occurred; and the value of the item. Seek instructions or advice.

Give any parties notice, if possible by fax, advising them that they may be held responsible.

Make duplicates of all notes and photographs of the incident, together with the loan form and CCD (see 46.2), for the broker and the loss adjuster.

40.9 In the event of damage only

In addition to the action set out in 40.8, inform the police if criminal damage is involved.

Secure the object and set it carefully aside, together with any pieces, sections, paint loss, particles, etc. Make sure that it is safe from the possibility of further damage or mishandling. All measures must be taken to mitigate the damage immediately, so as not to prejudice the possibility of a claim.

No attempts should be made to repair or restore the exhibit, without the approval of the broker, loss adjuster and – most importantly – the lender. It is important to remember that, under the 'process clause', an insurance company will not consider claims for damage inflicted during conservation. Artists restoring their own work should be aware of the clause before beginning restoration work.

Take a photograph of the object.

40.10 In the event of total loss

In addition to the action set out in 40.8, the police should be notified where theft or disappearance – even if only apparently 'mislaid' – is involved.

40.11 After the claim

If it is a relatively small claim, the brokers will advise the venue what to do, and will proceed on their own authority. If the claim is more substantial, the brokers will immediately contact the underwriters, who will appoint a loss adjuster.

If the loss adjuster accepts that damage to an object makes it a total loss and the underwriters make full payment, then the latter will take the object as salvage. Where a policy is on an agreed value basis, the insurers will pay to the Insured/owner the value agreed in the policy, in the event of a claim for total loss. In the event of a partial loss, the insurers will pay to the Insured/owner a percentage of the loss in value, based on the agreed value and the cost of restoration.

41

Indemnity

Heather Wilson

41.1 Government Indemnity Scheme

Indemnity is an arrangement whereby a borrower agrees to compensate an owner in the event of loss or damage to an item while on loan. In this section, 'owner' is used rather than lender (see 40.1); in a touring exhibition, the borrower might be the organizer or one of the venues.

The Government Indemnity Scheme (GIS) in the UK was introduced by the National Heritage Act 1980 and formalized earlier arrangements, whereby the British Government had agreed to accept the risks in respect of loans of material to the nineteen national museums and galleries (NMGs) directly funded by central government. These NMGs are:

- British Museum
- Imperial War Museum
- National Army Museum
- National Galleries of Scotland
- National Gallery
- National Maritime Museum
- National Museum of Wales
- National Museums and Galleries on Merseyside
- National Museums of Scotland
- National Portrait Gallery
- Natural History Museum
- Royal Air Force Museum
- Royal Armouries
- Science Museum
- Tate Gallery
- Ulster Folk and Transport Museum
- Ulster Museum
- Victoria and Albert Museum
- Wallace Collection.

GIS extended the cover the Arts Council enjoyed for loans to its exhibition programme, now National Touring Exhibitions (NTE, see 12.3), which was itself based on arrangements for the exhibitions toured by the Victoria and Albert Museum's Circulation Department. The National Heritage Act 1980 was, in fact, designed to make it easier for non-national museums to compensate for the demise of the Circulation Department in 1977.

'Non-national museums' are those museums and galleries not directly funded by central government, including those administered by local authorities, educational institutions and by independent trusts. The GIS does not cover loans made to commercial organizations, nor loans outside the UK.

41.2 Advantages and disadvantages

GIS now provides an alternative to full commercial cover in respect of:

- loans made from, to or between NMGs;
- loans to non-national museums;
- loans from, to and between NTE, the British Council, the Arts Council of Northern Ireland, the Arts Council of Wales and the Scottish Arts Council.

The advantage of indemnity over commercial insurance is that it can relieve the exhibition's budget of substantial insurance premiums (see 40.1). A venue may have to install new security systems or make other improvements to satisfy the Museums Security Adviser (see 42.1) and Environmental Adviser, both of whom are based at the Museums and Galleries Commission (MGC) and comment on GIS applications. Venues often use such requirements to carry out necessary but frequently-postponed improvements.

The disadvantage of GIS, especially for touring exhibitions, is that it can be administratively cumbersome because it has to be arranged venue by venue, not for the whole tour. Even so, the responsibility placed on the venue can help to reinforce its 'ownership' of the exhibition, in a way which is echoed by other aspects of touring where venues are now playing a more active part in protecting, publicizing and interpreting the exhibits (see 13.3).

Indemnity is arranged directly by the NMGs, NTE, British Council and the Arts Councils. Indemnity arrangements for all other loans made to and from non-national museums are arranged by the MGC. A copy of the application form and Guidance Notes for making an application to the MGC is available from the Capital Taxes Officer, Museums and Galleries Commission, 16 Queen Anne's Gate, London SW1H 9AA. Tel 0171 233 4200. Fax 0171 233 1709.

41.3 The organizer's role

With the exception of NTE, indemnity cover for a touring exhibition is normally arranged by each venue in turn, and not by the organizer.

Although it will usually apply for indemnity cover only for its own showing, the organizer has a crucial role in ensuring that the venues know what is required of them and that they have the necessary information to complete their applications in time.

It is not unusual for one or more venues to apply for indemnity, even though the organizer has decided to obtain commercial insurance. In this case, the organizer should still anticipate the information that venues will need in order to make an application.

The organizer should obtain a full description, photograph and current market valuation for each item.

Each exhibit should be examined, preferably before making a formal loan request, if possible before collection from the lender or at the latest immediately after collection (see 46.2). Aside from the risks of damage to an object that is not in acceptable condition, it should be noted that indemnity cover precludes damage caused by 'inherent vice or pre-existing flaw'.

Each venue should be provided with a 'non-nationals loans list' grouping all loans, except those from NMGs and from any of the venues that are also lending, ideally in the format required by the MGC so that it can be simply photocopied. This should be arranged in order of owner, and give the contact person, address of institution, name or title of exhibits.

Each venue should be provided with a similar loans list, which groups all loans from any of the other venues that are also lenders. Indemnity cannot be granted for the lender's own objects while they are the responsibility of the lender, i.e. while on display at the lender's premises. The organizer must be aware of the status of each venue, since indemnity procedures will vary if non-national museums and NMGs are to take part in the tour (see Figure 41.1).

The organizer must also be aware of the status of each lending institution, and provide each venue with a separate list of exhibits from every NMG that is a lender, with full details of whom to contact in the NMG about lending and indemnity arrangements.

The organizer must ensure that the contact person at each venue is aware of the specific indemnity arrangements which the venue will need to make (see 17.12).

41.4 Applications

Each non-national venue will decide whether it makes an application for indemnity or whether it arranges and offers commercial insurance cover for its showing and for an agreed period before the opening date and after the closing date.

A single application form to the MGC will cover all loans from non-national sources. Much of the information on the exhibition and the tour and on the condition and value of individual exhibits will be provided by the organizer, but the venue will add information on its own facilities and resources.

In addition, each venue will need to complete a form for every national collection from which a loan is requested. In this case, the information on its own facilities and resources will often be provided on a facilities report (see 38.3).

Indemnity may be granted to cover transport, storage, display, installation and dismantling, but not restoration or conservation. A venue should not assume that indemnity will automatically be granted, simply because it has already been granted to another venue. In processing applications for indemnity, the MGC will consider each venue's arrangements for security, environmental control, transport, etc. Each venue should agree with the organizer the environmental conditions that are appropriate and consistent (see 43.3). Environmental data should be obtained for at least one week from the period in the previous year which is equivalent to the proposed dates of showing (see 38.18).

Each venue is expected to arrange indemnity cover for one 'leg' of transport, as well as cover for any storage, installation, display, etc. at that venue. There should be agreement as to whether the first or last venue will be responsible for two 'legs'. Normal practice is to make the organizer, as the first venue, responsible for the initial and final transport. Agreement will need to be reached, and any special arrangements made (including changes to the length of indemnity cover) if there is a gap in the tour, when the exhibition has to be moved to or stored at either of the venues next to the break.

Applications for indemnity cover for loans to a non-national museum from non-national sources (including private individuals, commercial organizations and all sources outside the UK) must be forwarded to the MGC at least three months in advance of the date on which indemnity is due to begin. If cover is required

Venue – national

Source of loan	Indemnity arranged by	Contact
National	No indemnity – Lender bears risk	Registrar
Non-national	Borrower	
Government funded body	No indemnity – Lender bears risk	Lender
Non-UK source	Borrower	
Royal Collections	No indemnity – Undertaking given by the Borrower that the Royal Collections will be compensated in the event of loss or damage.	

Venue – non-national

Source of loan	Indemnity arranged by	Contact
National	Lender	Registrar
Non-national	MGC	MGC
Government funded body	Lender	Lender
Non-UK source	MGC	MGC
Royal Collections	No indemnity – Undertaking given by the Borrower that the Royal Collections will be compensated in the event of loss or damage.	

Figure 41.1

for collecting exhibits, the application must arrive three months before this operation begins, not three months before the exhibition opens.

Unlike other indemnifiers, the MGC will not have immediate access to or complete records of the exhibits, so it is essential that the MGC be given as much prior warning as possible of any large, unusual or very valuable exhibits. All applications must be made with all the necessary information. As with a late application, an incomplete one may mean that a venue will not receive the necessary cover.

Indemnities arranged by the MGC require each venue to agree to meet, for the duration of the indemnity granted in respect of that venue, the minimum liability (or 'first loss') in respect of each item. At present (1995), the minimum liability is £200 for each item valued at £4000 and below, and £200 plus 1 per cent of the value for each item valued in excess of £4000. If it is specifically requested on the loan form, a lender may agree to waive the right to receive the sum equivalent to the minimum liability, but normally venues take out a separate commercial insurance policy or extend their existing cover to cover this liability. If the lender's valuation has not been accepted for the purposes of indemnity, commercial insurance should also provide any 'excess' or 'top-up' cover required.

41.5 The period of cover

When indemnity has been granted, it is the responsibility of each venue to notify the MGC or other indemnifier of any variations in the list of indemnified items, valuations, dates of loan, arrangements for public access, security, transport and environmental control. With a loan from an NMG, lender and indemnifier are the same. The NMG will make certain requirements and expect to be kept informed of anything which affects its loan(s) and indemnity cover. In the same way, the MGC requires each venue to check and report any loss or damage, as if it were a lender itself.

A standard procedure for checking the condition and reporting any changes should be followed rigorously and consistently (see 46.1).

The organizer, lender and indemnifier should be notified immediately of any changes outside the agreed limits for temperature and humidity (see 43.5).

If damage is noticed, the lender, organizer and indemnifier should be notified at once. Unless immediate remedial action is required to stabilize the condition of the exhibit or to prevent further immediate deterioration, no conservation or restoration should be undertaken without the prior approval of both the lender and the indemnifier.

If the exhibit has to be taken off display, the indemnifier should be informed.

If there is a theft, the police should be informed at once, and the lender and indemnifier informed as soon as possible thereafter. A full report of the circumstances in which the theft occurred, or was likely to have occurred, and details of how, when and by whom the theft was noticed, should be prepared and forwarded to the indemnifier.

42

Security

Bryan Dovey

42.1 General principles

Exhibits in touring exhibitions must be kept in conditions that are at least as secure as those they normally enjoy. An exhibition can present a thief with the opportunity to steal a number of related works from one place, instead of attacking the different premises where they are normally kept.

It is a common mistake for organizers and lenders to specify that a venue should provide 24-hour patrolling, without taking into account the balance that the venue might have achieved between a strong security perimeter, an effective alarm system and adequate invigilation.

To provide a level of security acceptable to most lenders, venues should adopt and implement the Museums and Galleries Commission's security policy. This policy is the standard against which is measured a venue's suitability to receive loans from the national collections or cover from the Government Indemnity Scheme (see 41.4).

Copies of the policy are freely available from the MGC, which can also provide detailed specifications for many of the measures recommended below. Contact the Museums Security Adviser, Museums and Galleries Commission, 16 Queen Anne's Gate, London SW1H 9AA. Tel 0171 233 4200. Fax 0171 233 3686.

42.2 Strengthening the security perimeter

Roof, walls and floor of a venue must be capable of resisting a determined physical attack for at least the amount of time needed for the police or security staff to respond to the activation of an intruder alarm system (see 42.4).

Walls should be of reinforced concrete at least 12 cm (4.5") thick or cement mortar brickwork at least 23 cm (9") thick. The security perimeter must include the roof, which should be of reinforced concrete or of slate or tiles laid to close-boarded timber. The perimeter must also include the floors, ceilings and walls where there are other occupants in the building below, above or alongside the display areas.

External walls and – where the weight can be accommodated – ceilings can be reinforced by fixing a cladding of 4.04 mm Expamet (expanded metal grille no. 1576) sandwiched between two layers of 18 mm plywood. Fixing should be by coach-bolts at 15 cm (6") centres. Internal walls, ceilings and floors may dispense with the layer of plywood facing the space being protected.

42.3 Protecting the openings

Most burglars use windows, doors and roof-lights to gain entry. Unwanted openings should be blocked up. New brickwork should be tied to the surrounding wall. Steel plate and other materials can be used, provided fixing bolts are at right angles to the direction in which force might be applied.

Normally, defences will be fitted internally, so that the appropriate alarm sensor can be attached. Self-coiling steel shutters, collapsible gates, fixed iron or steel bars and plywood shutters are the most useful devices. Where appearance is important, internal secondary glazing should be used, consisting of 13.4 mm glass-clad polycarbonate bonded to steel frames that are bolted to the wall.

Many older buildings are fitted with internal wooden shutters to glazed doors and windows. These can be strengthened, preferably with sheet steel on the outer face, wrapped round all four edges of the leaf. The thickness of the steel will depend on the ability of the shutter to carry the extra weight. Additional (and heavier) hinges should be fixed to the masonry, and steel locking bars should also be fixed to the masonry with a padlock.

Doors not amenable to secondary defences should be replaced, with steel or iron doors or wooden doors laminated or clad with 16 gauge steel sheet. The least acceptable external door is solid hardwood or hardcore quality that is a minimum of 44 mm (2") thick. External doors should not have glazed panels. They should have three hinges to carry the additional weight, and should open outwards, i.e. toward the direction of any attack. Hinge bolts are essential in outward opening doors because of the vulnerability of the hinges.

There should be at least one mortise lock conforming to BS 3621. Where two locks are recommended, they should be spaced equally along the door edge. Multi-bolt systems, which shoot bolts on all four edges of a door, provide more resistance. The strength of the door frame and of its fixing to the wall must be equal to the strength of the door and its locks.

42.4 Intruder alarm systems

The deterrent value of an alarm system depends on whether a thief can enter and escape before the police or security staff arrive. The system must be designed to support the mechanical and structural defences. It should signal an alarm to a monitoring station as soon as an attack occurs and before intrusion is completed.

The system should be constantly monitored, so that the loss of signal – through tampering with the system or cutting the telephone lines – results in an alarm in the monitoring station. Constant monitoring, e.g. via British Telecom's RedCARE, is available at a small extra cost to normal maintenance arrangements.

Two common descriptions are used to describe alarm systems. 'Perimeter protection' includes those devices activated by an attack on the security perimeter. 'Trap protection' describes devices activated by the presence of an intruder within the perimeter. Venues require both, but perimeter protection will be of primary importance.

A specialist (who can be recommended by the Museums Security Adviser, see 42.1) will normally prepare a specification that is unique to a particular building, but a typical system might consist of:

- external doors fitted with magnetic reed contacts and 'lace-wired' on the inner face, if a wooden door;
- all internal mechanical defences fitted with a shock sensor, e.g. inertia switch or vibration sensor;
- glazed areas without internal defences fitted with break-glass sensors (except in the case of laminated glass, which needs special sensors);
- any internal walls adjoining adjacent premises that present an abnormal risk fitted with wall shock sensors;
- focal points of movement, e.g. corridors and staircases, fitted with volumetric sensors, e.g. P(assive) I(nfra) R(ed), microwave or ultrasonic devices;
- selected internal doors, e.g. stores, fitted with magnetic reed contacts;
- portable personal attack devices issued to staff as necessary;
- all devices to be controlled by a modern control box, with a fully-monitored communication module;
- bell or siren boxes fitted to outside of premises, as recommended by installers.

If a fire detector/alarm system is also being installed, it will be cost-effective to use the same installer for both systems and to use a single communication module (see 27.6).

42.5 Installing the exhibition

Since more than 60 per cent of all museum thefts occur during opening hours, time and effort taken to provide a secure display will be worthwhile.

The 'Abloy' range of locks currently provide the widest selection available for display cases. Never theless, avoid the use of locks carried by the glazing, as they are susceptible to attack. Use more than one lock on long stretches of frame (see 21.8).

'Security' screws needing a special screwdriver are useful to bolster the locking system of a case and to hang medium- to small-scale paintings using mirror plates.

Battery-powered alarm sensors giving a local alarm are useful for detecting entry into cases or into room-settings. For the latter use, they can be obtained with a twelve-word spoken message of the user's choice.

Barriers, ropes, platforms and even furniture can be used to create a space between visitors and sensitive exhibits. The space provided enables attendants to see quickly when a visitor gets too close to an exhibit.

Installation and dismantling periods need to be carefully supervised, and access restricted to authorized persons. Staff should lock themselves in the exhibition gallery where possible, or use temporary doors and screens in an open-plan situation.

If night guarding is an agreed part of the security plan, it should cover the whole period the exhibits are on the premises.

42.6 Invigilation

An exhibition must be supervised for the whole period that the public is admitted. The ideal is one person per manageable space, and the terms of a Government Indemnity may insist on this level of invigilation.

This level can be reduced if the exhibits can be given good physical protection, e.g. cases with thief-resistant features such as strengthened glazing and local alarms.

Invigilation may be by full-time, paid security attendants or by unpaid volunteers. All should be trained and then briefed for each exhibition, preferably by the person responsible for the showing so that their interest in the exhibits is aroused. It is useful to have a diagram recording the layout of exhibits, to provide the discipline of an active check at the beginning and end of a shift, and to identify immediately any exhibit that may be missing. A set of photographs of the installation is also useful.

Police crime prevention officers can be asked to brief invigilators on the local crime situation, the methods thieves use, and the exhibits that might attract thieves or protestors.

Venues should have a daily routine of inspecting all exhibits and display cases to identify any signs of tampering. Some thefts are committed over a number of days, and routine checks will reveal evidence of tampering with adhesive between glass edges or removal of screws.

Formal openings, receptions, private views and other special events (lectures, performances, etc.) all need to be supervised to at least the same standard as normal opening hours. Some events may need even more supervision (see 26.12).

42.7 Other security procedures

During a showing of an exhibition, venues should not relax their procedures to cover key security, reception of visitors and facilities afforded to researchers. Venues that do not have such procedures should introduce them.

Possession of keys, including those with the exhibition (e.g. for display cases, see 21.8) should be reduced to an absolute minimum, and keys should be locked in a secure cabinet when the venue closes. The only keys taken away from the venue should be the safe keys and those required for emergency call-out key-holders. An issue procedure should ensure that all keys are returned at closing time. Procedures which involve identity cards that are issued to individuals call for strict routines but are less time-consuming.

Visitors, researchers and contractors all require regulation and supervision. Visitor passes should be used, but will only be useful if staff are prepared to interrogate people without passes in any restricted areas. Researchers should be supervised, and care taken to prevent bags and cases from being taken into stores or special examination rooms.

43

The venue's environment

May Cassar

43.1 Environmental continuity in touring exhibitions

The following is aimed primarily at managers of venues which receive touring exhibitions. It is essentially about how venues can meet their responsibilities to care for exhibits on loan to them. However, defining, achieving and sustaining appropriate conditions require careful planning and frank communication between the venues and the organizer. Consequently, this section is also relevant to the organizer, who will need to ensure that the required conditions can be met by all the venues, to identify potential problems at individual venues, and even to assist them in achieving appropriate conditions.

Environmental deterioration is any damage that may result from unsuitable temperature or humidity (see 39.12, 39.13). The risk of environmental deterioration is heightened when an exhibit is moved any distance from its permanent location. The answer is not to deny access afforded by touring exhibitions, but to assess and manage the risks as far as possible. For touring exhibitions, this is best done by defining, achieving and sustaining environmental continuity and stability for all exhibits for the time that they are away from their permanent locations.

Textbooks usually recommend a relative humidity of 50 per cent or 55 per cent with a range of plus or minus 5 per cent. For some materials (e.g. metal, textiles and paper), drier conditions are often recommended. Temperature levels are usually established for the human comfort, at around 19°C plus or minus 1°C in winter ranging to 24°C plus or minus 1°C in summer. It is also recommended that these levels be maintained even while a gallery is closed to the public, because a drop in temperature may cause a rise in relative humidity.

However, actual conditions will vary to a greater or lesser degree between the place where a loan is normally kept and the venues in a tour. As a result, the aim must be to achieve environmental continuity and stability, first, by approximating to the average condition of the normal location and the venues, and secondly, by ensuring that any changes are as small as possible and as slow as possible.

43.2 Defining the needs

Each venue should obtain from the organizer the following information as early as possible:

A complete list of exhibits, containing a description of the size, weight (if relevant) and the main construction materials of each item (see 7.3). The list should be scanned immediately for unusual materials or combinations of materials that are potential problems. Contemporary art can sometimes present considerable challenges in this respect.

A draft of the condition check docket that will be used for the tour. Any modifications that the venue would like to propose in content and presentation of the form should be sent to the organizer as soon as possible. The condition of individual items can then be checked by their lenders using the tour's condition check dockets (see 46.2).

Data which records the environment near the items requested for loan in their permanent location. This should be from the previous year but for the same period that the exhibition will be shown. If a lender is unable to provide the organizer with this information, they should agree a period of monitoring of relative humidity and temperature, light and ultraviolet radiation (if appropriate) near the items, in order to build up a representative environmental profile. Note any peculiar events that might affect the readings. For example, is the equipment in a corner which might have its own micro-climate, near a source of heat (radiator, south-facing window or heat-emitting lamp), or in a draught between doors or near an air-duct?

Environmental monitoring data for the same period as its showing, but from the previous year, from the venue on either side of the recipient's showing. As part of its facilities report, each venue should provide information which will show maxima and minima and the fastest rate of change over a fixed period of time (see 38.18).

43.3 Achieving the right conditions

The purpose of collecting the information in Section 43.2 is to enable informed decisions to be made on the balance to be found between the environmental needs of the exhibits and what is possible for individual venues to achieve within existing resources. It will be necessary for the organizer to compare the conditions that venues can offer and to assess their ability to adapt these conditions to provide the optimum thread of continuity from showing to showing. The organizer may also have to check what flexibility the lenders will accept in terms of continuous and stable conditions which may be on the edge or even outside the ranges given in the textbooks.

Agree the limits within which relative humidity is allowed to fluctuate, and an acceptable rate of change. For example, the normal conditions in which an exhibit is kept should not fluctuate more than 10 per cent over a 24-hour period. It is generally accepted that many materials are unaffected by fluctuations in relative humidity that last less than an hour, so be prepared to discuss and compromise!

Agree the limits within which the temperature is allowed to fluctuate, and an acceptable rate of change. Temperature may vary quite widely to suit human comfort, as long as relative humidity has been controlled.

Compare the measures that should be taken to provide stable conditions with the control options that are realistically available. Air-conditioning is not the 'be-all-and-end-all' of environmental control. It implies a long-term commitment of considerable resources in time, money and expertise if it is to perform according to the design intent. Air-conditioning can be designed to cover every possible eventuality in terms of weather conditions and occupancy levels, but at tremendous capital, running and maintenance costs. Since compromises are always necessary, why not consider a localized, more user-friendly approach to environmental control?

Consider first how environmental stability for exhibits might be achieved or improved by the use of passive measures. The creation of micro-environments for vulnerable exhibits is the most cost-effective and sustainable way of achieving this. These measures include zoning of spaces such as isolating rooms by closing doors, using display cases for three-dimensional exhibits, glazing and backing two-dimensional exhibits, and crates to protect exhibits in transit (see 21.9, 45.2).

Consider the use of environmental control equipment, such as humidifiers and dehumidifiers only to fine-tune passive measures. Equipment should not be relied upon completely to achieve the desired conditions. Consider whether humidifiers are being used to compensate for dry conditions created by inadequate control of a heating system and excessive heat emissions from light sources. Extensive use of dehumidifiers may be a sign that all is not well with the building, for example rainwater may be leaking into the building or there may be problems with rising damp (see 44.2).

Provide appropriate storage conditions for packing materials and crates. They have a tremendous humidity-buffering capability which should be harnessed to stabilize conditions within crates or wrappings during transit (see 50.6).

Always bear in mind that the exhibits on display have different needs from the visiting public. Exhibits generally require stable relative humidity and cool conditions; people prefer fresh air and moderately warm conditions. Separate the two where possible by using solid transparent partitions in rooms or display cases for the vulnerable exhibits. This makes it much easier to provide the right conditions for both.

43.4 Sustaining environmental stability

Achieving appropriate environmental conditions should take into account that this is not just a demonstration to convince the lenders and the organizer that you are a responsible borrower. Environmental conditions during the showing of a touring exhibition need to be sustainable.

Compare what you are trying to achieve with a mountaineer scaling Everest and the planning, preparation, skill and equipment required to stay at the summit for just a few minutes. This is similar to aiming for 'ideal' or 'tight' environmental conditions without adequate technical and management support. Instead, consider the same mountaineer aiming for the lower elevations of Everest, and now there is time to pause, breathe, think and admire the view from a safe and wide plateau.

No responsible lender will wish a venue to try for 'tight' conditions that cannot be sustained, if the conditions to which the exhibit is accustomed are within the broad, sustainable band of environmental control which can be understood and managed by the users of the building.

43.5 During the showing

Devise a programme for periodic checking of the physical condition of exhibits on display, comparing them to their condition report on arrival, documenting any changes and informing the organizer and lender where appropriate (see 46.10).

Monitor environmental conditions continuously throughout the showing, to ensure that temperature and humidity remain within the agreed bands. The organizer, lender and other interested parties, e.g. the Government Indemnity Scheme, should be notified immediately of any changes outside the agreed bands (see 41.5). Equipment should be regularly checked and calibrated.

Take any necessary measures to stabilize temperature and humidity, which may include steps such as leaving a heating system switched on at night (relative humidity rises in a cooling interior), providing a cloakroom to keep wet raincoats out of the exhibition space, and installing lighting which emits less heat.

Include the exhibits in a touring exhibition in the venue's disaster plan, which sets out procedures in the event of an emergency such as fire or flood (see 7.16). The venue should rehearse these procedures at least once during the showing.

43.6 Further reading

Cassar, M. *Environmental Management: Guidelines for Museums and Galleries*, 1995, Museums and Galleries Commission in association with Routledge, London.

44

Protection from flooding

Mary Heathcote

44.1 Basic principles

There are two main causes for the incursion of water into buildings: chronic neglect and catastrophe. The first can be avoided by diligent maintenance, and the effects of the second can be mitigated by appropriate preventive measures and by damage limitation.

The organizer must be satisfied that each venue in a tour is in good physical condition, and that a contingency plan for the rescue of exhibits in an emergency is in place.

44.2 Maintenance

A routine programme of maintenance for buildings used for the display and storage of exhibitions will ensure that rain-water is effectively and harmlessly carried away. The problems caused by leaking roofs, blocked or damaged guttering and down-pipes, and a neglected damp proof course will be obviated.

44.3 Flood-prone areas

Some buildings are particularly vulnerable, being located in low-lying land near rivers or the sea, and flooding emergencies can arise with the conjunction of unfavourable conditions, e.g. heavy rainfall and exceptionally high tides combining to prevent natural drainage and resulting in a rapidly rising water table and widespread flooding. It will be possible to identify such risks from known history and the topography of the site and to take intelligent preventive measures. It must be borne in mind, however, that the whole locality may be affected and the disaster not confined to the venue, in which case the emergency services will be stretched and their priorities may well differ from those of curators.

44.4 Preventive measures

Water damage can be instant and irreversible. In the event of flood or other incursions of water, any delay in allowing the water into contact with exhibits will be invaluable.

The organizer should ensure that all exhibits are wrapped in a water-proof material when they are being transported in and out of buildings and when they are in transit, to prevent accidental water damage. Other measures should also be considered, e.g. paintings fitted with a hardboard (preferably oil-tempered) back-board sealed with archival tape, not only preserves the exhibit by insulating it from changes in relative humidity (RH), but also protects it from direct contact with water, providing valuable breathing space.

In exhibitions, exhibits placed on plinths will give an extra margin of safety. In storage, exhibits must be stacked at least 15 cm (6") off the floor on pallets or strips of wood, and polythene sheeting should be placed above stored exhibits, between them and any plumbing pipes.

44.5 Contingency plan

The organizer should provide each venue with an insurance list with the values of the exhibits clearly stated (see 7.4), so that the venue can establish priorities for the rescue of exhibits in an emergency (see also 27.8). In establishing a contingency plan for the rescue and recovery of exhibits in case of flood, the procedure for the rescue and removal of exhibits will depend upon the nature of the catastrophe and the type of exhibit (see 7.16).

The contingency plan should provide for a stock of materials and equipment to be maintained on the premises for wrapping, protecting and recovering exhibits. Materials should include polythene sheeting, tissue, PH neutral blotting and absorbent paper. A vacuum cleaner capable of drawing up water is a useful piece of equipment to have available. Where there is leaking from above, polythene sheeting can be fixed between the leak and the affected exhibit(s), to channel the water to a less damaging area.

The contingency plan should ensure that a rescue team can be summoned at short notice. Wherever possible, exhibits should be removed to a salvage area away from the disaster zone. Each member of the team should be familiar with the layout of the building, should know where the stock of materials and equipment is kept, and should have been briefed or trained in the contingency plan. In smaller organizations with few staff, this may require a team of volunteers.

The contingency plan should ensure that the rescue team can be equipped with protective clothing such as disposable gloves, masks and overalls, because flood water may be contaminated by sewage. The wearing of wellington boots should be discouraged, since they can fill with water in deep flooding. Old shoes and old clothing should be worn.

The contingency plan should ensure that the emergency services are called if required. The fire brigade will pump out water and, if human life is not at risk, will work closely with responsible gallery staff to protect valuable exhibits. The guidance of gallery staff will be necessary to ensure that no further damage to exhibits is caused by the rescue operation.

44.6 After the flood

As soon as practicable, the venue should inform the organizer of the disaster and the action taken, together with an assessment of the situation. The organizer will inform lenders (individuals and institutions), owners and insurers and indemnifiers (see 40.8, 41.5).

The contingency plan should also include the immediate ordering of de-humidifiers from local shops. If there is a local catastrophe, there will be a shortage of pieces of equipment which will be vital in the recovery operation. Hot-air blowers are not suitable because of the excessive heat they create, and the use of calor gas heaters should be avoided because they emit moisture in operation. The use of de-humidifiers to extract water from the air and the ventilation of the space by means of fans on medium heat settings is recommended. Increased air circulation will discourage mould growth, which can spread by direct contact or airborne spores. Security may need to be enhanced if doors and windows which are normally closed are opened to improve air circulation.

The contingency plan should list the names and addresses of several conservators, so that a conservator can be called without delay (see 39.4). The organizer may also arrange for conservators to visit the venue and assess the damage and recommend action to the lenders, whose permissions must be given before any remedial work is undertaken. Water damage affects materials differently and appropriate remedial action will be required. Even if exhibits are not submerged or soaked, the relative humidity is greatly increased and damage can occur. Treatment should be carried out by a conservator, but specific emergency procedures may need to be carried out by untrained personnel. Emergency treatment should be carried out on-site in the following order: first, the most valuable; second, the least visibly damaged; and finally, the slightly damaged.

Mirror plates should be loosened to allow for free circulation of air behind wall-mounted exhibits. Textiles and other natural materials will be in danger of fungal attack, so air circulation should be increased, but care should be taken not to expose the exhibits to heat stress. Wood should be allowed to dry slowly in cool air. If the flood-water is contaminated by salt or sewage, stone should be washed with a mild phenolic/anti-bacterial solution, rinsed with plain warm water and allowed to dry in cool air. Metal should be washed in de-ionized water, avoiding heat stress.

Water-damaged paintings are highly vulnerable. Exhibits should be removed from the water, drained of surface water by tilting to one corner and laid flat, face-up in a place of safety. No attempt should be made to treat an exhibit showing signs of flaking, lifting or curling, softened or dissolved paint. Such a painting should be laid flat, face up in a place of safety.

Paintings which are not visibly damaged should be lain face down on blotting pads. The frame should be removed (canvases can shrink so forcefully that they can tear away from the stretcher). Protect the front of the exhibit with a layer of Japanese paper or tissue, ensuring that there are no wrinkles or ridges in the pad or tissue which could imprint on the paint surface, then sheets of blotting paper cut to fit inside the stretcher and the whole covered with a piece of thin ply or card, lightly weighted down. The blotting paper should be changed every ten minutes or so until it comes away nearly dry, then leave for 24 hours under blotting paper and weights in a well-ventilated and gently-heated atmosphere.

45

Packing

John Wm Morris

45.1 The need

The prime responsibility of anybody who instigates a touring exhibition must be the care of the exhibits. The aesthetic standard of the exhibition is transient; irreversible damage to the content is not. Correct packing is the most important element in ensuring that the exhibits end the tour in their original state. A correctly designed crate may make the difference between survival of an exhibit and its permanent loss after touring for a year or more. Please note that in this section, the word 'crate' is used as a collective noun to include the many sizes and forms of packing cases, crates and boxes used for packing exhibitions.

When exhibits are included in a touring exhibition, they leave the protection of their normal surroundings. Suitable packing methods, materials and vehicles are essential for transporting exhibits and associated display material safely between venues (see also 53.1). It is almost impossible to achieve optimum conditions at all times, and objects must be selected that can stand the rigours of packing and transportation.

No object should be moved without due consideration of the problems which will be encountered, and an assessment of the risks involved. Both general and specific requirements must be agreed and implemented before any object is moved. It is essential that sufficient of the exhibition budget is set aside to ensure haste-free progress from one operation to the next, without compromising good practice.

45.2 Factors determining packing methods and materials

The type of transport vehicles used to convey a touring exhibition must be known before deciding on the packing method to be used (see 53.9). All exhibits should be placed inside some form of protection. Crates can be purpose-made but, more often, will be re-used stock or hired.

Crates not only provide physical protection but define the micro-climate within (see 43.3). Where relatively large volumes of air are enclosed, care must be taken so that temperature changes do not modify humidity levels; in extreme conditions, condensation may form on the surface of exhibits. Packing systems should be designed to give sufficient buffering capacity to absorb the relatively small amounts of moisture present in the immediate enclosure. Many of the traditional materials used, e.g. wood or cardboard, will provide the absorbency required. The use of totally 'plastic wrap' packing environments should be avoided.

Before proceeding answer the following questions:

- What are the agreed requirements for packing and transporting the exhibition, including specific conservation measures?
- Are there sufficient trained staff available to pack the exhibits to the required standard and within the time allowed?
- Is sufficient protection afforded by simply wrapping an exhibit? For example, if dissimilar objects and display materials are to be transported in a single load, simple wrapping is unlikely to provide sufficient protection.
- Will exhibits need the protection of a crate and to what standard should it be constructed?
- Can all the crates used be lifted safely by manual labour, or will mechanical equipment be needed?

45.3 Required properties of packing materials

A packing material will be chosen for one or more properties that contribute to the protection of an exhibit. Some materials will be composite and fulfil more than one role, but the basic properties required of a packing material are:

Shock absorption. Most packing methods include a shock and vibration absorbing material. The energy of the destructive forces which would damage an object can be diverted into the distortion of the packing material. Some materials will only do this once and have no resilience, e.g. in a vehicle crash, the bodywork absorbs shock as it distorts, but unless mechanical force is used to regain the original shape, it will no longer provide protection.

Ease of conformation. In many instances, a packing material needs to conform to surfaces (see Figure 45.1). This may be a sheet of tissue paper used to wrap an object, or a piece of foam cut to a complex shape, which locates an exhibit in a packing case. Materials which are difficult to form or require special equipment should not be used in a touring exhibition, because replacement may be difficult at remote venues.

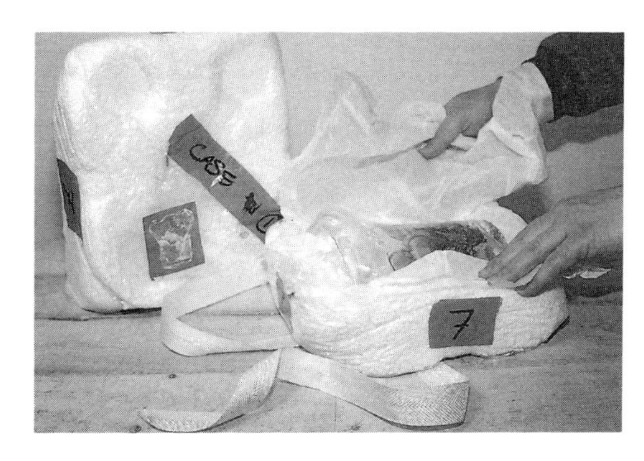

Figure 45.1 The packing of an item of 'Decorative Art' glass for a tour. A rubber-coated polystyrene bead has been used to provide a re-usable packing with close configuration. Several items were placed in a shock-resistant outer packing case.
(Courtesy of John Wm Morris)

Freedom from harm. When selecting a packing material always look out for adverse properties, such as:

- residual pollutants, e.g. isocyanate compounds used in the manufacture of plastic foam materials;
- dust, spore or fibres which would be harmful, e.g. from straw, dirty blankets, etc.;
- affinity to insects or rodents which will eat the exhibits between venues;
- materials which constitute a health risk to the packers, e.g. harmful vapours liberated from aerosol foam.

Useful properties. Look out for materials which are:

- light in weight and can be easily converted into the form required;
- economic to use and available in sufficient quantity;
- suitable for re-use from venue to venue;
- able to provide the correct environment for the exhibit.

45.4 Special conditions

With extremely delicate material or where vibration may be a problem (see 55.6), it may be necessary to calculate the environmental parameters provided by a crate with reference to shock absorption. The detailed procedure is beyond the scope of this work, but see the literature listed in 45.11.

It may be necessary to provide a record of the environmental conditions of the interior of a case during transit. It is possible to include data loggers which record humidity and temperature, and devices that monitor shock.

Certain exhibits may require separate micro climates or special provision against harmful pollution e.g. sulphur-absorbent fabrics to protect silver objects.

45.5 Crates

Packing will include one or more of the following layers of protection:

- a layer of wrapping protecting the surface of the exhibit.
- moisture-absorbing inner wrapping to assist with buffering against changes in relative humidity (RH).
- a waterproof outer layer.
- one or more sub-crates within a main crate.
- a layer of packing designed to insulate the exhibit.
- packing material to provide shock protection which will also act as thermal insulation.
- additional buffering against changes in relative humidity, e.g. packs of silica gel.
- insulation to the outer crate.
- a vapour and/or environmental barrier.
- a protective and secure outer crate.

These can be grouped into three distinct elements: surface protection for the exhibit; shock-absorbing materials; and the outer protective layer. With a travelling exhibition, there must be a realistic assessment of possible variation of conditions. A good crate design can assist with stabilizing conditions and provide a buffer against sudden environmental change.

45.6 Surface protection for the exhibit

If an exhibit has a particularly delicate surface, it may be possible to limit the points of restraint and avoid totally wrapping the surface. Where it is necessary to wrap the surface of an exhibit, care should be taken to find a non-abrasive material. The most common materials are:

- *Tissue paper.* Paper should be acid free.
- *Soft plastic films.* A polyester film such as melamine can be used where the absence of fibres is important: it has non-stick properties and can be used to protect the surface of fine art objects. Polythene sheeting attracts dirt, contains plasticizers and becomes acidic with age.
- *Soft fabrics.* Although expensive, fabric covers can be used over extended periods, and are an ideal method of protecting graphic panels. Covers should be washed before use and at regular intervals thereafter.
- *Net.* Mesh of different sizes can be used where it is necessary to hold packing materials close to the surface of a complex form, e.g. a large natural history model (see Figure 45.2).

45.7 Shock absorbing materials

Shock absorbing materials and insulators include the following:

Plastic and rubber foams. These are available in a wide range of materials with differing properties. They are easy to shape using craft knives and electric cutters (for limited use, a domestic electric carving knife will suffice). Guidance is available to compute the variables to give the required density and area of foam for a specified shock protection level: Messrs Zotefoam produce both a manual and a supporting programme for PCs which calculates thickness and area for a given load for Plastizote foam; and the Canadian Conservation Institute supplies a circular slide rule for protective package design. All foam materials offer some insulation due to the trapped air pockets within the structure. Foam material is often used to provide the support structure which locates an exhibit in a crate (see Figure 45.3). It can also be used to cushion the structural members necessary to locate heavy items. The dual property of insulator and shock absorber can be used to good advantage when designing packing. Polystyrene is a good insulator but may not offer sufficient shock absorbency. The problems associated with plastic and rubber foams include retained active com-

Figure 45.2 A fine meash fabric used in the construction industry retains a protective layer of tissue paper and Jiffy foam. Extra foam pads were sewn in place to protect delicate surfaces and areas of high relief, in this case the whale fins. (Courtesy of John Wm Morris)

Figure 45.3 A reconstructed foam was used to retain a heavy jardinière. Soft tissue, placed between the foam and the glazed surface to avoid scratching, was replaced at each venue. (Courtesy of John Wm Morris)

pounds which will 'gas-off' harmful substances, and plasticizers which can leach out into surrounding material. Foams which are made from reconstituted scrap material can contain pollutants. Fabrications can be built up using special adhesives, but care must be taken to vent the solvents from the work area and crate.

Polystyrene wafers and beads. These can be used as a means of separating small lightweight exhibits in a sub-crate. Problems include small particles of clinging dust which transfer to exhibits, and the migration of the objects through the wafers due to settlement. Poor shock resistance is afforded to heavier objects, and there is little to commend this form of packing.

Rubberized polystyrene bead. This is an adaptable packing material which equates to the semi-rigid configured packing used for the distribution of domestic articles.

Air-cap. Air-cap or bubble wrap is a satisfactory cushion material if the correct sized air-cap is used. Normally more than one layer is needed to obtain the desired protection. Problems include the rapid deflation of the 'bubbles' under a point load, e.g. at the corner of a picture frame, leaving no protection; and the static attraction of dust which can be transferred to exhibits during handling. This type of material will probably have to be replaced if the tour has several venues. In these circumstances, it may be more economic to invest in robust packing materials which will survive for the duration of the tour.

Resilient foams. These foams, e.g. Jiffy-Foam, are available in wide rolls of thin material and are easy to use. They can conform to exhibits with irregular shapes. Due to the resilient nature of the material, almost all the original protection returns after repeated compression. Problems include the static attraction of dust and easy tearing along the ridges of the material. To be effective, the foam must be positioned so that it cannot be displaced.

Cardboard. Corrugated cardboard can be used as a simple wrapping for robust exhibits, and has the advantage of low cost and wide availability. Its problems include the lack of resilience to repeated shock and poor configuration to three-dimensional objects.

Tissue paper. Frequently thought of as a wrapping material and not as a primary packing material, tissue paper can be a most effective shock absorber, when used in the form of air-containing pads. This method is widely used by the Victoria and Albert Museum for packing a diverse range of objects. Double layers of tissue paper are formed into a circular pad, held together by forming a tucked rim. Care is taken to trap air into the structure and, with multiple pads, 'nests' can be formed in a crate. This is a safe method to use with light objects and is very cost-effective, as the pads can be remade if they lose their resilience. Problems include the easy loss of small exhibits in the mass of tissue. Tissue paper must be kept clean, as dust and dirt retained on the surface create a mild sandpaper.

45.8 Outer protective layer

Requirements for the outer protective layer may include one or more of the following characteristics:

- protection from physical shock and penetration caused by handling equipment and impact from other cases;
- waterproof and, if necessary, fire proof;
- as light as possible, but retain sufficient strength under load;
- an integrated structure that will not distort when supporting other cases in a stack or when lifted by mechanical means;
- resistance to pilfering, with locks and anti-tamper seals to indicate unauthorized opening;
- the ability to be sealed and insulated to minimize changes in temperature and humidity, if required;
- any special handling provisions for placing or removing the exhibit within the container;
- construction of inert materials which will not conflict with the packed exhibits;
- painted in a light-reflective colour which will reduce thermal gain if left in sunlight.

Common materials for the outer protective layer are given below.

Timber. Wood is adaptable and can be worked with hand tools. It is available in many sections and a wide range of sheet materials, including plywood, blockboard and chipboard. It absorbs shock from rough handling, and can be repaired with hand tools. Its problems include weight, retention of moisture (leading to a high internal humidity when sealed) and glues used in the production of sheet materials which frequently contain harmful substances. The solution to the last two problems is to isolate by sealing the surface, or by the inclusion of vapour barriers – thin inert metal foils are useful for this purpose. Where there is any doubt, materials should be tested for adverse properties

Metal. Metal is easily formed into crates with an effective strength-to-weight ratio, offering good security and the potential for repeated use. Its problems include poor shock absorption, repair difficulties once distorted, rust from ferrous metals which can contaminate exhibits, and condensation particularly if transported by aircraft. Where possible, non-ferrous alloys should be used to avoid excessive weight.

Plastics. Plastic sheet is relatively inexpensive, waterproof, light and easily fabricated for special requirements. Plastic industrial crates are made in many sizes and can be adapted. Problems include the presence of plasticizers which can migrate from crates into the exhibits they are protecting, and a lack of resistance to mechanical damage. In the event of fire, the products of combustion and melt materials are very difficult to remove from exhibits.

Cardboard. Cardboard is inexpensive, relatively light and easily formed into crates. It can act as a buffer material by absorbing moisture, thus reducing the rate of change in humidity within a crate. Heavy-duty multi-ply cardboard sheet can be combined with wood frames and timber pallet bases to form a strong crate (see Figure 45.4). Its problems include the need for surface protection to make the crate waterproof because all strength is lost when wet, and lack of security and ease of attack because the material can be cut with a knife. Unless a special grade is specified, cardboard will be acidic, which will increase with age. Where exhibits are in crates for a relatively short time, no problems should be encountered.

Vegetable materials. Such materials are cheap and replaceable and provide adequate and flexible crates where woven, e.g. willow baskets and wicker hampers. Problems include the lack of resistance to weather, pilfering and pests.

Figure 45.4 Purpose-made, multi-ply cardboard boxes being used to transport a large skeletal dinosaur. The integrated pallet bases allow for mechanical handling, and the boxes are self-locating. (Courtesy of John Wm Morris)

45.9 Identification

Exhibits are at most risk when being handled or transported. Exhibits must be packed with sufficient care, and this includes providing adequate identification and documentation. Identification marks on the exterior of crates should include:

- a unique crate number (the same number should be repeated on the lid, to aid identification should it become separated from the crate);
- the name of the exhibition;
- the weight of the loaded crate;
- the name and address of the organizer;
- any special requirements, using the normal international protection markings for lifting points, no hooks, this way up, keep dry, etc.;
- markings to show the point of entry into the crate, e.g. which screws to remove first.

Much of this information will be repeated in the transport manifest (see 53.10).

45.10 During the tour

On arrival at the venue, it is often necessary to allow time for the exhibits to acclimatize, normally in the exhibition gallery, to the new environment. Where there is a delay between the arrival at the venue and installation, the packed exhibits should be stored in similar conditions to the exhibition area. Recent monitoring of exhibition transits has suggested that sealed containers and well-wrapped exhibits will retain their own micro climates for considerable periods and not acclimatize to their surroundings. It may be necessary gradually to ease wrappings to allow air exchange to take place. Conservation advice should be sought for the necessary environmental data on which to base this procedure.

The first items encountered when crates are opened should be a list of contents and instructions for unpacking. For opening crates and checking condition, see 46.8–46.10.

Packing materials are frequently lost and damaged during a tour. It is good practice to send spare stock with an exhibition and to replace any surface-protecting tissue at each venue.

After the showing, check that poor storage conditions have not affected the crates and packing materials, which should be taken to the exhibition area to acclimatize before any exhibits are repacked (see 50.6).

45.11 Further reading

British Museum. *A Guide to the Storage, Exhibition and Handling of Antiquities, Ethnography and Pictorial Art*, 1990 (2nd edition), British Museum Publications, London.

Mecklenburg, M. F. (ed.) *Art in Transit*, 1991, National Gallery, Washington.

Miles, C. E. 'Wood Coatings for Display and Storage Cases' in *Studies in Conservation*, 1986, vol. 31, no. 3, pp 114-124.

Morris, J. Wm. and Staniforth, S. (ed.) 'Packing of 3-Dimensional Objects' in *Safer Transport for Museum Objects*, 1985, UKIC, London: Meeting on Packing Cases Pre-prints.

Morris, J. Wm. 'Packing, Transport and Installation' in *Conservation and Circulation*, 1989, Touring Exhibitions Group Occasional Paper 2.

Morris, J. Wm. 'Travelling Exhibitions: a Team Manager's View of the Conservator's Role' in *The Conservator*, 1987, number 11.

46

Condition reporting

Jacqueline Ridge

46.1 A procedure for checking and reporting

Touring exhibitions present special problems because they involve numerous stages, different personnel and often separate insurance policies. Determining the suitability of an object to go on tour is an exercise in risk management. This risk can be effectively monitored by the condition check procedure, which is a formal system for checking the exhibits, the packing and the exhibition structure.

The procedure should be used before and after each movement to identify any damage, deterioration or infestation. It should record condition in a consistent way throughout the tour, to minimize misunderstandings between lender, organizer and venue. The condition of vulnerable or high-value exhibits should be checked by the lender's representative.

The loan of an exhibit should not result in a deterioration in its condition, and so requirements are frequently attached to an agreement to lend. These can be as simple as handling guidelines and packing needs, or can involve potentially more complicated issues, such as the provision of certain environmental conditions reflecting the exhibit's normal housing (see 43.3). Condition checking should act as a prompt for ensuring that these conditions are in place.

46.2 The condition check docket (CCD)

The CCD brings together all information relevant to the well-being of an exhibit. Ideally, one CCD should exist for each exhibit. Several objects might be recorded on one CCD where they are mounted to be displayed and transported as one unit, e.g. small drawings in one frame or a set of ceramic tiles.

A standard CCD can be used for most objects, whether they be two- or three-dimensional. Having the same form for all exhibits means that each venue has only to deal with a single format and will consequently be better able to record condition in a consistent way. A draft CCD should be sent to each venue in the tour, so that they will be familiar with the format before the exhibition arrives (see 43.2).

The organizer should provide lenders with one copy of its CCD for each exhibit being lent. Part of the CCD is an 'initial condition check' for the exhibit. This is a record of its condition prior to loan (see 46.4). The success of the condition check procedure will rely heavily on the quality of this first record, because all subsequent reports will be compared with it. If the lender does not carry out a detailed and accurate check prior to collection of the exhibit (see 37.5), then this task must be carried out on the organizer's premises or at the first venue, whichever is the earlier (see 36.9).

For the duration of the tour, the CCD should stay with the exhibit(s) to which it refers, and should be delegated to the venue and the carrier at the same time that the responsibility for the exhibit is formally handed from person to person. If the organizer or a courier wish to report a change of condition to the lender, then this should be by way of a photocopy of the CCD. The original CCD can be returned with the exhibit to the lender at the end of the tour, to join its documentation on the object.

46.3 Condition check docket: format and content

The following list of contents is not exhaustive but should provide sufficient scope for most exhibits. Sections can be tailored for different types of object. An example of a completed CCD is illustrated (see Figure 46.1).

Suggested format: A3 sheet of lightweight card, folded to make a four-page vertical A4 format, each kept in a polythene sleeve in a ring-binder wallet.

Although visually useful on the original, colour coding systems should be avoided. It must be possible to photocopy the CCD in the event that a lender has to be notified of damage or other change in the condition of an exhibit.

The same form can be used, omitting information from sections A and B as appropriate, for plinths, display cases and other display furniture.

First page:

SECTION A

- Identifies the exhibition: title, organizer, number of venues and dates.
- Identifies the exhibit (information pertaining to the owner): inventory number, artist/maker, title/name/brief description, size, number of parts.
- Identifies the exhibit (information pertaining to the exhibition): catalogue number, title, display case in which it is to be placed, method of display.

This section should be completed by the organizer.

SECTION B

- Identifies packing procedure, with reference to the exhibit and other items that may be packed with it: this should include the crate identification, internal packing materials, the method e.g. the order in which a multi-object crate should be packed or soft-wrap methods (see 45.9, 46.8).
- Provides brief but adequate details pertaining to necessary/agreed handling.
- Provides details concerning agreed display methods.
- Provides details of necessary and agreed environmental parameters.

This section should be completed by the organizer.

SECTION C

- Identifies the stage at which condition is checked: venue, date, name and position of checker.
- Records whether or not a change in condition or packing was noted.
- Notes environmental conditions at unpacking/packing: conditions should be recorded that may have a long-term effect on the exhibit.
- Records if notification procedure has been instigated (see 7.16).
- Records any changes agreed with the lender.

This section should be completed by each individual checker. If the organizer or a courier carries out the check, the venue should countersign any changes noted (see 51.4).

Second and third pages:

SECTION D

- Describes in writing the condition of the exhibit: the description should be short, to the point, providing an overall summary of the condition of the exhibit. Language should be clear and simple. Brevity is particularly important where an exhibition tours to venues where English is not the first language.
- Avoids the use of non-descriptive conservation terminology.
- Avoids a layout with boxes to be ticked, which, although useful for other purposes, can lead to unhelpful generalizations when describing condition.
- Avoids symbols that require a key, because they slow down the checking process and make reporting less accurate.
- Provides an image, which the person checking the exhibit can use to identify surface blemishes, distortions or disruptions, and upon which any changes of condition can be marked. The image might be a photograph, a photocopy of a photograph, an outline diagram or other means of visualizing the exhibit. If photographs are not available, then simple sketches of the exhibit or a standard outline for regular-shaped pieces can be used. It should be annotated to locate any problems. Photocopying an image onto gridded paper makes it easier to pinpoint a particular location, allowing a grid reference to be quoted in any written correspondence relating to a specific concern.
- Provides an image of sufficient quality to allow unambiguous identification of the object. Three-dimensional items should be represented by images taken from different viewpoints. Extra sheets should be added to the CCD if necessary, to display additional photographic details of complicated 3-D structures where many views are required.
- Provides ample margins (maximum 10 cm) around the image for notes to be added, to describe any marks on the image itself.

This section should be completed by the initial condition checker and annotated as required by subsequent checkers (and countersigned by the venues, if they do not carry out the check).

Fourth page:

SECTION C (continued from first page)

CONDITION CHECK DOCKET crate No: 6 catalogue No: 32

SECTION A completed by organiser

Exhibition Title: [illegible] Sculpture

Organisers: [illegible]

Number of venues: 4 Dates: 6/5/95 – 3/7/96

Lender: [illegible] Inventory/Accession No: [illegible]

Artist/Maker: Greco-Roman

Title/Exhibit Type: Bearded Man – Bust

Size (mm) H. 48 cm W. 31.5cm D. 24cm Number of parts: 1

SECTION B completed by organiser/initial checker

Packing: crate ☑ locked ☐ inner box ☐ face up ☐ face down ☐ multi object ☐
soft wrap ☐ polythene ☐ bubble wrap ☐ paper ☐ other:
corner protections ☐ glass taped ☐ all seams taped ☐ with plinthe ☐

Wrapping and arrangement in crate: (provide diagram if necessary)
[illegible] on side, do not invert sculpture
slides out – face forwards

Installation/display method: with courier ☐ without courier ☑
Agreed environmental parameters: (light, UV levels, RH) none
Agreed display method: display case ☑ with mount ☐ barriers ☐ hanging fitments provided ☐
other: on plinthe with perspex cover

Necessary agreed handling: gloves to be worn at all times,
NB weight 30kg

SECTION C completed by initial and all future checkers

Initial Condition Check (see Section D)
Place: [illegible] Before/after collection (del. as applicable)

Name/Position: J [illegible] – curator Date: [illegible]

Environmental conditions at checking and packing: 50% RH 17°C

Condition Check
Venue: Incoming/outgoing (del. as applicable)

Name/Position: Date:
Courier countersign: Changes noted:
Environmental conditions: Notification Procedure Instigated: Yes/No

Figure 46.1 Condition check docket.

SECTION D cont. completed by initial checker, annotated by future checkers

Attach or draw image/s of exhibit, annotate as appropriate. Date and initial all changes from initial check

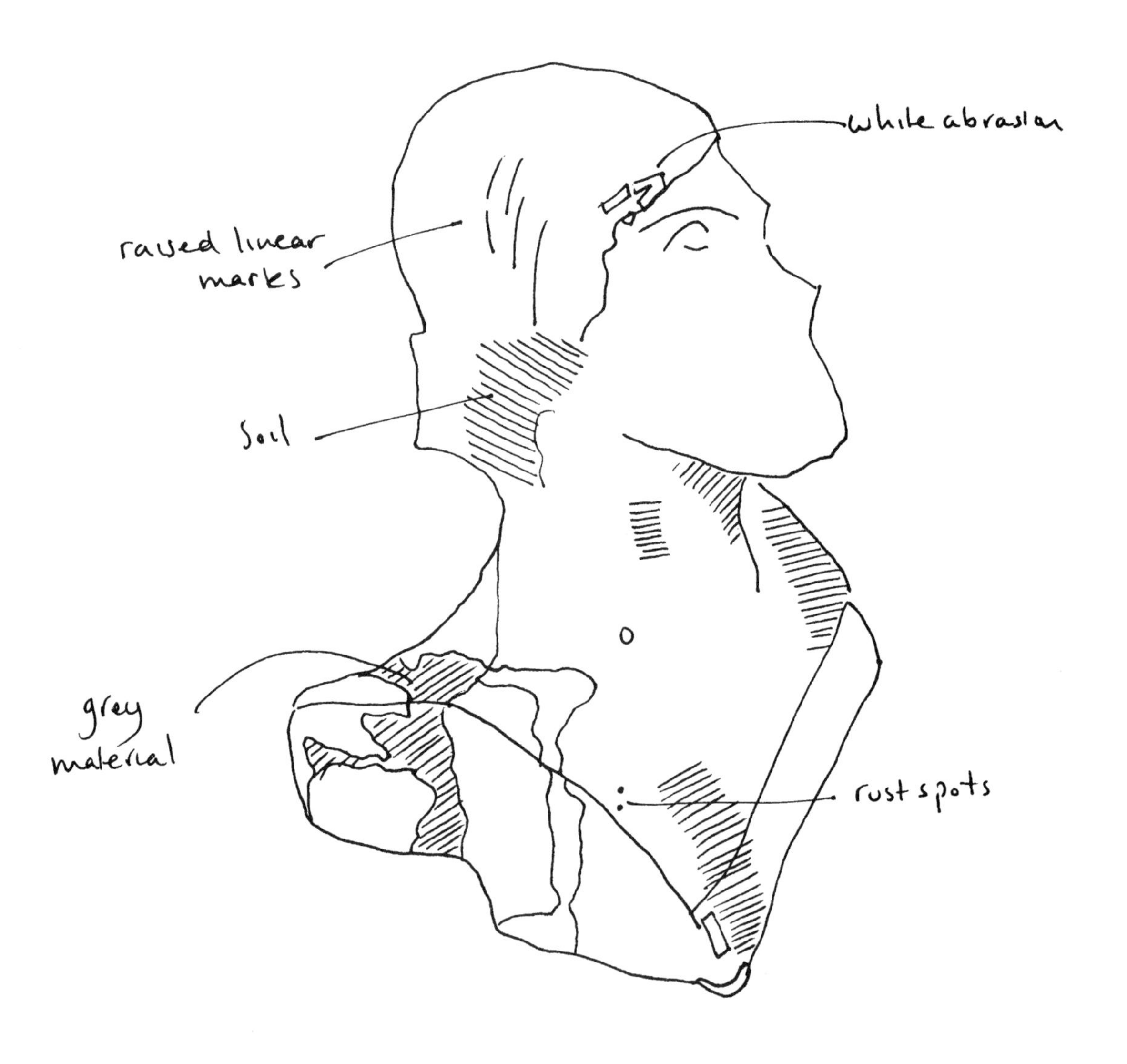

Figure 46.1 Condition check docket. (*Continued*)

<u>SECTION D</u> <u>cont.</u> completed by initial checker, annotated by future checkers

Attach or draw image/s of exhibit, annotate as appropriate. Date and initial all changes from initial check

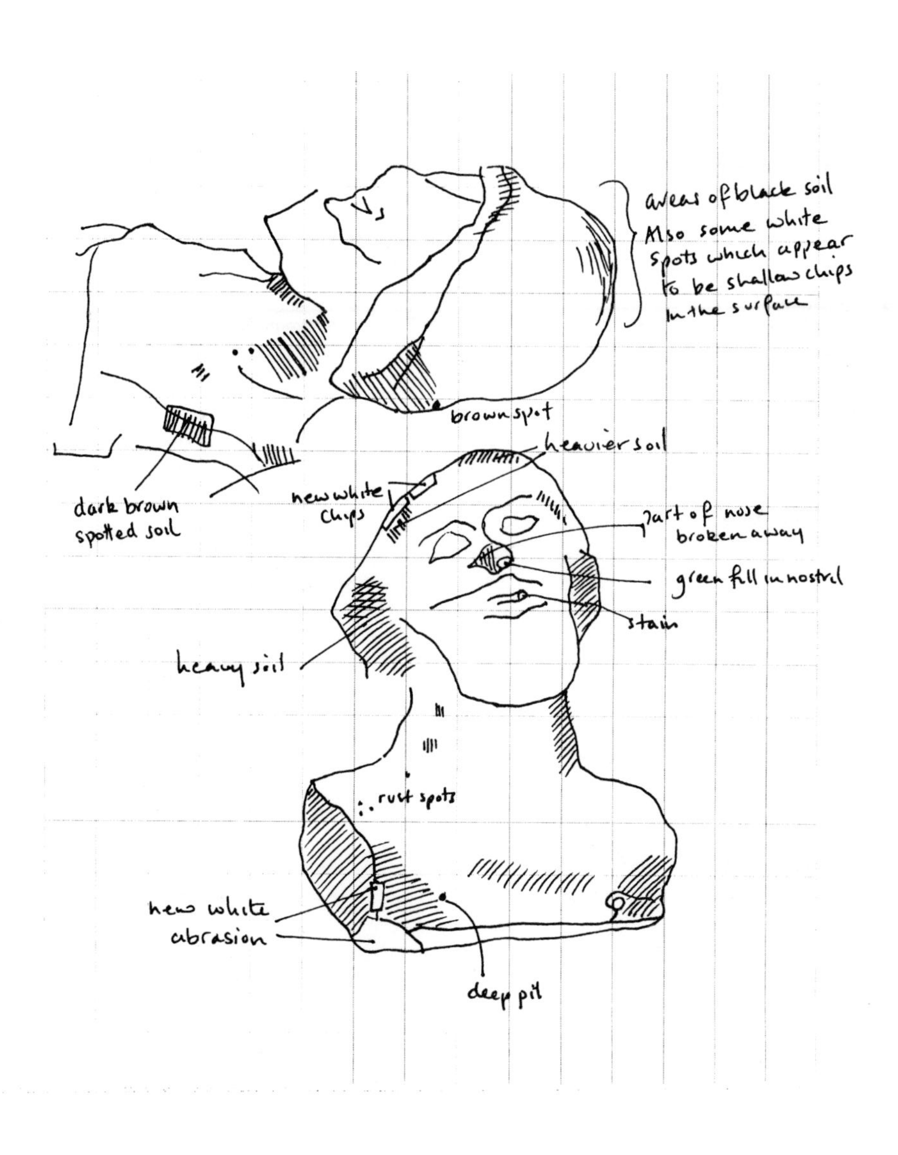

Figure 46.1 Condition check docket. (*Continued*)

SECTION C cont. completed by individual checkers

Condition Check
Venue: Incoming/outgoing (del. as applicable)
Name/Position: Date:
Courier countersign: Changes noted:
Environmental conditions: Notification procedure Instigated: Yes/No

---

Condition Check
Venue: Incoming/outgoing (del. as applicable)
Name/Position: Date:
Courier countersign: Changes noted:
Environmental conditions: Notification procedure Instigated: Yes/No

---

Condition Check
Venue: Incoming/outgoing (del. as applicable)
Name/Position: Date:
Courier countersign: Changes noted:
Environmental conditions: Notification procedure Instigated: Yes/No

---

Condition Check
Venue: Incoming/outgoing (del. as applicable)
Name/Position: Date:
Courier counstersign: Changes noted:
Environmental conditions: Notification procedure Instigated: Yes/No

---

Condition Check
Venue: Incoming/outgoing (del. as applicable)
Name/Position: Date:
Courier countersign: Changes noted:
Environmental conditions: Notification procedure Instigated: Yes/No

---

Condition Check
Venue: Incoming/outgoing (del. as applicable)
Name/Position: Date:
Courier countersign: Changes noted:
Environmental conditions: Notification procedure Instigated: Yes/No

---

Condition Check
Venue: Incoming/outgoing (del. as applicable)
Name/Position: Date:
Courier countersign: Changes noted:
Environmental conditions: Notification procedure Instigated: Yes/No

---

Figure 46.1 Condition check docket. (*Continued*)

46.4 Initial check: what, why, when and who

The initial check forms the basis of all subsequent checking and reporting. The report of this check must clearly identify damages, blemishes or surface features that could otherwise be construed as a change from the original state.

The report should reflect the condition in which the exhibit left the owner or lender, and should therefore be carried out as close to the time of collection as is feasible. If examined prior to collection, the exhibit should be packed and stored in a safe place until collected, to ensure no further change in condition. In this instance, the environmental conditions in which the exhibit was packed should be recorded on the CCD.

The check should be carried out by a conservator or other person qualified to identify clearly any problems associated with an exhibit. It may be appropriate for the organizer to employ a conservator to complete some or all of the initial checks, to ensure that appropriate and consistent information is gathered, and to save time and problems in future (see 39.1). However, conservators should not assume that a fellow conservator will be available at each venue, and the method of reporting condition at the initial check should not assume any prior knowledge of the exhibit.

46.5 Initial check: how

Examine the exhibit to familiarize yourself with it.

Annotate the image in section D of the CCD. Simple dots or hatching lines will be sufficient to indicate to future checkers that there is something here to look at. Add in the margin a brief descriptive note identifying the problem if appropriate.

Certain phenomena are straightforward to note initially, but are often difficult for future checkers to establish if there has been a change in their state, e.g. changes in tension of canvas or fabrics for paintings and textiles, cockling of a paper support, pinpoint flaking of a gilded frame, movements in cracks and splits in wood objects. If these factors are fundamental to the safety of the exhibit, then a detailed pictorial record with measurable parameters must be provided. In these cases, it may be appropriate for a courier who is very familiar with the exhibit to examine it (see 51.2).

Compile a brief written description of the condition of the object. The written section provides an overview for the person at each venue who will be examining the exhibit for the first time. Include comments relating to recent conservation treatment, if this will help to warn of potential problems that the exhibit may experience, e.g. a comment to the effect that part of a painting has been consolidated to stabilize flaking paint.

Note where there is an absence of a frequently-observed condition, e.g. if a gilded frame has no minor gilding loss because it has just been re-gilded, if a new backboard has been attached and therefore there are no scuffs on the reverse, or if new Perspex has been fitted and has no scratches. Similarly, note if a painting, work on paper or textile has no planar distortions.

Conversely, note phenomena that may be very extensive and not possible to mark, e.g. if a gilded frame is severely desiccated and prone to minute gilding loss. 'Generally discoloured throughout' may be sufficient if a work on paper has severe discolouration from foxing. In these instances, the lender will be acknowledging an inherent problem, and the phenomena are not considered a reason for not lending.

46.6 Tips on materials

When checking the condition of an exhibit, be aware of the materials it is composed of. Pay particular attention to junctions where two different materials meet: there will be an inevitable structural antagonism at this point, which is likely to become a point of weakness and thus be vulnerable to change. Always look for loose particles on the surface or in the wrapping. In itself, this is a damage, but it will also indicate the type of potential problems to be encountered. Condition checking may involve some handling of the exhibit: handling should be kept to a minimum, and instructions should be followed. The use of clean gloves is nearly always essential: fine rubber gloves may be more suitable in certain instances to avoid catching delicate or friable surfaces. A recent change or damage looks new in most cases: check for fresh surface deposits and the lighter or brighter colour of newly-exposed material.

The following is a list of common problems associated with a range of material types that may occur during or after the loan. The list is not intended to be exhaustive, and should not circumvent the need for specialists to be brought in to check condition when appropriate.

Wood (e.g. sculpture, furniture, panel paintings, craft items, ethnographic exhibits, models). Splits, joins, splinters, cracks: note where they stop. Scratches and gouges. Warps, lifting veneers, loose joints, loose or lost fittings, loose old repairs, lifting old repairs: check if surrounding material has been recently disrupted. Staining of surface, bloom or crazing in varnish/coating. Insect damage: holes old or new, fresh frass (wood powder), mould growth, surface bloom. (See also clear coatings, below.)

Stone (e.g. sculpture, archaeological exhibits). Scratches, gouges, scuffs, stains, lost fragments, chips, crumbling, old repairs, loose old repairs, cracks and splits, finger prints, staining, surface corrosion (white fluffy substance on marble).

Metal (e.g. sculpture, decorative arts, medals, plaques, craft exhibits, ethnographic items, costume details, jewellery). Scratches, dents, lost sections, old repairs, loose old repairs, joints, rivets, loose solders, opening of joints, loose attached sections or junctions with other materials. Surface irregularities: pitting, discolouration, tarnish, darkening of metal (occurs fast when a protective surface coating is lost, especially on silver). Corrosion products: irregular powder and/or hard nodular deposits standing proud of the surface, with localized colour differences from normal surface. Weak threads or chains. Shattered stones, with movement in mount. Flaking pearls.

Textiles (e.g. costumes, banners, craft items, paintings on canvas). Tears, splits, loose threads, holes, broken or loose stitching, lost or loose attached trimmings (beading, stitching, appliqué). Staining, dust in fibres, creasing, loss of pile from velvet. Mould, fungus, mildew. Planar distortions, over-tension in canvas support, localized bulges, canvas draws at corners. Damage to conservation work, e.g. adhesive lining lifting, stitching to support broken, cockling of lining or textile. Other materials, e.g. rubber, leather or metal, disintegrating or corroding.

Glass (e.g. decorative arts, sculpture, crafts, jewellery, stained glass). Cracks, pieces or components missing, visible surface irregularities, staining, abrasions, ingrained dirt, salt growths, crizzling, corrosion, moisture. Breaks in leading or solder, glass moving within lead, copper ties insecure, lead corrosion, paint or enamel flaking.

Plastics (e.g. decorative arts, sculpture, painting supports, models, craft and household items, costume, furniture). Scratches, dents, splits, warps, fingerprints, sweating, smell of chemicals, effect on other components, discolouration.

Painted and gilded surfaces (e.g. easel paintings, frames, works on paper, illuminated manuscripts, archival material, polychrome sculpture, furniture, textiles, models). Lifting or raised paint areas, marked cracking, actual losses in paint layer, crumbling paint surface. Check areas associated with scratches, splits, joins or old repairs and fillings. Mould. Bloom or blanching (whitening). Random variations in surface gloss. Staining. Insect damage.

Clear surface coatings (e.g. varnish, polish, unpainted surfaces). Staining of surface, bloom or crazing in varnish/coating, scratches, scuffs, powdering, changes in surface gloss.

Ceramics (e.g. sculpture, decorative arts, craft objects, plaques). Cracks, chips, old repairs, loose repairs, missing parts, staining.

46.7 Specific problems

The following summary lists typical problems that might be noted with common types of exhibit.

Books suffer considerably from inappropriate handling. Check coverboards, joints, sewing and spine. Normally it is not necessary to check every page, but watch for detached and creased pages, also soiling, foxing, discolouration and mould. The CCD should make a detailed report on the page on view, and general comments on the entire structure, especially where there is a specific problem of a type likely to worsen.

Works on paper, parchment and vellum (e.g. prints, drawings, watercolours, collage, pastels, photographs, manuscripts). Cockling/undulations (or absence of) in paper support. Splitting/pulling apart of paper fibres from over-tension: check round old repairs. Bulging of mount in frame. Detaching at joints of a multi-section image. Lifting from back support. Staining. Discoloured pigment. Pigment loss: pigment transfer to glazing where image/support touching glazing; loose pigment at bottom of mount. Crazing/flaking of photographic emulsion.

Paintings. Planar distortions (or lack of) in canvas support, localized bulges, canvas draws at corners and edges, tears, holes, punctures, dents, scuffs, scratches. Warp of panel. Splits: check for new wood dust; if open, check associated paint areas. Lifting paint and tented/ridged paint. Paint loss. Mould. Insect damage: frass, cocoons, flight holes. For unframed items, check for fingerprints, grubbiness and dents and bulges at edges. Lifting paint, paint losses, tenting/ridged paint. Bloom (whitening) in varnish or paint layer.

Frames. Lost moulding. Extensive flaking on gilding. Exposed white gesso. Damage from past attachment of hanging fittings. Crushed corners, open mitres, fingerprints, knocks, scuffs and gouges. If the attachment of exhibit in frame is visible, check it is secure. General loose surface dirt.

Framed exhibits (e.g. easel paints, works on paper with or without mounts, photographs, papyrus and other exhibits framed behind glass). Slippage in frame: skewed image, powdered edge varnish. Image touching the glass: transfer of material to glazing, crushed varnish through point impact with glazing. Check for foreign material along inside of framing or mount. Staining on mount. Insects inside glazing. Exhibit bowing away from frame at edge. Glass slipping, cracked, chipped, dirty.

46.8 Before opening a crate or package

Familiarize yourself with the contents of the exhibition, and with the general conditions that have been agreed, e.g. environmental and security measures (see 42.6, 43.4).

Check the relevant CCD for any specific requirements for an exhibit agreed with the lender, and make sure that these are being fulfilled and implemented, e.g. that a courier should be present, that an exhibit should acclimatize in its case for 24 hours after arrival, that relative humidity is within agreed parameters or that gloves are worn for handling.

Check for any handling guidelines or packing information that indicates how to handle the exhibit in the most appropriate manner.

46.9 When opening a crate or package

Familiarize yourself with the list of the contents of each crate, which should be provided in a wallet attached to the inside of the lid.

With crates holding several items, it is useful if there is a diagram or description identifying the layering or position of the items, showing the precise sequence of unpacking and repacking. If this is not already in the wallet, then make careful notes for when you pack the crate again.

It is also useful to have a diagram or description where unpacking includes the removal of complex internal supports. Again, careful notes should be made for when you pack the crate, if such a diagram is not in the wallet.

Identify from the list of contents what and how many items are supposed to be in the packing: items are not always packed in the crates or packing intended for them. Proceed with the utmost caution, in the event that the wrong items have been placed there or in case packing has not been done properly, noting any pertinent information on the relevant CCD.

Observe carefully the type of packing materials used and how the exhibits and other items are packed: check the actual packing against that described in the CCD.

Examine carefully packing materials, insides of crates, etc. for detached fragments which may indicate damage.

Follow the agreed notification procedure, agree any changes and record them on the CCD, if the packing method is deemed inappropriate and seems to be causing a problem. If the person responsible for checking the condition of the exhibits is not present at the time of unpacking, then such changes should be brought to his/her attention.

46.10 Checking and reporting

Remember that the condition of each exhibit must be checked and reported before packing and collection at the end of a showing, as well as during unpacking after the arrival of the exhibition.

Provide sufficient space and light for examination and make sure that there are enough people to help. The person delegated by the organizer for this purpose should be present with the CCDs.

Unpack and fully check one exhibit or a small group of exhibits at a time. Make sure that there is adequate time to look at each exhibit, and that the pace is not forced by other staff.

Read the written description in section D of the CCD to gain an overview of the condition of the exhibit. Examine the exhibit, checking irregularities against the image(s) provided in section D of the CCD. If irregularities have not already been noted, annotate the image, dating and initialling your addition. If the organizer or a courier completes the CCD, any changes noted by that person should also be initialled by the venue's representative.

It is sometimes difficult to establish whether information is relevant or not. If in doubt, include it.

If a change in condition appears to be significant, follow the agreed notification procedures. The CCD should stay with the exhibit to which it refers throughout the tour. Whether it is the venue, the organizer or a courier who notes a change in condition, a photocopy should be made to send or take back to the lender. If changes are noted during dismantling, the venue should retain for its own records a photocopy of the CCD (which will, of course, go with the exhibit to the next venue).

For handling procedures, see 48.2 and subsequent parts.

47

Protection against pests

Bob Child

47.1 The problem

Pests, which include insects and vermin, are those biological agents that damage museum material either by feeding on it, or by attacking it for pupation sites or bedding, or because it is in the way. It is rare for short-term exhibitions to be affected by pests, owing to the short time scale. Both insect and other pest infestations need a long period of time to build up before becoming troublesome and damaging. However, it is common for exhibits to be a source of a pest outbreak when they are returned to their permanent home, by introducing insect pests into the storage area.

47.2 Inspecting the venue

The primary causes of insect and other pest infestations are a suitable source and access to the exhibits. Most insect infestations develop in birds' nests in attics, chimneys, window ledges, etc., and become a pest when they obtain access into the building through fireplaces, windows and roof spaces. When a touring exhibition is planned, the organizer should inspect the venue, looking particularly for signs of the following:

- birds' nests and birds roosting on chimneys, window sills, etc.;
- open fireplaces and adjacent attic access;
- rubbish accumulation and poor waste clearance;
- poor housekeeping and cleaning procedures.

47.3 Precautionary measures

All material used in a touring exhibition should be kept in a clean, dry, well-ventilated environment. Any suspect material, such as straw, bark or display material that may be infested at the time it is acquired, should be fumigated before being introduced into the exhibition. Traditionally, methyl bromide gas was used for fumigation, but now safer, non-toxic gases such as carbon dioxide can be used. Commercial firms such as Rentokil can advise on the best methods.

Where exhibitions use material that may be susceptible to pest attack, and the organizer or staff at one of the venues is concerned about a spread of an infestation, then insect traps are advisable and useful. 'Blunder' traps are non-toxic sticky traps that can give an early warning of the presence of insect pests. They are available from the present author. They should be placed around the exhibition, and any catch of insects should be noted and identified.

As part of the condition check procedure (see 46.5, 46.10), exhibits must be carefully checked for the presence of insect pests. Any exhibits suspected of infestation should be isolated from other exhibits. Crates and any packing material should also be kept separate (see 45.10). The lender should be contacted and approval should be obtained for any treatment or other action. The carrier should be notified, so that it can take action to ensure that its vehicles are not sources of infestation.

47.4 Training

Personnel responsible for touring exhibitions should have training and experience in the identification and control of insect and other pests. Anybody carrying out any pest control treatments must be trained in the use of the equipment and the handling of the chemicals involved.

47.5 Further reading and information

Pinniger, D. *Insect Pests in Museums*, 1994 (3rd edition), Archetype Press, London.

Storey, K. O. *Approaches to Pest Management in Museums*,

1985, Smithsonian Institution, Washington, USA.

Help and advice can be obtained from:

- The author of this section, who is an adviser on pest control to the National Trust and other institutions, and Head of Conservation at the National Museum of Wales, Cardiff CF1 3NP. Tel 01222 397951.
- D. Pinniger, who is a consultant entomologist with experience of insect pests in museums and historic houses, and who can be contacted at the Central Science Laboratory, London Road, Slough SL3 7HJ. Tel 01753 534626.

48

Handling

John Wm Morris

48.1 The importance of correct handling procedures

Once an exhibit is included in a touring exhibition it will be handled many times. On each occasion, the exhibit is removed from the protection of packing materials and is placed on exhibition, a process of high risk. It is, therefore, necessary to adopt safe working practices which minimize the risk of damage.

There are three key statements which need to be understood by persons who handle exhibits.

ALL COLLECTION OBJECTS ARE IRREPLACEABLE

CASH PAID BY INSURERS IS SMALL RECOMPENSE

RESTORATION IS MERELY COSMETIC TREATMENT

During each exhibition there are three distinct phases which involving handling. These differ both in location and the staff involved.

The pre-exhibition period. Selection of exhibits starts a planning process which must decide on the methods to be adopted for packing, handling and transport. The first practical handling commences as the exhibits are gathered together, which may be from a single source or very diverse locations. This work is often undertaken by staff under the direct control of the organizer.

The exhibition phase. It is during this phase that the greatest risk of damage exists. Each exhibit is subjected to repeated handling; in a semi-protected state as it is placed in, or taken out of crates; and in an unprotected state during installation. Frequently the venue staff will have no prior knowledge of the exhibits and must rely on the handling notes supplied by the organizer. It is also difficult for the organizer to determine the level of handling skills present at each venue. This work may be delegated to agents (see 52.8).

Return of the exhibits. It is essential that at the end of the tour all exhibits are carefully examined for handling damage. This task is impossible unless comparison can be made with both the original and subsequent exhibit condition reports (see 46.2). The task of final distribution to the lenders may be under the direct supervision of the organizer, the staff of the last venue, or a commercial carrier. Whoever is chosen, the level of competence of the staff used must be sufficient for the task. This is particularly important when returning exhibits to private lenders, who may require pictures to be rehung and large objects installed in their original locations (see 36.3).

48.2 Handling exhibits on arrival at a venue

Before delivery, contact should be made with the member of staff responsible for the installation of the exhibition in the venue. Advance warning should be given of the exact time of arrival and the number of staff required to assist with off-loading (see 17.10, 17.11). It is important to minimize the handling of exhibits both when in the transit packing and during installation. Handling starts from the moment that the delivery vehicle is unloaded.

If a third party is responsible for installing the exhibition at an unfamiliar venue, it is essential that all problems associated with the handling of the exhibits have been discussed in advance of delivery to the site. Points to raise include problems of vehicle access and the constraints of the building, e.g. narrow stairs and doors (see 38.7).

Make sure that the correct handling equipment and protective clothing are available, including any special equipment that needs to be hired, e.g. a crane for heavy exhibits. Floor surfaces may need to be protected from the wheels of trolleys and other handling equipment.

There should be a pre-determined order for the construction of the display-cases and other display structures, which should be completed before the exhibits are unpacked (see 49.7). With a complex exhibition, a detailed plan can help to avoid unnecessary extra handling of fixtures and exhibits. Exhibits should be unpacked in a logical order, their condition checked (see 46.10) and they should then be placed as soon as possible in their correct position.

48.3 Basic rules for the movement of exhibits within a venue

Think before hands touch the exhibit. Time is a very expensive commodity. We are often put under pressure to carry out a move in a short space of time. Thinking out the problem and planning the resources necessary is the whole basis of a satisfactory procedure and must be given sufficient time. Ignoring this step can result in injury to staff and damage to the exhibits.

Provide suitable protection. What level of protective packing is required to protect an exhibit for handling within the building? If an exhibit is to be removed for transport, is it safe to move the exhibit without temporary packing to a packing area, or must it be packed *in situ*? Is temporary packing available, and supports on which to 'rest' an exhibit that is being manually lifted?

Plan the route. Has a route been planned and checked, and all potential obstacles removed or otherwise taken into account (see 48.6)? The relocation should be documented, and a photographic record made if necessary.

Provide sufficient skilled staff (see 48.4).

Exclude the public. Can the public be controlled by barriers or warding staff where it is necessary to cross areas open to the public? Is there security and physical protection at the destination?

48.4 Staff

Team work is the key to successful handling of exhibits. If possible, the same staff should be used to handle an exhibition at all the venues. If this is not possible, ensure that each venue can field enough people with the appropriate skills. All the actions have to be carried out in a disciplined manner, and under the control of a single person. Staff working under pressure can damage exhibits, and it is necessary to allow sufficient time. The staff should:

- be sufficiently skilled for the task;
- have previously worked as a team;
- be fully briefed for the task;
- not be under pressure, due to a shortage of time or other demands;
- be able to provide sufficient physical strength to complete the task;
- be trained to keep their hands off delicate surfaces and wear gloves when necessary;
- have a safe place to smoke away from the exhibits (and non-smokers), if any of the staff are smokers.

48.5 The route

Many of the buildings used for exhibition purposes were designed for other uses, and have restricted access. The worst scenario is when large and heavy exhibits have to be moved through a building. A full survey should be made to discover all the points where problems will arise. It may also be necessary to protect the floors and walls to prevent damage to the interior decorations.

Take the following action, when it is intended to move an exhibit through the building:

- walk the whole route before the actual move takes place;
- check that all the exhibits, crates and mechanical handling equipment will clear the door openings and corridor bends;
- securely fix open all doors;
- position helpers at doors and at other restricted points on the route;
- establish firm control over the route to avoid conflict with the public;
- inform the public of the reason for any restrictions.

48.6 The exhibit

Most museum objects are old and suffer from a reduction in their former strength. Weakness is often the result of a previous break that has been badly repaired, which will give way when it is least expected. It is always necessary to fear the worst and decide how the parts can be retained if the exhibit shatters. Consider:

- the structure as a whole and determine the weak points;
- the distribution of weight: look out for exhibits with a high centre of gravity, which will be top-heavy;
- how to keep all the parts of a complex exhibit together, including labels, conservation reports and other documentation;
- how fragments will be contained within the packing if a breakage occurs.

48.7 The lift and carry

Lifting is a skill. Although we are doing it all the time, we normally do it badly. Staff should be trained in manual lifting techniques and be aware of current safety legislation. A team should be directed by a single person who controls all actions, to avoid people lifting at different times and causing strain to backs and joints. Accidents are frequently caused by a person or group trying to lift exhibits which are too heavy for their strength. The point at which specialist equipment and staff is required must be recognized.

Observe the following rules:

- One team leader should co-ordinate all action and give clear commands.
- The sequence of an action must be agreed and not left to argument during the move.
- If working alone, always use both hands so positioned as to give support under the main body of the exhibit.
- Be prepared to stop *en route* if necessary, and place the exhibit on a temporary padded support to allow the staff to rest.
- Work within the safe limit of the weakest member of the team.

48.8 Large and heavy exhibits

Large and heavy exhibits require special skills and equipment during installation. At the simplest level, a heavy exhibit could be defined as a lift for two men, approximately 50 kg (110 lb), but this is a poor definition because the effective weight can depend on the difficulty of grip, the distance of reach and how close it is possible to stand to the centre of gravity of the exhibit.

As exhibits increase in weight and bulk, categories can be defined on the basis of the type of equipment used, from exhibits that can be carried safely by hand using two or more people, to those requiring simple manually-operated equipment and those needing powered mechanical equipment used by the venue's staff, and finally to exhibits that require the assistance of specialist contractors and elaborate handling equipment.

Preparation obeys the rules for normal handling of exhibits, but with the added complication of possible severe damage to persons and property if an accident occurs.

48.9 Planning the move of a heavy exhibit

Select contractors well in advance, allowing ample time for the submission of tenders if required. Contractors will normally provide one or more of five functions: transport; lifting and special moving equipment; building support (e.g. where existing floors will not carry the load); site protection (e.g. the provision of temporary roads over lawns); and additional security to cover short term needs.

Equipment must be suitable for the job and fulfil all the statutory requirements, comply with good working practice and provide an adequate safe working load. Staff must be adequately trained in the use of such equipment.

Check the route to be traversed for floor loadings, both internally and externally. Do not forget the weight of the supports and lifting equipment; this can often exceed the weight of the exhibit to be moved.

Complete all pre-installation work, e.g. where an item has a support structure, in good time.

Consult appropriate authorities on the detailed plans of the operation, including senior members of staff; external contractors and sub-contractors; statutory undertakings, e.g. highways, police, telephones; and the users of adjacent properties.

48.10 Moving a heavy exhibit

Examine the exhibit in great detail. The points at which lifting straps and attachments can be made must be noted. Check the weight and estimate the centre of gravity. Ensure that the structural strength of a complex exhibit is assessed by a competent person. Do not assume that the initial strength of the exhibit is still present: metal fatigue and internal corrosion may be present; in wooden exhibits, rot or insect attack may have weakened the structure with no obvious surface damage.

The exhibit should be dismantled into the smallest possible component parts.

The most economic method is not necessarily the best solution for the safety of the item (see Figure 48.1). It can also be cheaper to hire expensive equipment for a short period than to tie up large numbers of staff for a longer period. Access can always be made through walls and by removing windows. This may be cheaper than complex moves within a restricted building.

Be prepared for possible complications due to adverse weather and for issuing special clothing to staff.

A large exhibit on the move may be newsworthy and attract publicity which, although welcome, may create problems of crowd control and require the provision of barriers to maintain safe distances.

When there are several large exhibits to install, the sequence in which objects are moved and installed becomes critical. One exhibit should never be lifted over another.

At all times, have a fail-safe policy.

All costings should allow for overtime, night working and include a generous contingency sum.

Try to learn by other people's experience, e.g. ask

Figure 48.1 Large dramatic objects create impact if included in touring exhibitions. Providing the correct handling equipment can, however, incur considerable additional cost. (Courtesy of Paul Howard)

other organizations that might have moved similar exhibits if they can recommend competent contractors.

48.11 The destination

An object may have been safely displayed in a museum for many years, only to be damaged the first time it is moved. Any move increases the risk of damage to an exhibit, so it is particularly important that the destination is safe.

The whole area should also be checked for faults that may occur in the future, with attention to both the environment and security (see 42.1, 43.4). Conditions change, so check for risks arising from the following:

- sunlight changes direction at a rate of fifteen degrees per hour;
- local heat levels can change, e.g. radiators can come on at the most unexpected times;
- relative humidity can change rapidly;
- the new location can be less secure and be subject to theft, vandalism and accidental damage.

48.12 If the worst happens

Remember that exhibits are most at risk when being handled or transported, and problems will arise from vibration, contact shock and changes in environment.

If a breakage or damage takes place, do not panic. It is impossible to work for a lifetime in a museum without encountering or causing damage to an object. The objective is to minimize these events by care at all times. Report what has happened, and ask for the assistance of a conservator.

If there is a breakage:

- Stop, rest the object and support loose fragments.
- Seal off the area.
- Send for a conservator.
- Inform the organizer about the damage and the action taken.
- Resist the temptation to pick up the pieces: do not sweep up fragments or place loose bits in a bag.

If there is no conservator immediately available:

- Place all the fragments on a clean tray or in a drawer.

If there are any small fragments, place a clean disposable bag on a vacuum cleaner and vacuum with a light pass over the area. Place the labelled bag with the larger fragments.

- Inform the organizer to arrange for conservation support.
- Do not attempt a repair or try to cover up the damage (see 7.16).

49

Installation

Julia Ellis

49.1 Basic principles

A successful touring exhibition means success throughout the whole tour. Perfection achieved at the opening venue is ultimately only a small contribution to the complex process of maintaining the well-being of individual exhibits and achieving the success of the exhibition as a whole, in terms of its communication and appeal to visitors.

It is important for a touring exhibition to be hired to appropriate venues and to be designed with flexibility, anticipating the need for accommodation in a variety of spaces. A proactive role on the part of the organizer is essential to these procedures.

The organizer of a touring exhibition should then take all possible steps to ensure that, at each of the venues, the exhibition is displayed to its best advantage, i.e. that aesthetic and interpretive statements are reinforced, visual impact maintained and conservation requirements met.

It is the organizer's responsibility to regulate the processes of installing and dismantling the exhibition at each of the venues, either through direct supervision or, when this is not possible, through providing written instructions and images as guidelines for curators and technicians.

49.2 Communication, the key to successful preparation

The organizer should establish and maintain lines of communication with venues from the earliest planning stages. Regular communication maintains the exhibition's profile in the venues' planning. Exchange of information will minimize friction between organizer and venue arising from any disparity between an exhibition's requirements and each venue's resources. Installation is greatly facilitated if venues have been informed and prepared by the organizer in advance of their showing.

The organizer should bear the following considerations in mind:

All material advertising the exhibition to potential venues should state requirements and responsibilities for display (e.g. floor area, wall space, light levels, environmental conditions and security) and transport (see 12.6).

Changes in gallery requirements may occur as the exhibition develops. Venues should be notified of all changes as they occur (see 17.1).

When showings are being discussed or when they are confirmed, floor plans should be obtained from each venue, showing gallery spaces and access routes. These should be used to inform both the design of the exhibition layout and the size and weight of transit crates (see 38.6, 38.7, 38.18).

Ideally, when exhibits have been selected, venues should be visited to ascertain: the feasibility of the proposed exhibition layout; gallery style, colour scheme and the visual strengths and weaknesses of the display area not evident from a plan; suitability of screens, plinths, display cases, etc.; relationship of the display area to the entrance and other galleries; visitor access and signposting plans; and access arrangements to the display area, particularly for exhibits which are large and/or heavy.

A venue should be advised in good time about any extra costs likely to be incurred in installing and dismantling an exhibition, so that it can budget for these costs. These might include: accommodation and subsistence for artists or couriers who will supervise the installation of particular exhibits (see 34.4, 51.6), or paint, fittings, packing and other material and equipment costs.

The venue should, in turn, communicate to the organizer:

Any re-location of the exhibition from the display area originally proposed.

Any planned building or redecoration work which might change the display area, the environmental or security conditions, or access. Most painting and drawing exhibitions will not involve elaborate design or display structures, but will depend for their effectiveness on the sensitive hanging of the exhibits. The decorative condition of the display area will be of great importance, and painting and refurbishing should be seen as an essential part of preparing for an exhibition and should be costed into the venue's budget.

Any staffing changes, especially changes in curatorial staff and reductions in technical staff or invigilators.

Until the tour begins, the organizer is responsible for providing each venue with regular updates on the development of the exhibition and the tour. A mechanism for doing this is provided by 'advance information' (see 17.1). For example, new work created by an artist for an exhibition may be a radical departure from previous work, and a dramatic change of scale will affect display requirements (see 34.1). Regular communication between artist and organizer and between organizer and venue is essential to ensure that all parties are fully aware of major changes in direction and can prepare for any consequences for display or storage and their cost implications.

49.3 Briefing the venues

Once the exhibition is open at its first place of showing, it is a tangible entity. Venues that would not normally visit the inaugural showing at some stage, should be strongly encouraged to do so, in order that they become more familiar with the exhibition and can better prepare for its arrival and promotion. It is extremely valuable for the organizer to arrange at this first showing a briefing for the venues, which should be addressed as much to technicians and education staff as to the curator or exhibition officer managing the reception of the exhibition.

The briefing allows the organizer to:

- discuss the rationale of the actual exhibition in relation to the original concept (see 4.4);
- draw attention to vulnerable exhibits or to those which involve complex mounting or assembly (see 48.6);
- show how display cases are erected and what fittings are used (see 21.3);
- demonstrate procedures and techniques, e.g. for handling, packing and checking condition (see 46.8–46.10);
- discuss the prospectus of educational materials provided by the organizer and perhaps see evidence of actual programmes (see 25.3).

The briefing is also a convenient moment to recap and confirm arrangements for transport, insurance, couriers, etc and to discuss implications including costs for the venues. It is an opportunity for the organizer to provide the venues with samples and specifications of any fabric or other material which may be required, and to hand them detailed information, e.g. where fittings can be obtained and what British Standard should apply to any paint to be used.

The briefing enables the venues to:

- build confidence in, and enthusiasm for, the reality of the exhibition, through shared ideas and response;
- visualize the exhibition in their own display areas, anticipating possible access and installation problems, which may not have been considered already and for which action can be agreed;
- promote knowledge and shared ownership of the exhibition within their institutions;
- plan education programmes and marketing strategies (see 25.5, 30.1).

The briefing will be an opportunity for the venues to consider and discuss how exhibits might be placed to maximize the impact of the exhibition. It is often easy to place single exhibits as dramatic centrepieces, but more care may be needed with smaller items which might, for example, be crowded into a corner or concentrated in a display case which is only visible from one side. The briefing should also help to avoid congestion where display cases are placed a short distance in front of a number of framed items on a wall, or where an audio–visual presentation or introductory texts might stop visitors for long periods (see 23.5).

It should be emphasized that the majority of venues will see the exhibition only once before their own showing, which may be some months later. The briefing is a taster only. People should not be expected to remember complex points or to make detailed notes. Where possible, the organizer should provide notes, and an additional set should be sent to arrive at each venue nearer in time to its showing.

49.4 The organizer as facilitator of the installation

In advance of the exhibition's arrival, the organizer should negotiate with each venue a timetable for installation and dismantling, and should be flexible to accommodate last-minute changes in plan which a venue may need to make. For an example of an installation schedule, see 8.4.

The 'hang' or display of the exhibition should be the result of a discussion of priorities and concerns between organizer and venue, to arrive at a solution which is satisfactory to all concerned. The organizer must remember that each venue is in the best position to know how its display area is used by visitors and will also need to take account of health and safety considerations (see 27.9).

The organizer's role in installing and dismantling the exhibition at each venue can vary from a physical presence, overseeing and participating, to simply being available at the other end of the telephone. This role should be clarified with the venue at the outset, e.g. stating if the organizer is the only person to handle the exhibits, the task of any couriers who are to be present, the extent of technical support required, etc. Organizers should normally supervise the dismantling of exhibitions if they have supervised installation. If this is not possible, the venue should allocate at least two members of staff to work with the organizer on installation, so that they can subsequently dismantle the exhibition to the organizer's standards.

For the courier's role, see 51.4.

49.5 The agent as facilitator of the installation

A specialist fine art agent (see 52.8) or museum service can help to make successful installations possible: they are likely to be familiar with access to particular venues and with the staff there; they understand venues' schedules and are experienced in working around them; and if they are used for more than one delivery, they build up a knowledge of handling the exhibition.

From the organizer's point of view, it is invaluable for one company to undertake all of the transport arrangements for a touring exhibition, but many venues prefer to use their own vans for financial reasons. This option can be discussed with venues at the briefing during the initial showing. Discussions can involve solutions such as distances being averaged during the tour, so that each venue pays the same proportion of the overall transport cost (see 53.5).

49.6 Identifying exhibits and other materials

The exhibition should be documented and labelled to be understood by venues in three distinct and consecutive stages: first, the crated state; second, the process of being unpacked; and third, the displayed state (and vice versa for dismantling). At each of these stages, the appearance of the exhibition will be very different. The key to successful installation is for the organizer to make the transitions from the first stage through to the final one as simple and obvious as possible for the venue.

See 45.9 and 53.10 for the identification of crates. See 46.9 for instructions on unpacking and packing. A second copy of the list of each crate's contents should be sent, together with a copy of the transport manifest, as part of the advance information to each venue (see 17.11). Display materials should be marked on undersurfaces, components numbered and parts to be joined together coded at junctions with letters or symbols (see 21.3). Exhibits should be identified using adhesive or tie-on labels with full regard to conservation requirements (see 39.1). Exhibit labels should have sufficient information to enable easy and unambiguous identification, using at least two points of reference (e.g. the number and the title used in the catalogue), and should relate to the inventory of exhibits (see 7.3) and individual condition check dockets (see 46.2).

49.7 Installation instructions

Identifying and labelling individual exhibits does not tell the venue how they should be installed and how they relate to one another. This information must be supplemented by full installation instructions, informing venues of the way in which exhibition sections work together, and giving detailed information on the finer points of the display of individual exhibits.

The instructions should vary the means of communication, using the best form for the purpose, e.g. the best means of providing a list is in written form whereas photographs (see 9.4) or a video is the ideal way of showing how sections of an exhibition should look and a diagram most clearly indicates how two display surfaces slot together. Particularly if the exhibition includes a number of display units, a proposed floorplan will illustrate the preferred layout, indicating relationships between exhibits while allowing sufficient space between display cases for the expected number of visitors and providing visible and unobstructed exits from the display area.

The organizer should clearly indicate all installation procedures, and should not presume that the venue has any prior knowledge of conservation requirements. The use of acid-free tissue paper or cotton gloves should be specified where necessary. Cleaning methods should be described, and appropriate utensils and materials provided, e.g. it is crucial to identify Perspex and to provide a suitable cleaner. Details of fittings should be given, e.g. whether mirror-plates are provided for exhibits that are to be hung on walls or screens and what size of screws should be used with them.

The order and sense of the instructions should follow that of the intended process of installation, e.g. assembly instructions for display structures should always precede information about unpacking crates which contain exhibits. It should be clear from the outset if display structures cannot be moved once erected.

The paint colour for plinths should be specified, preferably as a British Standard colour. The types of any standard display fittings should also be specified and possible suppliers identified. It is important for spare screws, fittings and light bulbs to travel with the exhibition itself and to be replaced as necessary. For equipment, see 23.9. For fire precautions, see 27.9.

50

Storage

John Wm Morris

50.1 Storage before and during the tour

Material which has been selected for a touring exhibition will normally have been on display or housed in long-term storage and will have been influenced by a particular environment. Over the duration of an exhibition, the exhibits will alternate between being on view, moving between venues and short periods of storage. An operation that is frequently overlooked is the safe storage and security of the exhibits, if there is a delay between unpacking and installation.

50.2 The organizer's responsibilities

At the planning stage of an exhibition, it is important to establish the correct environmental conditions for the exhibits (see 43.2). These conditions should not only apply in exhibition galleries but – a near impossibility – at all other times.

As the exhibits are gathered together, the organizer will have to provide storage that meets the prescribed standard.

All the packing materials and containers will need a period after manufacture to stabilize to these conditions and to vent-off residual chemicals used in manufacture, e.g. glues and paints (see 45.3).

When designing crates, the organizer must consider the means of handling within stores: venues will not have the same level of equipment, and there is always a danger of dropping, where heavy crates have to be manually handled.

The organizer should advise the venues on the area required to store the containers and non-exhibited material travelling with the exhibition.

Storage conditions will vary from venue to venue, and are difficult to predict in advance (see Figure 50.1). It is important, therefore, that the organizer should specify that exhibits which are sensitive to environmental conditions, should be protected and buffered by their transit cases or packing when in store. If necessary, special storage should be arranged (see 15.13, 52.9).

50.3 Storage conditions

Stores should provide stable conditions within the environmental range of humidity and temperature specified. Once placed in the store, all the exhibits, however packed, should be protected from vibration, impact, abrasion, flood and contamination. Stores should also provide security from theft, casual handling and tampering.

50.4 Guidelines for storage

Exhibits should never be stored on the floor. Shelves and pallet bases must have a minimum clearance of 15 cm (6") from the floor in case of flood (see 44.4).

Stored exhibits should be placed within the structure of shelves to avoid overhang into circulation gangways. Where the store employs mechanical handling, great care is needed to avoid impact damage, and only skilled staff should control equipment.

Some exhibits may be of considerable weight, and when concentrated in storage, impose high loadings to floors and shelves.

If larger exhibits are travelling with minimal packing, protection should be provided for all light-sensitive surfaces, e.g. fabric-covered furniture.

Great care must be taken to maintain security as exhibits are transferred between the storage area and exhibition gallery. Exhibits in open containers are at particular risk. Prior to sending any packing materials to store, check for accidental inclusion of small separated parts of exhibits.

Figure 50.1 Very few museums have spacious, clean and well-lit stores which can be used for temporary storage of touring exhibitions. (Courtesy of John Wm Morris)

50.5 Storage of unused exhibits and display materials

Due to variations in the space available, it may be necessary to limit the number of exhibits and reduce the display material. Provided lenders agree to storage on site (see 37.4), secure storage with a correct and monitored environment must be provided, and the position of spare exhibits noted on their condition check dockets (see 46.3) and in the venue's disaster plan (see 7.16).

50.6 Storage of packing material

As an exhibition is unpacked, great care should be taken with the packing material. The material for each exhibit should be kept together, either in the transit container, or a bag provided. A label should be attached to retain the link between the packing and exhibit. The material should then be transferred to clean storage with a similar environmental profile to the exhibition area (see 43.3). Do not use a damp external crate store frequented by vermin and insects. Before any exhibits are re-packed, check that poor storage conditions have not affected the containers and packing materials. It is possible to place monitoring equipment inside temporary sealed crates to check for adverse humidity.

50.7 Storage of equipment

Equipment travelling with an exhibition will also require safe storage. Where there are consumable items, e.g. light bulbs, these should be placed in an accessible position. If there are mechanical handling devices, beware of oil leaks that may contaminate adjacent areas.

50.8 Awaiting collection

If after packing it is necessary to store the exhibition before dispatch, the same standards of security and environment must be maintained.

51

Couriers

Kate Lowry

51.1 When is a courier necessary?

If an exhibit is of great value or is fragile, if specialized packing or installation is required, if the journey involves a number of trans-shipments or if the venue is unfamiliar, a lender will specify that a courier accompany the exhibit.

The requirement for a courier should be established in the loan agreement, which should also set out the arrangements for travel and subsistence and the costs that the organizer or venue must bear (see 51.6). The courier is the owner's representative, holding absolute authority for the security and safety of the exhibit until it is handed over to the venue.

Although the following is written from the point of view of the courier, it should also enable organizer and venues to anticipate the courier's requirements, to help to save time and cost.

51.2 Selecting a courier

The courier will probably be a curator, registrar or conservator of the lending institution. The courier should be experienced in handling and packing the exhibit, understand its condition and display requirements and be able to monitor the venue's environment. He/she must be firm but patient, able to make intelligent decisions quickly and preferably able to understand the language of the borrowing institution, in the case of loans overseas.

51.3 Preparing the courier

The courier should be familiar with the following information before departure to accompany or supervise an exhibit:

- condition check docket (see 46.4);
- packing specifications (see 45.6);
- handling requirements, e.g. travel upright/flat, hand carry, etc (see 48.2);
- facilities report describing the venue (see 38.2);
- loan agreement, including the lender's specifications and provisions to be made by the borrower (see 37.5);
- transport arrangements, e.g. agents (see 52.10) and carriers used and modes of transport involved (see 53.6);
- dates and times of transit, arrival or departure, unpacking and installation, or dismantling and packing (see 53.11, 53.12);
- customs arrangements, e.g. sealed in-house or checked at port (see 52.6);
- installation/display instructions (see 49.7).

The courier should take the following:

- a copy of the loan agreement (see 37.5);
- contact names, telephone and fax numbers and addresses of lender, organizer, venue, carrier and agent;
- a schedule of transit (see 53.7);
- a checklist of the exhibits with the numbers, sizes and weights of their crates (see 7.12, 45.9);
- insurance certificates, if appropriate;
- a note of handling instructions;
- condition check docket (see 46.8);
- loan receipt, for the borrower to sign;
- environmental monitoring equipment, e.g. hand-held thermohygrometer, light meter and UV monitor;
- camera;
- crate keys;
- customs invoice, if an overseas shipment;
- current passport and any relevant visas if travelling abroad.

51.4 The courier's duties

Before an outward journey, the courier should:

- ensure that cases are loaded into a lorry or container or onto an aircraft pallet correctly and tied securely (see 53.14, 54.4, 55.6);
- ensure that other items loaded with an exhibit will not place it in jeopardy, e.g. avoid transporting small exhibits with other heavier items, glazed display cases or wet or perishable items;
- ensure that environmental control is operating on road vehicles, where specified;
- check paperwork with the carrier, making a note of the pallet number in the case of air transport;
- obtain a signed receipt from the carrier.

During transit, the courier should:

- stay with the shipment at all times wherever possible, or ensure that a representative of the carrier or agent remains with it during meal breaks or at plane-side;
- strap into a seat adjacent to the courier any exhibit carried in the cabin of an aircraft;
- ensure that hand-carried loans are accompanied by an additional courier when travel is by car, taxi or train;
- do everything possible to reduce delays to a minimum, and prevent unnecessary changes in itinerary;
- decide whether transit should proceed if weather is hazardous or if transport or security provision is unsatisfactory;
- anticipate problems, to be ready to solve them as they arise, e.g. customs;
- ensure that the vehicle is locked and alarmed if it is left on the vehicle deck of a ferry (see 55.4);
- take photographs in the event of any accident affecting the shipment.

On arrival of the shipment, the courier should:

- be present when the shipment is unloaded (in the case of transport by air, this will probably be done by the agent);
- oversee the transfer of the shipment to the venue;
- check environmental conditions of exhibition, preparation and storage areas (see 43.5);
- leave crate overnight to acclimatize if necessary, in a secure location;
- unpack the exhibit only when the environmental and physical conditions are seen to be adequate (see 8.4);
- check the condition of the exhibit (see 46.10): the venue should countersign and retain the condition check docket, and the courier should be given a copy if there are changes that need to be reported back to the lender;
- oversee the installation of the exhibit, ensuring that all fittings or supports are adequate and that display cases are appropriate;
- check levels of light on the exhibit and get adjustments made where necessary (see 20.3);
- ensure that exhibits are not placed in vulnerable positions and that barriers are installed where necessary;
- obtain the venue's signature on the loan receipt, and leave a copy with the venue;
- if at all possible, the courier should not leave until the exhibit has been installed;
- ensure that the venue is aware that the exhibit should not be moved (except in an emergency), until the courier arrives to oversee the return.

A return or onward journey should be handled in the same manner as above, but in the reverse order. Before departure of the shipment, the courier should:

- check the condition of the exhibit and note any changes (see 46.10): the venue should countersign the condition check docket and be given a copy;
- re-pack the exhibit;
- sign and hand a receipt to the venue.

During transit, the courier should maintain the same vigilance over the security and well-being of the exhibit as on the outward journey.

51.5 The courier's report

At the completion of any transit, the courier will file a report which identifies any problems encountered during the journey and/or at the venue. This information should be filed by the name of the carrier, agent and/or venue, to inform any future shipments or loans. The report should be written so that relevant parts can be shown to the party concerned where necessary, to ensure that remedial action can be taken. It might take the form of a standard form which asks:

- name of carrier, and whether the courier would recommend using this carrier again;
- name of agent, and whether the courier would recommend using this agent again;
- name of venue, and whether the courier would recommend lending to this venue again;
- name of exhibition;
- loaned items;
- how satisfactory transport arrangements were;
- whether access into or out of the venue was satisfactory:
- how satisfactory security arrangements were;
- whether proper care was taken of the items when unpacking/packing and handling;
- whether the venue had complied with the loan con-

ditions, particularly in relation to temperature, relative humidity and light levels;
- how acceptable were the arrangements for hotel accommodation, travel and subsistence.

51.6 Budgeting for a courier

The organizer (or, if agreed, the venue) should budget for the following costs:

- any travel with the exhibit(s) not already covered in a carrier's costs;
- independent travel to collect an exhibit or to return home after a delivery, based on the most economic form of travel;
- accommodation during unpacking and installation (or dismantling and re-packing) in a two- or three-star hotel near to the venue;
- local transport and food included in a *per diem* sum in local currency, to be handed to the courier on his/her arrival.

51.7 Further reading

Cannon-Brookes, P. 'A Draft Code of Practice for Escorts and Couriers', in *International Journal of Museum Management and Curatorship*, 1982, pp. 41-60.

Rose, C. *Courierspeak*, 1993, Smithsonian Institution Press, Washington.

52

Agents for shipping, packing and technical services

Sarah Shalgosky

52.1 Why use shipping agents?

The decline of many museum-based technical services has encouraged the development of agents in the private sector who offer a wide range of services, from hire of display cases to installation of exhibitions. They offer expertise, facilities and contacts which an organizer may not have the resources to provide in-house.

In some cases, an agent may become the sole agent for a particular museum or gallery. Although a continuing relationship may have financial benefits, its main advantage is that each party knows and respects the standards of the other. Certainly, it is a relationship which develops and is tested over time.

In other cases, a gallery may appoint an agent on a more short-term basis, to carry out an unusually complicated operation for which it has not the resources or the expertise, for example managing a tour. Foreign transport presents particular problems and if an exhibition involves bringing exhibits from overseas, it is essential to secure the services of an agent in the foreign country or city concerned (see 15.13).

52.2 Costs

Contracting work out in this way only seems expensive if previously the costs of installation or packing or whatever were hidden within overall running costs. As more public institutions adopt a cost-centre approach, the cost of agents becomes competitive (see 9.7).

52.3 Identifying agents

Agents are not hard to find. Most will target their mailing lists at exhibition galleries and will regularly send information to museums and galleries, although not always to the appropriate person. Directors and conservators as well as organizers are usually the recipients of such unsolicited mail. Many agents advertise in the yearbooks published by Arts Review or the Museums Association (MA), in periodicals such as *Galleries* and *Museums Journal* or in publications such as *Artists' Newsletter's Directory of Exhibition Spaces*. The Suppliers and Services section of the *Museums Yearbook* indicates companies that are corporate members of the MA; it does not mean that they have been approved by the MA. Agents may also attend the trade fairs associated with professional conferences.

The Museums Security Adviser (MSA, see 42.1) used to recommend agents, but it proved impossible to conduct annual checks on ever-growing numbers, so this practice has been suspended. Any agent who cites approval by the MSA gained it some years ago and has not been checked since. Instead, the MSA recommends consulting curators and registrars in different institutions to compare experiences.

Usually an agent will be happy to visit potential clients to discuss their needs and to explain the facilities and services the agent can offer. Sometimes it is possible to visit the agent's premises to inspect storage or display furniture. An agent should be able to give the names of previous clients who can supply references regarding the standard and efficiency of their work. These are useful to identify not only the agent's general approach but also experience of a particular type of exhibition or exhibit. Quotations (i.e. fixed price) and estimates (i.e. subject to variables) are usually presented free of charge.

52.4 Selecting agents

When the organizer is making arrangements for an exhibit belonging to a museum or collector, it is advisable to ask if the lender has a preferred agent.

Discussion of this preference should elicit whether the agent is able to meet the standards required by the organizer, e.g. temperature/humidity-controlled transits or indemnified storage. Curators in other countries, particularly from larger institutions which regularly make foreign loans, are often well-informed about local and international shippers and packers. The organizer's preference should be balanced against that of the lender. The organizer should always ensure that the lender is happy with the choice before confirming arrangements with an agent. Some institutions may insist on a particular agent because the latter can provide a certain standard of care, e.g. vehicles with air-ride suspension.

The choice of an agent is determined by the particular requirements of the exhibition and/or the exhibits. To minimize risks, agents should always meet the highest standards in the following areas:

- confidentiality of all arrangements;
- knowledge of handling procedures for all exhibits;
- security and observation of security procedures;
- fire precautions and training in use of equipment;
- maintenance of vehicles, stores and equipment;
- emergency procedures;
- documentation of all transits, storage, etc

References from previous clients should cover some or all of these areas. The organizer can visit the agent, and ask for confirmation in writing if necessary.

The organizer should discuss the ability of the agent to meet particular requirements and their experience of similar work. If control of temperature and humidity is required, the organizer should be able to specify the parameters that are acceptable, and the agent should be able to provide proof, e.g. with thermohygrograph charts, that conditions can be kept within the agreed parameters.

Exhibits should be covered by insurance 'nail to nail' or 'shelf to shelf', with a clause renouncing recourse against carriers and packers and the organizer's agents and representatives. Agents must be aware that this cover exists. Otherwise they may refuse to handle the consignments or take out special insurance cover to protect themselves, incurring unnecessary costs to the organizer (see 40.5).

The organizer should check that the work will be done by the agent and its staff. If the work is to be sub-contracted, the agent should provide references relating to the sub-contractor's work and, if necessary, the organizer should contact the sub-contractor to discuss the task in detail. Sub-contracting does not necessarily denote either sub-standard work or paying over the odds for a certain job. Often agents are in touch with a wide range of highly-skilled, self-employed individuals who may offer them more advantageous rates than they would to an organizer they do not know.

52.5 Setting out requirements: transport

Before commissioning an agent, the organizer will have to identify the precise requirements of an exhibition or exhibit (see 53.6). Some conditions may be specified by lenders on loan forms or in discussion. The following checklist outlines the most common considerations for transport:

- air-ride suspension;
- temperature/humidity control of load area;
- tail lift;
- security to standard required for indemnified loads;
- height of load area (allowing for wrapping/crating);
- height of vehicle (for access to loading areas);
- maximum load weight;
- requirements for courier, e.g. overseeing loading/unloading;
- arrangements for part-loads (see 53.4);
- insurance arrangements;
- overnight arrangements (see 53.13);
- collection/delivery arrangements;
- timetable.

52.6 Setting out requirements: customs documentation

The following checklist outlines the most common requirements for clearance at ports:

- preparation of customs documentation (see 56.1);
- availability of agent at port of entry/exit;
- expeditious customs clearance;
- possibility of customs clearance at venues;
- availability of bonded storage at port of entry/exit;
- arrangements for courier, e.g. overseeing palletization;
- timetable.

52.7 Setting out requirements: packing

The following checklist outlines the most common considerations:

- type of wrapping/travel-frame/box/crate (see 45.2);
- risks, allowing for transport used and length of journeys (see 53.1);
- lender's precise specifications (see 37.5);
- documentation (see 45.9);
- instructions for venues;
- involvement of conservators in designing and specifying (see 39.5);

- particular circumstances, e.g. wet paint on newly-finished paintings;
- timetable.

52.8 Setting out requirements: installation/dismantling

The following checklist outlines the most common considerations for installing or dismantling an exhibition (see 48.1):

- number of staff required;
- equipment required;
- lender's requirements, e.g. presence of courier;
- handling guidelines;
- security provision;
- professional indemnity;
- timetable.

52.9 Setting out requirements: storage

The following checklist outlines the most common consideration for the storage of exhibition material (see 50.1):

- security arrangements;
- provision for access;
- insurance arrangements;
- temperature/humidity control;
- storage system e.g. racks, pigeon-holes, etc.;
- exhibits wrapped/unwrapped;
- length of storage;
- other exhibits in store.

52.10 Commissioning an agent

The time required by an agent will obviously depend on the amount of work to be done, but it is always as well to give as much notice as possible. This will enable the agent to fit the organizer's demands in with other commitments. Last minute jobs, inadequate information, queries, lack of specific instructions are all factors which contribute to high costs.

Involve the agent at the earliest possible stage. An agent may be necessary to cope with work the organizer cannot carry out, but there is no point making the job more difficult by leaving the task to the last minute. Don't expect the impossible, but give agents the information and the time they need to do the job properly. Always remember that miracles are more expensive than ordinary tasks.

Discussion of requirements and of the concomitant estimates or quotations often means that, by the time an organizer comes to commission an agent, the latter will already be familiar with the work to be done. Any factors (e.g. the number of personnel required, delivery by a certain time, no stops, etc) which may affect the agent's estimate or quotation should be discussed and agreed (e.g. by the agent setting out the basis of calculations for an extra day's work or extra mileage). The agent's quotation/estimate and details of possible extra costs should be confirmed in writing, as should the organizer's acceptance and details of all requirements and conditions.

The agent should be supplied with all information necessary for carrying out the task. For most tasks, the agent will need a complete list of exhibits with framed/wrapped/crated dimensions. Details of weights are necessary for air freight but will also be necessary for transport within the UK if the load is likely to exceed the axle weight of the vehicle. Contact details – names, addresses and telephone and fax numbers – of lenders or venues should also be supplied. Any special packing requirements should also be given and the preferred method of transport (air, road or rail) stated.

A timescale should be agreed and a schedule drawn up for the work.

The different responsibilities of the agent *vis-à-vis* the organizer and/or a courier should be discussed, identified and agreed. Sometimes the agent prefers to contact lenders or customs officials, while the organizer wants to control these arrangements. Sometimes it is more cost-effective for the organizer and not the agent to supply the packing materials.

If any work seems less than satisfactory, the organizer should contact the agent immediately for an explanation. If necessary, the organizer should make a complaint in writing. The written statement of requirements and conditions supplied by the organizer should provide a sound basis for discussion of the agent's failure to comply with the arrangements. Most agents recognise that a good reputation is vital to their continued success, and they guard it very carefully.

53

Road transport

Anne Buddle

53.1 Standards of care and protection

Safe transport is one of the most fundamental requirements in organizing exhibitions, for protecting exhibits from shock and excessive vibration, incorrect handling, sudden changes in environmental conditions and the risk of theft or damage.

The level of protection for exhibits in transit will depend on the perceived risks: the fragility and/or value of the exhibits, the length and complexity of the journey and the type of transport used. Ceramics, terracotta and wrought iron are fragile and must be well insulated against vibration and shock. Gold bars can sustain robust handling, but require armed protection against theft. Soft wrapping may suffice for the transport of a painting for 300 kilometres in an air-ride vehicle, but the same painting travelling as air cargo must be crated.

With advances in the science of conservation, requirements for the safe transport of exhibits have become more specific, and this is often perceived as being troublesome, unrealistic and costly. However, organizer, venue and carrier cannot afford to take risks, even if a lender seems satisfied with no packing.

By thinking laterally, a strategy can be developed to anticipate every risk and to prepare a course of action to counter it. If an accident does occur and the lender makes a claim, the organizer will at least be able to show evidence of care.

The organizer must be aware of existing standards in the venues participating in the tour, and should take responsibility on behalf of the lenders for encouraging higher standards where necessary. He or she should ensure that the carrier, the venues and any couriers understand and accept each other's contributions. The determining factor in any discussion of standards of care and protection should not be financial, political or personal convenience, but whatever action is best for the exhibit.

53.2 Planning

Before any meaningful discussion of transport arrangements can take place, a significant amount of information must be requested, gathered and collated. The organizer would normally coordinate and manage information contributed by all those involved – lender, organizer, venues and carrier (see 53.17).

Forward planning and open communications are essential to control and reduce costs. At the earliest stages of exhibition planning, it is good practice to set out 'worst case' scenarios. Be pessimistic at this stage, and do not assume that you will necessarily be able to avoid the costs of crate-making, couriers and special transport arrangements. As hard facts replace estimates and possibilities, there should be few surprises and no unforeseen extra costs.

Agents and carriers are experienced professionals, and should be consulted and involved at the earliest possible date (see 52.10). The organizer must define the extent to which the carrier will control the transport schedule, and must identify specific areas of responsibility to avoid confusion, duplication of effort and the inevitable extra costs.

53.3 Outline transport schedule

The basic minimum for the outline schedule would be as follows.

A provisional list of exhibits. This may simply list the type of object, e.g. table, ceramic figure, framed oil painting, together with a rough indication of size e.g. small (defined as below certain dimensions height × width × depth), middle (defined in a similar way) etc. and any exceptional sizes or weights.

An indication whether the estimate should include time and materials for packing, or whether it is anticipated that works will be packed ready for collection.

A provisional list of towns/areas from which collections might be made, with outline dates for collection and return.

A provisional list of towns/areas for the tour, with outline dates.

53.4 Outline transport budget

A provisional budget for the entire exhibition will often be needed well in advance, so that it can be submitted with the bid by the institution or department for the coming financial year. The outline schedule (see 53.3) is an important part of the budgeting process.

The schedule may be produced at short notice and with many queries still outstanding, but it can be used to obtain estimates from one or more carriers or to assess the implications for in-house technicians, packers and/or drivers. In the process, the schedule will be exposed to these professionals and will elicit their questions and comments. The more information is provided at this stage, the more realistic the estimate will be. A deadline should be specified for the return of the estimates.

Transport, especially international transport, is one of the most expensive elements of an exhibition. Costs depend on distance, number of journeys and the size, weight and fragility of the exhibits. The carrier's estimate may help to determine the number of exhibits that can be afforded, if the overall budget rules out more distant loans.

Combined shipments with shared couriers can be arranged, but last-minute changes can spoil such arrangements. With sufficient notice, carriers can sometimes offer savings by sharing loads, but care should be taken that a shared load will not involve unsuitable companion consignments or exposing fragile exhibits to extra travel. Any suggestion of inefficiency or lack of care will not inspire confidence among lenders or funding agencies, whose support is crucial to the success of any exhibition.

It is important that carriers know that exhibits will be covered by insurance 'nail to nail' or 'shelf to shelf' and that the cover includes a clause renouncing recourse against the organizer's agents and representatives. Otherwise, the carriers may take out their own insurance, incurring unnecessary costs to the organizers (see 40.3).

53.5 Selection of carrier

Ideally, one carrier will be used for the whole tour, to ensure consistency of care (see 49.5). The organizer should have the experience and authority to nominate a carrier, and should be able to justify his/her choice, whether or not the carrier is in-house, a museums service or a commercial company. This will be based on:

- past experience of the carrier's performance and reliability: seeking comments from registrars and exhibition officers elsewhere is always useful;
- the carrier's suitability for the specific task in hand, e.g. moving contemporary sculpture requires very different skills and techniques from packing and transporting a collection of ceramics or natural history specimens;
- confidence in their stated methods for packing and handling, where the organizer wishes to give responsibility for these areas, and insurance arrangements to reflect this;
- suitable vehicles and adequate staffing to do the job; and
- a fair price for the work.

Before any estimate is accepted and the carrier appointed, the organizer should discuss as many of the aspects of the estimate as necessary with the carriers tendering for the job. Curators, conservators, finance officers, in-house technical staff, etc should also be consulted to ensure that they also subscribe to the final decision. Lenders may request that a specific carrier handles the work.

The chosen carrier should be sent a formal letter of appointment. Some institutions insist on a contract. A letter should also be sent to the unsuccessful carriers, releasing them from a possible commitment at the dates mentioned.

53.6 Lenders' requirements

Accurate schedules and costs can be prepared once the number of the exhibits and their whereabouts, size, age, fragility and approximate value have been established. The organizer must now work with the appointed carrier to finalize the transport schedule, noting any specific requirements and conditions of loan and their implications for packing, handling or transport. For safe transport, the lender must ensure that the organizer and its carrier are fully briefed about the nature and requirements of the exhibit(s).

A lender's requirements are usually part of the conditions of loan, which must be agreed in writing well in advance, along with all associated costs (see 9.2, 37.5). By the time a carrier is appointed, lenders should have signed and returned their loan agreements including confirmation that they agree to lend to each venue. Some lenders will wish to receive separate agreements or assurances from every venue before they agree to lend to the first venue.

The loan agreement will specify any special requirements for insurance/indemnity. Lenders will normally expect to receive written confirmation of insurance arrangements before they release their objects (see 40.4). The loan agreement will also specify any special requirements for handling, packing and transport. This may include the request that a courier accompanies the shipment. Lenders may also make specific requirements concerning the dates and times for collection and return.

53.7 Refining the transport schedule

The carrier should provide the organizer with the following information for discussion and agreement, based on the above conditions and requirements:

The proposed method of packing and protection, e.g. soft-wrap, travel frame, carton, crate, pallet, hand-carry case. These proposals must reflect lenders' conditions of loan, and the organizer's notes on special requirements for handling and movement (see 45.2).

The number of men required to handle, lift and transport the exhibits safely. Any special equipment required, and who should provide this (see 48.2).

The proposed schedule and route for collections/deliveries, including arrangements for overnight stops, if applicable, and departure/arrival times of associated planes/boats for assessment and approval.

Details of proposed vehicles (see 52.5). For particularly valuable shipments, lenders may insist that their loans are divided between two or more shipments.

It is important that administrative and practical arrangements progress simultaneously, and inform each other. For example, if the exhibition is to be crated, not soft-wrapped, then the venue must be advised that more technical staff and/or equipment and more floor space will be required when the vehicle arrives, and suitable storage must be arranged for empty crates.

53.8 Measurements

Accurate measurements are essential to the efficient working of a transport schedule. Assembling this information is well worth the investment in time, because a guess may result in a costly disaster. The following information should be readily available:

- all three dimensions of each exhibit (height x width x depth) NB paintings are not two-dimensional;
- the total volume of the packed material, including an indication of the sizes and weights of heavier cases;
- measurements of doorways, arches, corridors and tight turning areas at every point of each route from the place of collection to the exhibit's next destination (see 38.7);
- internal measurements of the vehicle to be used, including clearance at the back door/s;
- overall measurement of the vehicle;
- height of the vehicle from the ground, and how this height relates to loading bays and platforms at the venues;
- the size and capacity of any tail lift.

53.9 The vehicle

Carriers have been responsive to the increased demands of conservators and curators for secure, air-ride, environmentally-controlled vehicles for the transport of exhibits. If environmental control is required, the parameters should be specified (see 52.4). Greater emphasis on Health and Safety and EC Regulations has encouraged the use of hydraulic and other equipment instead of muscle and manpower, and many more vehicles are now fitted with a tail-lift, in addition to air-ride and environmental control (see 52.5).

If a vehicle has none of these benefits, some lenders may insist on employing another carrier, with increased costs and overheads. Packing will be designed to offer protection in transit. If the vehicle is known to be without environmental control or air-ride, then packing should be modified to compensate for this (see the Canadian Conservation Institute's circular slide rule).

53.10 Transport manifest

The organizer should provide the carrier with a transport manifest, which is an itemized list of every separate package that is to be collected or delivered.

In the case of collections and returns, this will be the inventory of exhibits (see 7.3). Each object should have a unique reference name or number, e.g. the name of the artist and title of the painting; its medium, size and weight; any special condition of loan; notes of any particularly heavy, fragile or damaged works; and whether with or without packing.

In the case of an exhibition that has already been brought together, the transport manifest would be a list of each crate, box or other separately-packed item that is actually loaded or unloaded on vehicles. Crates should be marked on the exterior with a unique number (see 45.9).

The transport manifest will itemize each crate according to its number, giving dimensions, weights and any instructions on handling or the machinery to be used. It should be sent to the carrier to provide a checklist against which carrier and venue can sign a receipt when they take delivery of the consignment.

There should be a receipt for the collection and delivery of each separate consignment. The carrier should be advised about related documentation which will travel with the exhibition e.g. condition reports or packing notes.

53.11 Instructions for collection

For each item that has a separate point of collection, the organizer should provide the carrier with the following details of each collection address, i.e. each lender will be listed separately when individual exhibits are being collected but, once the tour has begun, only one address should be necessary for collecting the exhibition from each completed showing:

- name, address, telephone and fax number of lender or venue;
- contact name (if different), position and telephone/fax number;
- address for collection, together with additional instructions if the address is difficult to find or if there are potential hazards, e.g. unmade roads, narrow archways, blind corners, cobbled yards, steps up/down to entrance, narrow corridors, broken door-bells, etc.;
- convenient times for collection, and what arrangements are necessary if, for any reason, the vehicle arrives outside these times;
- any assistance available for loading, including after-hours;
- the need for, and availability of, lifting equipment;
- presence of a courier to accompany the shipment, and if so, whether the carrier should provide an agreed sum for the courier's subsistence.

53.12 Instructions for delivery

For each item that has a separate point of delivery, the organizer should provide the carrier with the following details for each delivery address, i.e. the next venue in a tour should be represented by one address only, but each lender will be listed separately when individual exhibits are returned at the end of the tour:

- name, address, telephone and fax number of destination; contact name (if different), position and telephone/fax number;
- instructions for advance warning of estimated time of arrival (ETA), e.g. phone when leaving the previous venue or at an agreed period of time before ETA;
- address for delivery, together with specific point of delivery, instructions, e.g. ring bell, report to control room and any additional details of difficulties or hazards (as 53.11);
- convenient times for delivery, and what arrangements are necessary if, for any reason, the vehicle arrives outside these times;
- any assistance and equipment available for unloading, including after-hours;
- any requirement to assist with unpacking; otherwise simply obtain a signature on the organizer's receipt;
- any requirement to see the courier to his/her hotel;
- arrangements for overnight parking for the vehicle, if necessary.

53.13 Parking arrangements

As far as possible, transits should be completed in one long day, rather than two shorter ones. Where overnight stops are necessary, parking arrangements should be made well in advance, especially if space is requested at another institution. Their security staff will require the following details:

- vehicle registration number;
- driver's name, and the names of any courier(s);
- ETA, and whether access to the building is required, for unloading and for storage and/or to use washing facilities;
- whether any objects will remain on the vehicle overnight;
- contact name and number in the event of an emergency;
- scheduled departure time.

Exhibits should not be left overnight on the vehicle unless (a) the driver(s) are able to sleep in the vehicle; or (b) the vehicle is locked, alarmed and parked in a secure compound, e.g. by arrangement at a police station. The van should be backed up against a wall to provide additional security for its contents.

Lender(s) must be informed of and agree with these arrangements.

53.14 Loading

When the vehicle is loaded, the heaviest works would normally be placed against the bulkhead, or equally distributed, against the sides of the vehicle. Crates should be loaded before soft-wrapped works, and free-standing work tied-off centrally if there is no space against the sides. Small works may be placed in cartons or crates, which are then easier to stabilize and secure. The driver or carrier should be experienced in the handling and loading of exhibition material, and his knowledge should be respected. If there are any special reasons for loading certain objects first or last, e.g. because one is required for a photocall on the day of arrival, then the driver should be advised well before he sizes up the consignment for loading.

In any vehicle, it must be possible to 'tie off' the load firmly and carefully, either to raives along the sides of the van and/or to rings or sprung poles in the body of the vehicle. Cotton webbing is preferable to coarser rope. Ratchet webbing, colour-coded for different strengths, can be tightened with greater control over the pressure exerted on the object or crate. Blankets or foam should be used to cushion the object on the floor, and to create a pad between one object and another. The driver (not the courier) is legally responsible for the safety of his load, and must therefore check that all is safely balanced and secured before he sets off (see 51.4).

53.15 During the transit

Two people (preferably two drivers) should always travel with an exhibition shipment. One of them must remain with the vehicle at all times. This is a condition of Government Indemnity cover (see 41.5) and of many insurance policies. The vehicle should be fitted with security locks (not merely standard fittings) and remain locked at all times. It should also be fitted with an alarm.

The drivers must be provided with emergency contact numbers, including out-of-hours numbers. If there is no mobile phone on board, one driver must immediately find the nearest telephone and report any emergency to the appointed contact.

The contact should be able to assess the implications for the safety of the exhibits, and for the schedule, assist in making arrangements for an unscheduled overnight stop in a secure area, and advise those awaiting the shipment of the situation (see 53.13).

In the event of damage to an object or objects, these should be moved as little as possible – and preferably not at all – until expert assistance arrives. The organizer should be informed immediately. Brief notes should be made at once, and a photograph taken if possible. A full report will then be required, and certainly within 24 hours if the incident occurred locally and 48 hours if it occurred abroad.

53.16 The venues' responsibilities

Each venue should ensure that the organizer and carrier are aware of critical in-house dates and deadlines which may affect the transport schedule.

For the delivery of the exhibition, this will include any changes in opening dates, any plans for private views, press views or special guests, whose presence might interrupt any 'last into the case' deliveries and installations. The organizer should be advised of the venue's deadline for completion of building work, especially any painting (see 49.2), and of the earliest date for access to the exhibition area. The venue should inform the organizer about any prior commitments for space in the arrival area and stores, and any foreseeable problems with staff shortages, whether technical or security.

For the collection of the exhibition, the venue should inform the organizer about any change in closing date, any technical work and/or photography required before exhibits are packed, any changes in the list of works and/or couriers travelling to the next venue, and any concerns about possible changes in condition of the exhibits.

The venue should plan for the arrival and departure of the exhibition, by scheduling technical staff for unloading and unpacking and for packing and loading, making provision for any overtime payments if necessary. Security staff should be advised, especially if deliveries are after hours. Time and staff should be allocated to make condition reports. Misplacing display case keys and keys for hand-carry cases can cause confusion and delays (see 42.7).

53.17 Documentation

In addition to frequent correspondence by phone, fax and letter, the following documents will be required at various stages in planning and executing any transport arrangements.

From the lender: the signed loan agreement, including valuation for each loan; a formal agreement to insurance/indemnity arrangements; and a condition report.

From the organizer: the hire agreement with each of the participating venues; confirmation of insurance/indemnity arrangements (in collaboration with the venues); contract with carriers; transport schedules (in collaboration with carriers and lenders); notes on packing; receipt for the collection and delivery of each exhibit; instructions about documentation travelling with the exhibition, e.g. condition reports, packing notes; emergency contact numbers; spare condition report forms and damage report forms for the carrier's use, e.g. when collecting from private individuals.

From the venue: facilities report; confirmation of insurance/indemnity arrangements; condition reports completed on arrival and departure and any additional notes of changes to an exhibit; any environmental statistics collected during the exhibition; receipts for any subsistence monies given to couriers; receipt for the delivery of the exhibition.

From the carrier: formal agreement on costs of transport with or without packing; signed receipts for all works collected or delivered; signed receipts for the collection of the exhibition from the venues; Customs documentation for international loans; ticketing and cargo bookings by road, air or sea; compliance with all transport regulations e.g. tachographs, standard rest periods, weight loading of vehicles, licences and MOT.

54

Air freight

Roy Pateman

54.1 Introduction

This section highlights the factors that must be taken into account when planning and considering air freight as a mode of transportation. It does not cover the movement of individual exhibits travelling as hand-luggage with a courier (see 51.4).

The introduction of the Boeing 747 (the Jumbo Jet) changed air freight into a method of transportation which has been more instrumental in the expansion of the exhibition than possibly any other factor this century. Previous to the 747, a succession of narrow-bodied aircraft from the DC-3 to the Boeing 707 were the only practical means of transportation for non-military cargo, but the size and load capacity of the 747 caused a revolution in air freight. When an aircraft became capable of accepting cargo which previously could only have been moved by road, a new era had arrived.

However, while this brought a new global network which linked major cities, restrictions do remain on lesser and/or shorter routes, because the 747 and subsequent wide-bodied aircraft are normally used only between major airports.

54.2 Aircraft type

Because of the small number of manufacturers worldwide, the variations in type of aircraft has been kept to a workable minimum. This is especially advantageous to the exhibition organizer, who can get to know the size and load capacity of specific aircraft, and who can be sure that the aircraft operating between London and Paris are also those used between Beijing and Tokyo.

Most aircraft today are built to three basic configurations: passenger, cargo or 'combi'. The first is constructed primarily for carrying passengers, and its cargo capacity is of secondary importance. The cargo aircraft gives all possible space available to the carriage of freight, and has very limited seating capacity (e.g. for couriers). The combi gives greater flexibility, in that the main deck is split, two-thirds being devoted to passengers, and one-third to cargo.

54.3 Size restrictions

Whichever the configuration, almost all aircraft are designed to have an upper and lower deck. On the all-passenger aircraft, the main (upper) deck is exclusively reserved for seating, leaving the lower deck to accommodate baggage and cargo. The height of lower-deck cargo holds will vary, from 155 cm (62") to as low as 95 cm (38"), depending on the type of aircraft used.

The ability to use the whole of the upper deck in the all-cargo configuration, or part of it in the Combi, makes it possible to send cases with heights ranging from 195 cm (78") to 298 cm (119"), again depending on the type of aircraft used.

Figures for cargo hold capacities are available in the various aircraft manuals, but these are best analysed by a shipping agent. Question your agent to ensure that the whole tour schedule will be possible for all the exhibits and that your crate construction will give the best use of available aircraft capacity.

It is almost certain that an intercontinental transit by a 747 freighter will need onward carriage by road for any tour within a continent, e.g. an exhibition from Australia would probably travel by road for a European tour. What may be a normal factor within Europe may, however, present a serious challenge to the viability of tours in South America, Asia and Africa, where impractical road journeys would be needed to link major cities.

54.4 Handling

Especially with small passenger aircraft, handling is a major problem because it is predominantly manual.

From the first reception at the airline warehouse, the shipment may be moved constantly, often with little regard to handling instructions 'Keep this way up', 'fragile' etc. It will then travel to the waiting aircraft, which may sometimes be over a mile from the cargo terminal, in a vehicle which has minimal means of restraining its load. At the plane side, the cases are loaded to suit the confines of the hold and not for the benefit of the shipment. That consignments arrive unscathed reflects more on the packing techniques used than on any care afforded in transit. This form of transport should only be used as a very last resort and then only when very resilient objects are being despatched.

By far the best method of cargo handling is through the use of a container or pallet, where mechanized loading dispenses with manual handling. The pallet is a flat aluminium platform, upon which a cargo is placed and restrained by loading straps and specially-designed loading nets. Protection from water damage is given by a plastic cover which is placed over the cargo when the pallet is loaded. The standard pallet size is 305 cm x 213 cm (120" x 84"), but cargo and combi aircraft will accommodate a larger pallet size of 610 cm x 213 cm.

The container is constructed with the same aluminium base, but has fixed sides and a top of fibreglass or aluminium. One side is open to allow loading, and is protected by a heavy-gauge plastic curtain, and further protected by a nylon net to restrain the cargo. As with the pallet, cargo can be secured within the container by straps, but this is sometimes difficult, because the locking rings within the container do not always move to accommodate the anchorage points best suited to the cargo. The container was designed for the small package, not the exhibition crate. Containers vary in size, according to the aircraft they are being used with. Agents will have full details of sizes available.

Once loaded with freight, both pallet and container are moved using roller bed tracks and hydraulic lifts. Manual handling is excluded, and heavy freight items can be moved smoothly and safely.

54.5 Protection from the weather

With due care and attention to the possible dangers, dispatch of even the most vulnerable object can be successfully achieved, provided the correct measures are taken. Because of security procedures, non-couriered or unsupervised shipments have to be delivered to the airline at least twelve hours before departure, and there is no control over where the consignment is kept.

An effective method of limiting the time that freight is held within the airport is to use couriers. The time from receipt of cargo to the departure of the aircraft can then be reduced to four hours for a reasonably-sized consignment (more time should be allowed for larger consignments). A similar period is required upon arrival to allow for unloading the aircraft, handling and customs clearance, prior to delivery to its destination.

Of the four hours, one is normally taken receiving the cargo into the airline warehouse and loading it onto pallets or into containers, or unloading them. Whether or not the cargo remains in the relative protection of the cargo shed for the remaining time depends on the aircraft's location and the airline's efficiency in loading and unloading the aircraft. Cargo may not be immediately loaded onto an aircraft. With priority being given to turning round the aircraft as quickly as possible, cargo will be brought out to the tarmac two to four hours prior to loading, and this waiting time on the tarmac can expose the container or pallet to extremes of weather.

Water penetration on the tarmac can be avoided by the simple expedient of placing the largest crates towards the centre of the pallet, to help the waterproof cover to shed rainwater. Covered containers are not the answer to this problem, since they are prone to damage and since holes can effectively drain into the container any puddles forming on the top of the unit.

54.6 Temperature

Once loaded in the aircraft, the shipment returns to a controlled environment which, while not at room temperature, is sufficiently warm to allow for the transport of day-old chicks and other vulnerable livestock. Temperature can be controlled in the lower-deck freight hold, but this is normally lowered, for the benefit of flowers and other perishables. Accurate monitoring of material during transit has proved conclusively that environmental stability can be maintained, provided suitable packing is provided (see 45.2).

54.7 Timing

Air-transportation is geared to speed and frequency for passenger travel. A service of several flights a day is the norm between most major international destinations for passenger-carrying aircraft, but combi or freighters may be less frequent. The human factor is also the guarantee of reliability inasmuch as airlines must operate strictly to time, because of fierce commercial competition and the air traffic space available. An all-cargo aircraft may have to give way to passenger-carrying aircraft on take-off and landing, but delays are usually less than an hour. Delays due to extreme weather conditions are relatively rare and are normally resolved quickly.

54.8 Costs

As with any superior form of transport, the cost of air freight exceeds that of slower modes by sea, rail or road. However, lower costs elsewhere should be taken into account, not least on insurance. Because of its lower risk and better claims record, insurance premiums for air freight are considerably lower than for surface transits.

The actual cost of air transit is based on a calculation of the consignment's weight in relation to the space it occupies within the aircraft. Space is the key factor, so it is important to consider the overall size of the crates to ensure cost efficiency. Extra centimetres on a crate will certainly increase costs dramatically.

55

Sea transport

Roy Pateman

55.1 Why use sea transport?

Most of a museum's collection was originally transported by sea, but the emergence of the wide-bodied aircraft has left shipment by sea largely redundant for the movement of exhibitions (see 54.1). However, there are still opportunities and advantages in returning to this form of transport.

The 'Roll-On Roll-Off' ferry has clear advantages over air-freight for short crossings, especially where overall journey time is short, and where the crates containing the exhibits remain sealed within the vehicle.

For longer journeys, transport by container ship may be a competitive alternative to air where time may not be vital. In some circumstances, sea transport may be the only viable method, if consignments are bulky and/or if airports cannot accommodate aircraft with sufficient capacity (see 54.3).

55.2 Roll-On Roll-Off (RO-RO) ferries

A RO-RO ferry is a ship designed to allow vehicles to drive straight on or off without further mechanical assistance, in contrast to the conventional ship which uses cranes or derricks to load and unload its freight.

Shipment by ferry is a basic and necessary form of transport for any island (or peninsular) nation. As with all forms of transport, the ferry has changed dramatically, and the European ferry, to cite one example, is now possibly twice or even three times as big as its forerunners of 25 years ago. As a result of the expansion of car ownership and foreign holidays, tonnages between 17 000 and 31 000 dwt are now common, sizes which compare with cruise liners. Clearly, the size of ferry available on any route is conditioned by the traffic to be carried: it may vary from a small five-vehicle carrier which may operate between the Scottish Isles, to the modern English Channel ferry, which now has a capacity to hold upward of 100 commercial vehicles.

55.3 On the quayside

Extra precautions are necessary to protect exhibits from humid and saline conditions before embarkation and after disembarkation. The insulation provided by the immediate packing around an exhibit and by the vehicle or the container should be sufficient to protect the exhibits from extreme weather conditions while waiting on the quayside before and after the crossing (see 45.2). The agent should ensure that the extent of risk is reduced, by avoiding delays at the dockside and ensuring rapid passage through customs (see 52.6).

55.4 Stowage on ferries

For conservation and security reasons, it is important to ensure, both at the booking stage and on the dockside, that the vehicle has an overriding right to travel, even if it means that car passenger traffic is rejected. On most routes, ferry companies will always give passenger traffic preference over cargo, so specific guarantees must be sought and obtained at the time of booking. The driver should always carry documentation to substantiate this guaranteed position.

The stowage of the vehicle itself is the most fundamental area of concern. Wherever possible, vehicles used for transporting exhibits should travel below deck on any ferry, in order to be protected from the elements. The only exceptions that may be tolerated to this rule are short river- or estuary-crossings. Even here it is important to consider the exposure to which the vehicle – and indirectly its contents – may be subjected during the crossing. Above-decks stowage is totally unacceptable for sea crossings. Because cargo-only ferries often have a configuration which allows for vehicles to travel above deck, it is most important to specify a below-decks position when booking a crossing, and to ensure that driver, courier and agent confirm this position before embarkation.

Before embarkation, the driver, courier or agent should also discuss with the ferry's loading officer the possibility of a position mid-beam and mid-ships, to help to reduce the stress on the exhibits as the ferry pitches and rolls.

On many ferries, air-conditioning and air-ride systems must be switched off, but on the longer routes ferry operators are increasingly providing the possibility of plugging into the ship's power supply. The carrier and/or the agent should ascertain if voltages are satisfactory, so that environmental control systems can continue to function during the crossing.

During the crossing, drivers and passengers are required to leave the vehicle decks until just before disembarkation. The crossing should be treated in the same way as secure storage for overnight stops during inland journeys (see 53.13). Where possible, the vehicle should be provided with physical seals to detect tampering, and it should be left securely locked and alarmed. It is often possible for a driver or courier to arrange with the ship's purser a periodic inspection of the vehicle.

55.5 Containers

As little as 30 years ago, transportation by sea entailed manual stowage of cargo into the ship's hold, which was both time-consuming and potentially dangerous. The revolution brought about by the introduction of the container ship has eliminated these drawbacks, and freight is now pre-loaded into containers prior to loading on to the vessel. A container ship is designed to accept basic unit sizes of 6 m or 12 m (20- or 40-feet) containers with a standard width and height of 2.4 m (8 feet). Within these parameters, it is possible to use a multitude of container designs.

The most practical design for transporting exhibitions is the general dry box cargo container. It is constructed in mild steel, and its rigidity is enhanced by a solid wood floor of 5 cm thickness. Access is obtained through a double door at one end which gives a height restriction of 2.25 m (90"). It is possible to exceed this height by using an open-top container, but this would require special stowage and the contents would be protected only by a tarpaulin over the top of the container.

In the period before it is loaded on a ship, a container may travel by rail and road and be stored in the open, and be subjected to a variety of climatic conditions. Under the sun, the temperature inside a container can be more than 20° higher than the air outside, and the container offers no protection either against low temperatures in the middle of winter. This problem may be countered by the use of a refrigerated box container. The overall capacity and design is similar to the general dry box cargo container, but it is insulated and it is fitted with an independently-generated temperature control unit. With these modifications, it is possible to maintain an internal temperature of 13°C.

The basic freight cost of sea transport is invariably more competitive than by air, but this advantage is balanced by higher insurance premiums (see 54.8). The use of equipment with a higher specification such as the refrigerated container will also reduce the cost advantage.

55.6 Packing a container

When using a container it is important to control the loading procedure. Even where a consignment does not fill the container, it is vital to avoid consolidation with other freight. Consolidation means that the consignment will be delivered to a freight terminal where the operator will maximize the space and load potential of the container. Decisions based on commercial expediency will be taken outside the organizer's supervision. The important benefit of the container is the ability to supervise the only physical handling of its contents that takes place at loading. Once the container is loaded, locked and sealed, its contents remain untouched until the final unloading.

A sea container loaded in – or delivered to – an inland city such as Birmingham, Zurich or Calgary will have to use other forms of surface transport to reach its destination. It may be delivered to the nearest rail terminal to make the journey by rail, in which case thought should be given to packing methods to counter the considerable vibration and shock to be encountered on rail freight journeys (see 45.4). If it is travelling by road, it will be important to provide similar packing and/or to specify that the trailer has air-ride suspension.

55.7 On the dockside

A container ship may have a turn-round time in port as short as 24 hours to unload its cargo and to load a new one. Operators must ensure that the ship does not incur extra costs by unnecessary delays, so containers start to arrive at the port up to seven days in advance of the ship's arrival.

Security is not normally a major problem, because the containers are held in a Customs Bonded area with stringent security measures, and because it is physically impossible to get access to the container while stacked in a receiving area holding over a hundred containers. However, climatic conditions should again be considered.

An agent can normally make special arrangements

to deliver or collect a container within hours of the respective departure or arrival of the ship, but only if it is a sole-use container (i.e. not consolidated, see 55.6).

55.8 The sea voyage(s)

A container ship will load containers both under deck and also stacked up to four high above deck. Where a general dry box cargo container is used, the agent should give clear and specific instructions to the shipping company to ensure its stowage below decks, to avoid the climatic dangers of stowage above deck. A refrigerated box does not need this instruction, because it will be loaded into a special position reserved for these units, below deck in an area of stability which is constantly monitored by the ship's crew.

Frequency of sailings depend on the route, with major ports having possibly weekly or fortnightly services and lesser ports offering monthly sailings. For an exhibition travelling by sea, the organizer and/or agent should be aware of the exact route and the service offered. The modern trend is to consolidate freight destined for another continent in one major 'gateway' port, by using feeder vessels which bring freight from smaller ports. For example, a container bound for Vancouver from London will first move from Felixstowe to Rotterdam, then on an ocean-going vessel to Los Angeles, and finally onward to Vancouver by feeder vessel. Control can therefore be lost for the longest part of the voyage – and the one with the greatest climatic extremes – unless a representative of the agent is on hand at each trans-shipment to ensure below-decks stowage.

The timetable for sea transport is measured in the terms of days, as opposed to hours when using air. Delays can also arise when feeder vessels are used: because they are smaller, their carrying capacity is restricted and they are more susceptible to delays through bad weather.

56

Import and export rules and regulations

Kevin Richardson

56.1 The European Union

Midnight on 31st December 1992 saw one of the most important developments in Customs and Excise procedures for many years. This was the abolition of customs controls over the import and export of virtually all commodities throughout what had been known as the European Community and what is now called the European Union (EU). Since then the movement of works of art and other 'cultural objects' between member states has become a far less complicated affair, although still subject to certain restrictions. From that time – and allowing for a few weeks' teething troubles – cultural objects were allowed to be transported from one European country to the next without customs involvement, intervention or, most importantly, taxes.

All at once there was no longer the need to complete lengthy and complicated customs documentation. Delays at the borders, which could often be in excess of twelve hours, were suddenly a thing of the past. Hastily arranged payments of Valued Added Tax (VAT) were no longer a consideration. In fact, so acute were the changes that those of us who had over the years come to expect – and indeed grown accustomed to – the often turbulent activities at the various frontier crossing points felt suddenly disorientated at the apparent ease with which cultural objects could travel around Europe.

However, when considering the possibility of moving cultural objects between member states, one must not be lured into a false sense of security. While procedures have certainly become a great deal less complicated, there still remain many issues which must be taken into consideration. From a Customs and Excise point of view, the main issues to consider when contemplating the movement between the UK and other member states of cultural objects, be it a single piece or an entire exhibition, are relatively straightforward:

Are any of the objects not of EU origin?
Are any of the objects covered by existing Customs control?
Are any of the objects subject to Department of National Heritage restrictions or do they appear on the endangered species listings?
Does the tour extend beyond the EU?
Are any of the venues exempted from Duty and/or VAT?

56.2 The definition of EU origin

This covers cultural objects which originated within the EU, e.g. a work of art wholly executed in one of the member states. It also covers objects which have at some time been imported into one of the member states and which have been subject to payment of either VAT or Duty or both at the time of the original import into what is now the European Union.

Touring exhibitions comprising entirely cultural objects of EU origin can travel between member states without customs formalities, provided the exhibits are not subject to other restrictions (see 56.3 and 56.4).

56.3 Export licences

When an exhibition tours between member states, customs authorities are responsible for controlling and maintaining that country's regulations governing the export of restricted goods. These regulations vary slightly between member states, but in general are governed by the age and value of the items when dealing with works of art or antiques. The purpose of these controls is to ensure, wherever possible, that objects important to a country's heritage are retained by that country. The export of cultural objects from the United Kingdom is controlled by the Export Licencing Unit of the Department of National Heritage (2-4

Figure 56.1 Values at or above which an export licence is required

(All items more than 50 years old)	*UK licence (£)*	*EU licence (£)*
Paintings in oil or tempera	119,000	119,000
Paintings in other media	39,600	119,000
Portraits of British historical persons[1]	6,000	119,000
Any antique item not shown below	39,600	39,600
Drawings on any medium and in any material	39,600	11,900
Original engravings, prints, serigraphs and original posters	39,600	11,900
Mosaics (other than archaeological or monument categories)	39,600	11,900
Original sculptures or statuary and copies produced by the same process as the original, (other than archaeological)	39,600	39,600
Archaeological material found in UK soil or UK territorial waters[2]	Zero	Zero
Archaeological material from outside UK. Elements of artistic, historical or religious monuments	39,600	Zero
– more than 50 years old but less than 100 years old[3]	39,600	Not EU
– more than 100 years old	39,600	Zero
Firearms more than 50 but less than 100 years old	39,600	39,600
Firearms 100 years old or more, and any other arms and armour more than 50 years old	20,000	39,600
Printed maps which are:		
– more than 50 but less than 200 years old	39,600	Not EU
– more than 200 years old	39,600	11,900
Books which are:		
– more than 50 but less than 100 years old	39,600	Not EU
– more than 100 years old	39,600	39,600
Incunabula	39,600	Zero
Means of transport which are:		
– more than 50 but less than 75 years old	39,600	Not EU
– more than 75 years old	39,600	39,600
Textiles (excluding carpets and tapestries)	6,000	39,600
Photographs, films and negatives thereof	6,000	11,900
Collections and specimens from zoological, botanical, mineralogical or anatomical collections	Not UK	39,600
Collections of historical, palaeontology, ethnographic or numismatic interest	Not UK	39,600
Manuscripts including maps and musical scores, singly or collections	Zero	Zero
Archives, of any kind, on any medium	Zero	Zero
Architectural, scientific and engineering drawings	Zero	11,900

Notes:
[1]A 'British historical person' is someone listed in the *Dictionary of National Biography* or *Who was Who*
[2]'Zero' means all items within that category require an export licence: but there is a discretion for objects of limited archaeological or scientific interest e.g. common Roman coins.
[3]'Not UK' or 'Not EU' means no UK (or EU) licence required.

Figure 56.1 List of objects for which export licences are required

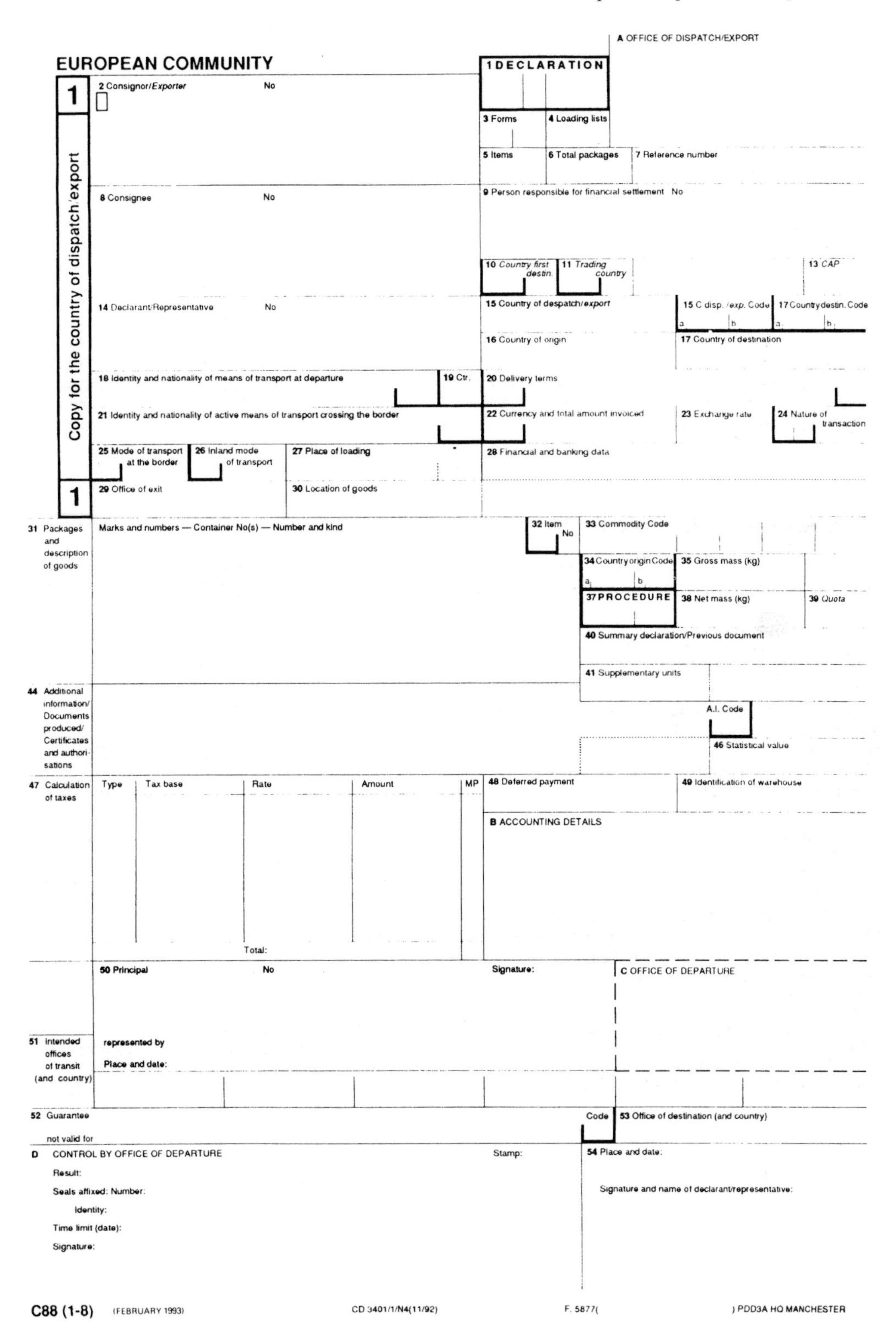

A OFFICE OF DISPATCH/EXPORT

EUROPEAN COMMUNITY

1 DECLARATION

1

Copy for the country of dispatch/export

2 Consignor/Exporter No

3 Forms

4 Loading lists

5 Items

6 Total packages

7 Reference number

8 Consignee No

9 Person responsible for financial settlement No

10 Country first destin.

11 Trading country

13 CAP

14 Declarant/Representative No

15 Country of despatch/export

15 C disp. /exp. Code

a b

17 Country destin. Code

a b

16 Country of origin

17 Country of destination

18 Identity and nationality of means of transport at departure

19 Ctr.

20 Delivery terms

21 Identity and nationality of active means of transport crossing the border

22 Currency and total amount invoiced

23 Exchange rate

24 Nature of transaction

25 Mode of transport at the border

26 Inland mode of transport

27 Place of loading

28 Financial and banking data

1

29 Office of exit

30 Location of goods

31 Packages and description of goods

Marks and numbers — Container No(s) — Number and kind

32 Item No

33 Commodity Code

34 Country origin Code

a b

35 Gross mass (kg)

37 PROCEDURE

38 Net mass (kg)

39 Quota

40 Summary declaration/Previous document

41 Supplementary units

44 Additional information/ Documents produced/ Certificates and authorisations

A.I. Code

46 Statistical value

47 Calculation of taxes

Type	Tax base	Rate	Amount	MP
		Total:		

48 Deferred payment

49 Identification of warehouse

B ACCOUNTING DETAILS

50 Principal No

Signature:

C OFFICE OF DEPARTURE

51 Intended offices of transit (and country)

represented by

Place and date:

52 Guarantee

not valid for

Code

53 Office of destination (and country)

D CONTROL BY OFFICE OF DEPARTURE

Stamp:

54 Place and date:

Result:

Seals affixed: Number:

Identity:

Time limit (date):

Signature:

Signature and name of declarant/representative:

C88 (1-8) (FEBRUARY 1993) CD 3401/1/N4(11/92) F. 5877( ) PDD3A HQ MANCHESTER

Figure 56.2 C88

Cockspur Street, London SW1Y 5DH. Tel 0171 211 6164/5/6/7) and policed by Customs and Excise. It usually takes eight weeks for a licence to be granted.

A UK licence is required for the movement of such objects within the EU. For a list of objects for which export licences are required, see Figure 56.1.

An EU licence is needed for the export of objects outside the European Union, where the objects are valued at or above certain limits. Figure 56.1 juxtaposes the limits required for UK and EU licences.

Note: a UK licence is required for the export outside the EU of objects where the UK limit is lower than the EU limit. For example, a portrait of a 'British historical person' might be valued at below the current EU limit of £119,000 and not require an EU licence, but the historical significance of the portrait will be protected by the lower threshold for UK licences.

If an object travels from another member state to the UK and then to a third venue outside the EU, the UK organizer must obtain from the Department of National Heritage a second EU licence showing only the non-EU destination. This licence is in addition to the one from the country of origin which shows both the EU and the non-EU destinations. This is because it is the responsibility of each member state to control the export of not only its own cultural objects but also all exports from the EU.

56.4 CITES permits

The Convention on International Trade in Endangered Species of Wild Fauna and Flora (CITES) governs the import and export of endangered animals and plants and all products derived from them. For example, an item of furniture which has ivory inlay, a piano with ivory keys, ivory chess pieces or a miniature painted on ivory will require a CITES permit in both the country of export and the country of import. In the UK, permits are issued by the Wildlife Trade Licensing Branch of the Department of the Environment (Tollgate House, Houlton Street, Bristol BS2 9DJ. Tel 0117 987 8000), and policed by Customs and Excise. It usually takes three to four weeks for the certificate to be granted.

56.5 Imports from outside the European Union

If the movement contains one or more items which are not of EU origin, then those items will be subject to customs control in the country of export, in any member state they are passing through and in the country of import. They will be subject to the usual Customs procedures, and require appropriate documentation. This will normally involve form C88 (see Figure 56.2), the various procedures for which are detailed in the Customs and Excise's 'bible', the *Integrated Tariff of the United Kingdom*.

Cultural objects imported from outside the EU will normally be liable to import duty and/or VAT at the port of entry into the EU. The current rate of import duty varies between member states but will gradually be unified so that the same rate applies to all members.

Some items, e.g. what the Customs and Excise define as 'antiques and collector's pieces', are eligible for relief provided certain requirements can be satisfied. Public Notice 712, available from local Customs and Excise offices, sets out these requirements.

Most National Museums and Galleries (NMGs, see 41.1) are exempt from import duty and VAT for goods temporarily imported for exhibition purposes. Cultural objects imported to these venues must comply with customs regulations and will remain under the control of Customs and Excise during the course of the exhibition. Normal customs procedures must be followed at the port of entry into the UK. Once satisfied that the correct procedures have been followed and that the venue is approved for the purpose of holding temporary exhibitions, Customs and Excise will hand over control from its port officer to the venue's local officer. The latter will maintain control over the imported material until it is moved to another approved venue or exported. Removal of the material from the venue is not allowed without the permission of the local officer. Public Notice 361 applies.

Cultural objects from outside the EU which tour to venues other than the NMGs can be exempted from import duty and VAT, provided that the appropriate documentation accompanies the objects during the tour. The customs authorities at the original point of entry into the European Union will need to be notified by the corresponding customs authorities at the point of exit, when the objects eventually leave the EU. This is normally done through the local shipping agents in the appropriate countries.

Valued added tax on works of art came into effect in the UK on 1 April 1973. Any work which was executed or remained in the artist's estate after this date is liable to VAT at 17.5% on import into the EU, unless it is for temporary exhibition at an approved venue. It used to be possible to import without paying VAT on works which had been executed or left the artists' estate before 1 April 1973. From 1 June 1995, VAT will also be levied on these works, initially at an effective rate of 2.5 per cent but gradually increasing over the next few years to reach a level agreed by the European Commission.

56.6 Shipping agents

It is important that everyone involved in the import and export of works of art, antiques or other cultural goods is aware of the basic procedures and requirements of licensing and customs authorities. For the UK, detailed information can be obtained from the various Public Notices issued by Customs and Excise and from the application guidelines produced by the Department of the Environment and the Department of National Heritage. Alternatively, shipping agents are good sources of information (see 52.6). They specialize in the export and import of cultural goods; they maintain contacts with their opposite numbers in other countries; and they keep up-to-date records of ever-changing requirements and regulations, in the United Kingdom, the European Union and elsewhere in the world.

Index